Dennett's Philosophy

A Comprehensive Assessment

Edited by Don Ross, Andrew Brook, and David Thompson

A Bradford Book
The MIT Press
Cambridge, Massachusetts
London, England

This book was set in New Baskerville by Achorn Graphic Services, Inc., on the Miles System.

Printed and bound in the United States of America.

Library of Congress Cataloging-in-Publication Data

Dennett's philosophy : a comprehensive assessment / edited by Don Ross, Andrew Brook, and David Thompson
     p.   cm.
"A Bradford book."
Includes bibliographical references and index.
ISBN 0-262-18200-9 (hc) — ISBN 0-262-68117-X (pbk.)
   1. Dennett, Daniel Clement—Congresses. I. Ross, Don, 1962– . II. Brook, Andrew. III. Thompson, David, 1941– .

B945.D394 D47 2000
194—dc21

                                                              00-039449

Contents

Contents

Contributors

Andrew Brook
Department of Philosophy
Director of the Center for
Interdisciplinary Studies
Carleton University
Ottawa, Canada

Timothy M. Crowe
Department of Zoology
Percy FitzPatrick Institute
University of Cape Town
Cape Town, South Africa

Daniel C. Dennett
Director of the Center for
Cognitive Studies
Tufts University
Medford, Massachusetts

Paul Dumouchel
Department of Philosophy
Université du Québec à Montréal
Montreal, Canada

Timothy Kenyon
Department of Philosophy
St. Andrews University
Fife, Scotland

Dan Lloyd
Department of Philosophy
Trinity College
Hartford, Connecticut

Ruth Garrett Millikan
Department of Philosophy
University of Connecticut
Storrs, Connecticut

T. Brian Mooney
School of Justice and Business Law
Edith Cowan University
Perth, Australia

Thomas W. Polger
Department of Philosophy
Duke University
Durham, North Carolina

David M. Rosenthal
Department of Philosophy
Graduate School, City University of
New York
New York, New York

Don Ross
School of Economics
University of Cape Town
Cape Town, South Africa

Contributors

William Seager
Department of Philosophy
University of Toronto
Scarborough, Canada

David L. Thompson
Department of Philosophy
Memorial University of
Newfoundland
St. John's, Canada

Christopher Viger
Department of Philosophy
Dalhousie University
Halifax, Canada

Preface

This book arose out of a conference, "Dennett's Philosophy," held at Memorial University, St. John's, Newfoundland, in November 1998. These chapters are very much the product of dialogue between Dennett and their authors, and among the authors. First drafts were discussed extensively at the conference, and all received replies from Dennett. Papers were then rewritten in light of these exchanges, after which Dennett composed the responses produced here.

In light of the close relationship between the conference and this book, it would seem appropriate to thank both those who helped with the organization of the first and those who helped in the production of the second.

The conference—and, therefore, this book—would not have come to be without Jennifer Dawe, who did a tremendous amount of practical work in organizing conference funding, and then the event itself. Joanne Myrick-Harris, Memorial's Conference Coordinator, gave invaluable assistance and organized registration, with the help of Diane Hussey. Jaymie Sheir handled communications and coordinated the event itself. Ken Byrne managed the conference website. James Bradley helped the organizing committee, and arranged a social program that kept the conference participants working very hard and in happy camaraderie, knowing that their collective labors would be regularly rewarded with collective fun. John Scott coordinated local fundraising. Funding was provided by the Social Sciences and Humanities Research Council of Canada, Kevin Keough (Memorial's Vice-President Research), Terry Murphy

(Memorial's Dean of Arts), John Martin (Deputy Vice-Chancellor of the University of Cape Town), Memorial's Department of Philosophy, and Labatt's Brewery.

With all of the above help we got as far as having the raw material for the book. Betty Stanton's support enabled this raw material to be refined for the reading public; we are sorry that its preparation immediately followed her retirement, making this one of the first post–Betty Bradford projects. Amy Brand tolerated some delays and encouraged us as press editor. Ken Byrne traveled from Newfoundland to Cape Town and served as Assistant Editor to Don Ross. Ken was assisted by Jongikaya Rabe and Andile Mgweba during the final stages of manuscript preparation. Robert Stainton helped with proofreading; our special thanks to him.

Judy Feldmann at MIT Press did such superb copyediting as to make the academic editors feel a bit useless at times. We now know why she was introduced to us as "MIT's Dennett-approved expert."

Carolyn Anderson handled the business end at the press. Given that publishers hold the gun relative to academics, we're grateful that at no time did we feel that Carolyn had it pointed at us.

Our warmest thanks go to the authors of these papers, including Dan Dennett. Their enthusiasm for the project, and their delight in one another's ideas, made this a genuine collective effort by a large team—a rare experience in the "solo heroics" atmosphere of professional philosophy.

Portions of the introduction appeared in *The Philosophers' Magazine*. Thanks to its editor, Julian Baggini, for feeding the informavores.

The book would also not have survived without e-mail. No fewer than three servers succumbed to viruses while storing the working copy, at which point it had to be reassembled by Brook in Canada and conveyed electronically to Ross in South Africa. A month before delivery of the manuscript, a thirty-ton crane fell on the computer science building at the University of Cape Town, pulverizing the University's communications infrastructure. Once again, Brook fished out the pieces of the text and the e-mails hummed. The book's appearance means that he is at last no longer on call against virtual and physical disasters. The fall of the crane caused rather a rush at the last, and threw a wildly inequitable domestic burden on Nelleke, for which loving thanks from DR.

1

Introduction: The Dennettian Stance

Don Ross

In November 1998, a group of fifteen scholars gathered at Memorial University in St. John's, Newfoundland, with Daniel C. Dennett, to study his corpus of books and articles as a set, and assess the extent to which the pieces fit together as a comprehensive philosophical system. In his work on consciousness, Dennett has considered puzzles over how the complex components of mental processing all seem to "come together" in serial, relatively coherent, narratives we tell ourselves about ourselves. At the conference, we stepped one level higher and asked "How do the complex components of Dennett's work on intentionality, consciousness, evolution, and ethics 'come together' into a coherent view of the world?"

"System-building" has had rather a bad odor among philosophers in the analytic tradition. This is hardly surprising: It is implicit in the very label "analytic," an approach that seeks to deconstruct (in the dictionary sense of the term) complex problems into manageable pieces. Now, Dennett has never claimed to be trying to build any sort of grand unified system in the way that, for example, Kant or Hegel did. But if one now turns back and reads his first book *Content and Consciousness* (1969), one finds in it the anticipatory seeds of most of his later work. The early book is among the first in analytic philosophy to even consider the problem of consciousness; furthermore, it does so within constraints drawn from what natural selection could plausibly design, another aspect of Dennett's approach that is now common, but was in 1969 almost unheard-of in philosophy. Dennett has since withdrawn or amended some of the specific hypotheses advanced in *Content and Consciousness,* but his then-original project has remained consistent with its aims. It is difficult to be as original in approach as Dennett then was and avoid implying a wide-ranging philosophical system, whether one has that intention or not.

It is unlikely that Dennett would ever be referred to as "a philosopher's philosopher," given the extent to which he eschews the analytic philosopher's main tool: the semiformal, quasi-deductive argument. Of course, many analytic philosophers, including, notably, Russell, Quine, Ryle, Lewis, and Fodor, have also used vivid examples, rhetorical questions, and wit to press for clearer thinking on various problems and for revisions to inherited conceptual schemes. However, in analytic contexts such persuasive devices have usually been intended to test conceptual distinctions against intuitions. The need for such distinctions, with which philosophy of course teems, usually arises from attempts to fix the scopes of terms used in deductive or semideductive arguments. In this atmosphere, Dennett's career-long barrage of "intuition pumps"—thought experiments, empirical examples, rhetorical challenges, which are difficult to place within the context of implicit formal arguments—has seemed to some philosophers to border on irresponsibility. Dennett, one often hears it said, is "slippery." In the present philosophical culture, this is at best an indicator of unease.

This book, like the conference from which it arose, is motivated by the conviction that Dennett's work is deeply serious, and that the manner in which his conversations with other philosophers have been conducted is itself of philosophical import. With one exception, these essays are written by philosophers, and their authors work in the typical philosophical style: They elucidate concepts, they split hairs, they test sets of premises for consistency of implications. However, all are predicated on the belief that Dennett's recent work is much more than a series of lively essays in popular science, and that it continues to offer some of the most significant contributions to professional philosophy available. Indeed, the authors here accepted a general challenge from the editors to contribute to a project that some of Dennett's intellectual critics—not to mention many who are sympathetic with his views—might find preposterous: to evaluate the extent to which Dennett's corpus comprises a coherent philosophical system. It must be left to the reader of this book to decide whether the ambition *was* preposterous. However, after providing a synopsis of the themes around which the volume is organized, I will offer and explain my own verdict; this will at least offer a point of departure to which a skeptical reader can react.

Among philosophers, Dennett continues to be best known for his distinctive theory of mental content, which has been with us for three decades now. Talk about "mental content" inevitably involves—is, perhaps, identical with—debates over theories of "intentionality." Such a theory's basic problem is "How is it that a state in a mind, brain, or mind/brain can be *about* something specific outside of itself?" Only once this general question has been answered with some plausible hypotheses can one then go on to usefully wonder how to assign *particular* content to particular mental states. Of course, different general hypotheses will generate different answers at the level of specific content-assignments. Dennett's general hypothesis, as advanced in two major collections of essays, *Brainstorms* (1981) and *The Intentional Stance* (1987), is that content is fixed by adopting the "intentional stance" toward a system, treating it for purposes of prediction and explanation as if it has beliefs, goals, and capacities that are related in a systematic way. Now, at first this seems circular: It does not appear informative to say "A system is deemed to have intentionality by virtue of having the intentional stance taken toward it." For this reason, Dennett has often been regarded as an *instrumentalist* about intentionality: We say that a system is a *mental* system just in case we find it useful for practical purposes to do so. In that case, it would not be obvious that intentionality exists in any scientific sense, its subconcepts—beliefs, desires, and so on—being merely artifacts of the way we find it natural to talk. Some philosophers, notably Paul Churchland and Richard Rorty, have defended exactly this view.

Dennett, however, has resisted the instrumentalist label. His basis for this resistance is that, essentially, "the way we find it natural to talk" is not something anyone *decided* or *chose;* it is a function of the way in which natural selection designed our brains and nervous systems. Of course, natural selection does not deliberately decide anything. As Dennett has emphasized throughout his career, natural selection is an engineer without foresight: It simply tries one design after another, and eliminates those that don't work as well, given their environmental niches, as competing designs. This is generally a poor engineering procedure given constraints of time and other resources; but natural selection has, effectively, all the time and resources in the world. Given this absence of economic limitations, blind trial-and-error is a *more* powerful technique than deliberation, because it allows a countless variety of avenues and contingencies to be investigated, rather than only those challenges that the deliberative engineer can anticipate. Thus, for Dennett, the ultimate source of types of human intentions is a designer we usually don't regard as having intentions at all, namely, natural selection. Dennett has worked strenuously to break apart what he regards as the overly close association between intentionality in general and *deliberative* intentionality. Thus too, in Dennett's opus *Consciousness Explained* (1991a), he develops his theory of the architecture supporting consciousness by applying the technique of "reverse engineering," that is, working backward from the "specifications" evident in our actual design, through the trajectory in "design space" followed by natural selection. Since natural selection cannot go back and reengineer a design, once environmental and morphological constraints start it down such a trajectory, the available room within design space shrinks tightly enough to permit reverse engineering to generate constrained and principled hypotheses.

Attaching such primacy to natural selection as a source of constraints on theories of intentionality and consciousness has led Dennett into explorations of the impact this has upon ethics and the possibility of free will. Put very broadly, Dennett's view is that Darwinian theory is a "universal acid" insofar as it dissolves any hope of establishing *transcendental* foundations for either morality or free will. However, he maintains in *Elbow Room* (1984), his book on free will, and in *Darwin's Dangerous Idea* (1995), that we should feel no need for such foundations in the first place. Since we are constrained by what natural selection has wrought, but since our deliberate actions also influence the region of design space open to biological—and, importantly, cultural—evolution, our sense that we have responsibility over our future, the exercise of which depends upon our reflectively chosen values, ensures that neither free will nor moral obligations are mere illusions. We have, as Dennett puts it, "all the free will worth wanting." This may seem reassuring, but it implies a problem that has echoes of Nietzschean existential freedom. If there is no transcendental foundation for ethics, we cannot hope to fall back on a set of predetermined rules that will advise us on what to do in every morally challenging situation. As discussed above, there are severe limitations on what can be achieved by deliberative engineering, which cannot anticipate all, or even most, contingencies that cultural evolution and chance might throw at us. Therefore, Dennett argues, the best sort of contribution ethicists can provide is a "moral first aid manual" (Dennett 1988), a basic toolkit of concepts flexible enough to permit exaptation to as wide a range as possible of new situations and challenges.

I have tried to sketch, in broad brushstrokes, the themes that recur in Dennett's work, and which give it its systematic appearance. After doing this at the conference, we then attempted to tug at any loose planks we could find in the edifice to see how well it could withstand pressure from various different directions. Is Dennett's "philosophical first aid manual" a sufficiently robust set of tools? (This metaphor seems apt, since it is obviously not a set of axiomatic first principles of the Spinozistic sort.) The fifteen plenary papers were divided among five sessions, on Evolution, Intentionality, Consciousness, Ontology, and Ethics/Free Will. Dennett replied to each paper. In addition, a number of poster submissions were displayed and commented upon by their authors. On the final morning, a roundtable was held at which themes that had reemerged repeatedly from session to session were subjected to further analysis and debate by all participants. The plenary papers, along with Dennett's replies, are now gathered here. (Sadly, Kathleen Akins's outstanding contribution was already claimed for another publication, and so does not appear in this book.)

The wide topical range of Dennett's work presented us with a challenge in organizing the Newfoundland conference, and in editing this book. On the one hand, we sought a group of papers that would jointly capture the full sweep of Dennett's professional interests. On the other hand, we certainly did not want a dozen papers all trying to synthesize his entire corpus. We decided not to commission papers by topic; instead, we invited contributors with an eye to achieving a match between the range of principal interests on which the panel had collectively published and Dennett's. Invitees were advised as to the intended overall product of the conference—an assessment of the extent to which Dennett's publications on an array of localized subjects fit together into a coherent philosophical view—but no suggestions were given as to the specific subjects of the papers. They were sorted into thematic blocks that became the basis for organizing the conference sessions and the sections of this book, only after all of the contributors had completed first drafts. We are satisfied that this trusting to chance—within pre-fixed constraints—was generally successful.

In all of Dennett's work, the possibility-space for psychological and biological mechanisms left open by natural selection fundamentally defines the conceptual terrain. The book therefore follows the order of presentation at the conference in opening with papers addressed to issues in the philosophy of biology. Tim *Crowe*, an evolutionary zoologist, presents a novel challenge to Dennett's adaptationism. The technique of explaining by simulated reverse engineering obviously requires the assumption that, although geological, geographical, and other contingencies determine the topology—both metaphorically and (often) literally—of evolutionary design space, our default principle must be that biological organs and behaviors exist because they are well adapted to an environment, and that this well-adaptedness explains their existence. This default principle has been challenged, most ferociously by Stephen Jay Gould, and the resulting debate between Gould and Dennett has been quite heated. Gould argues (at least, when at his most provocative) that events of speciation are mainly accidents, that is, nonadaptations. Crowe goes further: In his paper, he cites his own extensive research on African guineafowl to suggest that, from the gene's-eye point of view made famous by Dawkins (1976) and which Dennett accepts, speciation events are often *mal*adaptations, where, through pure accident, random ethological changes have reduced the sizes of the pools in which genes can operate. This seems to be a challenge that Dennett must meet if his method of hypothesis-formation is not to reduce to pure speculation. However, it is not obvious that Dennett must embrace Dawkins's "strong genic selectionism" for the sake of the rest of his philosophy, in which case Crowe's argument cuts no deeper than those of Gould, which Dennett has already sought to answer. In the second paper on evolution, Paul *Dumouchel* challenges Dennett from exactly the other side. If strong adaptationism is true, Dumouchel argues, then all of natural selection's moves through design space are "forced," and the room for cultural-evolutionary feedback pressures exploited by Dennett in his work on free will seems threatened. Dumouchel is not content with merely raising this problem; he also seeks to solve it, using first a well-crafted set of rhetorical questions that probe Dennett's concept of an evolutionary algorithm. He then goes on to suggest that Dennett's distinction between "Good Tricks" and "Forced Moves" involves us in "an antimony of natural reason." The style of the inquiry here is tightly Dennettian, torturing the distinction to see if it represents a difference that makes a difference, a favorite and recurring question posed by Dennett in several domains. Dennett makes no secret of the fact that he regards epistemological verificationism (as opposed to the obviously mistaken semantic verificationism defended by the logical empiricists) as a sound, indeed necessary, principle of good science.

Indeed, this issue was central in the discussions on consciousness. Dennett's most controversial claim about consciousness is that, in adjudicating between questions as to what information in the brain is processed "preconsciously" and what information is processed "postconsciously," there is no fact of the matter. Put more vividly, there is no discernible difference between "real seemings" and "mere seemings." When this distinction is denied, the point of talking about "seemings" disappears entirely: There is merely processed information, and judgments about the source and interpretation, in natural language, of that information. Here, the influence of Dennett's great mentor, Gilbert Ryle, shows clearly. At the conference, several speakers on themes related to consciousness tried to "domesticate" this radical implication of Dennett's view. Andrew *Brook* used this phrase explicitly. According to Brook, Dennett's "multiple-drafts" theory of consciousness is merely compatible with, but does not imply, the thesis that "seemings" have no place in a naturalistic ontology. If this is the case, however, it invites another question that would reverse Brook's moral: Does Dennett's epistemological verificationism imply the abandonment of "seemings," in which case the multiple-drafts model would be a demonstration that a neo-Rylean can tell a story that saves the phenomena? That verificationism is crucial to Dennett's project is suggested by his purely epistemological arguments to the effect that zombies, creatures behaviorally indistinguishable from conscious subjects but lacking phenomenal qualia, are incoherent posits. In his essay, Tom *Polger* argues that zombies, even if they are biologically impossible (as most contributors to the debate concede), nevertheless serve as useful conceptual fictions in testing the scope of psychological and neurological hypotheses. I think it fair to say that Dennett is not at all convinced by this argument, and that his verificationist premises, if accepted, block it more or less immediately. (See below for more on this point.) This fundamental epistemological divide has arisen repeatedly, though usually in unexpected and therefore enlightening ways. David *Thompson* attempts to persuade Dennett that he and Husserl have more in common than Dennett has elsewhere implied, since both deny that the content of a representation is an internal "seeming." I suspect that many philosophers will be surprised at how far Dennett, in his reply, is willing to go with this suggestion. That Dennett, Husserl, Thompson, and Brook are all naive realists about the contents of linguistically interpreted representations is clear. It is not at all clear, however, that a third-person verificationist such as Dennett could endorse the possibility of learning anything about the basis of consciousness through the Husserlian method of epoché. Indeed, it is difficult to see how, on Dennett's view, epoché could even be possible, since the subject has no available standpoint from which she could hope to *accurately* "bracket" the contents of consciousness.

If Brook, Thompson, and Polger try, in their different ways, to "domesticate" Dennett, other commentators on the themes of consciousness, intentionality, and ontology—which often run tightly together, as they do in Dennett's work—encourage him to break out of stockades that they take to be of his own making. Dan *Lloyd* amplifies Dennett's dissatisfaction with language-of-thought models by focusing on the nature of propositional content assignments "from outside." Lloyd agrees with Dennett that content cannot be fixed by trying to correlate it with some neo-Cartesian state, but he then takes the case further: We cannot gain a stable purchase on linguistically represented content unless we go beyond the organism and attend to its environmental locus. The problem, as Lloyd analyzes it, taking his cue directly from Dennett, is that many content-ascriptions refer to properties that exist only given the possibility of a detector of such properties. If, then, we do not consider minds *in situ,* we shall be driven all the way back to a Cartesian view about the ontological status of such properties: The sorts of objects we refer to by appeal to them will have no possible home but a (distributed) "Cartesian cineplex." Lloyd therefore advocates what he calls "phenomenal realism": Phenomena (e.g., those properties that depend on a potential detector for existence) exist in just the same sense as other properties, because, as a matter of fact, there are not only *potential* reliable detectors of them, but *actual* ones. If Lloyd is correct, however, that being realists about phenomenal properties while avoiding residual Cartesianism requires taking minds and relevant parts of the world as our systems for analysis, then the likelihood of any neat mapping between neural or perceptual content (or, to speak more cautiously, "sublinguistic content") and propositional content becomes vanishingly small. This suggestion urged by Lloyd, insofar as it requires an entire abandonment of the representational paradigm, would pull Dennett still closer to Husserl, or at least the version of Husserl described by Thompson.

Dennett has always explicitly embraced a robust Quinean naturalism. Naturalism, however, does not by itself decide between the naive realism of Brook and Thompson, and the "revisionist realism," if I may call it that, promoted by Lloyd. But another generic philosophical theme has recently been gaining increasing prominence in Dennett's work, a theme alluded to earlier: verificationism. Dennett calls his verificationism "mild" because it is not strict *semantic* verificationism of the Carnapian sort. However, several papers here, most notably Tim *Kenyon*'s and William *Seager*'s, argue that it has a great deal of bite. Kenyon maintains that both Dennett's anti-reductionism about the mental and his insistence on the under-determination of intentional properties by physical ones require verificationism, but not Quinean indeterminacy, a thesis couched in a realist idiom that Kenyon finds incompatible with the rest of Dennett's project. Seager, in an essay of dazzling sweep, studies the tension between naturalism and antireductionism. Seager's conclusion is that if Dennett wishes to maintain that types recognized from the intentional stance are as real as types recognized by physics, as he does (see Dennett 1991b), while avoiding a generalized antireal-ism, then he must adopt what Seager calls "surface metaphysics." If a thesis saves the phenomena, Seager argues, then there is nothing further the Dennettian can consistently ask of it in judging its status as a contender in the effort to describe reality. The objects referred to in physical theories then—and only then—come out as being on all fours with the objects referred to in the intentional idiom. This ontological parity between intentional and other sorts of objects is also sought in the paper by Don *Ross*, though I approach it by broad-ening the scope of the predicate "real," in accordance with some suggestions of Dennett's, rather than by directly deflating the meta-physical commitment involved in calling something "real." I argue for a view I call "Rainforest Realism" (the adjective *rainforest* deriv-ing from taking Quine's image of the metaphysician trimming our ontology of overgrowth as my foil). Like Seager and Lloyd, I defend the idea that if beliefs and other propositional attitudes are to be regarded as properly real, then all vestiges of ontological reduc-tionism must be scotched. I thus argue that Dennett should abandon the distinction between *illata,* that is, entities that exist entirely in-dependently of our conceptualization of the world, and *abstracta,* entities that depend on conceptualizations such as "taking the intentional stance." To avoid an infinite ontology, I then offer a definition of existence that reformulates Occam's Razor in infor-mation-theoretic terms, and ties pattern-existence to the physical possibility of a pattern-detector. This second aspect avoids meta-physical anthropocentrism, and is in accord with Lloyd's formula-tion of pattern-dependent existence, though more explicit. My primary concern with ontological matters, however, leads me to make less use of Dennett's epistemic verificationism than Kenyon or Seager. I suggest that if the papers of Lloyd, Kenyon, Ross, and Seager are taken together, one arrives at "radical Dennettianism"— or perhaps we should say "Ryleanism updated in light of cognitive science."

Chris *Viger* also addresses his paper to the nature of Dennett's realism about the patterns tracked from the intentional stance. Viger argues that Dennett is advancing not so much an ontological claim as an epistemological one, about the grounds that warrant confidence that a stance is conducive to adequate explanation. Again, verificationist principles play a crucial role in Viger's explication of Dennett's implicit epistemology. Viger's paper also seems complimentary to what I just labelled "radical Dennettianism."

Kenyon, as noted above, argues that Dennett's verificationism renders his thesis that content-fixation from the intentional stance is indeterminate unnecessary for interpreting his relevant intuition pumps, and so turns radical indeterminacy into a piece of gratuitous metaphysics. Dennett, in his reply, resists this attempt to systematize him, arguing that although the indeterminacy may not require or be required by his other leading theses, he nevertheless has good reasons—reflections on cases, as usual—for regarding it as true. Both Ruth *Millikan* and David *Rosenthal* argue, in different ways, for mitigating the force of this indeterminacy. Millikan's view, as outlined in Millikan (1984) and elaborated upon in Millikan (1993), is that the space within which meanings can range is fixed by natural functions, which are determined through asking what an organ, behavioral disposition, or signaling capacity was selected for. This thesis, according to which facts about evolution provide a basis for arriving at facts about the interpretation of intentional states, is among the most widely discussed contemporary approaches to the analysis of meaning, and owes a large—and often acknowledged—debt to Dennett's introduction of evolutionary foundations for the philosophy of mind in his first book, *Content and Consciousness* (1969). Despite their affinities, Millikan notes an important space of possible disagreement between them: Whereas Dennett insists on Quinean indeterminacy of meaning with respect to intentional states, Millikan supposes that indeterminacy is localized by evolutionary facts; indeed, this is the point of her so-called teleosemantics. She then seeks to diagnose a more general difference that underlies this relatively contained one. Dennett, she suggests, holds the intentional stance to be more basic than the design stance, whereas she takes the order of logical priority to be reversed. As in the case of Kenyon, then, Millikan's approach through the indeterminacy thesis leads her to highly general issues in the foundations of cognitive science and epistemology. In response, Dennett offers one of his more virtuoso intuition pumps, his "Quinean crossword puzzle." This is intended to suggest that although there can be irreducible indeterminacy of meaning, the space in which it can realistically arise is vanishingly small. This might appear to be a substantial concession to Millikan and to Kenyon. However, as Dennett's full reply makes clear, the issue of the logical relationship between the intentional and design stances is indeed deeper than the problems associated with indeterminacy to which it gives rise. Here, Dennett stands his ground. All philosophers of mind should find a great deal of insight into the views of both Millikan and Dennett in this dialogue, and it is sure to be much discussed over the next few years.

Rosenthal argues that although subcognitive content is indeed semantically indeterminate for the reasons that Dennett claims, judgments, as higher-order thoughts whose content is sharply constrained by the external demands and semantic richness of public language, are subject to only "garden-variety," as opposed to radical Davidsonian, indeterminacy. In this case, Dennett is again concerned less with indeterminacy per se than with the deeper assumptions that motivate Rosenthal's skepticism about it. In Dennett's view, Rosenthal's insistence that a conscious state must be a possible object of a higher-order thought extends application of the concept of "consciousness" beyond what is required for either scientific progress or philosophical clarity.

Finally, in a response to Dennett's various writings on ethics and free will, Brian *Mooney* relates Dennett's "moral first-aid manual" to similar themes found in both ancient and modern virtue ethics. Mooney's antiperfectionism seems well in accord with Dennett's views in this area, and is integrated into the broader Dennettian philosophy through reference to the idea that no preengineered "moral technology" could possibly compete with exaptation from a more flexible, multipurpose set of moral concepts, concepts that, furthermore, evolve under pressures of cultural selection.

In response to these essays, Daniel *Dennett* provides yet another inimitable example of his philosophical style. Considering these responses as a set will much help scholars seeking to evaluate the order of priority among his various philosophical commitments. However, although a distinctive philosophical style is evident here, the question as to whether it stems from an integrated *philosophy* in the classical sense is not explicitly addressed. Dennett's coyness in response to the attempts to fashion one—notable, for example, in the papers of Kenyon, Lloyd, Ross, and Seager—may make our editorial project of finding a system beneath the details seem to have been preposterous after all. In light of this, I will sketch an impression of my own sense of the unifying threads in Dennett's corpus, based mainly on the points of consensus found in these essays and in Dennett's replies to them.

Dennett himself has often disclaimed ambitions to systematicity, and a method that typically consists in attacking putative conceptual necessities through invocation of intuition pumps, against which these "necessities" are held to founder, hardly seems to be that of the system-builder. In *Consciousness Explained,* Dennett cites Ryle and Wittgenstein as his prime sources of philosophical inspiration; and it is difficult to find thinkers more skeptical of conceptual systems than that pair. However, Dennett's skepticism is primarily of the road-clearing variety associated with his third regularly acknowledged mentor, Quine. Unlike the cases of Ryle and the later Wittgenstein, Dennett offers a connected set of positive conceptual theories: of intentionality, of consciousness, of the narrative self, of the foundations of biology, and of the sources of the sense of free will. Furthermore, if one compares the instances of his skepticism, one finds a distinctive and common logical pattern uniting its targets: Almost all are rigid conceptual boundaries of one sort or another. Between the paradigmatically intentional and the paradigmatically nonintentional, Dennett tries to convince us, there is no sharp divide, but only a smooth gradation from the minded to the mindless. Within the sphere of the intentional, the same point is emphasized concerning the distinction between conscious minds and unconscious ones. When we think about the nature of evolution or about the problem of free will, Dennett would have us shake off false dichotomies descended from a basic one, that between absolute historical contingency and algorithmic determinism. Qualia are quined not because Dennett imagines that there is nothing it is like to be conscious, but because no clear demarcation can be drawn between representations of qualitative properties and representations of other sorts of states. This skepticism about "necessary" distinctions often cuts quite fine: Among the theses defended in *Consciousness Explained* that have provoked the most resistance is the claim that there is no fact of the matter as to whether nonveridical perceptual memory results from preconscious or postconscious misrepresentation.

Of course, Dennett is hardly the first philosopher to campaign against essentialism. Indeed, antiessentialism is the clearest theme uniting Ryle, Quine, and the later Wittgenstein. However, Dennett reacts against firm conceptual lines not simply on the basis of nominalistic temperament. The essentializing impulse that is a fundamental motivation behind much philosophical speculation is flatly at odds with naturalism, because it arises from the mistake of supposing that the structure of our logical and linguistic representational systems must map neatly onto the structure of the world. We not only do things with words, Dennett reminds us; words also do things with us. We could not have science without a digitalizing system that enables us to make and store precise measurements, and that allows for immense informational compression. However, this "von Neumann machine" that, according to Dennett, is the basis of the narrative sense of self and of all the grand (and awful) cultural and scientific projects that selves narrate, is also an impediment to science the moment one imagines that nature must have joints just where our system of words draws them. We draw sharp distinctions between animal classes, which is a sensible thing to do given the time-scale at which most of our observations and reasoning must guide us; but then we may suppose that when the biologist tells us that mammals are descended from reptiles, this implies the absurdity that some mammal did not have a mammal for a mother. The mistake here consists, of course, in thinking that there is some "mammalian essence" that processes of recombination and mutation miraculously crossed. Notice that this example, a favorite of Dennett's, must be interpreted in a certain way if it is to have its intended force. Every scientifically literate person has gotten used to the idea that an attempted refutation of Darwinism based on the "paradox of mammalian descent" would involve a failure to respect evolutionary gradualism. We might thus suppose that only the ignorant are prone to essentialistic blunders of this sort. However, the disposition to over-digitalize the world is ubiquitous, and unavoidable unless our thinking is both very careful and always open to correction. Even scientific geniuses, Dennett argues in *Darwin's Dangerous Idea*, often fall victim to implicit postulation of counter-naturalistic "skyhooks" when they must think inside the glacial pace of evolutionary change. Similarly, neuroscientists abolish the *ghostly* Cartesian theater but then frequently end up with something yet more wondrous: a *physical* Cartesian theater. Note, as an example, the crucial role that essentialism plays in the genesis of this last mistake. In the environmental settings about which we typically speak, representations are produced for the consumption of whole minds, and they have their impressive causal effects by virtue of such consumption. It becomes natural to think that suitability for processing by a mindful audience is part of what it *means* for something to be a representation. At that point, it becomes difficult to talk about inner representation without smuggling a cunning homunculus into our conception. And if one is studying the computational processes of, say, a peripheral perceptual module, so that banishing the homunculus is somebody else's job, it is easiest to simply live with ridiculous posits. These, however, are most pernicious when we are used to them. Consider the "occult" action at a distance that made Newton wary of attaching physical reality to gravitational force. A century after his death, the mystery was as great as ever, but few were much bothered by it anymore, since the concept was so demonstrably practical. The confusions bred of essentialism hide more easily in familiar conceptions than in novel ones. Thus, when Dennett tries to abolish the Cartesian theater, and venerable notions that travel with it, such as

Don Ross

that of a quale, this strikes many people as less intelligible than the quaint picture of the mind he seeks to overthrow.

Essentialism is an elusive target, because in the contemporary philosophical literature it is usually accidental. Few philosophers believe in metaphysical essences of the old sort. Even those who are persuaded that natural kind terms refer uniquely in all possible worlds buttress this logical essentialism with a naturalistic story about causal relations that must undergird the logical ones. This, I suggest, accounts in part for the unease with which Dennett's work is often viewed. Philosophers regularly accuse one another of having inadequately justified opinions, but it is implicit in many of Dennett's campaigns that his opponents don't quite *understand* the opinions they defend. Of course, the same could be said of Wittgenstein. But his critique of the philosophical project has the double screen of being aphoristic and of seldom associating any names with the views it undermines except Wittgenstein's own. Furthermore, given his vintage one can read him in his skeptical moments as aiming narrowly at positivism, a position no one has defended for years. However, I think that Dennett is correct in emphasizing his affinities with Wittgenstein. Both work through force of examples to cast doubt on the unintended essentialism that arises not from metaphysical convictions but from the nature of the philosophical enterprise. Most philosophical theories are precisely *about* the boundaries of concepts, and so must try to identify properties of types that can serve as centers of conceptual gravity, holding their associated concepts in place and apart. These may not be essences of the traditional sort, but they are useful for the same reason: They prevent concepts from sliding about when we are trying to do argumentative work with them. This *is* genuine utility, as Dennett nowhere denies. However, he is a pragmatist about concepts (and here Quine's influence shows itself at its most abstract level). Regimented concepts are useful precisely to the extent that they help us to investigate the nature of real processes that operate as they do independently of our conceptualizations (except where they involve intentions in irreducible causal roles; see Dennett's comments on Viger's essay). It is when he finds conceptual conservatism interfering with our ability to dissolve mysteries that Dennett reaches for his intuition pumps.

To maintain that conceptual joints can and should be trumped by nature's (typically fuzzy) ones is to endorse some version of realism or other. With respect to the question of just what sort of realism this is, relative to the traditional philosophical alternatives, Dennett is himself unsure. Several papers in this volume attempt to pin him down on this, but Dennett, in his concluding comments, declines to be pinned; "My ontological convictions," he says there, "are now in happy disarray." Since I am among those who try to force Dennett's intuitions, I risk abusing my editorial privilege in trying to diagnose the source of this disarray. I venture the hypothesis, however, that what causes Dennett's hesitation may be the fact that most of us attempt to force him to one or another philosophical *theory,* that is, a set of metaphysical propositions. Now, Dennett's work does not display the fanatical squeamishness about such propositions expressed by (for example) the logical positivists. However, he appears to be wary about them for the following general reason. A philosophical thesis must mainly appeal to the virtue of consistency among beliefs we are already disposed to hold on the basis of experience. Most such beliefs have a property that must be grounds for suspicion to a radical naturalist such as Dennett: They will have been entertained for long enough (at least by somebody) to have grown comfortable. This implies both that they will have settled into our belief corpus through being domesticated by our intuitions, and that they will have had some influence on that corpus through the process of making themselves at home. As memes, they are both parasitic residents of minds and part-authors of those very minds. Occasional memes promote skepticism about themselves (e.g., the philosopher's venerable "bent stick" meme), but most clearly do just the opposite. A philosophical system that tries to resolve inconsistencies among them will thus tend to conceptual conservatism. One of the best devices for removing local threats of inconsistency is to define concepts in such a way that their boundaries do not cross; and this, of course, is precisely the sort of move that calls forth Dennett's skeptical tactics.

What has all this to do with an attitude toward metaphysics? Organization of our concepts by a philosophical theory must come at a price, that of making them more resistant, through the strength of

Don Ross

mutual support, to overthrow in the face of novelties discovered by science. However, being *dangerous* is one of the important things that, according to Dennett, good science is *for*. Darwin's idea is dangerous because it threatens our conceptual structure more deeply than even most biologists realize. For Dennett, the fact that we are thus forced to revise and reconstruct that structure, including those parts of it relevant to ethics, is among the idea's greatest merits. Metaphysical habits, however, may throw up a buffer that interferes with the realization of this virtue, providing both a basis and an additional motivation for sheltering traditional concepts against the corrosive effects of more recent discoveries. Furthermore, metaphysical theories, if they are of any worth at all, must have implications for what we should expect to find in nature; and of course we tend to interpret findings according to expectations. There is little we can or should do about this natural cognitive disposition, but to privilege products of reflection over deliberate observation and experiment is to make that in which we are less confident the basis for evaluating that in which we should be more confident. And so, I suggest, Dennett is reluctant to accept metaphysical claims because he is skittish about the prospect of taking on board unnoticed implications that might conflict with some sound scientific conclusion, in which case he would, upon discovery of the conflict, have to go back and revisit everything he had thought while under the influence of such claims.

This attitude of Dennett's, then, reflects his commitment to empiricism. This empiricism, however, does not involve any endorsement of a "myth of the given," and so it is not the sort of empiricism that directly conflicts with realism (except locally, when it runs against Dennett's modest verificationism, as in the case of putative distinctions between states of consciousness that are too fine-grained for conscious awareness to track). Dennett's realism sometimes seems to be of the naive variety, as when, in *Consciousness Explained,* he takes the everyday manifold of macroscopic physical objects for granted, while at other times his concerns seem to be those of the scientific realist, as in "Real Patterns." In this volume, Seager tugs in the direction of Dennett's empiricist intuitions, Brook pulls with his naive realist ones, and Lloyd and Ross emphasize his scientific-realist moments. Among all of these countervailing pressures, Dennett mainly just tries to hold his boat in place—wherever, exactly, that place is. This, I think, suggests that we are looking in the wrong place if we try to settle the question of Dennett's wide philosophical attitude in the context of sets of metaphysical and/or epistemological propositions he might or might not endorse. There is, as I will discuss below, something like a Dennettian method, but this noun connotes both too much and too little: too much because Dennett's approach is neither original nor easily replicable as a procedure, and too little because his general attitude *does* involve *some* clear—and controversial—epistemological commitments. What Dennett offers the philosopher at the general level, I will now maintain, is best captured by first explicating a concept that has been of tremendous importance over the course of his career: that of a "stance."

When we adopt the physical or the design or the intentional stance towards a system or process, we are not, if we are true to Dennett's usage, simply viewing the system or process *as if* it were physical or designed or minded. We *are* doing that, of course, but it is not *all* we are doing. If it were, this would be straightforward instrumentalism, an epistemology Dennett has struggled to disown. We cannot seriously take the intentional stance toward a rock or an electron because the facts of the matter in these cases will not support our doing so. And we *must* take the design stance toward the agents depicted in history or economics because if we do not we will be missing the *real* patterns we must track if we wish to gain any understanding of what is going on in these domains. When Dennett and Millikan, in this volume, disagree about the circumstances necessary for assuming the design stance, they both take their differences of opinion to depend upon *facts*. There is—of course—a gradation of cases between the extremes of the "simply physical" and the "irreducibly intentional," instances where either stance could capture an aspect of reality missed by the other. This does not imply that our decision between them is *ever* independent of what is the case. A stance is a foregrounding of some (real) systematically related aspects of a system or process against a compensating backgrounding of other aspects. It is both possible and useful to pick out these sets of aspects *because* (as a matter of fact) the boundaries of patterns very frequently do not correspond to the boundaries of the naive realist's objects. If they always *did* correspond, the design and intentional stances would be worthless, though there would have been no selection pressure to design a community in which this could be thought; and if they never corresponded, the physical stance, which puts essential constraints on reasonable design- and intentional-stance accounts, would be inaccessible. Because physical objects are stable patterns, there is a reliable logical basis for further order, but because many patterns are not coextensive with physical objects (in any but a trivial sense of "physical object"), a sophisticated informavore must be designed to, or designed to learn to, track them. To be a tracker of patterns under more than one aspect-ualization is to be a taker of stances.

Now then: If we try to be precise in our use of the notion of a stance, so that "stance" is not simply a loose synonym of "perspective" or "attitude," what can we say about patterns in philosophical thought such that it might be appropriate to say that Dennett tries to track them from a distinctive stance? I have so far been approaching this question from one side by focusing on Dennett's theoretical commitments (or refusal of them). Let us now try to corner the quarry by bringing a sortie up the other side and examining Dennett's typical method. He begins by taking in mind a concept— intentionality, consciousness, free will, or one of the many logical offspring of these grand memes, for example, qualia—about which intuitions are unsure and on which philosophical energy has been spent. He then draws out of the philosophical traditions sets of properties that philosophers seem to have roughly agreed to be at least jointly necessary for the application of the concept in question. (This, of course, is an ideal moment for Dennett's targets to try to avoid the coming train by looking for ways in which his round-up of the herd has missed what is distinctive about *their own* view.) The object of inquiry thus identified, the battery of intuition pumps can fire: Dennett presents a series of real cases, and carefully imagined ones, in which . . . but now something completely different happens, to paraphrase Monty Python. A typical philosopher would, at this point, apply one or both of Mill's methods at the level of conceptual inquiry. That is, we would get an analysis according to which the necessary properties are all in place but our intuitions nevertheless refuse to assign the concept in question, or in which they do assign the concept but at least one of the necessary properties is missing; or we would be provided with instances of both sorts of case. Dennett, of course, often argues in this fashion, but when he is after big game he usually does another, quite distinctive thing: He asks us to imagine paramaterizing values for the putative property. (So it's colored? What shade? So it has discrete instantiations? How many?) The point of this sort of exercise is to lead us to doubt that we had actually imagined *literally* limning the concept in question in terms of the specified properties. (Do you *really* suppose, after all, that you form a mental image of a red thing in which the image is literally red? Surely not. And once you've been shown that your image also has no edges, and no depth, and so on . . . in what sense are you literally postulating an *image*? Do saltationists *really* imagine paradigmatic members of one species giving birth to paradigmatic members of another species? If so, they believe something that's simply nutty, even according to their own theoretical lights. If not, their saltationism is just Darwinian selection with the film sped up.)

This way of using thought experiments, when successful, does not just lead us to adjust our conceptual theories by shuffling putatively necessary properties about. It is intended to show us that we have been *utterly* confused about the concept in question, usually, exactly to the extent that we have framed it in an essentialistic way. The approach has famous antecedents, Berkeley's criticism of the concept of matter being an obvious example. In Dennett's case, however, it is the basic critical technique. Sometimes it is mustered in support of a claim to the effect that a concept is hopelessly incoherent; qualia or zombies, for example. More often, it is intended to clear the ground for a fresh start. Seldom, however, does reconstruction proceed by way of direct analysis. In light of what has been said above, this should not be surprising; Dennett's brand of antiessentialism would be inconsistent with efforts at replacing sets of supposedly necessary properties with others. The next move in a typical Dennettian campaign is to ask how the concept could possibly have arisen. This is not an exercise in philology, since most of the concepts that interest Dennett are not pure cultural artifacts; rather, their history encapsulates attempts to make sense of a biologically

designed but culturally interpreted and enhanced set of mechanisms, behaviors, or dispositions, such as language. Since the point
of these "how possibly" stories is to dispel mystery, attention shifts
from the concept that was the original object of investigation to the
natural processes which it is the concept's function to help us understand, explain, and predict. The eliminativist element sometimes associated with Dennett arises from the fact that he seldom explains
a concept in terms of other concepts. Rather, he tries to understand
the mechanism that gives rise to the phenomena (and I use the plural in earnest) that the original concept was intended to denote, and
to which the simplicity of the denotation relation lent a misleading
appearance of unity. Dennett is therefore frequently criticized on
grounds that his deconstructed concepts are not quite put back together; it is thus a well-known quip, the original authorship of which
I have not been able to trace, that "*Consciousness Explained* should
have been called '*Consciousness Explained Away.*'" But this sort of
complaint simply misunderstands the general project. For Dennett,
a concept that represents a partly biological phenomenon can only
be in good working order to the extent that it is *not* thought to denote a neatly unified type, since evolution does not and cannot
produce such things. A Dennettian conceptual reconstruction,
therefore, could not be thought by its author to have been successful
if it were a *perfect* reconstruction.

We may now turn directly to the nature of a possible "Dennettian
stance" toward the philosophical project. An aspect of the project,
which one might call "the Platonic stance," consists, like Dennett's,
in seeking to eliminate half-hidden inconsistencies in our uses of
concepts. To the extent that this involves erecting necessary-and-
sufficient-condition definitions of concepts that are intended to do
extraformal work for us, however, it must appear from the Dennettian stance to be a distorting exaggeration of a sound impulse. It is
an equally important task of philosophy to try to resist the sort of
rigid thinking that overdigitalization of reality encourages, and to try
to invest our thought-implements with a degree of fluidity suitable to
natural and cultural spaces in which there are few sharp lines but
many gentle gradations around basins of attraction in similarity
matrices. Hence Dennett's unease with large-scale philosophical

"-isms"—realism, instrumentalism, empiricism, and so forth—that are massively priorized commitments to build the conceptual grid within the limits of particular recipes. Hence in turn the fact that we cannot associate Dennett with a neat set of epistemological or metaphysical principles, at least outside of localized problem spaces. What we find in Dennett is a combination of an attitude, one that favors the piecemeal construction of a worldview using the box of epistemic kludges that the development of science has opportunistically collected (and that philosophers have, as is their wont, tried to forge into a single self-consistent "scientific method"), and a manner of critical technique and partial reconstruction that I have tried to sketch. Like the intentional and design stances that Dennett has spent three decades describing, this combination of attitude and rough procedure is consistently applicable without being reducible to a set of rules and principles, and emphasizes certain aspects of the philosophical project while shifting others into the background.

Dennett's, then, is certainly not a "system" in the classical sense of the term. However, the Dennettian stance has something important in common with the true philosophical systems: Like them, it can readily be applied to areas of philosophical inquiry that are outside of its original domains of application. Dennett has himself shown the way in his work on free will and in his occasional forays into moral philosophy. In normative domains, there are two leading ways of being rigid. Attempting to devise procedural rules for all possible contexts is one of them, and this theme is explored here in the dialogue between Dennett and Mooney. The other principal obstacle to taking morality seriously, and the more common one in applied contexts, is the same habit of mind that is Dennett's generic target as a philosopher: essentialism about types of people and/or actions. If we ask "Was that *really* a lie?" or "Is that *really* rape?" we might simply be expressing, in a compressed way, questions about whether a particular episode falls within a settled part of our normative sphere. However, this mode of rhetorical address can be dangerous, since, again, words do things with us. If we begin thinking that what matters *first* is whether an action does or does not have some essential properties by virtue of which it counts as an instance of lying or of rape, and that this decision, rather than careful reflection on the particular details of the episode in its context, is then the appropriate basis for determining a suitable response, we are likely to commit egregious sins of *both* forgiveness and intolerance. When types of people are essentialized, the danger is both greater and more obvious—so obvious, one might suppose, that only a person of dismally unreflective moral sensibilities could fall into the mistake. I am not so confident. In South Africa, where I live, there is a lively debate going on among intellectuals, journalists, and politicians over what constitutes a "real African," and the regularly touted necessary conditions almost invariably appeal to racial or cultural histories. The fact that these answers are not immediately seen as exposing the pernicious foolishness of the question suggests that the virtues of the Dennettian stance in public moral life need reinforcement.

Dennett's own views on normative matters reflect his general philosophical stance. Though he believes that the impulse to make moral judgments has and requires a biological basis, he is opposed to any principle that would elide over Hume's guillotine by supposing that we must "side with our genes." Dennett thus agrees with most philosophers in regarding the content of morality as a cultural product. However, whereas many philosophers feel compelled to block a threatened slide from this conclusion into moral skepticism through construction of complex procedural or metaphysical theories of moral justification, Dennett's reflections indicate serene unconcern with morality's metaphysical status, but some dissatisfaction with the way in which it is thought about and practised *in situ*. The recent direction of his work suggests that these interests now carry high cerebral fame with him: The last third of *Darwin's Dangerous Idea* is devoted to them, and his present book project revisits the issues of *Elbow Room* in an expanded theoretical setting. Might we soon have a set of new intuition pumps encouraging us to shed essentialistic habits in moral reflection, in preparation for the reconstruction of a "moral stance"? I have no inside information on where Dennett's current thinking on free will and responsibility is going, but the normative domain seems well suited to being understood by means of the "stance" stance. Morality deeply puzzles philosophers, and attracts much of their attention, for the same basic reason that the ontology of mind does: because it and its associated concepts do not drop easily into a naturalistic perspective. Dennett's approach to this difficulty where mind is concerned has been to urge the end of attempts at chiseling and torturing the concept until it can be wrenched into place; the mystery is instead to be dissolved indirectly, through showing that evolutionary design considerations are not only compatible with, but can actually explain the basis of, a plurality of stances that carve one world across different sets of joints. Might we best understand morality by first grasping in detail its biological basis, but then backgrounding Mother Nature's interests and viewing the web of—real—relationships between our own interests, obligations, and responsibilities from a "moral stance" that abstracts away from naturally designed functions while still acknowledging their causal potency by treating them as the principal elements of noise in our patterns of moral response and judgment? If Dennett himself has no inclinations in this direction, then it seems to me that some other philosopher who works inside the Dennettian stance might usefully give it a try.

These last reflections on Dennett and moral philosophy lead us to a more incidental, but certainly not unimportant, respect in which Dennett is reminiscent of the systematic philosophers. Like them, he has written something of importance on almost every subject of traditional philosophical attention (the exception being the nature of the *polis*). As noted above, few authors here reach for this broad scope—though Seager and Lloyd come close—and that is likely for the best. What gives these essays their unity is that all, with the possible exceptions of Crowe's and Polger's, work to a large extent from inside the Dennettian stance. This leads them to converge on a number of large themes. By way of illustration, no author here explicitly sets out to write on Dennett's brand of verificationism, yet several end up giving it pride of place from different angles. Thus Kenyon, while mainly concerned to argue that Dennett's theory of intentionality does not depend upon or imply Quinean indeterminacy and would, indeed, be better off traveling without it, finds it necessary to forge connections between Dennett's picture of meaning and those of Wright and Dummett. This is an innovation in the literature, and one that philosophers of semantics should find both surprising and worthy of further attention. The link is established by way of reflections on the relationship between realism and verificationism, something visited within different contexts by at least four other authors. In general, where verificationism is mentioned in this volume the tone is sympathetic. This is unusual, to say the least. Is the epistemology that has dared not speak its name for over two decades about to come out of the closet—and in alliance with realism, the very force that drove it underground in the first place?

Grand philosophical themes such as the foregoing are not what one would expect to find in a book about Dennett, and the organizers of the Newfoundland conference were surprised at the amount of attention they received. It did not seem to be anyone's impression that this resulted from a desire by participants to wander off topic. Perhaps we should hypothesize that it is not as easy to discuss philosophical issues in abstinence from classical problems as immersion in the Dennettian stance might have us think.

References

Dawkins, R. (1976). *The Selfish Gene*. Oxford: Oxford University Press.

Dennett, D. (1969). *Content and Consciousness*. London: Routledge.

Dennett, D. (1981). *Brainstorms*. Cambridge, Mass.: MIT Press. A Bradford Book.

Dennett, D. (1984). *Elbow Room*. Cambridge, Mass.: MIT Press. A Bradford Book.

Dennett, D. (1987). *The Intentional Stance*. Cambridge, Mass.: MIT Press. A Bradford Book.

Dennett, D. (1988). The moral first-aid manual. In *The Tanner Lectures on Human Values, VIII*, M. Walzer (ed.). Cambridge, Mass.: Cambridge University Press.

Dennett, D. (1991a). *Consciousness Explained*. Toronto: Little, Brown.

Dennett, D. (1991b). Real patterns. *Journal of Philosophy* 88: 27–51.

Dennett, D. (1995). *Darwin's Dangerous Idea*. New York: Simon and Schuster.

Millikan, R. (1984). *Language, Thought, and Other Biological Categories*. Cambridge, Mass.: MIT Press. A Bradford Book.

Millikan, R. (1993). *White Queen Psychology and Other Essays for Alice*. Cambridge, Mass.: MIT Press. A Bradford Book.

2

Daniel Dennett's Views on the Power and Pervasiveness of Natural Selection: An Evolutionary Biologist's Perspective

Timothy M. Crowe

A Philosophical Dichotomy

Since my undergraduate days in the mid-1960s, I have been exposed to a sharp philosophical dichotomy in evolutionary biology between selective determinism and historical contingency. By selective determinism I mean the potential for neo-Darwinian, natural selection to generate products (=species) that have remarkably similar biological "architectures," independent of their degree of evolutionary relatedness. Richard Dawkins (1976, 1982, 1986) is without question the most well-known proponent of the primacy, if not ubiquity and omnipotence, of natural selection as the driving force behind biological evolution. The fundamental assumptions underlying his position are that natural selection works through gradual, small-in-effect, step-by-step, genetic change and that, inevitably, it leads to design in the form of adaptations. Advocates of historical contingency, on the other hand, maintain that evolution (especially that which occurs at speciation) can be influenced by other factors in addition to natural selection and that it can sometimes occur in large steps. The other factors include historical forces and biological constraints (e.g., existing form, developmental canalization, indirect incidental effects of adaptation, immunity to selection, evolutionary setting, etc.) that can thwart or manipulate the direction of natural selection. Stephen Jay Gould (1980, 1982) is one of the leading champions of historical contingency as an additional causal factor in biotic evolution. He (1980, 119) has gone so far as to say that neo-Darwinism has "as an exclusive proposition . . . broken down on both its fundamental claims" (i.e., that natural selection acts via gradual, small-step, genetic change and that it inevitably leads to adaptation). More specifically, adaptations resulting from natural selection, like the spandrels essential to shore up the dome of the cathedral at San Marco, can be embellished with biological "artwork," to no apparent selective or adaptational advantage, thereby incidentally increasing biological diversity (Gould and Lewontin 1979).

Is Neo-Darwinism Passé?

In his various writings on evolutionary biology, epitomized in *Darwin's Dangerous Idea* (1995; hereafter DDI), Daniel Dennett argues eloquently and passionately for the omnipotence of selective determinism. Natural selection, he maintains, plays an essential role in the understanding of every biological event at every hierarchical level, from the creation of self-replicating macromolecules to evolutionary lineages. Quite simply, it is the sine qua non of evolution. The primary motive that drove Dennett to write DDI was his perception that many of his nonbiologist colleagues believe that neo-Darwinism is under scientific siege or has even been undermined by the scientific and semipopular writings of Gould and other advocates of historical contingency.

Dennett's Mission

In DDI, Dennett attempts to do three things: (1) to dispose of the requirement of, or recourse to, overriding, external, miraculous, godlike or Cartesian forces (="skyhooks") in explaining biological evolution; (2) to show that natural selection equals biological engineering driven by a foolproof, gradual, step-by-step, substrate-neutral, algorithmic design process; and (3) to prove that natural selection is a "universal acid" that has effects and applications well beyond biology to the extent that it "unifies the realm of life, meaning, and purpose within the realm of space and time, cause and effect, mechanism and physical law" (DDI, 21).

Does He Succeed?

This chapter has two purposes: (1) to express my views as an evolutionary biologist on the extent to which Dennett has achieved his three aims; and (2) to elucidate these views with an example based on the evolution of guineafowl (African gamebirds similar to chickens), a topic I have been researching for nearly thirty years. Gamebirds have been used time and again by evolutionary biologists, including Charles Darwin, to illustrate adaptations relating to topics such as territoriality, social dominance, sexual selection, kin selection, geographical adaptation, biological "weaponry," etc.

Aim 1: Cranes vs. Skyhooks   Dennett attempts to achieve his first aim by characterizing some of the products of natural selection, for example, sexual reproduction and competition, symbiosis, large brain size, and human language as evolutionary "cranes" firmly rooted in biological reality. These cranes can greatly enhance the efficacy and speed of adaptation via natural selection. Given enough time, they can help natural selection to produce all of the diversity expressed in extinct and extant organisms. There is no need to resort to evolutionary "skyhooks," that is, miraculous, godlike forces with no scientific basis, to explain any aspect or product of evolution.

I know of no evolutionary biologist, including Gould, who disputes the central importance of natural selection and its various cranes in the process of adaptation. Thus Dennett clearly achieves Aim 1.

Having said this, I cannot describe this achievement as a decisive scientific or philosophical victory over opponents with markedly different views. Gould and other advocates of a role for historical contingency try to do two things. First, they attempt to demonstrate that additional forces (beyond, not instead of or more important than, natural selection) can sometimes be involved in, and/or influence, the evolutionary process. Second, they present empirical evidence that evolutionary change, especially during speciation, can occur in large, effectively saltatory, steps. Although natural selection *sensu* Dawkins and Dennett is the universal explanation for adaptation, it is not the only way of generating biological diversity. For example, Gould and Niles Eldredge (Eldredge and Gould 1972; Gould and Eldredge 1993) have demonstrated from empirical, paleontological studies that evolution can be strikingly nongradual over evolutionary time, with eons of morphological stasis punctuated by bursts of change, presumably coincident with speciation events. This notion of saltatory evolution or speciation is supported by Orr and Coyne's (1992) finding that small genetic changes with large phenotypic effects play a significant role in evolution. Furthermore, Gould, like Richard Goldschmidt (1940) of "Hopeful Monster" fame, maintains that speciation events can be decidedly nonadaptive consequences of random genetic change or indirect effects of adaptations to living in novel habitats. I will give a possible example of how this might have happened later.

Aim 2: Does Natural Selection Equal Biological Engineering? Although biological evolution leading to adaptations clearly requires no recourse to skyhooks or "blind watchmakers," the equation of evolution by natural selection with engineering leading to design is unsubstantiated. This is because of the ways that natural selection works (and cannot work) and the differences between the products of engineering and biological evolution. True engineering involves skillful planning, research and development, and is about optimality and design aimed at solving problems.

No one, Dawkins and Dennett included, has demonstrated that biological evolution via natural selection has an R&D component or is anything other than a short-term, ad hoc, design-free process. Natural selection involves relatively poor reproductive performance or death of less-fit individuals, rather than the survival of the fittest along directed journeys up adaptational "ramps" to peaks of engineering optima in Design Space. More than likely, it is a long and winding road of trial, error, and ultimately, compromise. Remember, the units acted upon by natural selection are individual organisms. They survive and proliferate, to a greater or lesser extent, according to the combined fitness of, and interaction between, the genes that determine their form. In the end, it is their form (=phenotype) that has to cope with nature.

In some cases concerning molecules (e.g., for noncoding DNA), evolution can even occur essentially at random, independently of natural selection (Kimura 1983). In extreme cases, for example, the loss of flight by some island-dwelling birds and of eyes by cave-dwelling insects, it can follow an evolutionary "down-ramp" and even undermine the very design it has generated. The cranes of natural selection lift the fitness of individual organisms, demes, and populations, rather than developing biological design-features that are in reality effects of that upliftment. They do not find "good ways of solving problems that arise" (DDI, 133), but act as filters rather than drivers. Species are not, like Grand Prix racing cars, products of carefully thought out design based on R&D. They are make-shift, mosaic jalopies, the design of which is limited by the array of attributes evolutionarily accessible at the time. Thus Dennett fails to achieve Aim 2.

Aim 3: Is Natural Selection a Substrate-Neutral "Universal Acid"? Neo-Darwinian natural selection cannot be a substrate-neutral process. In biology, it requires very specific substrates, that is, the functional molecules known as genes: Mendel's Library, in Dennett's terms. Natural selection works by filtering out relatively less-fit, discrete, alternative genetic options, that is, alleles, from local populations. Indeed, it is the very absence of a precise counterpart to genes that best demonstrates that cultural evolution is not a process similar to biological evolution via natural selection. The substrates for cultural evolution, Richard Dawkins's memes (=ideas) (Dawkins 1982), simply do not qualify as cultural genes. Dawkins (1982, 112) and Dennett (DDI, 369) acknowledge this fact explicitly. This is because memes are not discrete entities that mutate at random, as do, for example, nucleotides (the basic building blocks of DNA and genes). In fact, mimetic mutation can be decidedly Lamarckian (=directed), being shaped by the popularity of a given meme. Memes are also often blends of two or more ideas that can be acquired or inherited in a decidedly non-Darwinian fashion. Therefore, Dennett is incorrect in maintaining that neo-Darwinian natural selection has played and continues to play an important role in shaping the development of human culture. Thus Dennett fails to achieve Aim 3.

Dennett is, nevertheless, correct when he states that natural selection has almost certainly contributed to the development of the core

Timothy M. Crowe

equipment necessary for culture, for example, the human brain and language. In practice, natural selection can help to create the potential to produce a television. However, other forces, for example, audience popularity and personality clashes between program producers and network executives, determine whether it's the Cosby Show or WWF wrestling that is shown on Wednesday evenings at 7 P.M. In fact, historical contingency may be a more fruitful starting point from which to develop a mechanism for cultural evolution.

An Example

Perhaps the best way to illustrate why I believe that both selective determinism and historical contingency collaborate to generate biological diversity is to give my scenario on the evolution and speciation of guineafowl. Guineafowl (*Galliformes: Numididae*) are African gamebirds similar to chickens. Before I can tell my "just-so" story, I first have to outline how the genera, species, and subspecies of guineafowl differ from one another.

What Makes a Guineafowl a Guineafowl?

Guineafowl differ from most other galliforms in having largely unfeathered heads and necks (Crowe 1978). One of the adaptations of this naked head and neck, at least in the helmeted guineafowl *Numida meleagris*, is the ability to cool relatively warm arterial blood being pumped upward to the brain from the heart within a car-radiator-like nexus of venules carrying relatively cool blood downward (Crowe and Crowe 1979; Crowe and Withers 1979). This "radiator" allows helmeted guineafowl to dump heat effectively under conditions of high ambient temperature (Withers and Crowe 1980), allowing them to forage and socialize throughout more of the hot African day. The helmeted guineafowl differs primarily from species in the three other genera of guineafowl in the color of the naked skin of its head, eyes, and other facial structures and adornments (Crowe 1978), and in the pitch of its advertisement cackle (Crowe et al. 1986). These morphological and behavioral characteristics are presumably functional components within the species' specific-mate recognition system (SMRS) (Paterson 1985), allowing helmeted guineafowl to instinctively distinguish conspecifics from members of other guineafowl species. The shape and color of these head adornments have no other obvious adaptive physiological or other functions.

The other prominent feature that distinguishes guineafowl from one another, the pitch of the advertisement calls, seems to be positively correlated with the openness of habitat (Crowe et al. 1986). For example, the black guineafowl *Agelastes niger*, which lives in primary rainforest, has a very low-pitched call. The call of the crested guineafowl *Guttera pucherani*, which lives in secondary forest and riverine bush, is somewhat higher pitched. The call of helmeted guineafowl, which live in open savanna habitat, is higher pitched still. Finally, that of the vulturine guineafowl *Acryllium vulturinum*, which lives in much more open desertic grass and bush land, has the highest pitch of all. One possible adaptive function for the variation in call pitch is that lower-pitched calls can penetrate thicker vegetation more effectively than high-pitched calls, which, in turn, function better in open habitats.

Within-Species Variation

Focusing on the helmeted guineafowl as a species, there is also striking, effectively qualitative geographical variation in head color and adornments among its various subspecies (Crowe 1978). For example, the west African subspecies has a very small helmet, white facial skin, rounded red wattles and very long, hairlike feathers confined to the midline of its nape and neck. The subspecies from the north-central savannas has a much larger helmet, blue facial skin, rounded blue wattles, and very short, feltlike feathers extending broadly over the nape and neck. The various subspecies from the southern savannas have much larger helmets, blue faces, pennant-shape wattles (blue with red tips), and, once again, long hairlike feathers confined to the midline of the nape and neck. None of this variation: (1) has any demonstrable adaptive value (Crowe 1979), (2) plays any role in specific-mate recognition (Elbin et al. 1986), or (3) inhibits inter-breeding between members of the various subspecies (Ghigi 1936).

For example, when domesticated helmeted guineafowl (derived from western Africa) are bred in captivity with members of other subspecies from as far afield as Somalia and eastern Africa (Ghigi 1936), or are released into populations of wild helmeted guineafowl in southern Africa (Walker et al., in prep.), they interbreed freely without any apparent loss of fertility. Indeed, within the zones of natural geographical contact between subspecies of this guineafowl, there is demonstrably free interbreeding, producing intergrades of all persuasions (Crowe 1978).

Crowe's "Just-So" Story

Now that we know how to identify the various forms of guineafowl, how might an evolutionary scenario based on both selective determinism and historical contingency account for their evolution and speciation?

Guineafowl appear to have been descended from ancestors that had feathered heads and lived, 90+ million years ago, in forested habitats in Gondwana, a megacontinent comprising South America, Africa, and Australasia (Mainardi 1963; Simonetta 1963; Holman 1964; Hudson et al. 1966; Cracraft 1972, 1981; Laskowski and Fitch 1979; Crowe 1988; Sibley and Ahlquist 1990; Kornegay et al. 1993; Crowe et al., in prep.). After Gondwana broke up into its present-day pieces, a still very much-forested Africa (Axelrod and Raven 1978) "drifted" northward, colliding some 17–20 million years ago with Eurasia. This collision caused marked changes in the African climate that, on average and progressively, favored the development of savannas and deserts at the expense of forested habitat (Axelrod and Raven 1978). This progressive climatic and vegetational change provided the necessary selective pressure that could have allowed natural selection to generate the proto-guineafowl with a naked head and neck, which could function more effectively in more open, hotter habitats. Now historical contingency clicks in as well.

Over evolutionary time, long-term climatic trends are clouded by shorter-term variation. In an African context, this means relatively microclimatic variation that allowed forests and savannas to spread and contract, forming island-like patches and fragments of one habitat or the other (Butzer 1967). It is within these islands that both selection-driven and neutral, incidental, and/or macromorphological change could have occurred (Kingdon 1989). By selection-driven change, I mean transformation of attributes like the pitch of the guineafowls' advertisement calls to allow them to function more effectively in their respective novel habitats. By neutral change, I mean the transformation of head adornments and coloration into states that characterize the various subspecies of Helmeted Guineafowl. Thus, like Gould and Lewontin's (1979) spandrels of San Marco, the functional, naked heads and necks of the proto-guineafowl could have provided a template that could have been embellished helter-skelter with apparently functionless head coloration and adornments, the differences among which are insufficient to undermine specific-mate recognition. However, in a few rare cases, perhaps as incidental, nonadaptive consequences of selection to function better in novel environments, changes in these adornments were of sufficient magnitude to breach the SMRS gap, creating, ultimately, the various species and genera of guineafowl.

In short, selective determinism driven by natural selection could have played the pivotal role in promoting the transformation of the ancestors of guineafowl into the precursor of the naked-headed creatures that have been the objects of my scientific obsession since the 1960s. However, the dynamic creation and reconnection of habitat islands, time and again, may have allowed selective determinism and historical contingency to "experiment" with various geographical isolates of guineafowl. Some of these experiments may have succeeded in generating the species we see today.

Is Speciation an Adaptive Process Driven Directly by Natural Selection?

Genetic species, at least species of sexual organisms, are cohesive gene pools bound together by the ability to interbreed (Mayr 1963; Paterson 1985; Templeton 1989). Indeed, if Paterson (1985) is correct, the "glue" that binds them are their SMRSs. Because of their central importance to successful interbreeding, the components of SMRSs should be under extremely strong stabilizing selection to "resist" change. So, if speciation requires a sufficient large change in an SMRS, how can this be an adaptive process driven directly by neo-Darwinian natural selection? Indeed, why would an individual organism or population "want" to cut itself off from the fullest spectrum of potential mates by speciating?

The answer is historical contingency *sensu* Gould and Lewontin (1979). Isolated populations of conspecifics under strong directional, or better still, bidirectional disruptive selection, can have their SMRSs change to function more efficiently in novel environments. If the change is of sufficient magnitude, when the transformed isolates come into contact again, they will not recognize one another as conspecifics. In effect, speciation can be an incidental, accidental, indirect, even maladaptive consequence of normal adaptation, a process that falls squarely within the realm of historical contingency. Furthermore, contrary to Dennett, such situations show that natural selection does not time and again produce the guaranteed results generated by an algorithmic process. This is because adaptive transformation of calls not involved with specific-mate recognition would not result in speciation, whereas similar changes in those that form part of an SMRS may. Thus quizzically, by taking only a gene's-eye, design-process view, Dennett underestimates the full potential (however inadvertent or undirected it might be) of natural selection.

What's the Real Problem?

I believe that the real problem behind what has descended into a war of words between Dennett, Gould, and their respective supporters stems from Dennett's determination for Gould to "come clean" in the semipopular literature and admit unambiguously the primacy (but not exclusivity) of natural selection in biological evolution. To achieve this aim, Dennett's negative comments on Gould's views have become increasingly strident (Dennett 1997). Gould, at least as far as I can tell from my literature searches, has not done this. He and supporters such as H. Allen Orr have, predictably, reacted to Dennett in kind, claiming foul. They maintain (Gould 1997a,b; Orr 1995) that their views on evolution are not an alternative, but rather a corrective adjunct, to the adaptationist, panselectionist program. The Gould "camp," on the other hand, might have reacted less disparagingly to what they characterize as Dennett's "one-process-fits-all" position, if he would admit the secondary importance of possible rapid nonselective and/or macromutational change, especially coincident with speciation. Is this too much to ask, given that even Charles Darwin admitted in the last edition of his *Origin of Species* that natural selection was not the exclusive means of evolution? Nevertheless, Dennett still sticks to his panselectionist position (Dennett 1997).

Where Do We Go from Here?

Clearly, the ongoing debate between extremists advocating selective determinism and panselection on the one hand versus historical contingency on the other will not be settled in the semipopular literature. Gould, Lewontin, and Orr are right in criticizing an ultra-adaptationist position that rests solely on clever "just-so" stories, is long on conjecture, short on empirical evidence, and dependent on the power and pervasiveness of one particular mode of evolution. Dennett (1997) also calls for more substance and less rhetoric in the quest for clear-cut answers relating to the causal basis of evolution. I will be the first to admit that, although it is based on some fairly solid descriptive, correlative, and experimental evidence, my evolutionary scenario for guineafowl is not much more than a just-so story. For example, if it could be shown that head adornments of the various subspecies of helmeted guineafowl might have some function akin to that of the unadorned naked head and neck, the influence of historical contingency may be downplayed or eliminated. Then I and other evolutionary story-tellers could remove words like "more than likely," "it is possible," and "could have caused" from our scenarios.

At present, however, my scientific research tells me that historical contingency has played a significant, but as yet unspecified and poorly quantified role in biological evolution, perhaps especially in speciation. The magnitude of its contribution requires much more empirical, especially experimental, research.

Timothy M. Crowe

Acknowledgments

My research on the evolution of guineafowl has been funded primarily by the Foundation for Research Development, the African Game-bird Research, Education and Development Trust, the University of Cape Town, and a range of natural history museums, especially the American Museum of Natural History. My attendance at this meeting honoring Daniel Dennett was funded, in part, by the Foundation for Research Development, the University of Cape Town, and the organizing committee (of the Dennett meeting). I thank Don Ross for inviting me to present this paper and commenting on its first draft and Daniel Dennett for his constructive rebuttal.

References

Axelrod, D. I. and Raven, P. H. (1978). Late Cretaceous and Tertiary vegetation history of Africa. *Monographie Biologica* 31: 77–130.

Butzer, K. W. (1967). Hypothetical rainfall and vegetation zones. In *Atlas of African Prehistory*, J. Desmond-Clark (ed.). London: University of Chicago Press.

Cracraft, J. (1972). The relationships of higher taxa of birds: Problems in phylogenetic reasoning. *Condor* 74: 379–392.

Cracraft, J. (1981). Towards a phylogenetic classification of the recent birds of the world (Class: *Aves*). *Auk* 98: 681–814.

Crowe, T. M. (1978). The evolution of guineafowl (*Galliformes, Phasianidae, Numidinae*): Taxonomy, phylogeny, speciation, and biogeography. *Ann. S. Afr. Mus.* 76: 43–136.

Crowe, T. M. (1979). Adaptive morphological variation in helmeted guineafowl *Numida meleagris* and crested guineafowl *Guttera pucherani*. *Ann. S. Afr. Mus.* 121: 313–320.

Crowe, T. M. (1988). Molecules vs. morphology in phylogenetics: A non-controversy. *Trans. Roy. Soc. S. Afr.* 46: 317–334.

Crowe, T. M. and Crowe, A. A. (1979). Anatomy of the vascular system of the head and neck of the helmeted guineafowl. *J. Zool., Lond.* 188: 221–233.

Crowe, T. M. and Withers, P. C. (1979). Brain temperature regulation in helmeted guineafowl. *S. Afr. J. Sci.* 75: 362–365.

Crowe, T. M., Keith, G. S., and Brown, L. H. (1986). Galliformes. In *Birds of Africa*, Vol. II, Urban, E., Fry, C. H., and Keith, G. S. (eds.). London: Academic Press.

Crowe, T. M., Bloomer, P., Randi, E., Lucchesi, V., Kimball, R., Braun, E., and Groth, J. G. (in prep.). Cladistics and classification of gamebirds: Effects of character selection, weighting and partitioning and missing data, or What kind of fowl am I? Department of Zoology, University of Cape Town.

Dawkins, R. (1976). The *Selfish Gene*. Oxford: Oxford University Press.

Dawkins, R. (1982). *The Extended Phenotype: The Gene as the Unit of Selection*. Oxford: Freeman.

Dawkins, R. (1986). *The Blind Watchmaker*. London: Longmans.

Dennett, D. C. (1995). *Darwin's Dangerous Idea: Evolution and the Meanings of Life*. New York: Simon and Schuster.

Dennett, D. C. (1997). To the editors. *The New York Review*. August 14, 1997: 64–65.

Elbin, S. B., Crowe T. M., and Graves, H. B. (1986). Reproductive behaviour of helmeted guineafowl [*Numida meleagris*]: Mating system and parental care. *Appl. Anim. Behav. Sci.* 16: 179–197.

Eldredge, N. and Gould, S. J. (1972). Punctuated equilibria: An alternative to phyletic gradualism. In *Models in Paleobiology*, Schopf, T. J. M. (ed.). San Francisco: Freeman, Cooper and Co.

Ghigi, A. (1936). *Galline di Faraone e Tacchini*. Milan: V. Hoepli.

Goldschmidt, R. B. (1940). *The Material Basis of Evolution*. Seattle: University of Washington Press.

Gould, S. J. (1980). Is a new and general theory of evolution emerging? *Paleobiology* 6: 119–130.

Gould, S. J. (1982). The meaning of punctuated equilibrium and its role in validating a hierarchical approach to macroevolution. In *Perspectives in Evolution*, Milkman, R. (ed.). Sunderland, Mass.: Sinauer Press.

Gould, S. J. (1997a). Darwinian fundamentalism. *The New York Review*. June 12, 1997: 34–37.

Gould, S. J. (1997b). Evolution: The pleasures of pluralism. *The New York Review*. June 26, 1997: 47–52.

Gould, S. J. and Eldredge, N. (1993). Punctuated equilibrium comes of age. *Nature* 366: 223–227.

Gould, S. J. and Lewontin, R. (1979). The spandrels of San Marco and the Panglossian paradigm: A critique of the adaptationist programme. *Proc. Roy. Soc.* B205: 581–598.

Holman, J. A. (1964). Osteology of gallinaceous birds. *Quart. J. Florida Acad. Sci.* 27(3): 230–252.

Hudson, G. E., Parker, R. A., Vanden Berge, J., and Lanzillotti, P. J. (1966). A numerical analysis of modifications of appendicular muscles of various genera of gallinaceous birds. *Amer. Midl. Natur.* 76(1): 1–83.

Kimura, M. (1983). *The Neutral Theory of Molecular Evolution.* Cambridge, Mass.: Cambridge University Press.

Kingdon, J. (1989). *Island Africa: The Evolution of Africa's Rare Animals and Plants.* Princeton: Princeton University Press.

Kornegay, J. R., Kocher, T. D., Williams, L. A., and Wilson, A. C. (1993). Pathways of lysozyme evolution inferred from sequences of cytochrome b in birds. *J. Mol. Evol.* 37: 367–379.

Laskowski, M. and Fitch, W. M. (1979). Evolution of avian ovomucoids and of birds. In *The Hierarchy of Life,* B. Fernholm, K. Bremer, and H. Jornvall (eds.). Amsterdam: Excerta Medica Publisher.

Mainardi, D. (1963). Immunological distances and phylogenetic relationships of birds. *Proc. 13th Intl. Orn. Congr.* 103–114.

Mayr, E. (1963). *Animal Species and Evolution.* Cambridge, Mass.: Harvard University Press.

Orr, H. A. (1995). Dennett's dangerous idea (review of *Darwin's Dangerous Idea,* by Daniel C. Dennett, New York: Simon and Schuster). *Evolution* 50: 467–472.

Orr, H. A. and Coyne, J. A. (1992). The genetics of adaptation: A reassessment. *Am. Nat.* 140: 725–842.

Paterson, H. E. H. (1985). The recognition concept of species. In *Species and Speciation,* Vrba, E. S. (ed.). Transvaal Museum Monograph No. 4. Pretoria: Transvaal Museum.

Sibley, C. G. and Ahlquist, J. E. (1990). *Phylogeny and Classification of Birds.* New Haven: Yale University Press.

Simonetta, A. M. (1963). Cinesi e morfologia del cranio negli uccelli non passeriformi. Studio su varie tendenze evolutive. Part I. *Arch. Zool. Ital. (Torino)* 48: 53–135.

Templeton, A. R. (1989). The meaning of species and speciation: A genetic perspective. In *Speciation and Its Consequences,* D. Otte and J. Endler (eds.). Sunderland, Mass.: Sinauer.

Walker, A. L., Ratcliffe, C. S., Bowie, R. C. K., and Crowe, T. M. (in prep.). Molecular evidence of interbreeding between wild and feral domestic helmeted guineafowl *Numida meleagris.* Department of Zoology, University of Cape Town.

Withers, P. C. and Crowe, T. M. (1980). Brain temperature fluctuations of helmeted guineafowl under semi-natural conditions. *Condor* 82: 99–101.

3

Good Tricks and Forced Moves, or, The Antinomy of Natural Reason

Paul Dumouchel

If consciousness is the result of evolution through natural selection, then borrowing two terms introduced in Daniel Dennett's *Darwin's Dangerous Idea* (1995), we may ask the question of whether it is a "Forced Move" or a "Good Trick." The dichotomy is of course not perfect. The choice is not exclusive, given that some Forced Moves are Good Tricks, though others are not, and presumably not all Good Tricks are Forced Moves. What the question really asks is whether consciousness is inevitable, a more or less unavoidable solution in a given situation X, a bottle-neck in design space; or is it a sufficient response, one that was to some extent selected by chance from among many different, but more or less equivalent, solutions to a given problem? How should one go about answering such a question? What is the problem or situation to which consciousness is a solution? Or should one even try to resolve this difficulty? Does the question mean anything? Is there any real (meaningful, interesting, important) difference between Forced Moves and Good Tricks?

1. At first blush the difference seems evident. Forced Moves, as their name says, are forced upon you, not necessarily because they are good, but because they are all there is. Good Tricks on the other hand are adopted (whether they were chosen or chanced upon is of little importance) because they are good. Yet, on closer inspection, especially in the domain that interests us here, evolution through natural selection, the issue appears somewhat different. Both Forced

Moves and Good Tricks are examples of what Dennett (1995, 96) has aptly named "retrospective coronations." This is not a very surprising conclusion concerning Forced Moves and Good Tricks given that, in evolution, everything is a "retrospective coronation"—everything, at least, that is not selected against, and for as long as it is not. The claim is nonetheless not empty. To say that Forced Moves and Good Tricks are retrospective coronations is to say that nothing is, as such, a Good Trick or a Forced Move independently of a given problem situation, context of selection or evolutionary history. Furthermore, it is to say that every Good Trick is a Forced Move, just like every Forced Move is your Best Trick. In any game the Best Trick is always your Forced Move; whether you are aware of it or not is a different question. In short, the difference between a Good Trick and a Forced Move, it seems, reflects nothing more than appeal to different possible degrees of insight into situations and different evaluations of how well we are currently doing. When we are happy with the results of what we do, our Trick is Good. If we are not, and if it seems nonetheless like the only thing we could have done, we will experience it as a Forced Move. The less complete our knowledge of the situation, the more likely we will be to attribute any success we may have to a Good Trick. As our knowledge grows, we will progressively come to see our Good Trick as a Forced Move, as the only rational possibility there is, all other options being fatal. It does not follow that the Move that is Forced upon us is Good in itself, but only that it is best in this context. This is the survival of the fittest, and the fittest, clearly, are those who survive. Is this circularity vicious? Not necessarily. But it does have some consequences. It entails, among other things, that there is no sense to the question: Could evolution have done otherwise? All Good Tricks are Forced Moves: Is this then a form of actualism? Not really, for the claim is epistemological rather than ontological. It is not that evolution could not have been different, but that in any and in every specific case of evolution there is no way to answer the question. "Is consciousness a Good Trick or a Forced Move?" is not a question that can be asked meaningfully.

2. Yet on a different reading, it seems like a highly sensible question. Not all Tricks are Good and not all Moves are Forced. In design space, some Moves are better than others and some Tricks are more or less indifferent. That is to say, though they are Good, there is a large class of other Tricks that could do just as well. Thus the question is, given the result of a particular selection process, was that result chosen because it is better than others, or is it one among many more or less equivalent solutions, and was chosen because it was the only good one available at that point in time? To make sense, this question requires that, in the particular case at hand, we be able to evaluate Good Tricks, of which there are potentially many, and Forced Moves, of which there are presumably fewer and perhaps only one, independently of the selection process and its particular result. If we can do this, and more generally, if we can do this in every case, we can ask some interesting new questions. For example: Is the path followed by evolution a series of Forced Moves through design space such that no matter what, no matter which selection pressures had existed, the result would have been the same? If the answer turns out to be yes, then it seems that natural selection is not what explains the particular path followed by evolution. According to this view, natural selection would be so constrained by the topology of the space it explores that it could not have given a result noticeably different from the one it did. This image, I take it, corresponds to some extent to the research project in which Stuart Kauffman (1993) is currently engaged and to at least one reading of the results he has reached to date. It is important to note, though, that the question makes sense only if it is possible to define the topology of design space, that is to say, to determine what is a good design independently of the selection process. Even if you can do this, the interpretation of the inability of natural selection to resist the constraints imposed by the topology of that space remains to some extent ambiguous. Does it mean that natural selection is a good search procedure that always hits on the best solutions in design space, or does it mean that whatever search procedure you used the result would have been the same? Only in the latter case would we be justified in having confidence in the assertion that natural selection is not the major force in evolution.

3. Which one is the best interpretation? Are Good Tricks and Forced Moves ultimately the same, given that there would be no way to determine what is a Good Trick independently of the selection process that forces certain moves upon us? Or, are they different? Doesn't natural selection sometimes force us to perform Moves that are not very Good Tricks? My claim so far has been that the two interpretations are different, so different that we cannot have it both ways. But is this really the case? Are they truly different or does the distinction between them simply reflect the limits of our knowledge, as was suggested above? There is a rather old, but nonetheless interesting, experiment that may help to clarify the issue. In the early 1960s, two mathematicians, D. Blackwell and D. Kendall (1964), imagined the following experimental set up. Take an urn in which you have put two balls, a black one and a white one. Draw one out at random, put it back into the urn and add to it another ball that is of the same color as the one you picked. How will the ratio of white balls to black ones evolve? After a short time (a few hundred draws) in which there are large variations in the populations of white and black balls, the ratio of the first to the second settles around some definite value, and as N, the total number of balls in the urn, grows, fluctuations around that value will decrease. The mildly surprising aspect of this experiment is that, if you run it again the ratio of black balls to white ones will always settle, after a while, at some definite value, but that value, whatever it is, will be different every time. If you run the experiment a large number of times, you will see that the determination of the value is random. The system does not show any bias whatsoever toward any value or values. Nonetheless once a particular value has been "chosen," it will always come to fixation after a period of fluctuations. As can be clearly seen, what that value is depends only on the history of the selection process, which is why it changes at each trial, and why nothing short of a catastrophe that brings about a modification in the existing ratio can allow a new value to appear. One (metaphorical) way of putting this is to say that the space in which the selected value evolves is perfectly flat. In that space, any point, that is, any possible value for the ratio of balls of different colors, is equally accessible. The value at which the systems settles in any one trial depends only on the history of the selection process during that trial. This form of selection is purely historical. The only thing that determines the probability that a ball of a given color will be selected at the next draw is the ratio of balls of different colors in the urn, and that for its part depends solely on past draws. To say that Good Tricks are Forced Moves is to say that the space in which natural selection functions is flat in this sense. Of course, during any one trial the landscape is modeled by the history of the selection process, but the space is not assumed to have any particular shape prior to that modeling. If, to the contrary, the landscape in which evolution takes place prior to the selection process has a topology with holes, rivers, mountain ridges, slopes, and valleys, then there can be sense in saying that Forced Moves are not all Good Tricks. For example, if it can be shown that there are some unavoidable pathways in that space, trajectories that will be adopted by any selection process, no matter how strong the selection force and no matter what the past history of the process has been, then we could identify some Tricks we might regard as Good, but which the selection process cannot reach.

4. Our original dichotomy can now be formulated in a somewhat crisper way. The first branch says that Forced Moves are Good Tricks, and adds that Forced Moves are Good Tricks because they are Forced Moves. The second branch asserts that not all Forced Moves are Good Tricks, and adds that those Good Tricks that are also Forced Moves are not Forced Moves because they are Good Tricks. The real difficulty, as I see it, is that while the first branch of the alternative is tautological, the second branch appears outright incoherent. Is it not evident that it is because certain moves are Good Tricks that natural selection is forcibly led to them? Not that these tricks are good in the absolute, but because they are best in the given context of selection. Can natural selection be "forced" to chose Bad Tricks? Conversely, if Good Tricks and Forced Moves can be pried apart, it would in principle be possible to show that it is because certain moves are good that they were selected, rather than conclude that it is because they were selected that they are good. I propose to call this alternative the *antinomy of natural reason,* and the solution I will advocate for it is a form of naturalized Kantianism. Given that intentionality and reason are products of natural selection, it is very likely, I will argue, that we should attempt to answer the question "Are all Good Tricks Forced Moves?" and it is necessary that we cannot. As Kant would have said, it is an illusion of reason to which it is moved by some of its fundamental interests. Furthermore, the fact that we cannot answer this question indirectly supports the claim that our intentionality and reason are products of natural selection. This may be called transcendental naturalism (for fun). In relationship with Dennett's dangerous ideas I see two benefits from this move, if it is sound. First, it puts and end to the "Panglossian paradigm" debate. The question is outside the reach of natural reason. Second, it gives more bite and consistency to the somewhat critical stance toward naturalized ethics Dennett adopts in the latter part of *Darwin's Dangerous Idea* (1995). The attitude we should adopt toward most forms of naturalized ethics, I suggest, is pretty much the one advanced by George C. Williams in "Mother Nature is a wicked old witch" (1993) and in "A sociobiological expansion of *Ethics and Evolution*" (1989). Thus, in this case also, just as for Kant, our incapacity to answer certain questions in the speculative field opens up new possibilities for pratical reason.

5. Consider any of Dennett's arguments against intrinsic intentionality and in favor of natural reasons or free-floating rationales. Natural selection, according to him, is a process through which certain things, events, and characteristics acquire a value, or rather, to use a term imported from chemistry, a "valence," a weight for an organism. In this way, deep, unoxygenated water is good for the most famous bacteria in philosophy and highly oxygenated surface water is bad for them. Any innovation in the organisms that enhances their ability to remain in deep water is good, though there is a very high chance that many of these innovations will be mixed blessings. They will have some drawback or other for the organisms. Imagine, for example, that such bacteria have predators that also crowd the deep bottom of the sea and avoid upper-level water. Then an innovation that would allow our prized bacterium to live in a slightly more oxygenated environment could be good for it, especially if its predators cannot follow it there. If the pressure from predation is high enough, and if that innovation is accessible, we can even expect such evolution to take place, unless of course extinction strikes first. This is a very frequent event in the biosphere as Dennett reminds us. Let's be generous, and grant that the ability to tolerate higher oxygen content will evolve. Now it is the capacity to shun deep unoxygenated water where predators lurk that is a good thing, not the ability to remain there. Clearly, what is a Good Trick for an organism depends on the selection process, the pressures to which it is subject, and its history of selection. All Good Tricks are also Forced Moves, not because no other choices were possible—on the contrary, many other choices were in fact made—but because none of them was retained by selection. Only the bearers of Good Tricks survive long enough to pass them on to their descendants. In such cases, there is no way to separate Good Tricks from Forced Moves. This separation becomes possible only with the appearance of organisms that possess a mechanism that permits vicarious exploration in the competition space of natural selection, what Dennett has called "Popperian creatures" (1995, 375). Given a few further complications, these creatures could be able to recognize some moves as good without always being able to implement them in reality. For such creatures, it makes sense for us to say that all Forced Moves are not Good Tricks, and, if you add a few more complications, it makes sense for them to say it, or at least it makes sense for us to say that they could experience it. This difference between Good Tricks and Forced Moves, it should be noticed, is purely local. It exists only within the space limited by the current selection process and only because certain points in that space that are accessible by the vicarious search procedure are not accessible "in person," so to say. I agree with Dennett that if a general vicarious search procedure confers a competitive advantage then it could evolve, and that we probably are the result of such an evolution. We have the ability to compare situations in the abstract, to frame problems in our minds, to design solutions for them, and to determine which solution is best. Best not only for this or that instance of the problem, but also the best solution given the most general specifications of the physical world, or the best solution in general and on average. If we are such creatures, endowed by natural selection with a general vicarious search mechanism, then it is a necessary part of that mechanism that we should try to determine what is best and what is good in itself, independently of all but the most general, timeless context. It is necessary because such an attempt simply reflects the fundamental interest of the mechanism, the reason it became established: its ability to frame solutions that can be applied over a large range of situations. But if the interests of that mechanism, like all interests, are products of natural selection, then it is a foregone conclusion that this mechanism will never succeed in absolutely sundering apart Good Tricks from Forced Moves. If Dennett is right concerning the evolution of reason through natural selection, then the belief that we can separate them is an unavoidable illusion. We have been designed by natural selection to separate Good Tricks from Forced Moves because there was a selective advantage in the capacity to design solutions that are not limited to a narrow range of difficulties. Yet because that separation was motivated by natural selection itself there is no way to say of the events making up evolution that they were chosen because they were Good Tricks rather than Forced Moves.

Adaptations have always been compared to the products of engineering. Before Darwin it was common to wonder: "How are such adaptations possible without foresight, without the wisdom of an all-powerful artificer?" Darwin's and all of modern biology's answer is that these "natural" products, these Good Tricks, are Forced Moves in a game of competition. If the game lasts a long time, involves a sufficient population, and investigates enough of the space of competition, these Moves are Forced to come out, they are bound to appear. If we are the products of this process and have an ability to vicariously explore this space at a much faster rate, then it is not surprising that we should come to similar solutions for similar problems, not surprising that "artificial" solutions and "natural" solutions should resemble each other so much. Thus it seems unavoidable that we are unable to provide a definitive criterion to determine what is a Good Trick independently of the fact that it is a Forced Move, and it also seems unavoidable that we be motivated to look for that criterion. The antinomy cannot be resolved. At the same time, reason learns something important about itself in this debate in which it exhausts its power.

6. What does reason learn? It learns that the debate cannot be resolved. That is to say, the *antinomy of natural reason* suggests a different reading of the old charge that Darwinian theory is tautologous. That question or problem is the fear that explanations through natural selection are empty. In its classical form the tautology of natural selection is that the survival of the fittest tells us nothing because we have no way to determine who are the fittest independently of the fact that they survived. Thus "survival of the fittest" means "survival of those who survive," not a very informative explanation!

The antinomy of natural reason suggests that, if natural selection is the major force that shaped evolution, including our own cognitive capacities, then we should expect that explanations through natural selection will tend to appear tautological. Given the hypothesis of evolution through natural selection, it is necessary that Good Tricks cannot ultimately be dissociated from Forced Moves, and yet that we should want to dissociate them, given the nature of that Good Trick which is our mind. Our cognitive abilities have been chosen precisely for their capacity to weaken the link between Good Tricks and Forced Moves, for their capacity to generalize, to find solutions that are not bound to one context only.

Classical solutions to the tautology problem reveal this fact about us. One solution, the propensity interpretation of fitness, consists in distinguishing those who actually survive from the fittest, that is to say, from those who have the highest degree of fitness understood as the greatest probability of survival, or, if you prefer, the greatest propensity to survive. This is done by determining the value of fitness independently of the selection process taking place in the present generation. There are two general ways to arrive at this value: either by attributing to each individual a fitness value (which is its probability of survival) on the basis of the past performance of the genome of which she is the bearer, or on the basis of her ecological fitness understood as an evaluation of an organism's ongoing performance in her environment. In this way, the fact that an individual is the fittest is no guarantee that she will survive. Thus it can be claimed that survival of the fittest is not tautological.

In the first case, fitness represents an individual's propensity to survive, not (tautologically) the fact that she survives. The meaning of selection from this point of view is the difference between past performance and present success. In many ways this is a very satisfactory definition of what selection does in each generation. Nonetheless, it is clear that fitness is defined here by past success. The propensity interpretation does not really respond to the charge of the tautology, it simply reminds us that past success is no more than a probability indicator with respect to future success. In other words, because fitness values are probability statements, the tautology, the equivalence between fitness and survival, cannot allow us to determine that those who are the fittest at time$_t$ will survive at time$_{t+1}$. Though this changes nothing about the logical issue, it indicates that even if the tautology is not informative and cannot be used in a constitutive way to determine which individuals or genomes are the fittest and which survive, it can play a regulative role and guide our research.

In the second case, ecological fitness, fitness is determined on the basis of the organism's performance in his environment. An example may help to illustrate this. Taking into account the energy expenditure for flight and foraging on one side, and the average calorie intake per time unit at every food stop on the other, it is possible, at least for certain species, to calculate a fly's optimal flight pattern in terms of average distance between food stops and average duration of stops. Empirical studies then permit the determination of which flies best approximate this optimal flight pattern and thus establish each fly's ecological fitness value for this characteristic. In principle, by reiterating these computations and empirical studies for every relevant characteristic, it is possible to discover the overall ecological fitness of every organism or genome. Though, for various reasons, this is in practice impossible to do, it nonetheless gives meaning to the idea that fitness is distinct from survival. Should this conclusion be resisted? I believe there are at least two closely interrelated reasons why it should.

First, suppose it turns out that flies who survive are not those who best approximate the optimal flight pattern. What conclusion should we draw from this? That the principle of natural selection is false? Any biologist will conclude to the contrary that selection pressure must be more important on some other characteristic that is in some way related to the flight pattern, and that the greater importance of the need to which this second characteristic corresponds is what explains the apparently suboptimal flight pattern. In more technical terms, the functional analysis that underlies this now falsified optimality hypothesis, will be revised. A new functional analysis will lead to a different optimality hypothesis, which, if we are lucky, can even be tested empirically. That such "ad hoc" hypotheses are always available is but another aspect of the practical impossibility of determining the overall ecological fitness of an individual. This impossibility is owing to the fact that there is no a priori way of deciding which "characteristics are relevant." Ultimately the only method of doing this is to take natural selection as our guide, and this is precisely what we do when we postulate the existence of another characteristic whose importance and interference with the realization of optimal flight patterns is what explains our empirical findings.

The second reason to believe that the idea of ecological fitness fails to determine fitness independently of survival is the way the optimality of a given characteristic is defined. Take flight pattern as an example: Which one is optimal? In the proposed case, the optimal flight pattern is the one that maximizes food intake for a given energy expenditure. But why is this flight pattern optimal? Clearly it is not optimal in and of itself. One can imagine many other flight patterns which under different circumstances would be optimal. For example the flight pattern that maximizes distance for food intake or even the flight pattern that maximizes the number of food stops. Deciding which flight pattern is optimal depends on what you think is the function or role of flight in relationship to survival. It is only once you have such a hypothesis that you can decide which flight pattern is a Good Trick.

In both cases, the propensity interpretation of fitness and ecological fitness, the tautology between fitness and survival plays a regulative role, guiding our explorations and suggesting hypotheses. But this regulative role does not justify our taking evolution through natural selection as constitutive of what is best. It does not justify our thinking that what is fit is what has survived.

7. In the preceding section, I argued against the claim that in the absence of an absolute separation between Good Tricks and Forced Moves we should reject the principle of natural selection as a tautology lacking all informative content. Using the Kantian distinction between the constitutive and the regulative roles of ideas, I tried to show that there is a regulative use of the tautology that is not only legitimate, but also fruitful and necessary, a Forced Move in the game of knowledge. This may be considered as a response to the first claim or thesis in the antinomy of natural reason, according to which the identity between Good Tricks and Forced Moves renders all attempts to distinguish them vain and meaningless. This is the rejection of the claim that the theory of natural selection obeys a Panglossian paradigm. In this last section, I want to address the antithesis in the antinomy of natural reason, the claim that the identity between Good Tricks and Forced Moves gives us a criterion to determine which Tricks are Good. More precisely, I want to argue that we should reject this antithesis also. Though this is not always transparent in the following discussion, the main targets here are the claims of sociobiology and naturalized ethics.

At least since *The Intentional Stance* (1987), Dennett has proposed, following Dawkins (1976), that we are machines built for the survival of our genes. This provocative claim has sometimes been interpreted as the expression of radical genetic determinism, as the expression of an extreme form of reductionism. Against this, Dennett has argued in *Darwin's Dangerous Idea* (1995) that in order to succeed in the competition for survival such machines would need to evolve their own goals and interests. In other words, it would be a Good Trick for the genes to give their survival machines some slack, some elbow room, and to rest satisfied with an overall, general convergence of interests between themselves and their survival machines, rather than exercising exact, constant supervision of all their moves. Given this, it is not surprising that genes are at times ready to sacrifice their vehicles in order to further their own survival. Nor should it be surprising if, at other times, it is the survival machines that are ready to give up on their genes in order to ensure their survival or simply their comfort (Martin 1998). The gene's-eyed view of evolution does not rule out goals and purposes that are not those of our genes. Furthermore, if, as Sober and Wilson (1998) forcibly argue, we should adopt a multilevel view of selection, then there are many reasons that a certain tension between our goals and those of our genes is precisely what we should expect.

Given this, there is no natural reason to believe that we should place the goals or purposes of our genes before our own, no reason to think that this would either be a Good Trick or a Forced Move. The identity between Good Tricks and Forced Moves is not constitutive, but only regulative. It does not allow us to determine a priori that some Trick is forced upon us, given that it is Good, or that some Move is Good, given that it is Forced. We can want something that is to some extent different from what evolution has produced so far, and different from the blind, mindless way in which it has produced it. The identity between Forced Moves and Good Tricks provides us with a definition, if you wish, but not with a criterion that allows us to determine which Tricks are ultimately Good for us. That remains an open question. The fundamental reason it remains an open question is not that only past performance can tell us which Move was Forced and which Trick was Good. To the contrary, we are endowed with a vicarious exploration mechanism whose goal and purpose is to anticipate the results of natural selection and provide us protection through this foresight. It is because that mechanism allows us to invent goals that are not those of natural selection that it was selected for in the first place. We can look into the consequences of these new objectives and purposes, inquire about their cost and stability, given who we are (or have been). Surely our foresight is limited and there is no need for us to be in an extremely pessimistic mood to judge that our innovations resemble blind variations more often than they reflect clear vision. This is our predicament. The belief that the answer to the question "Which tricks are good?" exists out there somewhere, in nature or in our past history of selection, will not put an end to this situation. It does not constitute a form of knowledge. Has the theory of natural selection anything to say about this difficulty of ours? Perhaps, when it reminds us that variation is the key to evolution.

References

Blackwell, D. and Kendall, D. (1964). The Martin boundary for Polya's urn scheme and application to stochastic population growth. *J. Appl. Prob.* 1: 284.

Dawkins, R. (1976). *The Selfish Gene.* Oxford: Oxford University Press.

Dennett, D. C. (1987). *The Intentional Stance.* Cambridge, Mass.: MIT Press. A Bradford Book.

Paul Dumouchel

Dennett, D. C. (1995). *Darwin's Dangerous Idea: Evolution and the Meanings of Life*. New York: Simon and Schuster.

Kauffman, S. (1993). *The Origins of Order: Self-Organisation and Selection in Evolution*. Oxford: Oxford University Press.

Martin, R. (1998). *Self-Concern: An Experiential Approach to What Matters in Survival*. Cambridge: Cambridge University Press.

Sober, E. and Wilson, D. S. (1998). *Unto Others: The Evolution and Psychology of Unselfish Behavior*. Cambridge, Mass.: Harvard University Press.

Williams, G. C. (1989). A sociobiological expansion of *Evolution and Ethics*. In *Evolution and Ethics*, J. Paradis and G. C. Williams (eds.). Princeton: Princeton University Press.

Williams, G. C. (1993). Mother Nature is a wicked old witch. In *Evolutionary Ethics*, M. H. Nitecki and D. Nitecki (eds.). Albany: New York State University Press.

4

Reading Mother Nature's Mind

Ruth Garrett Millikan

How does it happen that Dennett and I, both firm naturalists and believers in the relevance and importance of natural selection for understanding the human mind, should have come to such different conclusions about holism in the theory of meaning? I will explore the possibility that the difference stems from different understandings of the relation between the intentional stance and the design stance. Dennett takes the intentional stance to be more basic than the design stance. Ultimately it is through the eyes of the intentional stance that both human and natural design are interpreted. But the correctness of intentional-stance interpretation is not a completely determinate matter. There is always a degree of interpretive freedom in reading the minds, the purposes, both of Nature and of her children. The reason, or at least a reason, is that intentional interpretation is holistic, hence subject to Quinean/Davidsonian indeterminacy.[1] On the other hand, I take the design stance to be more basic than the intentional stance. Intentional attributions express our best guesses about the location of (read the next phrase transparently) effects of certain kinds of natural design. And although there is often indeterminacy, ambiguity, or vagueness concerning what it is that natural selection (or learning) has selected for, these indeterminacies and vaguenesses are local, not holistic. There is reason to suppose that the better portion of Nature's purposes and of the intentional states of her children are determinate in content within quite closely defined limits.

Ruth Garrett Millikan

I propose to defend my position as well as I can, so as to call from Dennett more precisely where our paths separate, if indeed they do.

Let me begin by remarking on a possible equivocation in the notion of the design stance. On the one hand, prediction from the design stance seems to be just predicting that a thing will indeed do what it was designed to do. Suppose I believe that this object over my head is a smoke alarm, that is, I believe it has been designed to sound an alarm if it encounters smoke. Without having any idea what is inside it, or how it is supposed to accomplish this task, from the design stance I may confidently predict that it will sound an alarm if it encounters smoke. On the other hand, Dennett often speaks of the design stance as though to use it one would need beliefs also about *how* a thing is designed accomplish its task(s). One would have to know, for example, not just that the tournament chess-playing computer is designed to win at chess, but something about the program it is designed to implement in order to win at chess. Shifting the example here makes the equivocation more difficult to spot, for it is evident in the case of the chess-playing computer, as it is not in the case of the smoke detector, that predicting that the device will actually accomplish its goal of winning from knowing only that is was designed to win would be a risky business. In this latter case, a reasonable prediction could proceed only by knowing something of *how* the machine was supposed to go about winning, for example, at minimum, that it was designed to win with legal moves. This makes it easy to assimilate what one must know in order to predict from the design stance to what one must know to give a Cummins-style functional analysis of how a system works (Cummins 1983).[2]

This threatened equivocation invites a sister one that lurks in the background of much current thinking about Cummins-style functional analysis. Although Cummins introduced his notion of functional analysis as explicitly *not* teleological, as *not* employing the word "function" in a way that connects with either purpose or etiology, he explained his idea by reference to what circuit diagrams, flow charts, and computer programs tell us about systems. But what these sorts of items, as found in the real world, generally tell us about actual systems is not how they do operate but how they were designed or intended to operate. The only reason for including a circuit diagram in the literature that comes with your clothes dryer is that there may come a time when your dryer fails to accord in its workings with this diagram, and then knowing how it was designed to work may help in repairing it. If you were to move from a look at the circuit diagram to a prediction about the effect of certain settings on the dryer's dials, that would be design stance prediction—prediction from a teleological stance—not a direct outcome of Cummins-style analysis. The circuit diagram is not a description of the actual dispositions of your particular dryer (a Cummins-style analysis), though one hopes it does accord with these dispositions. It is a description of the dispositions the dryer was intended to have.

What I will mean by "the design stance" in what follows is the teleological stance, not a Cummins-style stance. The design stance is the predictive stance that moves from what a thing *was* designed to do to a prediction that it *will* do that thing. On this account, design stance prediction is possible starting from beliefs about any aspect or aspects of a thing's design. It is possible starting with beliefs only about the most general "specs" for a thing's design, for example, the thing is designed, perhaps, to show the correct time, or to effect that the missile tracks its target. Compare here David Marr's "first level of analysis" or "task analysis" for his theory of vision (Marr 1982). Alternatively, it is possible starting with completely detailed knowledge of how a thing is designed to work, for example, of how the clock wheels are supposed to engage, or of the program the computer in the missile-tracker is intended to run, and so forth. Compare here Marr's higher levels of analysis.

Contrast the inferences that are involved when one makes a prediction from the intentional stance. Dennett does not define intentional systems with reference to origin. Rather, an intentional system is one that currently displays a certain pattern of behavior or, being more careful, is one that has a current *disposition* to display certain kinds of patterns of behavior. There is no need here to look too closely at what defines these patterns of behavior. Deferring to Dennett's use of "rational," I will call them "real rationality patterns," and note only something of what would seem to distinguish them from patterns of behavior that are "rational" merely in the sense of being reliably need-fulfilling, reliably gene-propagating or the like.

It is very rational for tortoises to grow shells and then to pull their heads inside when in danger. This is such a smart thing to do that tortoises have outlasted nearly every other largish kind of animal on earth. But tortoises themselves are not very smart. Nearly as old as the tortoise is the alligator/crocodile family, with members up to twelve feet long but with brains no bigger than a peanut. They too are built in smart ways but are not themselves very smart. Turtles and alligators are built such that they need not notice in much detail what situations they are in. They can handle most situations effectively with the same small stock of simple behavioral tricks. But there are other animals that care very much exactly what situations they are in, and are built to be able to change either themselves or the situations they are in accordingly. Only certain of the latter display "real rationality patterns."[3] Real rationality patterns are, roughly, dispositions to respond to a wide variety of environmental situations with a wide variety of wide-context-sensitive responses that promote the animal's interests. Especially, the ability to have the very same proximate external situation help to produce quite different but reliably helpful responses depending on the wider or more distal context the animal is in is a move toward displaying more ideal rationality patterns. Inevitably, it is a move toward giving "individual belief-like states *more to do*, in effect, by providing more and more different occasions for them to serve as premises for further reasoning" (Dennett 1987, 30).

What kind of inference is involved then when we make a prediction from the intentional stance? Dennett is very clear about some kinds of inferences that are not involved. To ascribe intentionality to a system is not to make any bets about how the Cummins-style analysis of the system will go. Certainly no intentional system is made of jelly inside, but one might contain the analogue of a huge how-should-I-respond-to-this-stimulation look-up chart, another a hugely intricate lattice that determines potentiations to potentiate potentiations to action, while a third processes mental sentences. Likely, many contain collages encompassing many different kinds of principles all operating at once.

Predictions from the intentional stance make no reference to actual internal mechanisms. Nor, it seems, do they make any reference to design in the historical sense. Dennett is clear that the intentional stance is separate from the design stance.[4] Attributions of intentionality go no deeper than claims about current patterns of external behavior. Thus prediction from the intentional stance seems to go from the attribution of rationality—attribution of the disposition to display real rationality patterns—directly to predictions about instances of such patterns. It has the form "All of O's behaviors fit the real rationality pattern, so O's next action will fit the real rationality pattern," or, allowing for idealization, "Most (many) of O's behaviors fit the rationality pattern so probably (perhaps) O's next behavior will fit the rationality pattern."

If this is the form of inference involved, it has two noteworthy peculiarities. First, it does not appear to be a form of inference that supports explanation. It seems to have the same general form as "All of the boys in this room were born on weekdays, so Johnny, being one of the boys in this room, was born on a weekday," which derives *that*, but does nothing to explain *why*, Johnny was born on a weekday. At most it explains why one should believe that he was, if one has a certain prior belief. Similarly, on this view, that O's behaviors fit the rationality pattern does not seem to explain why O behaves as O does, but merely why one should expect O to behave that way, given that one already believes O's actions fit the rationality pattern.

The second peculiarity of this pattern of inference is an unclarity about how one rationally acquires belief in the premises. "O's behaviors fit the rationality pattern" is short for "O has a disposition to produce (only, mainly, many) behaviors that fit the rationality pattern." But dispositions themselves are not, of course, directly observed. What is observed can only be a certain number of actual behaviors that are consonant with the possibility that they express a general disposition to fit the rationality pattern. We would like to treat the inference from some behaviors fitting the rationality pattern to all behaviors fitting the rationality pattern as a simple induction, of course. But fitting part of the rationality pattern is a very complex and rather disjunctive thing to do, not a simple thing like what emeralds do in support of the induction "all emeralds observed so far have been grue so the next emerald will be grue"! Compare:

"The ink marks on the very small part of this paper that I now can see look quite a lot like the queer configuration of streets right around Peter's house in Stockholm, so the marks on the rest of the paper will look like the rest of Stockholm." What makes us think that fitting some very small (a nearly vanishingly small) part of the rationality pattern is projectable to the whole?

Hint: What kind of history would one have to hypothesize for the part of the paper one sees in order rationally to make an inference to a map of the whole of Stockholm?

Why should partial exhibition of a rationality pattern, that is, apparent exhibition of a disposition to rationality, be a projectable predicate? Why, especially, if there are so "many internally different ways of skinning the behavioral cat" (Dennett 1994, 520)? If there are so many different ways, there must surely be many more ways to produce temporary *false* appearances of rationality patterns that would have failed to follow through in slightly different circumstances and will surely fail to follow through in the future. Is there nothing to go on, then, but the so-far-mysteriously-true meta-inductive premise that in the past, inferences from apparently-rational-at-t to apparently-rational-at-$t+1$ have often held up?

I think Dennett thinks this question is answered the same way I think it is. There is nothing that exhibits apparently rational patterns for any time or in any detail that was not designed to do so, either by natural selection, or by something that natural selection designed. Not only are there no swampmen, there are no apparent swampmen. There are no accidents that apparently exhibit coherent, rational behavior for a time but not owing to any underlying general dispositions to do so. That they should express certain kinds of[5] real rationality patterns is one of the "specs" for certain of nature's designs. That is, showing rationality patterns of one kind or another is often an excellent way to get yourself selected for, granted you don't have a strong enough shell or large and strong enough jaws to get by without.

True, Dennett takes spandrels (Gould and Lewontin 1979) and exaptations (Gould and Vrba 1982) seriously in this context. Sometimes what a thing was designed for is not a good guide to what it is used for, or what it is used for a good guide to what it was designed for (see especially Dennett 1990). Elsewhere I have argued against the importance of the notions of spandrels and exaptations in the context of determining biological functions (Millikan 1993, chapter 2; 1999. See also Godfrey-Smith 1994 and Dennett 1995). The case against true rationality dispositions being mere exaptations is much stronger than the general case, however. Real dispositions to exhibit rationality patterns are very sophisticated, subtle, finely tuned dispositions indeed, ridiculously improbable dispositions if not assumed to be shaped by natural selection. A spandrel or exaptation that resulted in a frog's being accidentally disposed to flick out its tongue in exactly the right direction in response to exactly the right sort of angle of motion of a fly image on its retina is (barely) conceivable. Then we might, I suppose, take the intentional stance toward the frog, saying that it (accidentally) knew when and at what angle a fly is passing and (accidentally) desired to eat flies. But this is exactly the kind of simple inflexible case, I believe, where Dennett would agree there is no use in talk of rationality. We are less likely to be misled if we talk only of reflexes.

Indeed, if some actual organism had acquired fully rational dispositions to behavior totally by accident, and if the observed appearances of rationality resulting from these dispositions were known by us to have resulted by accident, we would be foolish indeed to project these appearances into the future. Not knowing that the absurdly improbable—full and real rationality patterns without design—had indeed occurred, we would take it as far more likely that these were freakish false *appearances* of rationality resulting from accidental interactions of unsystematic features irrelevant to real rationality. Ridiculously unlikely that these features should continue to produce apparently rational outcomes in future. Clearly, exaptations for rationality would not be projectable.

If this is so, then predictions made from the intentional stance are really grounded implicitly in something like inference to the best explanation and out again. From enough apparently rational behavior one can infer design for rationality, just as one can infer design for seeing from good sight. And from design for rationality, one can infer real dispositions to rationality patterns, as opposed to mere temporary illusions of such dispositions.

It thus appears that the intentional stance must be underwritten by the design stance, rather than vice versa. Then too, the fact that the organism is rational, indicating that selection pressures have slowly designed it to be rational, serves as a genuine explanation of its behavioral patterns, not merely as a redescription of them. (Dretske would say that the explanation was by way of the "structuring cause" of the behavior—Dretske 1988.)

[I]magine posing scientists the following Swampman-style questions. Suppose that you discovered a thing that attracted iron but (the molecules inside were) . . . not m-aligned (like standard magnets). Would you call it a magnet? Or: suppose you discovered a thing that was not m-aligned but did attract iron. Would you call it a magnet? The physicists would reply that if they were confronted with either of these imaginary objects, they would have much more important things to worry about than what to call them. Their whole scientific picture depends on [this] . . . and the "fact" that it is logically possible to break this deep regularity is of vanishing interest to them. . . .
. . . If I ever encounter a plausible believer-candidate that violates [the idea that "a brain filled with jelly or sawdust could not sustain beliefs"], what to call it will be the least of my worries, since my whole theory of mind will be sunk. (Dennett 1994, 519)

Similarly, I should think, for rationality patterns not designed to be such by natural selection. Intentional systems are as essentially designed as magnets are aligned. An intentional system *is* a designed system. Rationality *is* something that has been selected for as such. Rationality is not, then, merely a disposition to display rationality patterns. It is not something that resides merely in the present dispositions of a thing.

If we wish to know how determinate in content our various mental states are, then, the question we should ask is, first, how determinate is it what natural selection has selected for? Second, given that what actual animals and their behaviors are like often strays quite far from what natural selection selects for, we should ask, how determinate in content are our various mental states when they stray from Nature's ideal?

It is crucial not to confuse the question whether what natural selection has selected for is determinate with the question of how well what has been selected for is determined by the evidence we can collect or have collected. This would confuse epistemological determinacy with ontological determinacy. Indeterminate evidence for history is not indeterminate history. What kind of indeterminacy might there be then in selection histories themselves?

A number of kinds of indeterminacies, I will soon argue. But there is one kind of indeterminacy that it seems to me will *not* be found. What will not be found, I believe, is any parallel to holistic Quinean/Davidsonian indeterminacy.

The indeterminacies that Quine argued for resulted from a very particular theory of linguistic meaning arising, originally, out of twentieth-century empiricists' struggles (Carnap, Norman Campbell, Reichenbach, Braithwaite, Hempel) to understand the language of theoretical science. The results were then applied to everyday language by philosophers such as Sellars, Feyerabend, and Quine and soon became dogma in empiricist circles: Concepts are nodes in an inference net or a sentence-association net receiving input from sense, predicting the ongoing course of sensory stimulations and guiding action decisions. The semantic content of any concept thus depends on the contents of the concepts inferentially surrounding it, even when the concept plays out part of its role in observation judgments or in desires that directly produce basic actions. Thus the meaning of any concept depends on the meaning of many other concepts, and indeterminacies result from a variety of possible kinds of holistic remappings. Of course Dennett does not accept this theory of thought, certainly not with its original realist interpretation as a theory of thought mechanics.[6] But it is worth noticing why a theory of this sort cannot possibly be applied realistically when we turn to the question of the determinacy of Nature's intentions.

One problem, of course, is the likelihood that this theory of mental semantics is in the end incoherent.[7] But supposing it coherent for the case of humans, there still would be no way to apply it realistically to the "purposes" of Nature. First, classical theories of the indeterminacy of meaning are theories about the nature of *representations,* including, of course, those that represent purposes and, on representational theories of mind, those that embody people's explicit beliefs and desires. But no one supposes that Nature anywhere represents her purposes (except, of course, insofar as her creatures are part of her and some of *them* may represent purposes). There is no sense in talk of a holistic remapping of Nature's beliefs and desires parallel to the classical theory of indeterminacy of translation, because if Nature has anything analogous to beliefs and desires, they are not represented. But second, and far more important, there is no sense in such talk *because there is nothing in Nature analogous to beliefs and nothing that so much as reminds one of inference.* Nature turns out products that easily remind us of products purposefully designed by humans. But there is nothing in the process by which she does so to remind us of beliefs, reasoning, inference nets, and so forth, hence of holistic remappings.

On Dennett's real-patternist theory of intentionality, the first disanalogy—Nature's failure to represent anything—is not relevant. But the second is decisive. The only way to read inference into Nature would be mechanically to interpret every product of natural design, such as an eye, with this sort of ritualistic formula: "Nature wanted her creature to see and she believed that employing such and such principles of optics and using such and such natural materials would enable it to see so (you see) that's just what she did!" Suppose we ignore Dennett's warnings against the barrenness of the intentional stance in cases where the supposed "individual belief-like states" are not given "*more to do.*" Still, that formula won't yield any "beliefs" the contents of which are unclear because of their dependence on the contents of surrounding "beliefs" and "desires." Similarly for Nature's "desires." Quinean holistic indeterminacy depends on the assumption of a very particular and peculiar theory of how human meanings are determined, a theory that very evidently does not apply to Nature's purposes, determined, as they are, by the facts of natural selection.

It is important, I have said, not to confuse indeterminacy in the evidence for selection pressures with indeterminacy in the pressures themselves. This, of course, is compatible with there being, in fact, indeterminacy in the selection pressures. But conflict or lack of clear direction in selection pressures is a completely different sort of thing from Quinean/Davidsonian holistic indeterminacy. Unclarity and conflict in selection pressures is *local,* at least in the sense required here. It has no tendency to contagion through any analogue of inference dispositions.

In Elliott Sober's terms, there is not just selection *of* features but selection *for* features [Sober 1984a]. And without this "discriminating" prowess of natural selection, we would not be able to sustain functional interpretations at all.

Certainly we can describe all processes of natural selection without appeal to such intentional language, but at enormous cost of cumbersomeness, lack of generality, and unwanted detail. We would miss the pattern that was there, the pattern that permits prediction and supports counterfactuals. The "why" questions we can ask about the engineering of our robot, which have answers that allude to the conscious, deliberate, explicit reasonings of the engineers (in most cases) have their parallels when the topic is organisms and their "engineering." (Dennett 1990, 189)

Not quite, I believe. If we dropped all talk of function or purpose in the biological world we would indeed be unable to discern most of the important patterns that are there. But talk of beliefs and "conscious, deliberate, explicit reasonings" would be otiose in biology. There is no need to drag the whole intentional stance into biology in order to perceive Nature's handiwork and the principles of natural design.

But these arguments do not settle the question we started with. That question concerned not whether holism was at work undermining determinacy in natural design generally, but whether it undermines determinacy in human beliefs and intentions. So far, I have argued only that if there is indeterminacy in human intention it is not rooted in the necessity of taking the intentional stance when interpreting nature as a whole. Nature does not have to be interpreted holistically, but perhaps people do.

Once again, it is important not to confuse epistemology with ontology. If it were true that the only way to guess the contents of another person's beliefs, desires, and intentions was by forming a hypothesis about the whole or large parts of the whole of that person's intentional attitudes, that would not make the contents themselves indeterminate. Nor, of course, should we inadvertently slip into the familiar view that our thoughts are indeterminate for Quinean reasons. That strange picture of thought might conceivably be true, but we certainly can't assume so, nor does Dennett usually do so. Rather, he has told us, there are many ways to skin the behavioral cat. Finally, that there are many ways to skin the behavioral cat does not mean, of course, that any individual cat does not have a determinate way to be skinned. The mechanism inside may be complex in the extreme, working in accordance with dozens of different principles each accounting for a different aspect or moment of the cat's rationality, but that just in itself would not cause indeterminacy any more than for bodily functions.

The theory of content I espouse for the whole person I espouse all the way in. The neurobiological theory of content is homuncular functionalism, to dress it in its most vivid metaphorical costume, and hence the very same principles of interpretation are used to endow subpersonal parts with contents as are used to endow whole persons. . . . The way in which personal-level attributions of belief and other intentional properties get confirmed (in the crunch) by subpersonal attributions of (nonordinary) intentional properties is roughly parallel to the way in which one might confirm one's attributions of culpable motives to, say, the British Empire, or the CIA, or IBM, by discovering a pattern of beliefs, desires, intentions, among the agents whose joint activity compose the actions, beliefs, and intentions of the superpersonal agent. (Dennett 1994, 528)

If this sort of technique were necessary in epistemological practice, however, that would not argue for a correlate no-fact-of-the-matter ontology. The rationality of the CIA, should that body happen to be rational, was surely not designed by natural selection, but the rationality of a person was so designed. Why not expect there to be some definite *principle* of design, then, that would determine what a person's mental representations were each intended by nature to mean?

Can we suppose, perhaps, that natural selection is as blind as we are when trying to see the insides of an organism's head? It can see only whether the emerging behavior is rational, not how it was caused to be rational. So is there no way of selecting for determinate principles on which to rest rationality, or for determinate vehicles to implement it? It is true, of course, that in a sense, all natural selection ever sees about any organism is whether it gets to the next generation or not—never how. The reliable result for every plant and animal, however, is good design, usually of a vast number of intricately interlocking inner parts, each working in accordance with entirely determinate principles. Occasionally Nature's designs are cumbersome or inelegant, and often they work only in rather specialized circumstances, but there are always good reasons why these designs work when they do. Moreover, evolutionary history characteristically displays progressive perfecting over the years of certain parts for certain roles. Clearly Nature has specific principles of operation for these mechanisms "in mind." Just as each animal is designed to make its living in a definite way, or in a definite set of alternative ways, each rational animal must be designed to be rational in some definite way, or perhaps in some large but definite set of alternative ways.

About Kripke's Pierre (Kripke 1979) Dennett says,

Which propositions, please, should be inscribed on Pierre's belief list? . . . Pierre is an imperfect believer, as we all are. . . . Psychological-attitude talk is a huge idealized oversimplification of the messy realities of psychology. Whenever push comes to shove in borderline cases, its demands become unanswerable. This is my pretty pernicious instrumentalism showing. . . . [P]ropositional attitude claims are so idealized that it is often impossible to say which approximation, if any, to use. . . . Biologists shrug when asked whether herring gulls and lesser black-backed gulls are different species. . . . How close to the [ideal] "specs" does something have to be to count as a genuine FM tuner? . . . [There is] a gradation of cases from truly embedded or encapsulated subdoxastic states to more and more versatile cognitive states. . . . (1994, 525–526)

It is tempting to fuss about details here. Why does the transition from truly embedded to more versatile cognitive states produce determinacy of content? Bee dances and rabbit thumps, each of which has only one thing to do, are not in the same pickle as Pierre's belief about London. And if the indeterminacies are rooted in holistic mappings, why should push come to shove in borderline cases rather than over the whole map? But forcing questions of this sort feels rather like squeezing soap. Instead, let me offer an alternative story about indeterminacy of content, and see with how much of it Dennett may agree.

Yes, there can be indeterminacy of biological function, even in a system's basic design. I don't have in mind here a biological trait that was originally designed for one purpose and now is used for another. Such a trait will generally be under current selection

Ruth Garrett Millikan

pressures to maintain its present form precisely for serving the new function, just as it originally invaded the gene pool under pressure to maintain this same form in service of the old function. Strictly speaking, of course, natural selection only selects, never designs, and having been selected once before for another function does not cancel its being in process of selection now for a new one—selection, that is, over less perfect variations and other accidental junk thrown up by mutation.[8] If there is indeterminacy at the transition from selection for one function to selection for the next, this is temporary and uninteresting indeterminacy, not really worthy of attention. More typically, the transition period probably finds it being selected for the service of both functions at once.

Interesting indeterminacy arises, however, when there is vacillation over alternating stretches of time or space in the selection pressures on a trait, say, from one short ice age through a warming period and into another, or from one kind of terrain that a species inhabits to an alternative terrain, so that its current form represents a compromise between two incompatible more ideal forms. Or it can arise when the trait is under selection pressures for two different functions at once, these pulling toward different forms for it. Thus the size and shape of the peacock's tail is, famously, assumed to be an awkward compromise between the functions of helping it fly and attracting a mate. Or imagine that a perceptual organ, or a neural response to a kind of sensory input, was torn by selection pressures between accurately carrying two somewhat different, not-quite-extensionally-equivalent, kinds of information, one needed for one purpose, the other for another purpose. It would seem then to carry equivocal content. Any such equivocation would be local, however, not holistic.

Another kind of content indeterminacy resting on basic design might better be called "vagueness." What does the frog's eye tell the frog's tongue? I have argued that it doesn't say "little ambient black speck here now" or "shadow now crossing the retina," because neither of these conditions is directly *causally* implicated in the process that moves from a directional flick of the tongue to arrival at the next generation of frogs (Millikan 1991a; see also Elder 1998). Neither is of relevance in the use to which the proffered information is put. But what exactly is the causal explanation of the efficacy of the flicking of the tongue when it does help the frog? Does the cause involve presence of a fly, or of nutrition for a frog, or of protein molecules *abc*? How abstractly should the content be described? What counts as the correct causal explanation is vague in a way that probably cannot be eliminated in any principled way. But again, the problem is local, not holistic.

Much more interesting is indeterminacy in content that arises when a creature's perceptual and cognitive mechanisms labor under conditions that are not normal for proper performance of their functions. In the last quotation above, Dennett seemed to portray Nature's sculpting of rational animals as aiming toward a single determinate ideal, the same for all intelligent species but, woefully, always missing that mark by a mile, even in our case. I propose instead, that those animals that are designed to collect together information from which to make inferences that govern certain of their behaviors are all perfectly designed rational animals. On the other hand, they are generally designed to use only specified kinds of information in this way. Moreover, they are designed to operate in this way only given certain quite definite supporting conditions, and these supporting conditions are often absent. It is not even coherent to suppose an animal designed to exhibit real rationality patterns in all possible worlds. Each is designed to handle only certain actual kinds of information, available only through certain actual media, that have actually been prevalent enough in its historical environment. Each is designed to use this information in the production of responses that lead to results reasonable for the animal, but lead there only given supporting conditions that have been prevalent enough in its historical environment. Let me illustrate.

Perceptual representations produced by the human eye may often be vague, but there is no reason to suppose they are, in the usual case, equivocal. They can become equivocal, however, if certain supporting conditions that historically have nearly always been present in the species' environment are artfully removed. This happens, for example, when you look through a stereoscope. Then you "see just one picture," but which one do you see, the one shown to your right eye or the one shown to your left? The object you "see" is equivocal between these two. The optometrist also has another piece of

Ruth Garrett Millikan

equipment through which you can see one picture as two, and with suitable preliminaries for adapting the eyes, the two may even appear different colors. Thus you can see (you can "visage"—Millikan 1991b) a contradiction without any awareness of this.

Kripke's Pierre thinks a contradiction without any awareness of this. How does this come about? Under the right conditions, our perceptual and cognitive systems are remarkably accurate in their ability to keep track of the identities of individuals, of natural kinds, of natural stuffs, and so forth. Indeed, they are designed so that they progressively learn to keep better and better track of identities of these sorts. We may learn to recognize each individual that we know in more and more ways with experience, under more conditions, by a greater diversity of symptoms or signs, and so forth. We may learn to recognize each of the natural kinds and stuffs with which we are acquainted in more and more ways over time (Millikan 1998a,b,c, 2000). How this happens is properly studied by developmental psychologists (and by the philosophy and history of science). As with all other biological mechanisms, however, the cognitive mechanisms that accomplish these tasks are not designed to work in all possible worlds, but only in the kind of world humans evolved in. Moreover, as with all other biological mechanisms, they were selected not because they always worked right, but because they worked better than competitors, for example, because they worked right under more conditions, or under conditions that were more prevalent. There will always be conditions under which they can be made to fail. For a simple example, although we are especially talented at recognizing people by remembering their faces, this ability assumes an environment in which different people have faces sufficiently different in just those ways by which we are designed to tell faces apart. Identical twins can confuse us, and if person-cloning became very common, we might face quite a serious problem.

Where failures to reidentify correctly have occurred we may have two thoughts of one thing (Pierre's thoughts of London) or one thought of two things (identical twins we have confused, mass and weight) or thoughts that are so equivocal as to have no definite object at all (phlogiston). And, to be sure, when our inner representational systems are corrupted in this manner, the "thoughts" that we have can no longer be unequivocally described in intentional idiom. But these problems are local, not holistic.[9]

Similar remarks apply to Anscomb's example of the person who says "Now I press button *A*" while reaching out and pressing button *B* (Anscomb 1963, 57, cited by Dennett 1990), and to Dennett's signaling "out" while he simultaneously shouted "safe" (Dennett 1990, 181). But all this has nothing to do with holism.

There are more extreme cases in which intentional description becomes inappropriate.

No one is perfectly rational, perfectly unforgetful, all observant, or invulnerable to fatigue, malfunction or design imperfection. This leads inevitably to circumstances beyond the power of the intentional strategy to describe, in much the same way that physical damage to an artifact, such as a telephone or an automobile, may render it indescribable by the normal design terminology for that artifact. How do you draw the schematic wiring diagram for an audio amplifier that has been partially melted, or how do you characterize the program state of a malfunctioning computer? In cases of even the most familiar cognitive pathology—where people seem to hold contradictory beliefs or to be deceiving themselves, for instance—the canons of interpretation of the intentional strategy fail to yield clear, stable verdicts about which beliefs and desires to attribute to a person. (Dennett 1987, 28)

This is certainly true and important. Design stance attributions are of no help in describing either sufficiently mutilated artifacts or sufficiently mutilated organisms. But Dennett continues thus:

Now a strong realist position on beliefs and desires would claim that in these cases the person in question really does have some particular beliefs and desires which the intentional strategy, as I have described it, is simply unable to divine. On the milder sort of realism I am advocating, there is no fact of the matter exactly which beliefs and desires a person has in these degenerate cases. . . . (1987, 28)

But the strong realist should not make such a claim. The strong realist who takes the contents of intentional states to be determined by phylogenetic and ontogenetic history is free to reject numerous behavior-influencing states as failing to have any content at all, and others as failing to have determinate content. What the strong realist must think is only that it is a determinate matter which of these states are contentless, which determinate, and which indeterminate.

If my remarks have been right, then we should expect it to be pretty definite *for the most part* what jobs the various inner parts and aspects of the perceptual and cognitive systems are designed to be doing, when and what they are supposed to be representing. Insofar as they are working in accordance with design, rather than smashed or laboring under conditions that fail to support them properly, they will represent what they were designed to represent given the circumstances. Or they will represent what they have learned or been tuned, in accordance with design, to represent given the circumstances. It is no accident that we think, for the most part, pretty unequivocal (though often rather vague) thoughts.

One more of Dennett's wonderfully apt examples deserves comment. A chess-playing computer, he famously says, may be correctly described as thinking that it ought to get its queen out early if that is its constant disposition, even if its program contains no such instruction (Dennett 1978, 107). It makes a difference, I believe, whether the disposition is a logical or merely a causal result of design. If a logical result, then it seems to be true that the computer was indeed designed to get its queen out early, even if that part of its design was not independently "selected for." Similarly, my digestive system was designed to digest, among other things, french fries and chocolate mousse, even though these aspects of its design were not independently selected for.

But there is also this kind of case. William has a way of insulting everyone he wants to impress by belittling their accomplishments over against his own. James has a way of winning people over by warmly admiring their children and pets, for he adores all children and animals perfectly sincerely and quite indiscriminately. These ways of William and James are not intentional any more than pointing your eyelashes toward your toes is purposive when you blink. These dispositions are real, and can form the basis of well-evidenced predictions of the effects of William's and James's behaviors. But systematic predictable effects of behaviors often do not have legitimate intentional descriptions or explanations. We all systematically and predictably depress the carpets on which we walk, and kick doctors who apply small rubber hammers just below our kneecaps. These effects are not correctly explained in intentional terms. Nor, without doubt, are a great many of the effects that traditional psycho-analysis attempted to explain in intentional terms. Has anyone yet proposed a Freudian explanation of the (clearly retaliatory) knee-jerk response?[10]

Notes

1. Dennett often refers to Davidson and, especially, to Quine's thesis on the indeterminacy of radical translation (Quine 1960, chapter 2), most relevantly for this discussion, perhaps, in Dennett (1987, 37–42; 1990, 180). Quine's thesis is that translation is *always* radically indeterminate. And should Quine's reasons for saying this hold up, no weaker conclusion would suffice. Dennett, on the other hand, seems to vacillate on the ubiquity of indeterminacy. For example, in (1990) he moves from saying on p. 180 that Quine claims that "*there may be no deeper facts* that settle the matter (of correct interpretation of people's intentional attitudes)" to saying in his footnote on this very sentence: "*That there are no such deeper facts* is also argued for at length in (Dennett 1987)" (italics mine). Part of what I hope for from this essay is clarification from Dennett which of these is really his own position and why. Not to preclude the possibility (recognized by my own position as well) that this very question may *happen* to have, or happen so far to have had, no determinate answer.

2. A Cummins-style analysis explains a complex capacity that a system has by showing how simpler capacities or dispositions possessed by it and/or by various of its parts add up to that capacity.

3. Peter Godfrey-Smith (1996) has an extended discussion of why intelligence is not, just in general, a good thing, that is, of why it is not always smart to be smart.

4. At (1987, 73), Dennett says, "One can view the intentional stance as a limiting case of the design stance: one predicts by taking on just one assumption about the design of the system in question: whatever the design is, it is optimal. This assumption can be seen at work whenever, in the midst of the design stance proper, a designer or design investigator inserts a frank homunculus (an intentional system as subsystem) in order to bridge a gap of ignorance." Being designed to do X in an optimal way is not, however, being designed to be rational. Recall the tortoises and the alligators.

5. I do not want to endorse the position that there is such a thing as the one perfect ideal of "rationality" in Dennett's sense of that term, to which different organisms approximate more or less closely. That the little thing plays a good game of chess does not give us reason to suppose it will be smart and keep itself away from harmful magnetic fields. Rather, there are many different kinds of smartness, many different ways to be smart and many different kinds of things to be smart about. Some of these ways are surely more versatile than others, but there is no single dimension or apex involved here. Perhaps Dennett agrees?

6. Dennett's theory of intentionality officially leaves it open, of course, that some intentional systems might actually work this way—better, perhaps, than sawdust inside.

7. This theory of meaning is decidedly parochial looked at from a historical perspective, and there are many signs of its slow demise. Recently Fodor and Lepore (1992) have summarized many strong arguments against holism in the theory of meaning. In Millikan (1984, 1993, 1998a,b,c) I have offered many details for construction of a decidedly nonholist theory of meaning for both language and thought.

8. For more recent reservations on this point, see Millikan (in prep.) and Schwartz (in prep).

9. I have argued that the problems tend to be local even in the case of developing scientific theory, see Millikan (1998c).

10. Thanks to Gunnar Björnsson for help with this essay.

References

Anscombe, G. E. M. (1963). *Intention*. 2nd ed. Oxford: Basil Blackwell.

Cummins, R. (1983). *The Nature of Psychological Explanation*. Cambridge, Mass.: MIT Press. A Bradford Book.

Dennett, D. C. (1978). *Brainstorms*. Cambridge, Mass.: MIT Press. A Bradford Book.

Dennett, D. C. (1987). *The Intentional Stance*. Cambridge, Mass.: MIT Press. A Bradford Book.

Dennett, D. C. (1990). The interpretation of texts, people, and other artifacts. *Philosophy and Phenomenological Research* 50: 177–194.

Dennett, D. C. (1991). *Consciousness Explained*. Boston: Little, Brown and Company.

Dennett, D. C. (1994). Get real, reply to my critics. *Philosophical Topics* 22, nos. 1 and 2.

Dennett, D. C. (1995). *Darwin's Dangerous Idea*. New York: Simon & Schuster.

Dretske, F. (1988). *Explaining Behavior*. Cambridge, Mass.: MIT Press. A Bradford Book.

Elder, C. (1998). What versus How in Naturally Selected Representations. *Mind* 107: 349–363.

Fodor, J. A. and Lepore, E. (1992). *Holism: A Shopper's Guide*. Cambridge, Mass.: Blackwell.

Godfrey-Smith, P. (1994). A Modern History Theory of Functions. *Nous* 28: 344–362.

Godfrey-Smith, P. (1996). *Complexity and the Function of Mind in Nature*. Cambridge: Cambridge University Press.

Gould, S. J. and Lewontin, R. C. (1979). The Spandrels of San Marco and the Panglossian program. *Proceedings of the Royal Society of London* 205: 281–288.

Gould, S. J. and Vrba, E. S. (1982). Exaptation—A missing term in the science of form. *Paleobiology* 8, no. 1: 4–15.

Kripke, S. A. (1979). A puzzle about belief. In *Meaning and Use*, A. Margalit (ed.). Dordrecht: Reidel.

Marr, D. (1982). *Vision.* San Francisco: W. H. Freeman.

Millikan, R. G. (1984). *Language, Thought, and Other Biological Categories.* Cambridge, Mass.: MIT Press. A Bradford Book.

Millikan, R. G. (1991a). Speaking up for Darwin. In *Meaning in Mind: Fodor and His Critics*, G. Rey and B. Loewer (eds.). Oxford: Blackwell.

Millikan, R. G. (1991b). Perceptual content and Fregean myth. *Mind* 100.4: 439–459.

Millikan, R. G. (1993). *White Queen Psychology and Other Essays for Alice.* Cambridge, Mass.: MIT Press. A Bradford Book.

Millikan, R. G. (1998a). A Common Structure for Concepts of Individuals, Stuffs, and Basic Kinds: More Mama, More Milk, and More Mouse. *Behavioral and Brain Sciences* 22, no. 1: 55–65.

Millikan, R. G. (1998b). With Enemies Like These I Don't Need Friends. *Behavioral and Brain Sciences* 22, no. 1: 89–100.

Millikan, R. G. (1998c). How We Make Our Ideas Clear. In the Tenth Annual Patrick Romanell Lecture, *Proceedings and Addresses of the American Philosophical Association* 11.

Millikan, R. G. (1999). Wings, spoons, pills, and quills: A pluralist theory of functions. *Journal of Philosophy* 96: 191–206.

Millikan, R. G. (2000). *On Clear and Confused Concepts: An Essay about Substance Concepts.* Cambridge, UK: Cambridge University Press.

Millikan, R. G. In prep. Cummins-functions/Millikan-functions. In *Functions in Philosophy of Biology and Philosophy of Psychology*, R. Cummins, A. Ariew, and M. Perlman (eds.). Oxford: Oxford University Press.

Quine, W. v. O. (1960). *Word and Object.* Cambridge, Mass.: MIT Press.

Schwartz, P. In prep. Proper Function and Recent Selection. In *Functions in Philosophy of Biology and Philosophy of Psychology*, R. Cummins, A. Ariew, and M. Perlman (eds.). Oxford: Oxford University Press.

Sober, E. (1984a). *The Nature of Selection.* Cambridge, Mass.: MIT Press. A Bradford Book.

Sober, E. (1984b). *Conceptual Issues in Evolutionary Biology.* Cambridge, Mass.: MIT Press. A Bradford Book.

5

Indeterminacy and Realism

Timothy Kenyon

Determinacy and Facts of the Matter[1]

What would have to be the case in order for mental properties to be real? Or, to introduce some complexities regarding negation, what does denying the reality of the mental amount to? One thing it might amount to is this: All our talk about beliefs and hopes and suspicions is on a par with talk of phlogiston or élan vital. Belief-desire discourse might appear explanatory, and might even be predictive when the phenomena are viewed at a sufficiently gross level, but such language will ultimately be eliminated from science and replaced with a correct etiology of human action. There are prima facie considerations speaking in favor of this line of thought—notably, the conceptual problems associated with naturalizing the mental, and a version of pessimistic meta-induction that identifies belief-desire psychology as humankind's first theory of behavior, and claims that we never get things right the first time.

   That is not the sort of antirealism I will be concerned with in the following discussion. Rather, I will examine a sort of antirealism intended to be consistent with the view that the idiom of intentional psychology is ineliminable. It is sometimes characterized as an instrumentalism, sometimes as a sort of abstract realism, and is difficult to label in light of its disparate allegiances. But on the presentation given by its chief advocate, Daniel Dennett, it is clear that the view takes its cue from Quine's indeterminacy thesis of meaning properties. I aim to summarize a problem characteristic of this sort of antirealism, the summary being both a reemphasis of some long-standing criticisms, and an attempt to draw out some tensions in intentional antirealism that have, I expect, been widely sensed, but not precisely spelled out. I conclude with some speculation on how to accommodate a form of intentional realism recovering some of the intuitions served by the indeterminacy thesis, without being committed to that doctrine. In particular, I wish to suggest an account of intentional states meeting many of the aims of Dennett's account, and yet which is effectively divorced from the indeterminacy thesis, properly so-called.

Some familiar background: Dennett's position is couched in terms of the *intentional stance,* from which one ascribes beliefs and desires to a system based upon its history (both phylogenic and ontogenic) and its niche in the world. Dennett, like Donald Davidson, proposes that the attribution of full rationality to the interpreted system is a necessary feature of belief-desire ascription; embracing this assumption, one may make reasonably accurate predictions about the object's behavior under the circumstances. Any system of which one can in fact make such predictions (like a frog, or a human) is an intentional system. But on this account, ascriptions of propositional attitudes to an intentional system are never determinately true, but rather only pragmatically constrained. Cases of misrepresentation, Dennett argues, are cases in which the practical constraints upon ascription fail to prefer one ascription over another, and such cases therefore reveal the thoroughgoing indeterminacy of belief-desire ascription.

The familiar example is of a frog taken out of its natural environment, placed in a laboratory, and shown a series of small dark shadows moving across a light background. The frog may shoot its tongue out at the spots. Consider the neural state causally responsible for the tongue-shooting: Does it have the representational content "fly"? If so, it is mistaken. But here is another construal that accounts for the frog's behavior: It believes it is shooting its tongue out at dark specks. It just does not discriminate flies from dark specks generally. If this is the case, the frog makes no error. The element of error, or misrepresentation, has disappeared on the broader interpretation. Dennett argues that the aspect of misrepresentation can always be dissolved in this manner,

> by adding disjunctions (the signal means something less demanding: fly or pellet or dark moving spot or slug of kind K or . . .) until we arrive back at the brute meaning of the signal type. . . . (1987, 84–87; see also 290–295; 302)

If there were a fact of the matter about what belief state the frog is really in, then there would necessarily be a chance that the frog holds an erroneous belief. But, since there appears to be at least one competing ascription on which there is no error, and no principled way to select one ascription as canonical, there seems to be no principled way to distinguish an error from a veridical perception. Thus there seems to be no such fact of the matter.

This line of thought has obvious affinities with another very famous one. Quine (1960) argues that ascriptions of meanings to utterances, and, by extension, ascriptions of contentful states to agents, are underdetermined in a fashion illustrating the strict indeterminacy of meaning-properties—that is, intentional properties. How, exactly, does the argument work? The story is a familiar one, so I will oversimplify: The enterprise of interpreting an agent only gets off the ground with the hypothesis of, broadly, the agent's ways of carving up the world. Such hypotheses, Quine claims, are analytical in character—they are not empirical hypotheses, and therefore not open to empirical confirmation or disconfirmation, because they are *functions*, from judgments about a body's movements to judgments about an agent's actions. Hence our ascriptions of content to agents' beliefs or utterances are felicitous only relative to some interpretive · function or other. For any finite set of behaviors, we may propose many competing ascriptive hypotheses, some of which stand in mutual contradiction, and yet which the behavioral evidence itself cannot in principle select between. So we should conclude that our tendency to settle on single interpretations reflects not the metaphysical distribution of intentional properties, but the norms encoded in the interpretive functions we employ. The world itself is strictly indeterminate with respect to intentional properties.

Such an antirealist instrumentalism threatens to commit its advocate to an error theory of folk psychology similar to J. L. Mackie's view of moral discourse, on which statements of moral obligation are taken to make implicit (and sometimes explicit) reference to moral properties in the world. To deny, as Mackie did, that there are such properties is therefore to be committed to the universal falsity of statements of the relevant class. But even if the idea that mental states are causal is not part of ordinary psychological discourse (as one might consider granting), the idea that they are real certainly seems to be. Associated, therefore, with the antirealist understanding of instrumentalism is the idea that certain domains of discourse deal mainly in useful fictions. In relation to folk psychology, those working in the Quinean tradition (like Dennett) are likely to agree with the useful component; their difficulty lies in bearing the weight of the "fiction" characterization. Whatever one's commitment to Quine's indeterminacy argument against intentional states (events, properties), one will recognize the unhappiness of the idea that our ascriptions of beliefs and desires are part of a pervasive but practically inescapable pattern of uttering falsehoods.

But suppose one bites the bullet and accepts the useful fictions idea, as Quine (1960) appeared to do.[2] What is immediately apparent is how robust a notion of truth such an error theory requires. Truth must be something more substantive than what is predictively and explanatorily rewarding, and systematically coherent, since these are presumably the properties of intentional ascription that make it useful though false. For my purposes there is nothing objectionable in such a notion of truth; all that matters is that the error theorist requires it in order to run the relevant contrast between the useful and the true. And this means there must be at least some regions of empirical discourse in which the attainment of such truth is the proper goal of inquiry. The claim that folk psychology only masquerades as an empirical discourse is bootless unless there are empirical discourses in good standing to serve as contrast cases. In Quine's view, physics is precisely such an empirical discourse in good standing.

Now we are in a position to point out how important it is that the argument for an instrumentalist reading of folk psychology does not generalize to all empirical discourse. Hence I observe that Noam

Chomsky's (1969) long-standing challenge to Quine on this very issue has not obviously been answered.

Chomsky points out that Quine does not make clear why the underdetermination of meaning ascriptions differs from that characteristic of empirical hypotheses generally.

> Quine has in mind a distinction between "normal induction," which in-
> volves no serious epistemological problem, and "hypothesis formation," or
> "theory construction," which does involve such a problem.
> . . . It is, to be sure, undeniable that if a system of "analytical hypotheses"
> goes beyond evidence then it is possible to conceive alternative hypotheses
> compatible with the evidence. . . . Thus the situation in the case of language
> . . . is, in this respect, no different from the case of physics. (Chomsky
> 1969, 61)

And Jerry Fodor and Ernest LePore (1992) argue in a similar vein
that the contrast between the semantical sciences and the other special sciences is a false one; so either there are also, say, no real geological facts, or there are perfectly robust psychological facts. (The
normal healthy adult is supposed to prefer the second disjunct.)

Challenged to make clear the sense in which content ascription
is subject to a truly radical underdetermination, Quine delivers the
following reply:

> Though linguistics is of course a part of the theory of nature, the indeter-
> minacy of translation is not just inherited as a special case of the under-
> determination of our theory of nature. It is parallel but additional. Thus,
> adopt for now my fully realistic attitude toward electrons (and the like)
> despite knowing that it is in principle methodologically under-determined.
> Consider, for this realistic point of view, the totality of truths of nature,
> known and unknown, observable and unobservable, past and future. The
> point about indeterminacy of translation is that it withstands even all this
> truth, the whole truth about nature. This is what I mean by saying that,
> where indeterminacy of translation applies, there is no real question of
> right choice; there is no fact of the matter even to within the acknowledged
> under-determination of a theory of nature. (Quine 1969, 303)

This is surely an unequivocal statement that the relevant distinction
obtains, but equally surely, it is no *more* than a statement. Chomsky's
question—why suppose that the underdetermination of content ascription is more exotic than that found everywhere?—is not answered by the claim, however emphatic, that there is indeed

something more radical at work in linguistics and psychology. The idea may be that there are two *levels* of underdetermination involved, one holding between observation sentences and the physics we choose, and another holding between the entities mandated by that physics and the psychology we choose. But apart from the obvious problematic assumption of an intimate relation between observation and physics, it is far from clear why two levels of underdetermination would generate outright indeterminacy, when one level would not. Alternatively, perhaps what Quine has in mind here is the distinction between the characteristically empirical underdetermination of the *general* fit between one whole language and another (i.e., does "Gavagai!" refer to something rabbity, or to affordable footwear?) and the additional question of which of many possible stimulus-equivalent referents a term picks out, even once a general translation has been decided (does "Gavagai!" refer to rabbits, or time-slices of rabbits, or . . . ?). This is more or less the distinction between meaning holism and ontological relativity, in Quine's terms. But if the latter is the "parallel but additional" consideration, it is not suited to bear out the indeterminacy thesis per se. For the point of that thesis, as I understand it, is that the broad permissiveness of translation—of which both holism and ontological relativity do serve as examples—is responsible for the failure of propositions to perform their essential function: being primitive truth-bearers. The permissiveness of translation is supposed to lead to cases in which two or more empirically adequate, *but mutually incompatible,* ascriptions are available; if one is true, the other must be false, and nothing but our preference chooses between them. Bearing this in mind, we may reply to Quine simply by noting that the second, parallel phenomenon rests wholly on the assumption that the available multiplicity of meanings all generate the *same* truth-value. To the extent that there is an additional consideration that Chomsky has missed, it is not one that points up a problem with semantic concepts, but rather merely illustrates that there are limits to how finely grained our referential capacities can be. Even within an empirically underdetermined translation, it may be indeterminate whether an utterance means "rabbit" or "undetached rabbit part." But even within an empirically underdetermined physical theory, at the finest grain it is indeterminate where, precisely, an electron is. In neither case (we may say on Chomsky's behalf) need we generalize to there being no facts of the matter across the entire discourse.

Quine and Dennett agree with Chomsky and Fodor that the analytical hypotheses involved in content ascription are "indispensable" (Quine 1960, 75), postulating intentional states that are *practically* determinate (Dennett 1987, 40–41); but they differ in taking the marginal cases—Twin Earth, frogs in laboratories, ontologies in which things consist of compact and contiguous slices—as illustrative of the entire class of ascriptions. The argument appears to be this: The cases of ascription in which underdetermination makes itself known show that the broad class of ascriptions are strictly indeterminate. It is then a pretty question why analogous considerations do not show the world to be indeterminate with respect to the properties figuring in all empirical theories.

It appears to be Quine's position that motivates Dennett's view of intentional states as abstracta (Dennett 1987, 40); but Chomsky gives reason to think that there is no clear way of spelling out what is radical about the underdetermination of the mental. If a compelling case cannot be made to the effect that intentional explanation is subject to an especially exotic variety of underdetermination, then either the argument to indeterminacy fails—so instrumentalism is unmotivated—or the argument generalizes to all empirical discourse—so the instrumentalist is committed to a global, and quite possibly incoherent, error-theoretic view. To the extent that the premise can be supported, and to the extent that a global error theory is unpalatable, such an argument undermines a useful fictions sort of instrumentalism.

To consolidate: Whatever the lesson to be learned from Quine's meaning holism, it cannot be that intentional ascriptions are universally false. Nor can it be that there is something otherwise amiss with linguistics and intentional psychology, in contrast with the other special sciences. The question for the antiidentity theorist is whether there is conceptual space in which to locate a realist metaphysics of propositional attitudes, based on the holist premise, without advancing a complete non sequitur. Since Dennett considers himself a realist toward the attitudes, this question is of some importance for him.

Indeterminate Realism?

Can one go on to be a realist about beliefs and desires, having taken the indeterminacy argument seriously? Is it enough to say, as Bo Dahlbom (1993, 2) says in Dennett's defense, that "even if 'sake' is a perfectly fine noun, there are no sakes," and let this be an analogy for psychological idiom? I expect that declaring an allegiance to realism about propositional attitudes and declining an error theory of psychological explanation is apt to seem ad hoc, once one has taken on board the indeterminacy thesis. I wish to suggest that both the antiphysicalist intuition and the realist intuition that Dennett accommodates among his stances are borne out by a view importantly distinct from the indeterminacy thesis. In particular, the Quinean picture of meaning is shot through with a sense of the following dilemma: Either meaning is wholly physically determined, or meaning is strictly indeterminate. Recognizing the element of normativity or interpretation in content ascription, the Quinean rejects the former disjunct, and takes the latter disjunct as her conclusion. I propose to free up some conceptual space by denying this dilemma from the outset, and see what sort of *via media* may be found. But this requires an explicit rejection of the idea that any normativist account of intentional psychology inevitably depends upon the notion of indeterminacy.[3]

As things stand, there certainly appears to be a tension in Dennett's use of the indeterminacy thesis. On one hand, he appeals to the thesis at crucial justificatory points (1975; 1987, 40; 1993, 217–218). On the other hand, he clearly balks at certain inferences that follow quite naturally; Dennett is sensitive to the possibility that his view implies the strict falsity of mental ascriptions and explanations when taken at face value. For at least this reason, we may regard Dennett as combining the quite different approaches of Quine and Gilbert Ryle. Just as Ryle (1949, 23) thought that quantification over mental states could be true "in one logical tone of voice," so Dennett claims that mental ascriptions can be true "with a grain of salt" (1987, 72).

Those uneasy with the suggestion that our theory of psychological explanation implicitly incorporates a theory of voices or a theory of salt will react sharply to Ryle's and Dennett's maneuver. The obvious objection is that we already have a word that means "true with a grain of salt" or "true in one logical tone of voice." That word is "false." This response, for all its bluntness, cannot easily be accused of unfairness, since neither Ryle nor Dennett says much about what it means to modify truth with voices or grains of salt. This is no reductio of the idea that truth could be qualified in the ways toward which Ryle and Dennett gesture; the charge is rather that a great deal more needs be said in order to make out such a qualification. In the absence of such a theory, Dennett's allusion to *veritas cum grano salis*, as he puts it with mock technicality, will ring hollow for many commentators (1987, 73).[4]

Nor is this problem mitigated by appending Dennett's sort of ontological pluralism to the indeterminacy thesis. Dennett employs a range of analogies to illustrate the ontological status he imputes to beliefs. For example, being in a belief state is more like being famous than like having a mass of five kilograms; there are clear-cut cases of being famous and being unknown, but there are also marginal cases in which to ask whether one is really famous is to ask for an inappropriate sharpening of a vague concept. Alternatively, he draws a parallel between beliefs and theoretical posits like centers of mass or the equator. Just as these notions are purely predictive in their applications, psychological states are abstracta employed to facilitate the prediction of the movements of certain physical systems. At the same time, we are entitled to think of beliefs as real to the same extent that money, centers of mass, and the Arctic Circle are real (see, e.g., 1994, 535).

To be sure, these analogies are striking and original. But when we get to the point of asking why, exactly, one is constrained to regard intentional states in this manner, things turn rhetorical. Are beliefs really the kind of things that could be fixed and determinate? Do we really think there has to be a fact of the matter about beliefs? According to Dennett, some things are apt to be viewed as determinate—*really* determinate—but beliefs are not such things. To suppose otherwise is to be an "Industrial Strength Realist" or a

"Hysterical Realist," as Dennett (with some provocation) labels Jerry Fodor and Georges Rey (1994, 530).

This attempt to tack realism onto the indeterminacy argument is, I think, the weakest link in Dennett's theory of mind. The Quinean way of carving up these issues does not easily accommodate the realist intuition Dennett advances; realism inevitably emerges as an inconsistent afterthought to a position apparently hostile to it. In taking the psychological to be strictly indeterminate, Dennett courts criticisms like that mounted by Jennifer Hornsby, who notes that "it is not easy to see how we could work to a lower standard in interpreting ourselves than in understanding anything else" (1997, 7). So the key move for the opponent of the particular class of identity theories to which Dennett objects, I will argue, is to give up the claim of indeterminacy and focus instead upon the relation between the epistemology of intentional psychology, and any putative metaphysics for the domain. The view properly regarded as the target of traditional intentional antirealism is a sort of physicalism on which the instantiation of some subvening physical property is, itself, metaphysically sufficient for the instantiation of a mental property. The Quinean tradition is mistaken in objecting to the idea that meaning facts have what we might call "special science standard" determinacy. But what can be challenged is the idea that the truth conditions for meaning statements are wholly physically determined. This, I submit, is the core of Dennett's negative program. It does not require the indeterminacy thesis.

The Proposal

Here is what I suggest: For anyone trying to illuminate the intuition that this strict sort of physicalism is misled, indeterminacy is a dead end. The line of thought that one ought to focus upon is both pervasive and generally undeveloped in the work of Quine and Dennett. It is their shared resistance, anchored partly in American pragmatism, to the idea of "differences that make no difference." This is the principle of reasoning for which both are widely and scathingly criticized: their verificationism. What the normativity of intentional ascription shows is not that content ascriptions are false or of universally indeterminate truth-value. What it shows is that *the truth conditions for content ascriptions cannot be purely physical, on pain of its being possible that there are psychological truths that are unverifiable in principle.* So if one has a defense of the right sort of verificationism, then one has a route from holism to a rejection of identity theories of mind, in the strict sense of "identity" to be contrasted with correlation. I offer three premises to construct that route.

The Knowability Argument

K1.   There is an essential behavioral element in intentional ascription.
K2.   Behavioral evidence, and evidence derivative upon behavioral evidence, need not always select between incompatible intentional ascriptions. Therefore,
K3.   There is no sense to be made of the idea of truths that transcend in principle our ability to know.[5]

Clearly some elaboration is called for. Suppose, as seems plausible, that there may be cases in which the total behavioral evidence is thoroughly ambiguous between recommending an intentional ascription F (S believes that Φ) and some distinct belief ascription G (S believes that not-Φ). Suppose further that P is one of perhaps indefinitely many physical properties subvening on the belief that Φ. Nevertheless, on the received view, the truth of "P obtains" might still be metaphysically sufficient for the truth of F. In other words, the truth of "P obtains" could well determine the truth of F even when, by assumption, all behavioral evidence falls short of rendering F knowable. The truth of this intentional ascription could, then, be unknowable in principle. Prescinding from some sort of conceptual reduction, there will be no way of inferring the truth of F from "P obtains," and thus there will be a truth about the relevant system's intentional state that in principle eludes us. If we have reason to think that the idea of evidence-transcendent truth is not cogent, then we may contrapose and conclude that the truth conditions for F cannot be given merely as "P obtains," for any physical property P.

This argument goes through only if "all behavioral evidence" really means "all evidence, period." But how radical is this requirement? Is K2 intended to suggest that, say, *neurology* could not be relevant to intentional ascription? That there can be no correlation of neurologically type-individuated states with intentionally type-individuated states? Dennett sometimes writes as if he believes holism to show this. Identifying a neurological event as the subject's believing that Φ "would itself be an exercise in Quinian radical translation," he argues, and so completely question-begging as a means of settling uncertain cases of ascription (Dennett 1993, 218). I disagree; we are not prevented a priori from settling *some* uncertain cases by means of neurology. Asymmetrical psychophysical type correlations are, I expect, perfectly possible in principle; recognizing this is an important step in ridding meaning holism of its perceived tendency toward a priori science. That a mental property M supervenes upon a collection of physical properties $P_i \ldots P_n$ is no more problematic for the antiidentity theorist than is the correlation between judgments of redness and a whole discontinuous range of light wavelengths, for someone concerned to deny the strict identifiability of red with those wavelengths or surfaces. Colors, like psychological states, may be multiply realizable, and in both cases empirical investigation may give us confidence in the inference, ceteris paribus, from a subvening base to the supervening property. But in neither case does it make sense for us to *rigidify* on the subvening base—to judge the subvening property metaphysically sufficient for the occurrence of the supervening property even at the expense of our standard epistemology of color or psychology. For intentional psychology, of course, the standard epistemology for ascription is behavior. To claim as K2 does that behavior is an essential element in any ascriptive practice is simply to observe that no neurological evidence could be introduced as relevant, except by our having psychophysical correlations worked out. And the project of establishing those correlations is quite clearly hostage, at every step, to our behavior-based judgments.

In contemporary philosophy of mind, emphasizing the central epistemic role of behavior is rather like admitting to being a liberal in American politics: You must immediately backtrack, qualify your position, and distance yourself from everyone else who ever said anything similar. But the idea is really quite benign. When we go looking for subvening bases of the belief that Φ, we can do nothing other than wait until our subject does something that leads us to ascribe the belief that Φ, and then record the accompanying possibilities for subvening properties.[6] We have here just the observation that, though we may aim at psychophysical correlations, all we can get are correlations between possible subvening bases on one hand, and psychological *ascriptions,* on the other. Consider again some suggestions from recent discussions of response-dependent accounts of color (Blackburn 1995; Boghossian and Velleman 1989; Wright 1992; Lewis 1997). I am exploiting something analogous to the intuition that no physical subvening base could comprise *red* if competent observers in favorable viewing conditions generally see it as green. That is, we might establish a correlation between red and some reflective surface, but its counting as a correlation is ultimately a function of the judgments agents make when encountering that surface. Appeal to the subvening base might override such judgments in *local* cases—poor lighting, incompetent observer, the thing really was red after all—but even then, its power to do so derives from a base class of correlation instances in which the red-judgments were made under intuitively better conditions. We could not make the subvening base criterial in such a fashion that it would then *generally* supersede the considered judgments of agents. By the same token, I expect that neurological evidence could often be relevant in deciding what a subject really believes. Why not? But our confidence in its relevance would be entirely derivative upon our confidence in those purely behavior-based judgments that served to establish the correlation in the first place. Neurological evidence could not generally supersede psychological ascriptive judgments based on behavior.[7]

If that is reasonable, then I have all I want for these purposes. For this is tantamount to the view that if there were intentional ascriptions with wholly physical truth conditions, then when all behavioral evidence failed to bear out the ascriptions, no evidence whatever could do so. If K3 can be made to go through, then we may reject the antecedent in favor of the view that the truth conditions for intentional ascriptions make essential reference to the judgments of ascribers. Propositional attitudes are constituted subjectively, in part; but they are no less real for all that.

Again, I will not—cannot—defend K3 in any great detail here; the argument can remain conditional upon there being such a defense to be had. Perhaps the lesson for those hoping to recover some element of Quine's metaphysics of meaning is that they have a greater stake than they may have realized in the debate over Michael Dummett's meaning-theoretic objections to the notion of evidence-transcendent truth. For now I will be satisfied if I have shown why the proposal I have sketched, to shift all emphasis from indeterminacy and focus instead upon the truth-conditions of intentional ascription, is one that ought to appeal to Quineans like Dennett and Davidson. Still, some brief comments about K3 are in order, and so I will close by anticipating an objection to the general strategy I have adopted.

My proposal, it might be said, only avoids Quine's problematic contrast between linguistics or psychology and the other sciences by relying on a broader antirealism smuggled in via verificationism; I have, in effect, grasped the nettle of a generalized antirealist view, despite questioning the coherence of this option in the early stages.

There is something right in this objection, but it has no bite for my position. I am indeed claiming that a general sort of antirealism is required to make sense of antiphysicalist intentional realism, but that general antirealism is not a generalized version of traditional intentional antirealism, understood as only aesthetically distinct from outright eliminativism. The semantic antirealism taken to underwrite K3 is not the perverse view that there exists nothing at all; it is rather a claim about the *nature* of what exists. Reality, it claims, is essentially knowable in principle—hence its verificationist component. But there *is* a reality. Indeed, the sort of antirealism I have in mind ought to seem distressingly reasonable to those who like to pound the table about the true facts and what is really the case. There is a dark side of the moon, there are colors, and there are beliefs; there are many, many things that neither we nor any of our descendants will ever know. It's just that there are no utterly unde-tectable planets, no completely invisible colors, and no undis-coverably true belief ascriptions. Even Georges Rey, the Hysterical Realist's Hysterical Realist, describes this sort of verificationist princi-ple as "a quite general form that many might find innocuous enough" (1994, 276). It is nevertheless strong enough to bear out, prima facie, the view that psychological states are both real and mind-dependent. If there are mind-independent regions of reality, the entities characteristic of intentional psychology are not found there.[8]

Notes

1. This paper benefited greatly from the insightful and spirited criticism of Ausonio Marras, whose generosity is much appreciated. Peter Clark, William Demopoulos, Paul Markwick, Jill MacIntosh, and Crispin Wright also provided very useful com-mentary. Any remaining errors are reluctantly claimed by the author.

2. That psychological explanation is both useful and false is clearly entailed by the following well-known passage from Quine: "Not that I would forswear daily use of intentional idioms, or maintain that they are practically dispensable. But they call, I think, for bifurcation in canonical notation. . . . If we are limning the true and ultimate structure of reality, the canonical scheme for us is the austere scheme that knows no quotation but direct quotation and no propositional attitudes but only the physical constitution and behavior of organisms" (1960, 221).

3. Dennett recognizes this objection, to be sure, and anticipates it with the claim that the burden of proof lies upon the objector to show why a view of the attitudes as abstracta is problematic (1994). He says, in effect: When you can tell me why it's fine to quantify over Wednesdays and ways of tying shoelaces, then I'll worry about the metaphysics of abstracta in folk psychology. I sympathize with this response, but many do not. If I am right in what follows, the lingering air of ad-hocery can be dispersed.

4. I cannot defend a verificationist notion of truth in this paper, nor will I try. But I observe that there is an established philosophical program which does defend such a notion: semantic antirealism, advanced primarily by Michael Dummett (1991), and, lately, Crispin Wright (1993).

5. Of course, I do not mean to suggest that there is no useful debate about whether one ought to be a "normativist" in the first place. But given the limits of the current discussion, there is no way of mounting a serious defense here of meaning holism itself. Still, for those willing to forgive a lengthy aside, here is an observation in favor of the holist intuition that inferential relations between belief-contents are (at least partly) constitutive of those contents. To show the strength of this intuition I turn to comments by Fodor in which he attacks an argument for meaning holism, given by Stephen Stich.

Stich cites the case of Mrs. T, an elderly and long-term sufferer of amnesia. When asked the fate of American President William McKinley, Mrs. T states that he was assassinated. But when immediately asked whether McKinley is dead, she cannot say (1983, 54–56). How could we ascribe to Mrs. T the belief that McKinley was assassinated? Stich uses this example as an "intuition pump." What is striking is how it succeeds in pumping Fodor's intuitions.

"What's uncontroversial about Mrs. T," Fodor replies, "is only that she forgot many things about death, assassination, and President McKinley and that she ceased to believe that McKinley was assassinated."

But what needs to be shown to make a case for meaning holism is that she ceased to believe that President McKinley was assassinated *because* she forgot many things about death, assassination, and President McKinley; indeed, that her forgetting many things about death, assassination, and President McKinley was *constitutive* of her ceasing to believe that he was assassinated (Fodor 1987, 62).

Why, though, is it *uncontroversial* that Mrs. T ceased to believe that President McKinley was assassinated? She says she believes it, after all. And Fodor, like the rest of us, has been given access only to Mrs. T's behavior with respect to the inferential neighbors of that belief. Unless the holist argument is correct, there are no obvious grounds for viewing Mrs. T as more likely not to have the belief than to have it. But Fodor is right: It is not merely likely, but downright uncontroversial, that she does not actually have the belief in question. Why? In brief, and to the detriment of Fodor's contrary claim: Because we have holist intuitions that run as deep as any about the mental.

At this point one wonders why, rhetorically speaking, Fodor would have said this at all. Surely it is just asking for trouble. But Fodor is deeply skeptical of arguments from epistemology to metaphysics; this is why he grants as much as he does in the Mrs. T case. If it is obvious that Mrs. T lacks the belief that McKinley was assassinated, this is because the observed breakdown of semantic liaisons is reliable *evidence* for— and not constitutive of—that lack. But in this case, Fodor is in a most awkward position. Having allowed (tacitly, at least) that holism reigns at the epistemic level, his metaphysical account of belief will have to explain how the facts can defy this epistemology, without at the same time placing the real representational facts beyond our ken.

6. The space of possibilities will be ludicrously large, of course, especially if we are externalists and must include elements of the environment in the subvening base. But that is no problem for me. I am prepared to grant possibility in principle to the correlation project; only the world is to blame if the project is impossible in practice.

7. For another perspective on applying the notion of response-dependence to intentional psychology, see Wright (1989).

8. A thesis in many ways supportive of this one is found, surprisingly enough, in Jerry Fodor's *Concepts* (1998). There the example of choice is the concept DOORKNOB; as a functional concept it evinces a particularly extreme multiple realizability (Fodor 1998, 147–50). Fodor sketches an account on which doorknobs are both mind-dependent and unambiguously real—an intriguing development in his thought, from my perspective, if a bit rich coming from someone who has tended to read the most implausible antirealism into any thesis claiming psychological states to be mind-dependent (see, for example, Fodor and Lepore 1992, 74).

In fact, Fodor even appeals to the case of color (though not the response-dependence literature) as an example of real things that are partially subjectively constituted; he extrapolates to doorknobs, and thence to all manner of artifacts and secondary properties. This I take to be an auspicious development, since a major theme of what I have argued is the congeniality of my view to realists of all but the most radical sort. On the other hand, Fodor is still just such a realist with respect to intentional psychology. He would utterly reject the idea that beliefs and desires are like colors and doorknobs, and would no doubt insist that propositional attitudes are mind-dependent, not in the way that doorknobs are mind-dependent, but in the way that doorknobs are doorknob-dependent. That is, if there were none, then there would be none—so big deal. My proposal, by contrast, is that the property of believing that *F* is relevantly similar in its mind-dependence to the property of being red, or the properties of being a clock, a doorknob, or a hammer.

References

Blackburn, S. (1995). Circles, finks, smells and biconditionals. *Philosophical Perspectives* 9, J. Tomberlin (ed.). Oxford: Blackwell.

Boghossian, P. and Velleman, D. (1989). Color as a secondary quality. *Mind* 97:89–104.

Chomsky, N. (1969). Quine's empirical assumptions. In *Words and Objections*, D. Davidson and J. Hintikka (eds.). Dordrecht: Reidel. 53–69.

Dahlbom, B. (1993). Editor's Introduction to *Dennett and His Critics*, B. Dahlbom (ed.). Oxford: Blackwell. 1–12.

Dennett, D. (1975). Brain writing and mind reading. In *Language, Mind, and Meaning*, K. Gunderson (ed.), *Minnesota Studies in Philosophy of Science* 7. Minneapolis: University of Minnesota Press.

Dennett, D. (1987). *The Intentional Stance*. Cambridge, Mass.: MIT Press. A Bradford Book.

Dennett, D. (1993). Back from the drawing board. In *Dennett and His Critics*, B. Dahlbom (ed.). Oxford: Blackwell. 203–235.

Dennett, D. (1994). Get real. *Philosophical Topics* 22:505–568.

Dummett, M. (1991). *The Logical Basis of Metaphysics*. Cambridge, Mass.: Harvard University Press.

Fodor, J. (1987). *Psychosemantics*. Cambridge, Mass.: MIT Press. A Bradford Book.

Fodor, J. (1998). *Concepts: Where Cognitive Science Went Wrong*. Oxford: Oxford University Press.

Fodor, J. and Lepore E. (1992). *Holism: A Shopper's Guide*. Oxford: Blackwell.

Timothy Kenyon

Hornsby, J. (1997). *Simple Mindedness: In Defense of Naïve Naturalism in the Philosophy of Mind.* Cambridge, Mass.: Harvard University Press.

Lewis, D. (1997). Finkish dispositions. *The Philosophical Quarterly* 47:143–158.

Quine, W. v. O. (1960). *Word and Object.* Cambridge, Mass.: MIT Press.

Quine, W. v. O. (1969). Reply to Chomsky. In *Words and Objections,* D. Davidson and J. Hintikka (eds.). Dordrecht: Reidel. 70–77.

Rey, G. (1994). Dennett's unrealistic psychology. *Philosophical Topics* 22:259–289.

Ryle, G. (1949). *The Concept of Mind.* Chicago: The University of Chicago Press.

Stich, S. (1983). *From Folk Psychology to Cognitive Science.* Cambridge, Mass.: MIT Press. A Bradford Book.

Wright, C. (1989). Wittgenstein's rule-following considerations and the central project of theoretical linguistics. In *Reflections on Chomsky,* A. George (ed.). Oxford: Blackwell. 233–264.

Wright, C. (1992). *Truth and Objectivity.* Cambridge, Mass.: Harvard University Press.

Wright, C. (1993). *Realism, Meaning, and Truth.* 2nd edition. Oxford: Blackwell.

6

Real Patterns and Surface Metaphysics

William Seager

The Naturalist Imperative

Naturalism is supposed to be a Good Thing. So good in fact that everybody wants to be a naturalist, no matter what their views might be.[1] Thus there is some confusion about what, exactly, naturalism is. In what follows, I am going to be pretty much, though not exclusively, concerned with the topics of intentionality and consciousness, which only deepens the confusion, for these are two areas—perhaps the *last* areas—where it remains possible to doubt the virtues of a naturalistic treatment.

If taken as an expression of the urge to avoid belief in the nonexistent and the false, who would deny the virtue of naturalism? But if the nonexistent and the false are frankly magical entities like the vital spirit, Cartesian consciousnesses, immaterial bearers of meaning, or a supernatural source of intrinsic intentionality, how strong a bulwark is required to save us from error? Does not the consistent trend across more than three hundred years of modern scientific investigation provide us with sufficient evidence to ensure, at least, the supervenience of the phenomena of life, meaning, intentionality, and consciousness upon the natural processes of the world? Although the precise grounds and details of these supervenience relations remain very uncertain, it cannot be seriously doubted that all these phenomena (along with innumerable less controversial examples) are at bottom "fully natural."

Naturalism expresses more than a faith in, but also the desire to *enter into* the orderly community of the *real* sciences. This religious feeling comes in familiar varieties: At one extreme, the fundamentalist Unitarian is remembered for the doctrine of the unity of science, which espoused the outright reduction of every field of knowledge to physics, reserving for all that resisted reduction the ontological hell of nonexistence. At the other extreme we find the New Age liberal theology of *mere* supervenience, unaccompanied by any attempt at reductive analysis, whose hell is the hell of vacuity and quietism.

Between these extremes falls a more hopeful and optimistically temperate naturalism, which requires neither outright reduction to fundamental science nor yet an empty faith in the naturalist outlook. The rules of this naturalism are straightforward and remain at heart reductionist in spirit: They require us to provide an explanation of the target phenomenon (be it intentionality, consciousness, or plain old chemistry) in terms of *Something Else* that is irreproachably "natural" and that does not itself appeal to or depend upon features of the target. The rules of this hopeful naturalism can be codified as follows.

The Rules

X has been *naturalized* iff

(1) *X* has been explained in terms of Something Else.

(2) The Something Else does not essentially involve *X*.

(3) The Something Else is *properly* natural.

This notion of naturalization has several virtues. It is reasonably clear and is directly and quite properly aimed at the *scientific* integration of the naturalizer's targets. After all, it would seem very strange if not perverse first to embrace the scientific view of the world and then boast about how there are some phenomena that defy all attempts to give an account of how they fit into that worldview. In terms of the idea of supervenience, the need for an explication of the supervenience relation between target and base domains is obvious (otherwise, to generalize a remark of Simon Blackburn's, supervenience is part of the problem rather than part of the solution). Still, there is no guarantee that such explications must be forthcoming, and I'll label any view that *denies* the possibility of a Rule-based naturalization (for some domain) *mysterianism*.[2]

The Rules evidently comport well with the several successful naturalizations we already have in hand. Consider chemistry. Although there is no prospect of a full-fledged reduction of chemistry to physics, it is pretty clear that quantum mechanics has succeeded in naturalizing chemistry according to the Rules. Chemical interactions are explicable in physical terms, not in their full detail, but in their very *nature*. I believe that the process of heredity has been (or is very close to being) similarly naturalized by the biochemical understanding of genetics. And while no one knows how life originated on earth (let alone anywhere else) the phenomenon of life certainly seems to be a reasonable goal for naturalization, which will likely be attained quite soon.

It is not only scientific domains that have been naturalized; "weather," "storm," "rain" are hardly scientific terms, but the weather has been explicated by the study of fluid dynamics, and it is only an—unfortunately inevitable and over-hyped—inability to collect and process enough data that prevents accurate and reasonably long-term weather prediction. This list could be long extended, but as we ascend toward more complex phenomena we find ourselves forced to say that we see "how naturalization would go" rather than being able to trot out a triumphant naturalization. Allowing for this weaker sense of naturalization, it seems to me that now, at the end of the twentieth century, it is *only* in the case of the mind (or certain of its features) that we lack a good sense of how naturalization should go.[3]

Nonetheless, the attempt to present naturalist theories of mind goes back a long way, at least to Plato. Recall in the *Theaetetus* Plato's analogical gropings toward a theory of knowledge, which can easily be seen as an early effort to naturalize intentionality, in the relevant sense of following the Rules. You will remember that Plato likens mental content, under the guise of knowledge, first to impressions in a block of wax and then to a set of captive birds which remain free to fly about the aviary of the mind. Such models unfortunately end up breaking the Rules. For example, the birds can stand in for mental contents only if there is some way to recognize them, and this notion of recognition clearly threatens to be viciously intentional. That is, as Plato explains, we can't account for the difference between one of these natural items expressing or signifying a truth as opposed to a falsehood (what Plato calls "knowledge" and "ignorance" respectively) unless some intermediate step of recognizing the import of these items falls between the occurrence of the item and its significance. But of such an intermediate step Plato wisely notes, in the voice of a "destructive critic": "are you going to tell me that there are yet further pieces of knowledge about your pieces of knowledge and ignorance, and that their owner keeps these shut up in yet another of your ridiculous aviaries or waxen blocks. . . . On that showing you will find yourselves perpetually driven round in a circle and never getting any further" (Plato c. 368/1961, 200b–c). In honor of this early failure, let's call the violation of Rule 2 *Plato's problem*.

Many attempts at naturalization have been accused of succumbing to Plato's problem. To see how this goes in a modern setting, I want briefly to consider two nontrivial examples.

The first is Ruth Millikan's theory of intentionality, sometimes called biosemantics. The theory depends upon an account of *functions* that, very roughly, sees the function of X as what provides the *explanation* of why Xs have been "reproductively successful" within a population (very abstractly conceived of course; this account goes far beyond familiar biological functions). Intentionality is then understood in terms of the functions of "symbols" to carry information. Of course, lots of things—potential symbols, so to speak—are reliably hooked up to features of the world (smoke and fire, to take a common example), but only for those hookups in which it is the *function* of the candidate symbol to carry information will there be any intentionality or meaning. A little more precisely: Y *means* X if X is the basic factor explaining (in an evolutionary or quasi-evolutionary way) the continued existence and historical proliferation of *interpretations* of Ys (by the relevant interpreting "devices"). Such explanations are what Millikan calls normal explanations, and these pick out what she labels the proper function of the sign, or, in her own inimitable prose: "the most dominant notion of what is signed by signs is derived by reference to the *direct* proper function of these signs themselves, hence to resulting adapted proper functions of interpreting devices qua taking these signs as immediate adaptors" (1984, 43).

An example will make this clearer (I borrow the example from Robert Cummins's discussion of Millikan's theory in Cummins 1989): In the famous "dance" of the honey bees the orientation of the dance is a sign of where nectar-bearing flowers are. Why? Because the interpretation of the dance by other bees as indicating the presence of such flowers in the appropriate direction explains why the dance proliferated and continues into the present. It may be objected that a huge range of factors actually helped to establish the bee dance. True; but it was the presence of flowers that the dance was "selected for,"[4] not, say, the absence of predators in a sufficiently large number of cases where bees were inclined to forage after observing a sister's dance, or, equivalently, it is not by appeal to the past absence of predators that one can make clear why the dance persisted and proliferated.

Note, by the way, that the reference to interpreting devices prevents just anything with a proper function from becoming a sign— that is, it blocks a version of pansemanticism that might threaten Millikan's view with vacuity. For example, the heart has as its proper function the pumping of blood, and the word "red" has as its proper function the indicating of red, but only the latter operates through and essentially through interpreters. That is, whereas the explanation of the proliferation of sign devices needs to make reference to the interaction between sign producers and "consumers," there is no such need in explanations of the proliferation of features that possess "nonsemantical" proper functions. Of course, the idea that *interpretation* is an essential feature of the operation of signs awkwardly recalls the difficulty Plato found in the wax-block and caged-birds models of thought. In general the notion of an interpreter device must itself be given an entirely nonintentional explanation, most likely in terms of the behavior that helped, and continues to help, to "fix" the sign into the interpreters' world. This is not a trivial task; but according to the Rules, the complete naturalization of intentionality requires a nonintentional treatment of interpreters. I am sure in practice this condition will be extremely difficult to fulfill, for it amounts to no less than providing a noncognitive theory of the interpreters' sign-response behavior. It strikes me that if we could provide such accounts we would not be just one step closer to naturalizing intentionality, but would have already succeeded in naturalizing intentionality. In the case of the bees, it is of course tempting to suppose that they respond to their sisters' dances in a "mechanical" way without the intervention of beliefs (or other cognitive states) about or genuine interpretations of these dances, but no one can yet claim to understand the basis of such a mechanism.

It has been argued, however, that biosemantics—in common with all the other theories on offer—may encounter difficulties solving a core problem that faces any account of intentionality, namely, the problem of assigning the *properly specific* information to particular symbols. Crudely speaking, the problem is to distinguish the proper meaning of "horse," that is, *horses,* from other possible meanings that seem identically capable of reproducing themselves within a reproductive family of symbol systems, for example, *horse or anything indistinguishable from a horse to twentieth-century science.* As the growing intricacy of the attempts to solve it attest, this problem is deeper than it looks. But as we've seen, biosemantics has a ready response that is quite plausible. It may be that the reproducing symbol system couldn't care less about the difference between these two possible meanings since there is nothing in the use of the symbol "horse" that could have distinguished them, but it is ludicrous to claim that the two meanings are equally good *explanations* of why "horse" is connected to what it is connected to (save for any who happen to believe that there are, and have been, clever alien or robot horses interspersed with the genuine article—but that is a *ludicrous* belief).

Now Plato's problem reappears. On this view of biosemantics, it is impossible to understand how symbols connect to the world without understanding what *explanation* is; the notion of explanation is a key component of the workings of the theory. It is unfortunately all too clear that the notion of explanation is implicitly intentional. We could caricature the theory somewhat as follows: Symbol *S* means *O* just in case the proper explanation of S's role involves appeal to S's carrying the information that O. Since S carries lots of information besides O we need some mechanism to narrow down the field. But if the mechanism explicitly appeals to what is a "good explanation" then we have succumbed to Plato's problem. (We might still have a good theory of how symbols function, but, like Grice's theory of meaning, it could not be employed in the project of naturalizing intentionality.)

Contrast this case with one where there is a clear victory for naturalization: chemistry. One of the most important chemical properties of an element is its *valence,* which was originally defined as the number of atoms of hydrogen the element could combine with (so, oxygen has a valence of 2). Lots of chemistry could at least be organized, if not explained, by use of this idea. But of course the urge to naturalize arose with the question of exactly what valence *is.* And it turns out that everything the old chemists were going on about with their talk of valence as a fundamental chemical property of elements can be accounted for by the physical structure of atoms, in particular in terms of the structure of the outer electron shells. This means that someone could (albeit inefficiently) learn what valence is without bothering about developing a prior acquaintance with chemistry—there is no need to understand chemistry in order to understand the physics of valence. I am strongly inclined, however, to think that no one could understand the physical account of valence without already understanding what explanation is supposed to be, that is, without knowing about how minds connect information together, find certain things interesting and relevant, etc. (This does not interfere with the naturalization of chemistry since these intentional notions are not chemical notions.) I am also inclined to think that this seemingly innocuous fact is very important to the project of naturalizing the mind, and in fact probably makes it impossible. Although this naturalizing story *is* a good explanation of valence, *that* it is a good explanation is not part of what makes it the proper story about valence—the world sees to that all by itself. Biosemantics can't let the world do its job since the world can't distinguish between problematic contents (that's why there is a problem about specifying content in the first place). Thus biosemantics makes its explicit appeal to the canons of good explanation. Part of what makes "horse" mean *horse* is that this *explains* why "horse"-symbols proliferated, and this appeal violates Rule 2.

Another well-known and highly developed theory of content is that of Jerry Fodor (see Fodor 1992). This theory—unlike, as I think, Millikan's—has as its explicit aim the production of a theory that abides by the Rules. Fodor solves our *horse* versus *horse or anything indistinguishable from a horse to twentieth-century science* problem by appeal to what he calls asymmetrical counterfactual dependence. The idea is that instances of *horse or anything indistinguishable from a horse to twentieth-century science* would not cause instances of "horse" unless instances of *horse* do (and did) cause instances of "horse," but *not* vice versa. Of course, it is very hard to believe that we do have asymmetric dependence in this case, but leave that aside (along with a host of more or less technical difficulties, for samples of which see Adams and Aizawa 1993 or Seager 1993). We are interested in Plato's problem, and it perhaps arises here when we consider whether the appeal to counterfactuals in Fodor's theory secretly invokes some of the very notions that the theory is supposed to be naturalizing. Arguably it does, since arguably the kind of counterfactuals the theory needs do not have any determinate truth conditions independent of the *goals* of explanation (thus there is a weak affinity between Millikan and Fodor here). There might be some counterfactuals that have, so to speak, world-limited truth conditions (what Putnam 1992 called strict counterfactuals), but it is, to say the least, unlikely that instances of *horse or anything indistinguishable from a horse to twentieth-century science* would not cause instances of "horse" unless instances of *horse* do cause instances of "horse" is an example of one of them. You can't tell whether this counterfactual is true unless you understand the context in which it is to be evaluated, and you can't discover this context unless you understand how counterfactuals are interest-relative, and *interest* is a thoroughly intentional notion. Another way to put this: Fodor needs to know the truth-value of certain counterfactuals. Unfortunately, these counterfactuals don't have a truth value simpliciter but only relative to a "context of evaluation." The notion of a "context of evaluation" is itself an intentional notion, and to the extent that the theory appeals to it, it violates Rule 2.[5]

Notice that, as in the case of biosemantics' use of the notion of explanation, an appeal to counterfactuals (even nonstrict ones) is no barrier to naturalization in general, since in almost all cases of naturalization the appeal to an intentional notion would not violate the Rules (since the target would not be itself intentional).

Naturalism and Dennett

Even if you accept the Rules of naturalization, there are still different ways to play the game. For example, the failure to naturalize something could be seen not as a failure of the scientific worldview, but rather as the *discovery* that the target was chimerical. Not only is the history of science replete with well-known examples of this; it is commonly occasioned by our growth of general knowledge about the world (of course, such growth is highly conditioned by scientific progress). There is no scientific proof that demon possession is unreal (so far as I know—and may we continue to be preserved—there has never been any attempt at a scientific demonology), but the idea has somehow fallen by the wayside. The trend of this eliminative history reinforces the respectability of our Rule-defined notion of naturalization. It seems that wherever we have seen no prospect of naturalization we have preferred elimination to ontological inflation.[6]

Thus it is curious that Dennett, who by and large writes from a perspective that clearly endorses the scientific view of the world and that is supposed to be noneliminativist, espouses a theory of intentionality that blocks the naturalization of the mind. Although Dennett's theory of the intentional stance is by now intricate and subtle, it remains essential to it that the mental states of a subject, *S*, be understood as states (no doubt physical states, probably of *S*'s brain) whose *mentality* resides in their underpinning an intentional interpretation of *S*. Now, on just about anybody's view, the mental states do the job of generating behavior that can be interpreted from the intentional stance, but for most theorists the mentalistic interpretation is parasitic upon the *mental properties* of these states. It is because they are mental that we can successfully interpret them (or their possessor) as having a mind. Fundamentally, Dennett sees things the other way around: It is because we can (perhaps, if we are to grapple successfully with the behavior, even *must*) interpret these states (or their possessor) as mentalistic that they are mental. To take a favorite example, the internal states of a chess-playing computer are *about* chess because we can interpret the machine as playing a (reasonably good) game of chess. The straightforwardness of the example notwithstanding, it would be a *deep* metaphysical error to seek any intrinsically chess-aimed intentional states within the mechanism—an error that Dennett sees being everywhere committed in the philosophy of mind.

The problem of "original intentionality" is thus dodged, but part of the cost of this success is the loss of naturalization. (It remains open whether outright falsehood is another, and higher, cost of Dennett's views.) The notions of "interpretation," "intentional stance," "predictive purposes," etc., are one and all notions that generate another case of Plato's problem. This is formally obvious, but let's be clear how the problem arises. It is not that, as a matter of fact so to speak, mental state ascriptions are parasitic upon behavior that can be interpreted mentalistically; the problem of naturalization is that we cannot *explain* what mental states *are* without appeal to notions shot through with their own mentalistic implications. You can't understand what a mind is unless you already know what a mind is, since you can't understand mentality without understanding the intentional stance, which requires you to already understand a host of essentially mentalistic concepts. Another approach to this is via the comparison of the case of the mind with that of chemistry; the two are entirely dissimilar. One can imagine learning chemistry by learning its naturalization along with a host of defined terms— at the end one would really know what chemistry was about, although after this beginning, because of typical problems of complexity, one would have to learn to "think chemically" to get anywhere in chemical studies. According to Dennett, you can't do this for the mind, since you'd already have to know what a mind was to "get" the intentional stance.

Understanding Dennett's failure (or refusal) to naturalize the mind might clarify other issues. One example is the long-standing debate between Donald Davidson and Jaegwon Kim about reductionism. Davidson's *anomalous monism* rejects the naturalizability of the mind (and for reasons not altogether unlike Dennett's) but Davidson famously accepted the supervenience of the mental upon the physical, whereupon Kim presented a variety of arguments to show that supervenience entails reducibility, construed as necessary co-extension of properties (see Davidson 1970; Kim 1978, 1989). But if we pay attention to the Rules we see that reducibility need not entail naturalizability. Even if for each mental property there were a physical property nomologically necessarily coextensive with it, this would not suffice for naturalization unless this co-extension relation served to *explain* what mentality *was*. Somewhat curiously, naturalization is *both* weaker and stronger than reducibility as we are construing it here. For a relation much less strong than reducibility can underwrite an *explanation* of one domain in terms of another (or an explication of how the one domain supervenes upon the other), but even a necessary co-extension between domains is not sufficient, all by itself, for explanation (recall the example of the height of the flagpole and the length of its shadow—though there is obviously a necessary co-extension between these the latter cannot explain the former).[7] In the case of the mind, if some of the concepts needed to explain the mind are themselves mentalistic, then naturalization will be impossible, whether or not any relation of co-extension holds between mental and physical properties. I thus urge that we interpret Davidson's remark that even if we discovered relations of co-extension between certain mental and physical states, we would have no reason to believe it was not an accident as the claim that the discovery of the co-extension would not serve to explain the mind in physical terms. Davidson's claim here can be put in old-fashioned language: discovering the neural "correlates" of mental states does not *explain* the physicality of the mind. This seems worth emphasizing since many have fallen into the trap of believing that the successful discovery of a pretty complete set of robust mental-physical correlations would amount to naturalization.

All this seems to lead to the rather nice result that the failure to naturalize the mind does not mean that the mind is nonphysical, although it does entail that the mind is physically inexplicable, which is to say that the failure to naturalize does lead to a version of mysterianism.

For reasons I cannot understand, mysterianism tends to be a vilified, rather than merely criticized, doctrine, but there are several forms that deserve to be distinguished. One may hold that it is impossible to naturalize the mind because of certain inherent conceptual limitations of the human mind (see McGinn 1989). Since at present we have no real understanding of the nature and creation of concepts themselves, let alone the limits of human conceptual machinery, it is hard to assess the merits of this claim. McGinn's argument depends upon quite strong assumptions about the nature of concepts and their genesis, assumptions which are far from assured. Nonetheless, it seems plausible to suppose that there is some limit to our ability to understand the world, and if so, it is an empirical question whether the scientific naturalization of the mind transcends this limit.

Another form of mysterianism rests content with the neural-mental correlations, declaring them to be "brute facts," incapable of explanation by *any* science aided by however powerful a conceptual system. Ironically (given his views on the first type of mysterianism), it is possible that Owen Flanagan promotes this position when he says "some patterns of neural activity result in phenomenological experience; other patterns do not. The story bottoms out there" (1992, 58). I have some trouble understanding how a feature of the world that manifests itself (so far as we know) only when vast numbers of complex neural units interact in quite special ways can be at the "bottom" of the story of the world. The bottom of this story ought to reside in the very simplest features of the world; thus the charge of the electron is perhaps a candidate for being a brute fact, but not the sensations brought about by electrical current.

There is yet another form of mysterianism, which I call *methodological mysterianism,* and which I have been urging above. It is possible that it is the conditions of naturalization that block naturalization. I take this to be so—Rule 2 cannot be satisfied in the case of the mind (intentionality, meaning, content, etc.) since a variety of mentalistic notions must be understood in order for any explanation to be given. This is universally a condition upon explanation, but it matters not at all to the project of naturalization throughout all domains that are remote from mentality (as discussed above, the naturalization of chemistry is not blocked by the fact that any explanation of chemistry in "purely physical" terms assumes that there is either an explicit or a more or less implicit understanding of explanation, the context of explanation, the notion of intelligibility, etc.).

While I think that methodological mysterianism is a *general* impediment to the naturalization of the mind, and in fact could explain the so-called explanatory gap between matter and consciousness and thus ease our qualms about accepting the identification of mental and physical states despite this unbridgeable gap, I won't expand on that here. For there are more specific versions of methodological mysterianism, and Dennett's view of mind is one of them. Insofar as notions such as *interpretation, explanatory and predictive purposes,* and the like are required to understand what minds are, Rule 2 cannot be fulfilled, but not, on the face of it, because of any ontological or conceptual problems. This is a kind of methodological mysterianism.

However, despite the fact that Dennett's views set up only a methodological block to naturalization, one might remain unsatisfied. The mind *is* physical at bottom, and there must be some account of what this amounts to, mustn't there? Yes, and no.

What Can Be Explained, or Darwin to the Rescue

Anyone who read the, shall we say, heated exchange between Dennett and Stephen Jay Gould about *Darwin's Dangerous Idea* (which begins with Gould 1997) will have noticed, among other things, that Dennett has a strong commitment to optimality, or adaptationist, explanations in evolution. Dennett vigorously defends adaptationist thinking with a set of arguments internal to evolutionary theorizing, but the importance of optimality for his philosophy stems from a deeper source.

Adaptationism is needed to save Dennett from a much stronger form of mysterianism about the mind than the mere methodological mysterianism I ascribed to him above. Suppose that one felt the opposing pulls of an interpretationist or intentional stance theory of mind (or of mental states) as well as the residual attraction of a Rule-based project of naturalization. Strictly speaking, the former would preclude the latter, but there might remain something central to the favored picture of the mind that could be plausibly naturalized. Dennett's scheme is perfectly set up for such a maneuver.

The nature of the intentional stance requires that there be appropriate input into the engine of interpretation, and this input is behavior—generally speaking, extremely complex behavior (and at the higher end, mostly verbal behavior). At least to a first approximation behavior can be described in nonmentalistic language, although the more complex interpretable behavior becomes the less sense can be made of it from outside the intentional stance. So one might be tempted to ask for the nonintentional description of behavior that licenses the ascription of mental states in the hope for a Rule-based naturalization of mind on the basis of such nonmentalistically described behavior. But since this strategy is simply behaviorism in a "metaphysical" guise, it is abundantly clear that it cannot succeed. Furthermore, if it *could* succeed we would have no reason to cleave to the intentional stance as our theory of mind; we would have fully succeeded in naturalizing the mind (at least on the assumption that the physical mechanisms of behavior generation are naturalizable, an assumption that is entirely plausible on almost everybody's view). And, even leaving aside the devastating critique behaviorism has been subject to, there is simply no hope of this, since the behaviorists would have to understand and more or less covertly deploy a host of intentional concepts (such as, to reiterate, explanatory purpose, predictive goals, relative intelligibility, etc.) in order to understand their behavioristic theory of the mind. Thus the full naturalization of the mind would have failed, falling victim, as so many attempts do, to Plato's problem, in particular to the version of it that supports methodological mysterianism.

In any event, there is another path. We cannot explain the mind in terms of behavior (or behavioral disposition, behavioral patterns, or whatever), yet the intentional stance still takes behavior to be the foundation of mind; actions are interpreted *behavior*, where the behavior at issue can be, as a matter of fact, nonmentalistically described. And it is possible to ask for a scientific account of the origin of systems that can display behavior sufficiently rich to deserve (require?) intentional interpretation. Here we can get a lift up from Darwin.

Crudely speaking, the claim is that evolution can explain the genesis of organisms capable of ever-richer patterns of behavior, including behavior susceptible to intentional description. Once this claim is in place we seem to have an account of the origin of mind from "mere matter" even though we lack a "proper" Rule-based naturalization of mind; call such an account a *quasi-naturalization.* There is an air of sleight of hand here, but this may stem from incompletely suppressed hankerings after Rule-based naturalization. Consider Dennett's account of the "birth of meaning," which he traces back to the earliest beginnings of life on earth whereupon arose the possibility of "exercising the option of adopting the perspective from which errors might be discerned" (Dennett 1995, 203). What perspective, you might ask, and who is adopting it? It is we, enminded creatures, who adopt the perspective, but the errors are found in the primordial replicators' failures to reproduce themselves *exactly,* and that *is* where the errors are, isn't it? One could hardly chide the early replicators for failing to take the error-discerning perspective (you might as well complain that it's your golf ball's fault for going into the rough, though indeed it is the thing sitting in the tall grass). Still, there is a long way from faulty molecular transcription to folk psychology. Is there any *account* of the genesis of behavior patterns that tend toward deserving a mentalistic interpretation?

I'm not sure that Dennett has ever ventured to demonstrate that folk psychological interpretability is a natural product of the evolution of complex organisms. From one point of view, the early part of chapter 7 of *Consciousness Explained* (Dennett 1991a) is close to such an attempt (see also Dennett 1975). A crude story more directly aimed at integrating folk psychology and evolution might go something like this. Organisms that are more successful at replication will proliferate at the expense of the less successful. We can expect that organisms will have to compete for the resources necessary for replication (and it is this competition that will drive the creation of complexity in organisms). So the more successful replicators will out-compete their rivals. What will this amount to? It is not hard to believe that the more successful organisms will appear (at least) to make more of an effort to get the resources (this could work in a variety of ways; they might be better at finding resources, or keeping resources, or taking resources away from other organisms—ancient, not always honorable, and still familiar strategies). That is to say (almost) that the successful organisms will give, within the initially stringent limits of their behavioral capacities, indications of *wanting* the resources necessary for replication. The usefulness of some method of tracking resources is clear and could (did) lead to the concomitant development of sensory organs. From the point of view of developing folk-psychologically chacterizable organisms, the birth of sense organs is the birth of *belief*. Since the only value of such tracking mechanisms is to ensure that the "desired" resources are obtained, there is a natural ground for the basic pattern of rationality that grounds folk psychology: Organisms will want what they need and believe what is true (albeit within a very restricted domain). Although very crude, some such story seems not implausible as a ground of at least a quasi- or pseudo-psychological characterizability. We have no trouble looking even at ants from a folk-psychological perspective. (Actually it's rather hard not to look at them this way unless we make a conscious effort.)[8]

There are other clues that there is this kind of evolutionary story to be told. It seems to me striking that organisms that are extremely different by almost any measure often engage in behavior patterns that cry out for a similar sort of (pseudo-)psychological interpretation. Here is one such example. The Scottish red deer and the African funnel-web spider exhibit striking similarities in behavior. In the rutting season, stags in possession of a harem are likely to be challenged by intruder males. Their bouts typically involve "roaring contests" (where each apparently tries to out-roar the other), "parallel walks" (where the stags walk along beside each other for varying lengths of time), and, occasionally, fighting. Pretty clearly, the precursor activities aid each stag in assessing the fighting ability of the other. This information exchange and its point could easily be expressed in folk-psychological terms, and in fact it is difficult not to think of these animals as engaged in a variety of cognitive tasks (and surely such higher mammals really are "cogitating"). Moving to another order of organism, the female funnel-web spiders contest webs, and their typical bouts involve the following: "(i) 'locating'; orienting movements, and palpation of the web . . . (ii) 'signaling'; lengthy exchanges of vibratory and visual displays . . . (iii) 'threat'; running or lunging toward an opponent. (iv) 'contact' . . ." (Maynard Smith 1982, 115–116). The point of the precursor activities again seems clearly to enable each spider to assess the fighting ability of the other (and possibly the value of the web).[9] A description of a typical encounter in terms of belief and desire would not be hard to produce. Although both the style and function of these behavior patterns in deer and spider are strikingly similar and in themselves equally susceptible to psychological characterization, it does not seem very likely that these creatures share any significant neural structure, state, or process that accounts for it. The mammalian brain of the deer is immense and densely connected compared with the paltry brain of the arthropod, yet both, in the appropriate environments, produce "psychologically equivalent" behavior. This is, of course, not to say that the spider is the intellectual equal of the deer; in fact, the greater the disparity between deer and spider the better for the point I'm trying to make, which is that psychologically characterizable behavior is a fat evolutionary target, that Mother Nature would have trouble missing once she started building organisms of any appreciable complexity.[10]

So perhaps we can allow that behavior suitable for interpretation from the intentional stance is the natural by-product of the evolution of complexity in organisms. There remains a wide gulf between the animals and ourselves. The *human* intentional stance is incomparably more complex, subtle, and intricate than that required for the interpretation of animals, as is the behavior interpreted by the human stance (as Dennett has frequently emphasized). A problem looms here. In light of the gulf between animal and human mentality as indexed by behavioral differences, it is possible to maintain that although "basic" psychological characterizability is one of evolution's natural products, the human mind, with all its *distinctive* features, is *not* a product of selection. This would threaten even the weak naturalization of the mind, which Dennett's view can still allow, leaving the mind (the human mind at least) an accident of nature.

If it should turn out that the features that distinguish human from animal mentality are *spandrels* (that is, accidental and unsought for by-products of independent development), then we shall have no evolutionary account of the patterns of human behavior after all. We would then be forced to say, first, that no account of the mind can be given except in terms that presuppose mind, and second, the best account of why creatures with minds like ours arose is that it was a lucky accident, perhaps, if we have still more luck, building upon the foundations of animal cognition. Though not as extreme as, for example, McGinn's, this would be a quite robust form of mysterianism: You can't understand the mind in scientific terms and it arose by a fluke of nature.

An extreme, and extremely implausible, example can illuminate the problem. Suppose that the growth of the human brain into that which supports our distinctive mentality was occasioned by selection pressure for blood cooling, completely independent of cognitive function. That is, we were doing just fine with our ape-brain, but the move on to the savanna forced development of better heat-dissipation methods—so we shed our fur and grew our brains. As a purely accidental by-product of this brain growth we suddenly "woke up," became conscious, and invented tools, language, and culture. According to this tale, although the complex behavior distinctive of human intelligence emerged out of this brain growth, its accidental nature leaves the radical change evolutionarily inexplicable. Now, my story is ridiculous (there is more chance of the reverse being true, that brain growth provided better cooling as the accidental, but useful, concomitant to cognition-driven growth), but the more "accidental" the brain changes underpinning human intellect (or, equally from the intentional stance, the behavior distinctive of human intellect), the more mysterian becomes our account of the mind.

How much of the human mind is the accidental result of neurological change occasioned by noncognitively driven changes? Unfortunately, neither the question nor the proper method of answering it is very clear. Gould (1997), for one, is willing to assert that "adaptationism [is] a particularly dubious approach to human behavior," since many, if not most, universal behaviors are probably spandrels, often co-opted later in human history for important secondary functions. The human brain is the most complicated device for reasoning and calculating, and for expressing emotion, that has ever evolved on earth. Natural selection made the human brain big, but most of our mental properties and potentials may be spandrels—that is, nonadaptive side consequences of building a device with such structural complexity (Gould 1997).

On the other hand, if we are allowed to use *language* as the index of achievement of the human mind, there seems to be evidence of structural change in the brain aimed at supporting linguistic functions (see Deacon 1997). Could language be a spandrel? Here is one place where the unclarity mentioned above intrudes. As Dennett points out, from a certain point of view, all—certainly most—of the features of highly evolved organisms probably began as spandrels, but if one has to go back a very long way to spot the spandrel nature of the feature then there is an intervening adaptationist story of the development of the completed feature from the initial "spandrel" that certainly *looks* like it provides an evolutionary explanation of that feature. Furthermore, even if language developed from some neurological feature unrelated to linguistic function in some more interesting sense (for example, if the supporting feature is very recent), what grounds are there for thinking that this unrelated function was noncognitive? Both Deacon (1997) and Donald (1991), for example, suggest that a prelinguistic but *symbolic* function spurred the unusual development of the frontal cortex which now supports language. Perhaps there is an evolutionary story of the development of abstract symbolic abilities that is analogous to the story of the development of sensory organs. If so, then there is some possibility of extending the quasi-naturalist account of elementary folk psychology to the level of the human mind. I take it that one of the basic projects of "evolutionary psychology" is, or should be, to bridge this gap. And though it has its detractors, it is too early to tell whether evolutionary psychology will fail at this task (though it is a much harder job than, for example, explaining why more men than women are philanderers or why men murder more often than women—the sort of thing most evolutionary psychology seems to spend most of its time on).

One might think that Dennett has another option here, which is to run the quasi-naturalization at a different level. Perhaps much of what is distinctive about the human mind has been produced by the human mind via the development of *memes*, a process that is itself susceptible to adaptationist explanation. But there are two problems here. In the first place, it is unlikely that the analogy between genetics and natural selection on the one hand and the propagation and development of memes between and within human minds on the other is more than superficial. Genes are nicely atomistic and discretely compositional; ideas are not. So a memetics based on the model of genetics probably won't go very far. The second problem is worse, at least from the naturalist's perspective. Memes are products and inhabitants of mind *as such*. We have no understanding of them except as units of meaning. Thus, if we plug them into the quasi-naturalist story we are trying to develop, we once again fall victim to Plato's problem. The previous project avoided this by looking for an account of the behavior patterns that sustained interpretation from the intentional stance. This behavior was supposed to be characterizable in nonmentalistic terms, and we were supposed to be able to see how natural selection could mold behavior thus characterized into appropriate—mentalistically interpretable—forms (recall that, even on the most optimistic assessment of this project, *full* naturalization fails since we always presuppose the intentional stance itself). This is not to say that the meme-story is not worth telling or somehow illegitimate, but that it cannot replace the original, evolution-based, quasi-naturalist program.

That program seems to me coherent, fruitful, and integrated in a variety of interesting ways with a host of "cognitive sciences" (biology and neuroscience as well as AI and psychology). To summarize: It takes as given the intentional stance, that is, our core mentalistic notions by which we interpret the behavior of our fellows (and ourselves). Thus it must forsake Rule-based naturalization. The resulting mysterianism is, I argued above, a kind of methodological mysterianism, which is general and unavoidable. It leaves behind an outstanding debt to the scientific worldview, which can be only partially repaid by an evolutionary account of the genesis of the behavior patterns that are the targets of the intentional stance. To the degree to which this promised account lapses into appeals to accidents or spandrels, the underpinnings of mind remain mysterious.[11] Notice that there are two *kinds* of mystery here. One is the methodological mysterianism which stems from the fact that there is no way to explain the mind except in terms that essentially depend upon other mentalistic concepts. The second is the more familiar sort, wherein an evolutionary account of the genesis of certain behavioral capacities may be difficult or impossible to come by. We can hope to overcome the second sort of mystery, but never the first. It is my hope that methodological mysterianism is entirely safe for human consumption (and might be a pleasant and relaxing brew). I want to conclude however with my fear that it is not, which leads to a strange and interesting confluence of views.

Patterns and Metaphysics

The question, at bottom, is whether methodological mysterianism has any impact upon our metaphysics. I mean by metaphysics simply our general picture of the world, our picture of how things "hang together" in the large. The picture behind the Rules of naturalization is such a metaphysics and one that is very powerful and compelling—call it the scientific picture of the world (or SPW for short). What is the SPW? Here is a sketch (which should not be unfamiliar).

To begin at the Beginning, we have a pretty good idea of how our universe began, though we await the long anticipated marriage of quantum mechanics with general relativity for the *really* early details of creation. The theory of the Big Bang reveals how matter originated and suggests how early inhomogeneities in energy distribution led to star and galaxy formation. We know how stellar processes create the heavier elements and how massive dying stars "fertilize" space with these newly generated elements. Such second-generation material forms new stars and planetary systems some of which are lucky enough to have planets orbiting neither too far nor too close to their sun, and possess the chemical mix required for life.

No one knows how life originated on earth (let alone anywhere else), but this is a scientific question. Those toiling on the creation of a scientific metaphysics have no reason to deny that life is just a matter of complex chemistry. From, as it were, the bottom up, chemistry itself is understood as the natural outcome of the physical interactions of the atoms' various constituents. Life is the pinnacle of chemical complexity.

Within the realm of living things the hierarchy of chemical complexity is again extended, from very simple structures not fully alive to exceedingly complex creatures, some of whom aspire to produce science and the SPW. What is more, we possess an exceptionally elegant theory of how biological complexity arises. Again the SPW integrates the top-down and bottom-up perspective. From the top, the theory of evolution tells us how organisms become more complex, so long as complexity is reproductively advantageous (which it evidently was within many of the environments the earth has provided over the last three billion years). From the bottom, we have forged an indissoluble connection between chemistry and genetics, which has revealed the chemical basis of life and evolution.

Take anything you like: a galaxy, a person, a flounder, an atom, an economy—it seems that anything can be *resolved* into the fundamental physical constituents, processes, and events that determine its activity.[12] Although innumerable difficult questions arise at every stage of resolution, and there is no practical prospect of *knowing* the full details of the physical resolution of anything much more complex than even a simple atom, the picture is clear. And since the *world* has no need to know the details but just runs along *because* the details are the way they are, the problems *we* have understanding complex systems in terms of fundamental physics are quite irrelevant to the metaphysics of the SPW.

Here's a thought experiment to help assess one's attitude to the SPW. Imagine a computer simulation of a part of the world. First restrict attention to something "simple"—say, a pendulum swinging on the moon. The simulation covers a restricted region of space and time (though "boundary conditions" can be set up to represent external influence), and must be defined solely in terms of fundamental physical attributes. The programmer is *not* permitted gross parameters such as the mass or the length of the pendulum, or the lunar gravitational force, but must write her code in terms of the really basic physics. (It might help to imagine the code written in terms of the properties of the atoms of the pendulum, its support structure and moon, though these are not really physically basic.) [13] The SPW predicts that the simulation—appropriately displayed— will reveal a pendulum swinging above the lunar surface. Now up the ante. Imagine simulating a more complex situation, for example, a child's birthday party. Do you think the simulation would mimic the actual party? Though there is, of course, no prospect of ever being able to develop such simulations, I think the notion is perfectly well defined (or could be with a little more effort). I venture to maintain that what we know about the world strongly suggests that such a simulation would "re-generate" both the action of the pendulum and the behavior of the children. I think that one way of understanding the task of physics is exactly as the development of a theory of the fundamental features of the world whose simulation would meet this challenge. In any event, if you think the simulation would agree with reality, you believe in the SPW. [14]

The problem I'm worrying about emerges upon consideration of the status, within the SPW, of the myriad of high-level explanatory structures ubiquitous throughout science and ordinary life, of which the primary example is the complex behavior interpreted by the intentional stance. These Dennett calls patterns.

Inhabiting a curious zone midway between, as it were, objectivity and subjectivity, patterns are *there* to be seen, but have *no function* if they are not seen. [15] By the former, I mean that patterns are not just in the eye of the beholder; they are really in the world and provide us with an indispensable and powerful explanatory and predictive grip on the world. By the latter, I mean that the *only* role they have in the world is to help organize the experience of those conscious beings who invent them and then think in terms of them. That is, although the world is rightly described as exemplifying a host of patterns, the world has no use for them. In terms of our thought experiment, high-level patterns do not need to be coded into the world-simulation in order to ensure the accuracy of the simulation, and this is just because it is the fundamental features of the world that organize the world into all the patterns it exemplifies, and they do this all by themselves, with no help from "top-down" causation. Doubtless there is a harmless sense of "top-down causation" that is perfectly acceptable, appropriate for use within pattern-bound explanations. For example, we can explain the location of a particular atom by reference to the *intentions* of the operator of a scanning tunneling electron microscope. But we know that those very intentions are elusively accommodated within a vastly intricate web of microstates that, within their environment, "push" the target atom to its final location. Intentions, like planets, animals, and molecules, have no need to be specially written into the code of the world-simulation.

We could define "radical emergence" as the hypothesis that the world-simulation will fail, save for the addition of certain high-level, complexity-induced properties ready to step in and "make a difference" at various critical junctures.[16] The SPW, then, is the denial of radical emergence. The SPW says that the world generates complexity out of simplicity, but never dreams that complexity itself has powers that outrun its source. There is another notion that is sometimes confused with radical emergence but is quite distinct, which I'll call *explanatory emergence*. This is the doctrine that complexity does outrun the *explanatory resources* provided by an *understanding* of the simple. Explanatory emergence is compatible with radical emergence but obviously does not entail it.

Now we can see that the Rules of naturalization express the hope that explanatory emergence is false, or, rather, that it is not wholly true; that there is an *explanation* of every high-level phenomenon in at least slightly lower-level terms (and thus by a chain of explanations the world will be unified in accordance with the ultimate primacy of its fundamental physical features).[17] By and large, this hope has been fulfilled. Explanation is a less stringent formal requirement than outright reduction,[18] and the SPW is chock full of Rule-based explications of high-level phenomena, all of them tending to follow explanatory pathways back toward the truly fundamental features described in physics. The explanations that Rule-based naturalization require are the sort that let us understand what a phenomenon *is* in lower-level terms, but they are not required to be so strong as to replace high-level discourse. We do, I think, understand what chemistry is in terms of physics, but it is not possible, and there is no desire, to replace chemical talk with purely physical talk. In terms of our world-simulation thought experiment, we can express all this very simply—we would expect to see chemistry (or simulated chemistry) at work in the simulation even though no chemistry was coded into the simulation. Our belief in this feature of the imaginary simulation is an expression of our belief that there is no radical chemical emergence. And though perhaps we don't know *for sure* that radical emergence is false, that's where the smart money has gone for the last four hundred years.

But we've seen that Rule-based naturalization can fail in ways more insidious than radical emergence. Because of Plato's problem, the theory that mind is to be properly understood in terms of interpretation from the intentional stance precludes Rule-based naturalization. Dennett's ideas about patterns involve a generalization of the interpretationist scheme, for patterns are explanatory posits, useful only from a point of view that understands them (bearing in mind that understanding comes in degrees).

Perhaps this is disputable. Isn't the world full of patterns in use by a host of systems to which we would be unlikely to ascribe minds? For example, don't some moths have eye-shaped patches on their wings the function of which is to startle predators, thus giving the moth an extra fraction of a second to escape being eaten? Doesn't this work—doesn't it *have* to work—via the predator's *recognition* of the patches as eyes? Well, is the moth *trying* to scare the predators when she flashes her wings? Of course, at some point mind does intrude and we do have recognition and intentional deception. And there we have the patterns taken up and understood by the only thing that can understand, appreciate, or perceive patterns—minds. Precisely where the changeover from nonmind to mind occurs is a vexed question (even allowing that the distinction will be fuzzy), but what matters is the point that *patterns* have no role to play in the world unless and until they are taken up in understanding by minds.

Does evolution work by discovering, creating, and arranging patterns? We understand evolution as a "search" for optimality, but the search is blind. Any intentionality ascribed to nature is entirely and only metaphorical, the appreciation of which is dependent upon a prior understanding of mind. The patterns we see in evolution are there, but are there only to be *seen*. Nothing but mind can see them and only mind "needs" them. Evolutionary theory is a way of apprehending parts of the world that brilliantly highlight certain more or less enduring patterns to be found in the "dance of the atoms." *We* need the idea of evolution to understand the world, but the *world* has no need of it; the world—not even the bio-logical parts of it—is not being driven by evolutionary properties. Predator-prey relations will be revealed in our imagined world-simu-lation of an environment in precisely the form they take in the world itself; the Hardy-Weinberg law will emerge from the quark/lepton sea of our simulation with not a jot of evolutionary theory needed in the underlying program (unless of course, and perish the thought, evolutionary properties are more than just benignly emergent).

Leaving aside the metaphors of "Mother Nature," it is clear that we have at least the good beginning of a Rule-based naturalization of evolution, and though this will never eliminate our need to under-stand the world in evolutionary terms, it does reveal to us what evolu-tion is in physical terms.

I've argued that it is not the existence of patterns but the *function* of them that is mind-dependent. Perhaps this is made clearer by focusing on an interesting feature of some patterns—they can exist and retain their explanatory usefulness even when their naturaliza-tion reveals them to be *less* than we thought they were. (Here we see the source of the curious attraction-repulsion that Dennett's views have for eliminativism about the mind.)

Consider, for instance, the Coriolis force, which gunnery officers have long had to take into account when computing the trajectory of long-range cannon shells. (A host of other activities "require" cognizance of the Coriolis force as well.) This is a benignly emergent property of the earth, or any other rotating system. But there is no such force; it is an artifact of a certain viewpoint. At least, if we really thought there were such a force, with its own causal efficacy, the world would end up being a much stranger place than we had imag-ined. Just think of it: Rotate a system and a brand new force magically appears out of nowhere, stop the rotation and the force instantly disappears. That is radical emergence with a vengeance. Luckily, there is no need to posit such a force. The Coriolis phenomena are related to the underlying physical processes in a reasonably simple way—in fact simple enough for us to comprehend quite "directly." We can give a perfect Rule-based naturalization of the "force" that reveals it to be nonexistent! But the pattern retains its usefulness, and no one faced with the problem of understanding how objects move over the earth is going to give it up. And, of course, the world-simulation automatically duplicates Coriolis force behavior patterns from the bottom up.

The final problem to address here emerges from the mind-dependence of the function of patterns: Since patterns function only to help minds organize their experience of the world, they would appear to be metaphysically otiose. We have the fundamental physical structure of the world, and, according to the SPW, this is quite sufficient all by itself to generate all the patterns that mind can appreciate. Furthermore, the vast majority of patterns seem to be susceptible to Rule-based naturalization, some of these approaching old-time strict reductions, others allowing only a chain of less strict explanations that reveal the principles by which the underlying physics generates the patterns at issue. But whether or to what degree we believe in explanatory emergence is an epistemological question. The *metaphysics* of the SPW is clear and austere. Helping itself to all of modern science, it is a comprehensive and grand view of the world incorporating every day new and exciting science linking everything from quarks to galaxies. It would, in fact, be perfect if it weren't for mind itself. (Consciousness really is the heart of the problem, for patterns are required only insofar as there is conscious apprehension of them—the SPW does a perfectly good job on unconscious apprehension.)

The more general view of how patterns function in explanation (of which the intentional stance is but one example—we see now that there is, in effect, the "chemical stance," the "biological stance," the "Freudian stance," etc.) reveals that the methodological mysterianism we encountered above may, after all, be in conflict with the SPW. Methodological mysterianism tells us directly that the mind is an explanatorily emergent phenomenon. Very well, we say, but mind nonetheless *is* a physical phenomenon at bottom. Unfortunately we cannot rest there. Mind cannot be "just another" pattern.

If it were, it would be metaphysically otiose. But it cannot be, since the role of patterns within the world depends upon minds' appreciation of them. This seems to be another version of Plato's problem: We cannot explain mind as pattern since pattern depends upon mind. The SPW likes to "dissolve" patterns into the swirling micromachinery of the world, but the application of this strategy to the mind yields not an account of the place of mind in the world but rather an eviction of mind from the world. But the SPW actually *requires* minds as a part of its overall picture of the world. *Other* patterns can be integrated into the SPW as structures noticeable to minds. Given minds, this strategy works well and smooths over the few disagreeable aspects of the SPW's otherwise very attractive picture of the world summed up by our simulation thought experiment. But minds themselves cannot be similarly integrated without falling into a vicious circularity.

It would put too much stress on the SPW to admit that the mind is, in its terms, utterly inexplicable or completely outside of its purview. Perhaps one could fall back to the position that the link between the basic physical features of the world and mind is a "brute fact," but this is unattractive for at least two reasons. One we discussed above: The notion that there are "brute emergences" linked to the formation of certainly highly complex material structures is entirely unappealing and utterly at odds with the outlook of the SPW. (In fact, the metaphysics of patterns is the replacement of the idea of emergence as a feature of the world and seems altogether superior an account.) A second difficulty is that such a brute emergent must be entirely inefficacious insofar as the SPW rejects, as I think it must, radical emergence.

I can only suggest that the solution is perhaps to recognize that the metaphysical picture of the world that accords with the pattern-based view of explanation is in the end radically unlike the SPW. I think one philosopher who draws a version of this conclusion is John Haugeland (1993), but the effort I've expended in drawing this out so long stems from a general sense I have from all of Dennett's writings that the SPW is rather attractive to him.[19] What might an alternative metaphysics, more in keeping with the pattern-based theory of explanation, look like?

I call it *surface metaphysics* (SM is, I'm afraid, an all too appropriate abbreviation for it). It begins with the claim that our basic physics is no less a "pattern" (or an appreciation of certain patterns) than any other theory. And it assumes that patterns are built out of the experiences of conscious "observers." Since the patterns that "correspond" to mature scientific theories are very remote from experience, SM allows that patterns are built up recursively, out of preexisting patterns (or such patterns plus experiences).[20] We must also allow that minds are themselves molded by the patterns they take up, so that experiences are not "patternless" but are more or less infected with the patterns passed down to us through the ages, both from earlier human efforts and even the efforts of our (enminded) ancestors (these patterns are, of course, the memes, content-infected right from the start).

Even at such an early stage of development, SM is recognizably empiricist, but it is a modern empiricism incorporating the so-called theory-ladenness of observation. The attitude toward science that SM ought to espouse has, I think, already been developed at length and with great elegance, though perhaps with not much persuasiveness, by Bas van Fraassen (1980) in a view he calls *constructive empiricism*. On such a view, science is in the business of generating models that help us manage the experienced world, and is no route to the metaphysical or even—surprisingly, but there is no escape from the conclusion—the physical depths. It seems that there may be a deep connection between constructive empiricism and the mind-body problem, creating the interesting possibility that the problem of consciousness will provide additional support for the kind of scientific antirealism (or "arealism") constructive empiricism enjoins. So far as I know the debates about van Fraassen's work have not explored this territory. The contortions—ever more convoluted—that philosophers have gone through to find an acceptable link between matter and mind may be a sign that a common assumption is being dangerously overstressed. Perhaps that assumption is scientific realism.

Thus I'm urging that Dennett ought to take consciousness and the experienced world as the foundation of existence and forthrightly dismiss the demand for an explanation of *them* in scientific or quasi-scientific terms. He ought to regard science as explicable in terms of mind rather than mind in terms of science. This would be in line with the methodological mysterianism inherent in the interpretationist theory of mind based upon the intentional stance as well as the more general pattern-based theory of explanation. Dennett does seem to be willing to take "intentional interpretation" as a primitive element of his theory, and this notion is of course a mentalistic one. His theory of consciousness is dependent upon this notion and so is infected with mentalistic concepts.

At the same time, SM does not deny the indispensable importance of scientific models and goes so far as to endorse a theory of explanation that re-legitimates all of our scientific explanations (essentially—maybe distastefully—by cutting explanation off from *truth;* here the echoes of Dennett's own "instrumentalism" about mentality are clear.)[21] We can have our science, but we can't have the SPW. This would be the end of an old dream, the dream that energized the whole scientific revolution, but a view of the world that takes mind or "patterns" (which are dependent upon mentalistic concepts for their understanding) as basic may require no less.

Notes

1. For example, John McDowell denies that he is a physicalist but nonetheless regards his view of mind as naturalistic. David Chalmers goes so far as to label his own view "naturalistic dualism"!

2. The name is borrowed from Owen Flanagan's characterization of a well-known particular instance of such a view (see Flanagan 1992, 109ff.).

3. Perhaps a caveat or two are in order here. It is among the things that *ought* to be naturalized that the mind stands as, at present, especially problematic. It is not clear to me that we need to worry about naturalizing numbers, and other abstractions, though it does seem that all these things can probably be understood in terms of minds and the thoughts they contain. Roughly speaking, what ought to be naturalized are the things that "push and shove"; those things that make things happen in the world. If numbers, for example, should somehow fall into this category we'll just have to embrace supernaturalism and find the world a *much* stranger place than we thought. (But even here, wouldn't the oddity of the imagined situation come down to how *minds* come into contact with numbers and the like?) On the other hand, metaphysics won't let us go here. Isn't it *properties* that cause things, and aren't properties abstract objects? I would say rather that it is things having properties (that is, more or less, *events*) that cause, and property instances—at least those that make things happen—are just the sort of thing that ought to be naturalized. Outside the

Real Patterns and Surface Metaphysics

realm of the abstract, the ultimate source of existence itself must remain mysterious, short of a physics that emerges out of pure mathematics. The naturalist rests content with finding the ground of all things in the presumed fundamental structure of the world.

4. For the distinction between "selection for" and "selection of" see Sober 1984, 97ff. Please note that Plato's problem looms already—*selection for* is an intensional notion and it is very unclear that appeal to it could be a legitimate part of a naturalization of intentionality.

5. My criticism of Fodor overlooks a feature of Fodor's theory that might provide an answer to Plato's problem, namely, his appeal to laws of nature construed as relations between properties. This is supposed to make it an "objective fact" that there is the appropriate relation between the word "horse" and *horses*. I doubt that this really makes any difference because I doubt that there are such relations independent of interest-bound constraints on the set of possible worlds we are allowed to look at (it seems clear to me, at least, that there are nomologically possible worlds not too distant from the actual world where the "horse"-*horse* link is quite different).

6. Such a strategy—in various forms—has of course been explicitly defended with respect to the mind, perhaps first by Quine (1960, 264ff. and 1966), followed by Feyerabend (1963), Rorty (1965), and later by Paul Churchland (1981).

7. Except in very special explanatory contexts (if, for example, we imagine that someone built a pole with the intention of having a shadow of a certain length we might be able to produce a situation in which the length of the shadow did explain the height; see van Fraassen 1980, 132ff. for an attempt at such an example). Philosophy itself is a particularly clear instance of the need for an understanding of the explanatory context. Any teacher of philosophy will recognize that one of the stumbling blocks facing beginning students is that they just don't "get it"—they don't see what philosophy is trying to do (this is usually especially evident in the inappropriate use of examples). The clearer it becomes that every explanation presupposes an *understanding* of the explanatory context, the clearer it is that the mind can never be naturalized according to the Rules.

8. I have given a more detailed account of this argument is Seager (1990). There I claim that what virtually guarantees the creation of psychologically characterizable organisms is evolution's development of creatures that fulfill the theory of teleology espoused by Taylor (1964), MacKenzie (1972), and Bennett (1976). Once organisms can exploit what Bennett calls the "conditional properties of the environment" they will be, more or less, psychologically characterizable.

9. But there is evidence against this in favor of the view that only the owner of the web knows its value (Maynard Smith 1982, 116).

10. To be fair to the vegetable kingdom, plants are also pretty complex. The kind of complexity that matters is that stemming from a kind of "information-laden" interaction with the environment, especially with other organisms and mediated by sensory organs rather like our own. To some extent plants fulfill these conditions too, but it is also true that some weak psychological characterizations of plants are not foreign to us. As soon as we notice that plants are capable of certain sorts of movement, we speak of plants "trying" to get to the light, or spreading roots because they "want" water.

11. It is of course possible to believe that the physical properties of the brain generate all of our behavior. Everyone *does* believe this already. The problem is to extract from the neural details an *explanation* of our behavioral capacities, and specifically those behavioral capacities that underwrite the ascriptions of mind of the intentional stance as applied to complex, distinctively human behavior. I suspect that the gap is too large here, and the project would be akin to *understanding* plate tectonics in terms of quantum chromodynamics. The beauty of the adaptationist story is (or would be) that it tells us why the neural details *have* to generate psychologically characterizable behavioral capacities. Then we can happily dig away explaining how neurons account for little bits and pieces of these capacities.

12. It may be worth noting here that this is not an endorsement of so-called part-whole reductionism. We know from quantum mechanics that the states of "wholes" are not simple functions of the states of their parts but this does not tell against the characterization given in the text. Quantum mechanics is a *celebration* of how the interactions of things can be understood—rigorously understood—to yield new features. It is, if you like, the mathematical theory of emergence.

13. Real versions of something like my imaginary scenario now exist and are already fruitful. For example, there are computer models of quantum chromodynamics that can compute the theoretically predicted masses of various quark-constituted subatomic particles (see Weingarten 1996). The ultimately insuperable problem of computational intractability is all too evident, for realizing these calculations required the development of special mathematical techniques, the assembling of a dedicated, parallel supercomputer especially designed for the necessary sorts of calculations (a computer capable of 11 billion arithmetical operations per second) and roughly a year of continuous computing. Weingarten reports that a special two-year calculation revealed the existence of a previously unrecognized particle, whose existence could be verified by examining past records from particle accelerator experiments. Modeling the interactions of particles would be a much more challenging task, suggesting to the imagination computational projects analogous to the construction of medieval cathedrals, involving thousands of workers over many decades.

14. Some would be inclined to say that we already have one computer running the perfect simulation: the world itself (see Deutsch 1997). This is another way to test your attitude. If you think this idea must be right, that the world, at least, is a powerful enough "simulator" and that the "machine language" it's running on is basic physics, then you believe in the SPW.

15. Note that Dennett says "These patterns are objective—they are there to be detected—but from our point of view they are not out there independent of us, since they are patterns composed partly of our 'subjective' reactions to what is out there, they are the patterns made to order for our narcissistic concerns" (1987, 39).

16. Such a view was once very popular, especially among British philosophers. See for example Morgan (1923) or Broad (1925). For an overview see McLaughlin (1992).

17. Bear in mind that "*x* explains *y*" is *not* a transitive relation. Nonetheless, a chain of linking explanations suffices for an appreciation of the world's unity; our slogan could be "the world is one, science is not."

18. We might define "reductive emergence" as the claim that there are high-level phenomena that cannot be strictly reduced to low-level phenomena, where reduction is conceived in classical terms (i.e., the high-level laws are to be strictly derived from low-level theory plus the "bridge laws" that provide extensional definitions of the high-level phenomena at issue). I think most would accept reductive emergence, which entails the explanatory indispensability of high-level theory. The combination of reductive emergence plus the denial of radical emergence might be called "benign emergence," which is, I think, the generally accepted position today. But I stress that reductive emergence does not entail explanatory emergence.

19. I note that in "Real Patterns" (1991b) Dennett gestures admiringly toward Arthur Fine's Natural Ontological Attitude as an appropriate version of scientific realism (see Fine 1986). The interpretation of NOA is far from clear but it would seem to support the SPW as outlined. Crudely speaking, NOA asserts that if, for example, you want to know if electrons exist you should go and ask a physicist (rather than a metaphysicist, i.e., a philosopher). NOA is an attempt to banish metaphysics from philosophy of science. Whether or not that is a good idea, it is obviously not a good way to draw out a metaphysical picture of the world that is based upon science (and if NOA firmly rejects this project then it will end up being not so far from the arealist position I am advocating). Similarly, if you want to know if the total behavior of the world is generated from the fundamental physical structures you should go and ask a physicist—and you know what the answer would be. It seems quite clear that a basic goal of physics is to discover *the* physics that underwrites the SPW, and the physicists have had immense success at this.

20. To be a little more precise: A pattern is defined as (1) any salient set of experiences, (2) any salient set of patterns, (3) any salient set of patterns plus experiences. Of course it would be hard to define "salience" here.

21. It is interesting that van Fraassen sees his "instrumentalist" (officially constructive empiricist) approach to science growing from the bottom up (quantum mechanics is a haven for scientific antirealism). Perhaps instrumentalism can also grow from the top down, from an argument based upon a pattern-based notion of explanation. (For more on how the explanatory power of experimental science can be integrated with a nonrealist outlook see my 1995.)

References

Adams, F., and K. Aizawa (1993). Fodorian Semantics, Pathologies, and "Block's Problem." *Minds and Machines* 3, 1: 97–104.

Bennett, J. (1976). *Linguistic Behavior.* Cambridge: Cambridge University Press.

Broad, C. D. (1925). *The Mind and Its Place in Nature.* London: Paul, Trench, Trubner.

Churchland, P. (1981). Eliminative Materialism and the Propositional Attitude. *Journal of Philosophy* 78: 67–90.

Cummins, R. (1989). *Meaning and Mental Representation.* Cambridge, Mass.: MIT Press. A Bradford Book.

Davidson, D. (1970). Mental Events. In *Experience and Theory*, L. Foster and J. Swanson (eds.). Amherst: University of Massachusetts Press. Reprinted in Davidson's *Essays on Actions and Events*, Oxford: Oxford University Press, 1980.

Deacon, T. (1997). *The Symbolic Species: The Co-Evolution of Language and the Brain*. New York: W. W. Norton.

Dennett, D. C. (1975). Why the Law of Effect Will Not Go Away. *Journal of the Theory of Social Behavior* 2: 169–187. Reprinted in Dennett's *Brainstorms*. Cambridge, Mass.: MIT Press, 1981.

Dennett, D. C. (1987). *The Intentional Stance*. Cambridge, Mass.: MIT Press. A Bradford Book.

Dennett, D. C. (1991a). *Consciousness Explained*. Boston: Little, Brown and Co.

Dennett, D. C. (1991b). Real Patterns. *Journal of Philosophy* 88: 27–51.

Dennett, D. C. (1995). *Darwin's Dangerous Idea*. New York: Simon and Schuster.

Deutsch, D. (1997). *The Fabric of Reality*. New York: Allen Lane.

Donald, M. (1991). *Origins of the Modern Mind: Three Stages in the Evolution of Culture and Cognition*. Cambridge, Mass.: Harvard University Press.

Feyerabend, P. (1963). Materialism and the Mind-Body Problem. *The Review of Metaphysics* 17: 49–66.

Flanagan, O. (1992). *Consciousness Reconsidered*. Cambridge, Mass.: MIT Press. A Bradford Book.

Fodor, J. (1992). *A Theory of Content and Other Essays*. Cambridge, Mass.: MIT Press. A Bradford Book.

Gould, S. J. (1997). Darwinian fundamentalism. *New York Review of Books*, June 12.

Haugeland, J. (1993). Pattern and Being. In *Dennett and His Critics*, B. Dahlbohm (ed.). Cambridge, Mass.: Blackwell.

Kim, J. (1978). Supervenience and Nomological Incommensurables. *American Philosophical Quarterly* 15: 149–156.

Kim, J. (1989). The Myth of Nonreductive Materialism. *Proceedings of the American Philosophical Association* 63: 31–47.

MacKenzie, A. (1972). *An Analysis of Purposive Behavior*. Ann Arbor, Mich.: University Microfilms.

Maynard Smith, J. (1982). *Evolution and the Theory of Games*. Cambridge: Cambridge University Press.

McGinn, C. (1989). Can we solve the mind-body problem? *Mind* 98: 349–366. Reprinted in McGinn's *The Problem of Consciousness*, Oxford: Blackwell, 1991.

McLaughlin, B. (1992). The Rise and Fall of British Emergentism. In *Emergence or Reduction: Essays on the Prospects of Nonreductive Physicalism*, A. Beckermann, H. Flohr, and J. Kim (eds.). Berlin: W. de Gruyter.

Millikan, R. (1984). *Language, Thought, and Other Biological Categories*. Cambridge, Mass.: MIT Press. A Bradford Book.

Morgan, C. L. (1923). *Emergent Evolution*. London: Routledge and Kegan Paul.

Plato (c. 368/1961). *Theaetetus* (trans. F. M. Cornford). In *The Collected Dialogues of Plato*, E. Hamilton and H. Cairns (eds.). Princeton: Princeton University Press.

Putnam, H. (1992). *Renewing Philosophy*. Cambridge, Mass.: Harvard University Press.

Quine, W. v. O. (1960). *Word and Object*. Cambridge, Mass.: MIT Press.

Quine, W. v. O. (1966). On Mental Entities. In Quine's *The Ways of Paradox*. New York: Random House.

Rorty, R. (1965). Mind-body identity, privacy, and categories. *The Review of Metaphysics* 19: 24–54.

Seager, W. (1990). Instrumentalism in Psychology. *International Studies in the Philosophy of Science* 4, 2: 1990.

Seager, W. (1993). Fodor's Theory of Content: Problems and Objections. *Philosophy of Science* 60, 2: 262–277.

Seager, W. (1995). Ground Truth and Virtual Reality: Hacking vs. van Fraassen. *Philosophy of Science* 62: 459–488.

Sober, E. (1984). *The Nature of Selection: Evolutionary Theory in Philosophical Focus*. Cambridge, Mass.: MIT Press. A Bradford Book.

Taylor, C. (1964). *The Explanation of Behavior*. London: Routledge and Kegan Paul.

Weingarten, D. (1996). Quarks by Computer. *Scientific American* 274, 2: 116–120.

van Fraassen, B. (1980). *The Scientific Image*. Oxford: Oxford University Press.

7

Where Do Dennett's Stances Stand? Explaining Our Kind of Mind

Christopher Viger

Introduction

What is the ontological status of entities posited by or referred to in Dennett's various stances? In particular, how does the ontological status of entities posited by or referred to in the intentional stance contrast with the status of those things posited by or referred to in the physical stance, and what is entailed in the differences? (I will say nothing about the design stance in this paper.) Physical entities have a privileged place in the philosophy of mind. The mental either can be eliminated altogether, identified with something physical, or at least supervenes on the physical in the sense that there can be no change in some mental respect without some physical change. The privilege of the physical stance is that it alone includes terms that refer to "the furniture of the physical world" (Dennett 1987, 72).[1] So where does that leave the things referred to in or posited by the intentional stance? There are two readings of Dennett's intentional stance,[2] which I claim result from different agendas in the characterization of the intentional stance in Dennett's writings. On one reading, Dennett is an instrumentalist; on the other he is a small "r" realist. I propose to make explicit Dennett's two agendas, and how the distinct readings of his position come out of these. I will then suggest that there is an interpretation of Dennett's characterization of the entities posited by the intentional stance from which he can be seen as offering a single view, consistent with both of these agendas, despite the distinct readings of his work they suggest. I think this will clear up some confusions about Dennett's approach to problems in the philosophy of mind, a nonreductive approach that can help elucidate the nature of our kind of mind.

Instrumentalist Reading of the Intentional Stance

In "Fodor's Guide to Mental Representation" (Fodor 1990, 3–29), Fodor characterizes Dennett's position as instrumentalism—a variety of antirealism—and quickly dismisses it because he takes instrumentalism to be a quite implausible view.[3] "You could take[4] an *instrumentalist* view of intentional explanation. You could hold that though there are, *strictly speaking*, no such things as beliefs and desires, still talking as though there were some often leads to confirmed behavioral predictions. . . . The most extensively worked-out version of instrumentalism about the attitudes in the recent literature is surely owing to D. C. Dennett" (Fodor 1990, 6–8, emphasis in original). No doubt, Fodor has passages such as the following in mind: "Lingering doubts about whether the chess-playing computer *really* has beliefs and desires are misplaced; for the definition of intentional systems I have given does not say that intentional systems *really* have beliefs and desires, but that one can explain and predict their behavior by *ascribing* beliefs and desires to them" (Dennett 1978, 7, emphasis in original); or, "My *ism* is whatever *ism* serious realists adopt with regard to centers of gravity and the like, since I think beliefs . . . are *like that*—in being *abstracta* rather than part of the 'furniture of the physical world' and in being attributed in statements that are *true* only if we exempt them from a certain familiar standard of literality" (Dennett 1987, 72). It is this move of characterizing beliefs and desires as abstracta, in contrast with the "furniture of the physical world," that has led to Dennett being labeled an instrumentalist, because in addition Dennett holds the view that "[t]he actual internal states that cause behavior will not be functionally individuated, even up to an approximation, the way belief/desire psychology carves things up" (ibid., 71).[5] Dennett seems to reject even token identity of beliefs and desires with physi-

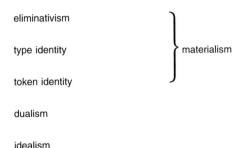

Figure 7.1
Standard taxonomy of ontological positions in the philosophy of mind

cal states. But if beliefs and desires are mere abstractions that cannot be identified even token-wise with anything physical, they have no place in the causal nexus of the physical world, so they are not really real.[6]

The standard taxonomy of ontological positions in the philosophy of mind[7] simply leaves no room for any kind of realism concerning intentional states and properties if one is, like Dennett, a materialist who rejects the identity, even token-wise, of the mental with the physical. The positions are discrete and exclusive possibilities. One cannot be two-thirds eliminativist, one-third token physicalist. Since Dennett is a materialist, his characterization of beliefs and desires as abstracta disassociates them from physical entities, thereby banishing them from reality; the intentional stance is nothing more than a useful heuristic, according to the standard taxonomy, which is to say that Dennett's view is instrumentalist.[8]

Dennett's agenda in characterizing beliefs and desires as abstracta is not primarily to advance an ontological thesis; rather it is to elucidate the nature of intentional *explanation*. That beliefs and desires are abstracta does not itself exclude them from the domain of the physical stance. After all, physics often refers to abstract patterns and relations; beliefs and desires are like centers of gravity in being abstracta. But to understand the nature of intentional explanation it is essential to understand that beliefs and desires are abstracta, and to that end it is important to know what Dennett means by abstracta.

Abstracta are contrasted with the "furniture of the physical world." A tempting way to understand this contrast is ontologically, distinguishing the real from the merely useful, in which case Dennett is an instrumentalist about abstracta. On this reading, abstracta are distinct from illata in that illata are theoretical entities postulated as corresponding to physical entities, whereas abstracta are not supposed to correspond to anything. But to put the contrast this way is to *presuppose* that Dennett is advancing an ontological thesis. The contrast can also be captured as follows. Illata and abstracta are both theoretically posited entities, but they play different roles within the explanatory practice in which they are posited. The nature of an abstract entity is given entirely by the theory; there is nothing *empirical* to discover about it.[9] Illata on the other hand are such that they can be investigated empirically, and such investigation could reveal something about them that is not given in the theory. Now this way of putting the contrast can also be read ontologically, so that illata, but not abstracta, are "there to be investigated"; but the contrast need not be so read. The contrast can be a general elucidation of our explanatory practices. The entities we posit within an explanatory practice can play different roles within that practice, which we characterize in terms of illata and abstracta. That is, the difference between illata and abstracta *just is* their role in an explanatory practice, and not their ontological status. Illata and abstracta are, after all, equally theoretically posited entities, which on this view captures their ontological status.[10]

If we distinguish abstracta from illata in that abstracta are prescribed by a given explanatory practice, then entities posited under idealizing assumptions must be abstracta, since there is nothing empirical to be discovered about such entities. For example, no experiment could ever tell us anything about *ideal* gases. Thus a key feature of abstracta for Dennett's purposes is that they figure in explanans incorporating certain idealizations made in the context of an explanatory practice. "Optimality assumptions are popular ploys in many disciplines" (Dennett 1987, 277). It is the particular idealizations one makes that distinguish various explanatory practices. What makes beliefs and desires distinct from abstract nonmental entities is the nature of the idealization that one makes in ascribing them.

Systems are ascribed beliefs and desires only under the idealizing assumption that those systems are *rational*. It is only through the filter of rationality considerations that intentional patterns are visible, and it is for this reason that beliefs and desires have no place in physical explanations.[11] As Ryle (1949) taught us, to suppose they do is to make a category mistake. However, physical explanations do not exhaust explanatory practice. Perhaps the most central notion in Dennett's philosophy is that we can engage in distinct explanatory practices by adopting different stances; beliefs and desires are the sorts of things that figure in *intentional explanations,* and we engage in intentional explanation by making rationality assumptions about what we are explaining. Thus, in my view, Dennett's starting point is intentional explanation. Its autonomy derives from the rationality assumption, which distinguishes the intentional stance from the physical stance. But the idealization of the rationality of systems demands that beliefs and desires be characterized as abstracta, hence Dennett so characterizes them.

Notice that if I am correct in holding that Dennett characterizes beliefs and desires as abstracta primarily to elucidate the nature of intentional explanation, then Dennett's view is committed to intentional explanation. That is, the legitimacy of intentional explanation is not in question; it is a genuine explanatory practice. In elucidating the nature of that explanatory practice, Dennett has accepted, perhaps too easily at times, what are ostensibly the ontological implications of his view. Since intentional explanation is grounded in idealized rationality, the characteristic entities posited in intentional explanatory practice—beliefs and desires—are abstracta; so in accordance with the standard taxonomy of positions available to materialists, Dennett has, at times, accepted the label instrumentalism for his view. It is not a label that sits particularly well with him, however, for his own intuition is that beliefs and desires *are* real. "I have let myself be called an instrumentalist for a half-dozen years (so it's my own fault), but I am not at all happy with the guilt-by-association I have thereby acquired" (Dennett 1987, 71). Since instrumentalism is inconsistent with his view of intentional phenomena as real, Dennett has had a second agenda in characterizing the intentional stance: to distance himself from instrumentalism.

Small "r" realist Reading of the Intentional Stance

When Dennett's concerns are ontological, he characterizes his position as a kind of moderate realism concerning beliefs and desires. This position is most famously advanced in "Real Patterns" (Dennett 1991). What Dennett is explicitly rejecting in characterizing his position that beliefs and desires are abstracta as moderate realism is the standard taxonomy of ontological positions available to a materialist; that is, the forced choice between some kind of identity thesis and eliminativism. On Dennett's view there are real patterns in behavior that are visible from, and only from, the intentional stance. What explains these patterns is that systems that exhibit them have certain behavioral dispositions, multiply realized over different systems and over a single system at different times. Behavioral dispositions that explain intentional regularities just are beliefs and desires. The underlying mechanisms that realize behavioral dispositions are physical mechanisms (at least neurological), and for this reason Dennett is a materialist. But Dennett resists the identification, even the token identification, of a behavioral disposition with an underlying mechanism realizing that disposition. Beliefs and desires qua behavioral dispositions are real, but they are not the underlying mechanisms realizing those dispositions.[12]

But how can a materialist hold that beliefs and desires are real if they are not at least token identical with something physical? In rejecting the standard taxonomy is Dennett suggesting some kind of semirealism? Is Dennett a new mysterian, suggesting some kind of ontological spectrum of being, an inverted version of Plato's degrees of being, in which the physical is most real, and increasingly abstract objects are less real? Of course not. Dennett is simply challenging the strong ontological intuition people have with regard to mental states and properties. As Jerry Fodor puts this intuition: "If the semantic and the intentional are real properties of things, it must be in virtue of their identity with (or maybe their supervenience on?) properties that are themselves *neither* intentional *nor* semantic. If aboutness is real, it must be really something else" (Fodor 1987, 97, emphasis in original). The standard taxonomy of ontological positions concerning mental states and properties is grounded in this intuition; philosophers disagree about the ontological status of mental states and properties, but most do not disagree about the standard taxonomy of ontological positions concerning the mental or the intuition that grounds this taxonomy. Dennett, on the other hand, rejects both.

Dennett questions the intuition that intentional states and properties are real only if they can be identified with something physical by providing examples of abstracta for which we have no comparable intuition. Lines of latitude and centers of gravity are familiar examples that Dennett offers to try to shake our intuition. But his point is not that abstract objects are real in general, so qua abstract objects belief and desires are real. His point is rather a deeper one about the nature of scientific explanation. Many different kinds of things are real, where kinds are determined in the context of the explanatory practice that posits them. When we are confronted with the question of what exists, we must fall back on our explanatory practices. The only answer we have—indeed the only answer we *can* have—to the question of what exists is whatever our best theories tell us exists. And when our best theories are deficient, we may need to revise what we are prepared to say exists. This is not to say that what is real is what we say is real, of course, but to note how our explanatory practices are the source of our ontological commitments. In general, we are ontologically committed to the entities posited by *well-confirmed* explanatory practices; if "a model attributes a state to an organism, then insofar as we accept the model we are ontologically committed to the state" (Fodor 1975, 51). Dennett's rejection of the standard taxonomy collapses the distinction between instrumentalism and moderate realism according to that taxonomy, since a useful heuristic is useful precisely because it is predictively successful, in which case we are ontologically committed to the referents of its characteristic terms. Intentional explanation *is* a predictively successful explanatory practice;[13] hence the intentional stance is not merely a useful heuristic—as it would be from an instrumentalist view of intentional explanation according to the standard taxonomy—since we are ontologically committed to the entities posited by it in virtue of its explanatory success.[14] That is to say, our ontological commitment to beliefs and desires derives from the success of intentional explanation.

There is simply no room, then, to contrast the existential status of beliefs and desires with the existential status of entities posited by physics. Beliefs and desires are as ontologically secure as electrons or gravitational fields, for it is nothing more than the predictive success of physics that grounds our commitment to the entities that our physical theories posit.[15] We see now why the physical stance is a genuine stance, on the same footing as the intentional stance in terms of what it ontologically commits us to, and not a privileged vantage point in the ontological sphere from which all judgments of existence are to be made. Physics is grounded in the world of observables, rocks and trees and planets and measuring devices, and posits theoretical entities to explain the behavior of those observables. The success of physical explanation ontologically commits us to the theoretical entities. *In the same way, and for the same metatheoretic reasons,* we are ontologically committed to propositional attitudes. Intentional explanation, like physics, is grounded in the world of observables, in this case human and animal bodies, and perhaps certain artifacts,[16] and again as in physics, entities are posited to explain the behavior of those observables, in this case by the intentional stance. The abstractness of the entities we posit depends on the idealizations we make in positing them, but their being abstract is not relevant to our ontological commitment to them, which depends entirely on the success of the explanatory practice from which we posit their existence. Now clearly what exists is independent of our explanatory practices, as evidenced by the failure of some explanatory practices. Sometimes the world kicks back. Certain explanatory practices simply fail to capture any structure in the world, so our predictions based on such practices fail, and we lose our ontological commitment to the entities they posit. We no longer believe in the existence of phlogiston or ether because we cannot make successful predictions about what we will observe by positing their existence. And for the same reasons, we do not believe in demons that can temporarily take control of human and animal bodies.[17]

If I am right that Dennett has presented the intentional stance with distinct agendas, then we can see that he has advanced a stable position, rather than distinct views in tension with each other. Dennett is a realist about beliefs and desires, just as he is a realist about many other things. Reality does not come in varying degrees; entities we posit from our explanatory practices either exist or they do not, and the world indicates to us what exists by either confirming or disconfirming our predictions. In characterizing beliefs and desires as abstracta, Dennett can be read as elucidating the nature of intentional explanation and not advancing an ontological thesis. To be sure, there are varying degrees of abstractness; but since abstractness itself is inherently tied to explanatory practices and the idealizations that ground those practices, the characterization of an entity as abstract is a psychological claim about us, about our kind of mind, and not an ontological claim about the world, on this view. Degrees of abstractness do not correspond to degrees of being, and it is only in supposing that they do correspond, while recognizing that reality has no degrees, that Dennett's characterization of beliefs and desires as abstracta is tantamount to instrumentalism, from the standard taxonomy. In rejecting the standard taxonomy, Dennett has given us an opportunity: a new way to understand our kind of mind.

Our Kind of Mind

We saw above that both the intentional stance and the physical stance are grounded in observables, putting both stances on an equal footing in terms of what they ontologically commit us to. That is, the characteristic entities that are posited by these stances are posited to explain observable phenomena. So in one important respect observables constitute "the furniture of the physical world" for our kind of mind. Our engagement with the world is such that we perceive it in terms of objects, which are paradigmatically physical—but physical in the sense of *folk physics,* not theoretical physics, which makes idealizations and posits theoretical entities to explain the behavior of observables every bit as much as the intentional stance; our kind of mind is so constituted that we cannot help but see the world in terms of objects. Dennett's account of the evolution of minds sheds some light on why this may be so (Dennett 1995, 370–383; 1996, 83–117).

Dennett distinguishes four kinds of minds. Creatures with Darwinian minds learn, as a species, at the school of hard knocks. They are entirely hard-wired. Those creatures hard-wired with beneficial responses to the objects they encounter—beneficial in the sense that the responses promote a creature's survival—live to reproduce and pass on this hard-wiring; those not so fortunate make a quick exit from the evolutionary stage. Each successive generation will acquire the best behaviors from their parents' generation, and in this way the species learns; but since each creature is totally hard-wired, it cannot modify its behavior. Creatures with Skinnerian minds are much better suited to survive because they can learn in the school of hard knocks on their own. For a given stimulus, a creature has options as to how it will behave; though which option it chooses is initially random. If the creature is lucky enough to survive its first few guesses, the feedback from the environment can be used to modify future behavior in ways advantageous to survival. Again survival depends on appropriately responding to objects encountered, but the Skinnerians are more likely to produce appropriate responses because there is some flexibility in how they respond. Creatures with Popperian minds can internalize the school of hard knocks, which, as Popper said, "permits (their) hypotheses to die in (their) stead." These creatures test out possible behaviors against an internal model of the world, according to Dennett. Based on predicted responses of the environment given by their models, these creatures can modify their behavior without waiting for environmental feedback. Of course, these modifications are only as good as the models, so Popperians need reliable representations of both the objects they are likely to encounter and the effects that behaviors they might produce will have in the presence of those objects. Finally, there are creatures with Gregorian minds, which possess *mind* tools that allow them to improve the internal models upon which their success depends. Languages are particularly powerful mind tools. One of the resources that languages provide us with is an ability to explicitly represent hypothetical situations by using the material and subjunctive conditionals. Competing hypotheses can be tested so that disconfirmed hypotheses are immediately dropped from the internal model, thereby improving the overall model we have. Creatures with our kind of mind can wonder why predictions we make based on our models are successful, engaging us in explanatory practices from which we posit theoretical entities to explain observable phenomena. We cannot help but see the world in terms of the objects of folk physics because of our evolutionary history, but our kind of mind, largely because of language, is not constrained to understand the world purely in terms of those objects.

Our kind of mind, by its very nature, understands the world as comprising objective observables and theoretical entities—we cannot help that—and as we understand the world, beliefs and desires and other denizens of the intentional realm are posited theoretical entities. In particular, they are abstracta because they are posited under the idealization of rationality. To treat them as either observables or illata is to make a category mistake, not of ontology but in explanatory practice. Furthermore, because beliefs and desires are posited only under the idealization of rationality, they do not belong to the explanatory practice of physics. To treat them as physical is also to make a category mistake in explanatory practice. Now it is important to realize that interpreting Dennett's characterization of beliefs and desires as something other than an ontological thesis does not by itself solve any of the long-standing problems in the philosophy of mind, such as mental causation, mental content, concept acquisition, or agency. However, in elucidating the nature of intentional explanation, Dennett has also advanced a nonreductive approach to studying our kind of mind, which suggests that some attempts to solve these problems are ill fated, precisely because they treat beliefs and desires as if they have a place in physical explanations. For example, on this view, mental content will not be accounted for in terms of causal relations between neural structures and physical entities, relations that belong to our physical (biological) explanatory practice. Nor will mental causation be explained in terms of physical causation; supposing that it must be so explained has led to widespread fears that mental states and properties are epiphenomenal, what Fodor calls "epiphobia" (Fodor 1990, 137).

Christopher Viger

The problem, however, is that we are attempting to explain the causal relations of one explanatory practice, intentional psychology, in terms of the causal relations posited by another explanatory practice, physics. When distinct explanatory practices are cross-applied, hybrid monsters result.

Finally, notice that the distinction between posited theoretical entities and objective observables in terms of which our kind of mind necessarily understands the world depends on our particular sensory organs and our explanatory practices; hence that distinction need not be ontologically realized in the world, in that not all kinds of minds need make that same distinction. Perhaps discerning complex dispositional or social patterns and the relational features of objects will confer survival advantages in the future. In such a case we might evolve to perceive what we now take to be abstract relations. Mathematics has made a conceptual shift in this direction in moving from set-theoretic foundations to category theory, where the crucial difference is that a set is defined in terms of its elements—the objects it contains—whereas categories are determined relationally by the arrows going into and coming out from each category. If evolution were to take such a path, the next kind of mind might experience as observables theoretical entities we posit from our explanatory practices. Observables for such minds might include beliefs and desires as well as gravitational fields and virtual particles. The world would not change, but how minds perceive the world would. Creatures with this next kind of mind might then develop a single explanatory practice that includes physical and intentional items, though it would not correspond to either our physical or our intentional explanations, of course. Our philosophical debates about the ontological status of beliefs and desires might seem to creatures with the next kind of mind as a debate about the ontological status of written words, pictograms, or smoke signals would seem to us. Creatures with this kind of mind might find patterns in their observables that we cannot even grasp,[18] and posit new theoretical entities to explain those complex patterns. Then their philosophers might debate the ontological status of these theoretical entities; or creatures with the next kind of mind might not engage in philosophy.

Notes

1. Dennett takes this expression from Friedman (1981, 4).

2. Davies (1995) also makes this point.

3. Hornsby also finds Fodor's quick dismissal of Dennett's view unsatisfying (Hornsby 1997, 168–170).

4. The text reads "taken," which I assume is an error.

5. For another expression of this view see Dennett (1987, 75–76).

6. For contrasting views, see Burge (1986), Burge (1993), Hornsby (1997), and Pietroski (2000).

7. See figure 7.1 for the standard taxonomy of ontological positions.

8. I do not mean to suggest that Dennett does not accept that he views intentional explanation as a useful heurisitic—indeed, he promotes that view; but as we will see, this does not have the same ontological force as instrumentalism according to the standard taxonomy.

9. It is useful to think about numbers in this context, since in most ontologies they are real, though nothing empirical can be discovered about numbers. This also makes clear that the claim is not that there is *nothing* to be discovered about abstracta.

10. Note that I am not asserting that Dennett has ever made explicit the idea that he is not advancing an ontological thesis in characterizing beliefs and desires as abstracta, nor that he has always clearly separated the ontological from the nonontological readings of that characterization. My point is simply that the nonontological reading *is* implicitly offered and that it renders a consistent interpretation of Dennett's views.

11. Of course, Dennett also takes holism and normativity to be marks of the mental. However, normativity of the mental presupposes rationality, and holism only precludes type identity (pace Davidson).

12. It is on this point where Dennett parts company with Stalnaker (1984), for example, who holds a dispositional view of propositional attitudes but attempts to give a naturalistic account of the attitudes in order to solve Brentano's problem.

13. Haugeland makes this point by arguing that there are three distinct types of explanation, each of which is scientifically rigorous. In his terminology, intentional explanation is an instance of systematic explanation, which is characterized by the organized cooperative interaction of specified structures having specified abilities in virtue of their structure (Haugeland 1978, 12–13).

14. Davies also attributes this view to Dennett (Davies 1995, 304–305).

15. It is important to note here that electrons are traditionally taken to be illata, and to emphasize that the abstracta-illata distinction is not the source of our ontological

144
Christopher Viger

commitments, on this view. My own view is that electrons are, in fact, abstracta given modern quantum theory, but this position is not relevant to the main point in the text.

16. I qualify artifacts, for it is not clear to me that any rationalizing assumption is made in predicting the behavior of a thermostat, for example.

17. This example is particularly illuminating. We are confronted with the problem of explaining the behavior of something of a kind we normally adopt the intentional stance toward, under conditions in which the rationality assumption fails. We must then adopt a different stance from which to predict its behavior. As it turns out, the design stance is more predictively successful than the demonic stance, so we are ontologically committed to neural structures having certain functions and not to demons.

18. Of course, this suggests that we are cognitively closed to such patterns. Notice, however, that this is not cognitive closure of the sort to which Dennett objects. Dennett accepts that some things (patterns) may be beyond our cognitive horizons. What he objects to is the possibility that we can understand a question but not the answer to that question (personal communication).

References

Burge, T. (1986). Individualism and psychology. *Philosophical Review* 95: 3–46.

Burge, T. (1993). Mind-body causation and explanatory practice. In Heil and Mele (1993).

Dahlbom, B. (1993). *Dennett and His Critics*. Cambridge, Mass.: Blackwell.

Davidson, D. (1970). Mental events. In Davidson (1980).

Davidson, D. (1980). *Essays in Actions and Events*. Oxford: Clarendon Press.

Davies, D. (1995). Dennett's stance on intentional realism. *Southern Journal of Philosophy* 33: 299–312.

Dennett, D. C. (1978). *Brainstorms: Philosophical Essays on Mind and Psychology*. Cambridge, Mass.: MIT Press. A Bradford Book.

Dennett, D. C. (1987). *The Intentional Stance*. Cambridge, Mass.: MIT Press. A Bradford Book.

Dennett, D. C. (1991). Real patterns. *Journal of Philosophy* 88: 27–51.

Dennett, D. C. (1995). *Darwin's Dangerous Idea: Evolution and the Meanings of Life*. New York: Simon and Schuster.

Dennett, D. C. (1996). *Kinds of Minds: Towards an Understanding of Consciousness*. London: Weidenfeld and Nicolson.

Fodor, J. (1975). *The Language of Thought*. Cambridge, Mass.: Harvard University Press.

Fodor, J. (1981). *Representations: Philosophical Essays on the Foundations of Cognitive Science.* Cambridge, Mass.: MIT Press. A Bradford Book.

Fodor, J. (1987). *Psychosemantics: The Problem of Meaning in the Philosophy of Mind.* Cambridge, Mass.: MIT Press. A Bradford Book.

Fodor, J. (1990). *A Theory of Content and Other Essays.* Cambridge, Mass.: MIT Press. A Bradford Book.

Friedman, M. (1981). Theoretical explanation. In Healey 1981.

Haugeland, J. (1978). The nature and plausibility of cognitivism. *The Behavioral and Brain Sciences* 2: 215–260. Reprinted in Haugeland (1998), 9–25.

Haugeland, J. (1998). *Having Thought: Essays in the Metaphysics of Mind.* Cambridge, Mass.: Harvard University Press.

Healey, R., ed. (1981). *Reduction, Time and Reality: Studies in the Philosophy of the Natural Sciences.* Cambridge: Cambridge University Press.

Heil, J. and Mele, A., eds. (1993). *Mental Causation.* Oxford: Clarendon.

Hornsby, J. (1997). *Simple Mindedness: In Defense of Naive Naturalism in the Philosophy of Mind.* Cambridge, Mass.: Harvard University Press.

Pietroski, P. (2000) *Causing Actions.* New York: Oxford University Press.

Putnam, H. (1988). *Representation and Reality.* Cambridge, Mass.: The MIT Press.

Ryle, G. (1949). *The Concept of Mind.* Chicago: The University of Chicago Press.

Stalnaker, R. (1984). *Inquiry.* Cambridge, Mass.: MIT Press. A Bradford Book.

8

Rainforest Realism: A Dennettian Theory of Existence

Don Ross

Both John Haugeland (1993) and Richard Rorty (1993) read Dennett's 1991 paper "Real Patterns" as an exercise in fundamental ontology. They are right. As Haugeland (1993, 53) says, "Ostensibly, it is prompted by questions about the reality of intentional states. . . . But these are pretexts: the issue is not intentionality at all, but rather *being*. . . . Intentional states are just a special case, and there can be other special cases as well, the status of which we will be able to understand once we understand the ontology of patterns more generally." This slightly alarms Dennett. "I wouldn't want to trot out *my* ontology," he worries,

and then find I had to spend the rest of my life defending or revising *it*, instead of getting on with what are to me the genuinely puzzling issues— like the nature of consciousness, or selves, or free will. . . . When and if professional ontologists agree on the ontological status of all my puzzle examples, my bluff will be well and truly called; I will feel a genuine obligation to make things clear to them in their terms, for they will have figured out something fundamental. (1993, 212)

"Professional ontologists" will not, of course, reach any consensus on Dennett's "puzzle examples," or "intuition pumps," as he more commonly calls them, unless they are motivated to take them seriously. Haugeland and Rorty *do* take the intuition pumps trotted forth in "Real Patterns" seriously, and so they should; for Haugeland is quite right that their intended implications with respect to how we should think about intentional states generalize. As I have argued in detail elsewhere (Ross 1995), for example, they help to unlock serious and enduring puzzles with respect to the domain and nature of microeconomic theory. In what follows, I will attempt to develop a general definition of existence out of them. Fortunately for Dennett's concerns about his future activities, I do not expect to produce unanimous agreement among ontologists, so *I* can occupy myself with revising and defending the proposed definition while Dennett concentrates on his preferred targets. However, I, at least, wish to call Dennett's bluff for myself, since I believe, for reasons to be explained, that his position on intentionality requires the cogency of the ontological thesis that "Real Patterns" suggests but stops short of consistently propounding.

I hope to alarm Dennett further by constructing an "ism" out of this ontology. Dennett dislikes having "isms" assigned to his views, as these generally carry connotations that go beyond claims with which he wishes to associate himself (Dennett 1993, 212). However, my proposed "ism," which I shall unveil later in the paper, is a new one, and so rolls with no historical moss. But it does require that a distinction exploited in "Real Patterns," that between illata and abstracta, be abandoned. Rorty (1993), I should note, takes the same view, but with quite different ends in mind. For Rorty, the distinction should collapse because the deeper distinction that motivates drawing it in the first place, that between realism and irrealism, should give way in the face of a radical pragmatism. "Dennett," Rorty writes, "wants to say that it is as silly to ask whether beliefs are real as to ask whether his lost sock centre is real. I quite agree, but not for Dennett's reasons. My reason is that it is silly to ask whether *anything* is real—as opposed to asking whether it is useful to talk about, spatially locatable, spatially divisible, easily identified, made out of atoms, good to eat, etc." (Rorty 1993, 197–198). Dennett rejects this intended friendly amendment: "There *is* a fact of the matter about whether Oswald and Ruby were in cahoots, even if it forever eludes us. It is not *just* a matter of which story plays well to which audiences, and I would say the same about all the usual quarries of empirical investigation" (Dennett 1993, 234). This passage can be read in no other way than as an affirmation of realism. As such, it is consistent with Dennett's adventures over the years in trying to evade the charge that his theory of intentionality is an instrumentalist one. Dennett (1993, 210) suggests that his struggles in this respect have been motivated by his ambition to avoid "isms" in general. However, there is a less purely personal reason why Dennett—and the rest of us—should be wary of instrumentalism: It reduces explanation to psychological satisfaction, since a theory that generates correct predictions, or, more broadly, "saves the phenomena," on the basis of false assumptions provides no explanations at all unless we suppose that being in possession of an explanation is simply a feeling of contentment, thus allowing us to say that those who are unaware of the falsehood of the assumptions in the theory are provided by it with explanations. Consistent instrumentalists, such as Friedman (1953), bite the bullet and deny that explanation is a goal of science at all. However, this view is not consistent with the actual history of science, where predictively inferior theories have often been preferred to predictively superior ones because the former, by virtue of relying on more plausible assumptions, show greater explanatory promise. To put this point in a way that is directly germane to the present debate, if Dennett embraces instrumentalism, then *Consciousness Explained* succeeds in its ambition, but trivially; not because it dissolves puzzles about consciousness by calling into question *mistaken* assumptions that generate the puzzles, but simply because it brings about a state of satisfaction in Dennett and some of his readers. I should think that Dennett does not intend his magnum opus to be taken as a *mere* meditation. Furthermore, "Real Patterns" is best read as the culmination of a series of earlier, unpersuasive attempts by Dennett to show that his "stance" theory with respect to intentional states does not imply instrumentalism about them. Dennett's 1981 paper "True Believers" (reprinted in *The Intentional Stance*) is a salient example. Its argument fails because it depends on a premise to the effect that we should make a Quinean ontological commitment to intentional states on the grounds that to treat them as real is useful. This, however, is circular; one cannot deny instrumentalism by an appeal to radical pragmatism, because radical pragmatism just *is* instrumentalism under another label. Dennett's only available strategy, the one he finally adopts in "Real Patterns," is to do what he finds distasteful: motivate a variety of realism that is compatible with the "stance" theory of intentional states, but which avoids being ad hoc by not itself depending on the "stance" theory it is designed to protect. I now wish to argue that the strategy begun in "Real Patterns" is successful—but only if the distinction between illata and abstracta is denied. This denial, I will maintain, is necessary to *save* realism, not, pace Rorty, to make the point of such salvation go away.

What primarily raises the specter of instrumentalism for Dennett's theory of intentionality is his radical antireductionism. Since most philosophers of mind these days are antireductionists, some discussion of what motivates my use of the adjective "radical" is required. The classic arguments against mind/brain identity theory, such as those of Putnam (1975) and Fodor (1974), which concluded that the types over which psychological generalizations quantify are never likely to admit of description by reference to types recognized in neurophysiology, led to the widespread embrace of functionalism, and to attempts at developing a precise account of mind/brain supervenience. Functionalism and supervenience hypotheses are, respectively, the epistemological and the ontological sides of "nonreductive materialism," since the former is a view about how mental states are to be individuated, and the second tries to explain how they can be said to exist, as nonphysical entities, in a material world. Of course, Dennett is a prototypical functionalist, and so has no quarrel with the epistemological mainstream. However, for reasons to be explained, I will henceforth refer to those who embrace the *conjunction* of functionalism and supervenience as *quasi-reductionists*. Quasi-reductionism, I will argue, is no more satisfactory than reductionism, and this is true not only within the philosophy of mind, but within philosophy of science generally. What is needed— by Dennett in particular, and by all of us who are persuaded that he is right about intentional states—is a stable doctrine of *genuine* antireductionism. Three requirements on such a doctrine make its development challenging: (1) It must not violate materialism; (2) it must not run afoul of Occam's Razor; and (3) it must not assign differential status to illata and abstracta, if the latter gain their "reality" *merely* through being predictively useful constructs out of the former, for that is to embrace instrumentalism with respect to abstracta. Since I will argue that there is no defensible basis for distinguishing between illata and abstracta except by appeal to instrumentalist intuitions, it follows that the distinction should not be drawn at all.

A crucial step in motivating the need for an ontological position that meets the above objectives is an indication of why those who cling to supervenience hypotheses are quasi-reductionists. One means of doing this is to contrast quasireductionists with their original opponents, unabashed reductionists. Historically, reductionism has rested on two general motivations. The first is a confused descendant of Occam's Razor. The Razor insists that we not grant existence to redundant entities: *If* we can explain and predict the etiologies, causal capacities, and dispositions of a composite entity entirely by reference to the etiologies, capacities, and dispositions of its components, then, from the point of view of scientific generalization, the composite is, at best, an anthropomorphically centered artifact, something to which we refer only for purposes of descriptive economy, perhaps because of our peculiar epistemic limitations. This is sometimes mistakenly interpreted as implying that our ultimate scientific ontology should be *small*. Quine, notably, has often encouraged this confusion (without any such intention, a point to which I will return) through his persistent appeal to "jungle-clearing" metaphors in his descriptions of the ontologist's enterprise. At the end of *Word and Object* (1960), the scientist is assigned the job of populating our ontology, while the naturalistic philosopher should follow as a sort of janitor, "smoothing kinks, lopping off vestigial growths, clearing ontological slums" (275). Elsewhere, Quine says that "cognitive discourse at its most drily literal is largely a refinement . . . characteristic of the neatly worked inner stretches of science. It is an open space in the tropical jungle, created by clearing tropes away" (Quine 1978, 162). Since the ontology I will be defending is lush and leafy, Quine's metaphors will provide the foil for the name of the metaphysic I wish to urge upon Dennett: *Rainforest Realism*.[1]

Quine is, most emphatically, no epistemological reductionist. However, he is the strongest sort of ontological reductionist, in the sense that, for him, nothing ultimately exists but physical particles, even if our epistemic limitations and practical purposes shall forever lead us to refer to various ensembles of them. This kind of physicalism, however, does not derive from arguments, but from Democritean faith, a point which Quine acknowledges when he writes that

> Physical objects are conceptually imported . . . not by definition in terms of experience, but simply as irreducible posits, comparable, epistemologically, to the gods of Homer. For my part, I do, qua, lay physicist, believe in physical objects and not in Homer's gods; and I consider it a scientific error to believe otherwise. But in point of epistemological footing the physical objects and the gods differ only in degree and not in kind. (Quine 1953, 44)

Most of us (I hope) share this Democritean faith; but to reserve attribution of existence to particles on these grounds, along with an appeal to instrumental reinforcement, is in fact to eschew metaphysics in favor of a pragmatic epistemology, which is what Quine really intends; hence his preference for talk of "entities to which we are ontologically committed" as a surrogate for "existence." However, I suggest that there are solid naturalistic grounds, the sort of which a Quinean should approve, for defending a "primacy of physics" thesis that does not require a version of metaphysical reductionism resting only on Democritean faith plus a pragmatist epistemology. The naturalistic argument is this: If there is *one* metaphysical presupposition that has been observed throughout the history of science, and across all its branches, it is that the generalizations of the special sciences must not contradict those of physics, whereas no symmetrical limitation holds in the opposite direction. And it is a fundamental axiom of naturalism that philosophers of science must not seek to legislatively override uniformities of scientific practice, since we have no transcendental first principles available to us on the basis of which we could justifiably do so. (This, of course, is the central point of Quine's "Epistemology Naturalized," 1969, 69–90.) Therefore, an adequate naturalistic metaphysics of science should both be consistent with, and ultimately explain, this asymmetric relationship between physics and other sciences. Appeal to a distinction between illata and abstracta is one means of trying to do this: If physics describes illata, while other sciences describe abstracta that must be constructed on the basis of them, then the "primacy of physics" axiom is duly explained. However, as I am in the process of arguing, this only works by resort to either instrumentalism or reductionism, both of which Dennett rightly rejects. Therefore, the peculiar privilege accorded to physics in the history of science does not provide an acceptable basis for the distinction. I shall return to this issue, and to the precise nature of the "primacy of physics" thesis that a naturalistic argument *does* justify, later. For the moment, we must return to the main subargument at hand, namely, the case against reductionism and its quasi-reductionistic successor theses.

The classic defense of reductionism is Oppenheim and Putnam (1958). Their argument, given its vintage, is surprisingly naturalistic in character. Quite simply, it rests inductively on the claim that scientific progress has consisted, most fundamentally, in the achievement of reductions, at both the intratheoretic and the intertheoretic levels. Oppenheim and Putnam distinguish six "basic" levels of organization in nature distinguished by science as of their date of writing. These are (6) social groups, (5) multicellular organisms, (4) cells, (3) molecules, (2) atoms, and (1) elementary particles. They then cite specific examples of empirical work in an effort to show that progress has consisted in, and shows every sign of continuing to consist in, predicting and explaining the etiologies, capacities, and dispositions (henceforth ECDs) of entities at each level in terms of ECDs of entities at the next lowest level. Space does not permit a thorough review of the "encouraging trends" toward continuation of this pattern, which they perceive from their survey of the state of science in 1958. I must therefore content myself, here, with the bold claim that *all* their prognostications appear, from the state of scientific play in 1998, to have been disconfirmed.[2] As Kitcher (1984) argues, even where the reductionist agenda looked *most* promising in 1958, namely, between levels (5) through (3), it has failed, since the neo-Mendelian concepts used by ecologists and population geneticists are not reducible to the basic concepts of molecular genetics. The mid–1980s campaign against reductionism in psychology constitutes, if ultimately successful, a refutation of another aspect of the reductionist program, specifically, that between levels (5) and (4). Reduction between levels (6) and (5) hinges on the fate of methodological individualism, which has generally fallen on hard times among social scientists. Ross and LaCasse (1995) argue that it has been implicitly abandoned even in microeconomics, the social science that Oppenheim and Putnam cite as the prime locus of supposedly assured reduction at the (6) to (5) level. The generalizations of chemistry show no signs of being expressible in terms of the language of microphysics, and the investigation of the substructures of the atomic nucleus may help to explain, but exhibit no trend toward supplanting, the generalizations of particle-field physics. In general, then, the past four decades of scientific development have not been kind to Oppenheim and Putnam's "working hypothesis."

There thus seem to be no persuasive grounds for clinging to reductionism, especially given Fodor's (1974) powerful argument against its general logic. As noted above, however, there is a solid naturalistic basis for retaining materialism, namely, the fact that no special science has ever sanctioned generalizations that violate the fundamental generalizations of the physics of its day.[3] Given the general turn against classical reductionism, the fact that the primacy of physics axiom is still respected throughout the sciences has been the principal motivation—and the one I will discuss here—for the development of supervenience hypotheses.[4] If all nonreducible types must nevertheless have, as their extensions, sets of physical tokens, then this both explains and justifies the primacy of physics axiom. The most sophisticated attempts at developing a definition of supervenience have concerned the relation between the mind and the brain. (See Kim 1995 and the papers in Savellos and Yalcin 1995.) These attempts have encountered serious difficulties, to the point where Kim, the most dogged of the definition-forgers, has come to doubt that a version of supervenience adequate for preserving materialism does not imply reductionism after all (Kim 1989). This does not settle the matter, because, as Marras (1993) points out, there are varieties of supervenience hypotheses that Kim's 1989 argument does not consider. I will not pursue this debate, however, because my grounds for regarding advocates of supervenience as quasireductionists do not depend on its outcome. My objection to supervenience doctrines is that they *either* presuppose a dubious scientific metaphysics *or* implicitly divide the world into two sorts of properties, and then assign all of the enduring clusters of properties recognized by sciences other than physics, but not by the conceptual vocabulary of physics, a kind of "second-class" status. In particular, they follow Reichenbach in cleaving the world into illata and abstracta.

My reasons for believing this are as follows. Why does an advocate of supervenience wish to ascribe reality to the properties of supervening types? The answer to this question typically runs along the following lines. It is the task of science to produce nomic generalizations (that is, laws). The disjunction of tokens that forms the supervenience base for a supervenient type will generally not support counterfactuals that hold throughout logical space; hence, even if we could identify the full disjunction of tokens for a supervenient type, the disjunctive object in question could not be plugged into the counterfactual-supporting laws of the higher-level science in question. This concern, however, rests upon two highly questionable assumptions about the ambitions of science, and of the special sciences in particular. First, it will cut no ice with those who are persuaded, as I am, by Cartwright's (1983, 1989) arguments to the effect that the success of science (including physics) does *not* consist in the production of true nomic generalizations. Rather, it consists in the identification and measurement of causal capacities of particulars, upon which both the typologies and the (context-sensitive) approximations expressed in generalizations are parasitic. Second, it depends on the belief that the generalizations of all of the special sciences are intended to apply across all possible worlds. Why should one hold such a belief? It finds no basis in the actual history of any special science, with the possible exception of physics itself. (I say "*possible* exception" here because it can plausibly be argued that, since we have no possible epistemological basis for applying the generalizations of physics across the boundaries of temporal singularities, such as the Big Bang, or spatial singularities, such as black holes, even these generalizations do not fall within the scope of universal quantifiers, regardless of whether one is or is not persuaded by Cartwright's arguments that physics does not produce true laws even within the boundaries of singularities.) The only sound motivation for the belief I can think of is that it would be true, as a matter of semantics, *if* sciences are sets of theories and theories are extensions of sets of axioms. However, Hacking (1983 and elsewhere) has cast powerful doubt, independent of Cartwright's arguments, on the first idea, and the failure of Carnap's mature version of logical empiricism was effectively a refutation of the second one. Unless an advocate of supervenience is prepared to accept the burden of defending these assumptions about science—which is a very tall order—her defense of the reality of supervenient types threatens to collapse into instrumentalism: Our special sciences generalize over supervenient types *only* because we lack the epistemic resources necessary for identifying their disjunctive supervenience bases.[5] On this view, the objects over which the sciences generalize are rendered into two sets: abstracta, the domain of the special sciences, and illata, the domain of physics. Furthermore, and most importantly in the present context, abstracta come out as ultimately anthropocentric. But Dennett's well-motivated desire to avoid this conclusion where intentional states are concerned is just where we came in.

Let me now summarize the set of conclusions at which we have arrived: Reductionism is (probably) false, quasi-reductionism is unstable, and instrumentalism (obviously) holds the ontologies of most special sciences to be anthropocentric. If this is correct, then we find ourselves faced with a bullet that several philosophers, such as Rosenberg (1992, 1994) and Dupré (1993), have recently bitten without discomfort: We can simply allow that adoption of an instrumentalistic stance need not impugn the scientific legitimacy of a discipline so long as the tasks served by the instruments are neither sociopolitical advantages for elites (a charge Dupré levels at economics), nor mere mathematical tractability for its own sake (in which event a science retreats from the domain of the empirical, the charge Rosenberg levels at economics). Dennett, however, does not and should not bite this bullet. Although the history of science does not, as noted, show a general trend toward reductionism, it *does* demonstrate an implicit presupposition that if the types over which a theory generalizes turn out to be anthropocentically motivated, then progress consists partly in seeking and achieving their elimination. Dennett (1991b, 51) may be right in his claim that Churchland's eliminativism with respect to the propositional attitudes is a "presumptive thesis way out in front of the empirical support [it requires]." However, if the argument I have made to this point is accepted, and given Dennett's commitment to antireductionism where intentional states are concerned, then, were he to follow the path of Rosenberg and Dupré, he would be committed to the implication that we should be doing our damnedest to achieve Churchland's ambition. No attitude, however, could be further from that which is most central to Dennett's theory of intentionality.

"Real Patterns" is clear evidence that Dennett recognizes, at least implicitly, the difficulty, along with the need, of stabilizing the volatile brew of antireductionism, radical naturalism, and realism if his stance theory of the intentions is to be viable. The intuition pumps provided in "Real Patterns" are precisely intended to shake a comfortable instrumentalist's confidence that the regularities tracked by intentional psychology (and, by implication, other special sciences such as biology and economics; see Ross 1995) have no existence independent of our predictive purposes and epistemic limitations. However, he stops short of pronouncing himself a realist, concluding the paper by asking rhetorically "Is the view I am defending here a sort of instrumentalism or a sort of realism?" In answer, he says "I think that the view itself is clearer than either of the labels, so I shall leave that question to anyone who still finds illumination in them" (1991b, 51). As I have been at pains to show up to this point, this is a cop-out: The labels *do* denote distinguishable positions, and adopting one or another of them has implications. If Dennett's position is in fact instrumentalist, then he must, at risk of self-contradiction, join Churchland in doubting that the objects of intentional psychology are *real* patterns, and should, being the deeply committed naturalist that he is, also follow Churchland in identifying progress in the study of behavior with the extent to which we can successfully eliminate them.

However, Dennett is not *entirely* unwilling to label himself. In the opening paragraphs of "Real Patterns," he calls himself a "mild realist" (Dennett 1991b, 50), in the context of comparing the degree of his realism with those of Fodor, Churchland, Davidson, and Rorty. In Dennett (1993, 212–213), he concedes that this "was at least a tactical mistake." It is, I believe, worse than that: Use of the adjective "mild" to refer to realism about intentional states, when coupled with naive realism about illata, invites Dennett's reader to interpret him as suggesting that there could be differential degrees of reality in which objects or types might partake. Now, as Andrew Brook has suggested to me in correspondence, perhaps this is how Dennett *should* be read. *Consciousness Explained,* as Brook points out, is written in the idiom of naive realism about the objects of the heterophenomenological world (rocks, building, people, chairs, and so on). These, then, could be the illata. Theoretical objects posited by science, including both psychological types and such physical types as centers of gravity (Dennett's favorite analogical example) are then the abstracta. This allows the distinction to be drawn in a way that implies neither ontological reductionism nor epistemological instrumentalism. However, this interpretation of Dennett's discussion as depending on a commitment to naive, as opposed to scientific, realism seems deeply inconsistent with Dennett's larger project. On what basis could a philosopher be a naive realist about, for example, rocks, while rejecting naive realism about, for example, "desires that *p*"? The point of naive realism, after all, is to take the phenomenal world as given, and then to relate the world described by science to that manifest image. Dennett's leading career project, however, has consisted in encouraging us to radically revise our manifest image of the psychological domain suggested by auto-phenomenology. In light of the revisions to our manifest image of the physical world demanded by twentieth-century physics, it would seem bizarrely ad hoc and unmotivated to adopt naive realism with respect to the physical, while campaigning against it in the domain of the psychological.

It therefore seems to me to be more charitable to read Dennett's discussion in "Real Patterns" as an intervention in the debate between *scientific* realists and antirealists. This interpretation is supported by Dennett's choice of membership in his selected contrast class against which he describes his own position. Both Churchland and Fodor, for example, two members of this contrast class who figure most prominently in Dennett's discussion, are clearly concerned with the attitude that scientific realists should take toward intentional states; Churchland, especially, is not in the least concerned with what naive realists should or should not regard as real. Furthermore, as careful attention to the discussion in "Real Patterns" makes clear, the force of the adjective "mild" is (in contrast with the views of Fodor and Churchland) a reference to Dennett's position with respect to reductionism. Fodor's realism is "strong" because he would deny reality to intentional states unless they reduce to computational states, and Churchland's realism is also "strong" because he denies that intentional states are real on the grounds that they don't reduce to anything. Rorty's realism is described as "milder than mild," but here the basis of measurement has changed, since Rorty's irrealism, as noted above, is driven by his radical pragmatism, rather than by any particular view on the question of reducibility. Rorty, after all, is the original eliminativist where propositional attitudes are concerned, and his motivations for eliminativism are a subset of Churchland's (see Rorty 1965). Given these confusions, what sort of sense should we make of Dennett's placing himself (along with Davidson) in the middle of this scale? The clue, I suggest, lies in Dennett's misdirected appeal to the abstracta-illata distinction. Dennett wishes to hold that (some) abstracta are real, regardless of whether they can be reduced. But, in that case, what is the basis for the distinction in the first place? If we search for it in adherence by Dennett to naive realism, his discussion here would egregiously beg the question against both Fodor and Churchland. Dennett is innocent of the charge of question-begging if we suppose that his basis for appealing to the illata-abstracta distinction is the familiar one I discussed above, namely, the view that each token of an abstract type is identical to some physical particular or other. However, we now have Dennett out of the fire in preparation for the frying pan. Implicit adherence to token-physicalism would seem to make Dennett's *ontological* position identical to Fodor's; their disagreement, where intentional states are concerned, would on this interpretation lie in the fact that Fodor is an internalist whereas Dennett is an externalist. But this can't be squared with another aspect of Dennett's realism, which he uses to justify calling it "mild," namely, his belief in the irreducibile indeterminacy of content-ascriptions from the intentional stance. Dennett (1991b, 46–48) says that his realism is "slightly milder" than Davidson's because, on Dennett's view, but not on Davidson's, there is an ineliminable element of indeterminacy in assigning token-identities to particular intentional states; it is for this reason that the reality of the psychological lies in patterns rather than in the conjunction of their applications. It is this initially peculiar, but persuasively argued, claim that makes Dennett's antireductionism *radical*, in a way that Fodor's (and Davidson's) is not.

We now may examine the implications of the conjunction of two propositions to which, I have argued, Dennett is fundamentally committed:

(1)   (Some) abstracta are real;

(2)   (Some) tokens of real abstracta are not identical with any illata.

Perhaps Dennett *would* prefer to embrace the bizarre idea that reality admits of degrees, with a base level of illata serving as "bedrock reality"—the "realest of the real," as it were. In that case, however, I fail to see how Dennett's denial of instrumentalism is anything but a *mere* rejection of the label, rather than the substance of that position. If he genuinely wishes to deny instrumentalism with respect to intentional states and other entities he calls abstracta, then he has no consistent basis for drawing a distinction between abstracta and illata at all. This, I think, is all to the good, since Dennett's actual, and deeply innovative, way around instrumentalism does not require the distinction. This innovation, as we shall see in a moment, is to be found in Dennett's use of the technical concept of information to limn the boundaries of the real. This innovation rescues Dennett from the quasi-reductionism to which his endorsement of Reichenbach's distinction threatens to lead him, but which it is precisely the point of his "mild realism" to avoid. Dennett can escape from the tangle of threatening inconsistencies upon which I have elaborated only by taking his radical antireductionism to its logical conclusion: instead of vaguely imagining a "quasi-real" world of abstracta floating, in some unspecified way, above a world of "really real" illata, he must endorse the view that reality is composed of real patterns *all the way down*. Through his use of information-theoretic concepts, he has, perhaps without clearly noticing, given himself the means of doing this, without resort to the sort of anthropocentric perspectivalism that must inevitably slide into instrumentalism.

To see how this works in detail, we first must use the intuition pumps supplied in "Real Patterns" to extract what Dennett shies from doing: providing an ontological theory. This is the theory that I wish to dub *Rainforest Realism*. What is sought is, in effect, a replacement for the naturalist's account of existence famously offered by Quine, that "To be is to be the value of a variable in our body of best-confirmed scientific theory." The spirit of Quine's definition is to be preserved, but we must abandon the literal slogan as soon as we give up, as I have urged (in common with Dennett; see Dennett 1993, 219) that we should, the view that scientific knowledge is a collection of axiomatizable theories. I regret, however, that the proposed replacement I have derived directly from Dennett's reflections and examples lacks the pith of Quine's, and so is bound to be less effective as a meme. At any rate, here is Rainforest Realism:

To be is to be a real pattern; and a pattern is real if

(i) it is projectible under at least one physically possible perspective, and

(ii) it encodes information about at least one structure of events or entities S where that encoding is more efficient, in information-theoretic terms, than the bit-map encoding of S, and where for at least one of the physically possible perspectives under which the pattern is projectible, there exists an aspect of S that cannot be tracked unless the encoding is recovered from the perspective in question.

I must, obviously, elaborate on the point of each of these two necessary conditions for pattern-reality, now identified with existence itself. Clause (i), in granting reality to patterns that can be tracked from all physically *possible* perspectives, effectively denies that a non-reductionist, perspectival ontology is necessarily anthropocentric. If we define the set of physically possible perspectives as the set of perspectives available in the possible worlds that are nearby according to physics,[6] then this explains and justifies the primacy of physics axiom exactly as it has in fact been observed in the special sciences. (It is also consistent with Dennett's rejection of arguments such as Chalmers's 1996 insistence that we must take the possibility of zombies seriously merely because they are logically possible, and

Jackson's 1982 defense of irreducible qualia on the basis of the fact that color-deprived but otherwise neuroscientifically omniscient Mary is logically possible. As Dennett 1991a argues, neither zombies nor Mary are physically possible.) Clause (ii) then *ensures* that our ontology is neither anthropocentric nor infinite by reformulating Occam's razor in information-theoretic terms. It blocks ontological redundancy in two senses. First, it excludes pure semantic artifacts, such as arbitrary conjunctions of real patterns; no properties of the object "my left nostril and the Namibian government and Miles Davis's last solo" are projectable under any compression smaller than the bit-map expression of the conjunction of the most efficient description of each individual conjunct. Second, and more interestingly, it blocks anthropocentrism—and thus denies instrumentalism—by holding that if there is a physically possible perspective from which some phenomenon recognized by our current working ontology could be more efficiently represented under an alternative ontology, then our current ontology is false, regardless of whether we are or are not, or shall ever be, aware of the existence of the alternative possible perspective in question. There are facts of the matter, grounded in computability theory, about the compressibility of information. There are also facts of the matter, grounded in the conjunction of thermodynamics and the topology of space-time, about whether a signal can or cannot be sent from one point in the universe to another. This is why Rainforest Realism *is* a variety of *realism*. It is not, however, a realism of the desert, since unless (contrary to our present evidence) the progress of science vindicates Oppenheim and Putnam after all, we should expect the large range of physically possible perspectives to imply an enormous ontology. As noted earlier, however, though size per se may matter to Hollywood and to Texans, it does not matter to Occam.

Not only do I claim that Dennett *must* accept Rainforest Realism for the sake of consistency, I also suggest that he should welcome it, his general distaste for "isms" notwithstanding. The view is stringently naturalistic; just as Quine intended in his definition of existence, it leaves the job of populating our ontology entirely up to empirical science. Indeed, as noted above, it actually allows for the possibility that reductionism or eliminativism could be empirically vindicated; so although it deliberately allows room for current anti-reductionistic expectations, it doesn't impose them a priori. Furthermore, in contrast with supervenience hypotheses, it incorporates the weakest possible form of materialism—which, I suggest, is the only thing Dennett could *consistently* intend in calling himself a "mild realist." This is just what we should wish of a philosophy of science that, following Quine's lead, draws its conclusions from reflection on the history and practice of science. To expect the generalizations of the special sciences to apply counterfactually across all of logical space, or even, as in the case of Chalmers's zombies, physically possible but (by Chalmers's own admission) enormously physically remote space, would be to impose an unmanageable burden upon them; and when this is done, as Dennett has often observed, it exposes them perpetually and inescapably to far-fetched philosophical "refutations." At a stroke, Rainforest Realism puts Chalmers's zombies, Jackson's Mary, and Searle's Chinese room exactly where, according to Dennett, they belong: in the space of pure philosophical toys, of no relevance to theories in empirical cognitive science.

It may be supposed that to define existence in terms of information-theory in order to save the coherence of Dennett's philosophy of mind is a very strange basis on which to defend an extravagant metaphysical claim. However, there are independent arguments for the claim, which are presented at length in Ross and Zawidzki (1994). An important anticipation of it can be found in Schrödinger (1967). Interestingly, in light of his otherwise extreme dialectical polarization with respect to Dennett's position on consciousness, Chalmers (1996) also views the suggestion with cautious but enthusiastic hope. The core intuition behind the claim can be stated briefly as follows. To *exist,* is essentially, to persist as a distinguishable entity for a long enough period of time that measurement of a set of distinguishing properties is possible using some physically possible property-detector. But in this statement of a vague (though, I submit, highly intuitively natural) conception, fundamental appeal to information has already been introduced by reference to "property-detection." If nothing with measurable properties could persist, then, given acceptance of a mild and sensible degree of verificationism—a degree of verificationism *demanded* by Quinean naturalism—there would exist only one thing: undifferentiated everything, the pure Aristotelean plenum. The second law of thermodynamics implies that, all else being equal, this would be the ontology we should expect. Of course, all else is not equal: The distribution of mass/energy resulting from the Big Bang is such that in the actual world, all manner of cabbages and kings can ward off entropic pressures for (relative to the capacities of similarly enduring measurement devices) impressive periods of time. Furthermore, through adoption of Schrödinger's formulation of thermodynamics in terms of *neg*entropy, we can move smoothly back and forth from definitions cast in terms of thermodynamics to definitions expressed in mathematical information theory. Therefore, expressing a conception of existence-in-general in information-theoretic terms captures exactly what we should want in justifying ascription of an existence claim concerning some particular entity or type of entity: persistence against increasing entropy, and distinguishability-in-principle from the rest of the background universe. Now, *if* a theory of existence this generic can be formulated, then everything that exists should be said to do so in these terms and on this basis. Since the formulation I have essayed above makes no reference to any particular class of detectors privileged by unusually sophisticated computational capacities (e.g., people in general, or the institutional apparatus of scientific inquiry), it follows that, from this generic perspective, the distinction between illata and abstracta is otiose. Dennett's struggle to find a place in our scientific ontology for types of intentional states, while avoiding both reductionism and instrumentalism, suggests something further: that the distinction is not only unnecessary, but positively dangerous, since it encourages ontological pseudo-problems when we come to deal with types of patterns the detection of which *does* require unusual sorts of computational capacities of the sort we (so far) find instantiated only in our own mind/brains. Suddenly, at that point, we are tempted to suppose that whereas some types of entities, the putative illata, exist independently of *our* detection of them, other types are constructed by us, strictly for *our* purposes, out of these ontological (as opposed to epistemological) "givens." The temptation to endorse ontological reductionism, or epistemological instrumentalism, or both, then immediately looms. Dennett's sound intuitions have led him to resist both temptations, despite regular flirtations with them over the years. I have tried, in this paper, to show him, and the rest of us, how to consistently avoid both: find their source, in the abstracta-illata distinction, and purge it from our intuitions.

Rainforest Realism is intended to call Dennett's bluff; it challenges him to admit that his puzzles and intuition-pumps *do* drive us toward a comprehensive metaphysic. I have argued that, at the small cost of abandoning the abstracta-illata distinction, he has available to him an ontological thesis that weaves his special varieties of antireductionism, naturalism, and realism into a consistent whole. As stressed, I do not propose the doctrine of Rainforest Realism merely as a means of making Dennett consistent. Since I believe that Dennett's theories of intentionality and consciousness are broadly correct, if Rainforest Realism is required to undergird them, then I believe that we should all be Rainforest Realists. Furthermore, since Rainforest Realism has arguments in its favor that are independent of Dennett's work in the philosophy of psychology, its endorsement might allow him to proceed more successfully with his preferred puzzles of less sweeping scope. In describing his general approach to philosophy, Dennett (1993, 204) says "Philosophers are supposed to try to hit home runs, and I guess sometimes that's why I'm misunderstood. I seldom swing for the fences; I try to scratch out my runs by a more modest collection of bunts, grounders and aggressive base-running." The bunts and grounders have scored many runs over the course of Dennett's career, but I have argued in this paper that the base-running has at times been a trifle too aggressive: He has not infrequently been caught stealing. The present paper unabashedly swings for the fences; and so I suggest to Dennett that, where matters of ontology are concerned, he wait patiently on second, from where he can safely be brought home with, if not a home run, at least a solid line drive to the outfield.[7]

Notes

1. I owe Rachel Barney credit and thanks for this meme. Naturally, I hope that her coinage will enjoy a fecund existence in the memesphere.

2. This discontinuity is interesting. Should we infer from it that pursuit of interlevel reduction was epistemically fruitful up to some threshold encountered in the middle of the twentieth century, or, with Kuhn, that Oppenheim and Putnam read their history of science selectively? I incline, eccentrically, toward the former view; but a defense of this inclination is a subject for another occasion.

3. I avoid talk of "laws" because, with Cartwright (1983), I doubt that any science has ever produced, or could produce, a true law in the strict and traditional sense of the term.

4. The major motivation for supervenience hypotheses that I will *not* discuss is the view that all causation must ultimately operate at the microphysical level. This, however, seems to have nothing to support it beyond the same Democritean faith that grounds Quine's ontological physicalism, and so, in the context of the present debate, leads us in a circle.

5. The defender of supervenience cannot fall back here upon Fodor's (1974) argument to the effect that these limitations are logical rather than contingent, since that argument depends on one of the premises here being denied, namely, that physics produces true nomic generalizations.

6. By "worlds that are nearby according to physics," I mean whichever worlds lie within the intended scope of the generalizations of physics. Trying to precisely fix this scope would be, obviously, a fool's errand. However, the scope in question clearly includes many nonactual worlds, since the generalizations of physics are intended to support various counterfactuals, but excludes worlds that are *merely* logically possible. It also excludes aspects of the actual world that are treated by physics as lying beyond the boundaries of singularities.

7. I wish to thank the following people who have critically commented on earlier drafts of the present paper: Stuart Barnum, Andy Brook, Steve Clark, Murray Clarke, John Collier, Paul Dumouchel, Cliff Hooker, Rob Stainton, and Tad Zawidzki. I am also grateful to Daniel Dennett, Brian Mooney, and the participants at the Newfoundland conference in November 1998, for illuminating conversations on the various issues germane to my argument.

References

Cartwright, N. (1983). *How the Laws of Physics Lie*. Oxford: Oxford University Press.

Cartwright, N. (1989). *Nature's Capacities and Their Measurement*. Oxford: Oxford University Press.

Chalmers, D. (1996). *The Conscious Mind*. Oxford: Oxford University Press.

Dennett, D. (1981). True believers. In *Scientific Explanation*, A. Heath (ed.). Oxford: Oxford University Press.

Dennett, D. (1991a). *Consciousness Explained*. Boston: Little Brown.

Dennett, D. (1991b). Real patterns. *Journal of Philosophy* 88: 27–51.

Dennett, D. (1993). Back from the drawing board. In *Dennett and His Critics*, B. Dahlbom (ed.). Cambridge, Mass.: Blackwell.

Dupré, J. (1993). *The Disorder of Things*. Cambridge, Mass.: Harvard University Press.

Fodor, J. (1974). Special sciences. *Synthese* 28: 77–115.

Friedman, M. (1953). *Essays in Positive Economics*. Chicago: University of Chicago Press.

Hacking, I. (1983). *Representing and Intervening*. Cambridge, Mass.: Cambridge University Press.

Haugeland, J. (1993). Pattern and being. In *Dennett and His Critics*, B. Dahlbom (ed.). Cambridge, Mass.: Blackwell.

Jackson, F. (1982). Epiphenomenal qualia. *Philosophical Quarterly* 32: 127–136.

Kim, J. (1989). The myth of nonreductive materialism. *Proceedings and Addresses of the American Philosophical Association* 63: 31–47.

Kim, J. (1995). *Supervenience and Mind*. Cambridge: Cambridge University Press.

Kitcher, P. (1984). 1953 and all that: A tale of two sciences. *Philosophical Review* 93: 335–373.

Marras, A. (1993). Psychophysical supervenience and nonreductive materialism. *Synthese* 95: 275–304.

Oppenheim, P. and Putnam, H. (1958). Unity of science as a working hypothesis. In *Minnesota Studies in the Philosophy of Science*, v. 2, H. Feigl, M. Scriven, and G. Maxwell, (eds.), 3–36. Minneapolis: University of Minnesota Press.

Putnam, H. (1975). *Mind, Language, and Reality*. Cambridge, Mass.: Cambridge University Press.

Quine, W. v. O. (1953). Two dogmas of empricism. In Quine, *From a Logical Point of View*. Cambridge, Mass.: Harvard University Press.

Quine, W. v. O. (1960). *Word and Object*. Cambridge, Mass.: MIT Press.

Quine, W. v. O. (1969). Epistemology naturalized. In Quine, *Ontological Relativity and Other Essays*. New York: Columbia University Press.

Quine, W. v. O. (1978). A postscript on metaphor. *Critical Inquiry* 5: 161–162.

Rorty, R. (1965). Mind-body identity, privacy, and categories. *Review of Metaphysics* 19: 124–154.

Rorty, R. (1993). Holism, intrinsicality, and the ambition of transcendence. In *Dennett and His Critics*, B. Dahlbom (ed.). Cambridge, Mass.: Blackwell.

Rosenberg, A. (1992). *Economics: Mathematical Politics or Science of Diminishing Returns?* Chicago: University of Chicago Press.

168

Don Ross

Rosenberg, A. (1994). *Instrumental Biology, or The Disunity of Science*. Chicago: University of Chicago Press.

Ross, D. (1995). Real patterns and the ontological foundations of microeconomics. *Economics and Philosophy* 11: 113–136.

Ross, D. and Zawidzki, T. (1994). Information and teleosemantics. *Southern Journal of Philosophy* 32: 393–419.

Ross, D. and LaCasse, C. (1995). Towards a new philosophy of positive economics. *Dialogue* 34: 467–493.

Savellos, E. and Yalçin, Ü., eds. (1995). *Supervenience: New Essays*. Cambridge: Cambridge University Press.

Schrödinger, E. (1967). *What Is Life? and Mind and Matter*. Cambridge: Cambridge University Press.

9

Popping the Thought Balloon

Dan Lloyd

Ain't Misbelieving[1]

Non sunt multiplicanda entia praeter necessitatum. The patron saint of
Anglo-American philosophy might well be William of Occam, who
with his legendary razor undercut the ever-present impulse to
reify dispositions, processes, capacities, and correlations, trans-
forming them into discrete enduring things, black boxes to be
presupposed, discussed, and finally taken for granted. But for a
really close shave, one should choose Dennett, who out-occams Occam by not just holding the line on new entities, but by resolutely
cutting the extant ontological inventory. Over the years many a familiar entity has suffered *redennettia ad absurdum,* of the following
rough form:

1. Many people believe in the existence of *x*.
2. *X* has (or should have) properties *P . . .* , if it is indeed the *x*
that many people believe in.
3. Nothing with properties *P . . .* does/could exist.
4. Therefore, *x* does not exist, or better,
5. Therefore, *x* exists but has few or none of the properties
commonly believed of it. (Instead, it has the properties *Q. . . .*)

For his reductio Dennett draws from a repertoire of rhetorical and
argumentative strategies:

3A. Intuition pumps: You really can imagine the world without x if you only try a little harder. (And here's a story to help. . . .)

3B. Analogies: x is very like the utterly disreputable y, which scientists/philosophers/everyone have long cast off or would cast off instantly if its existence were seriously proposed.

3C. Skeptical disjunctions: The properties ascribed to x are initially vague. The attempt to resolve which of P . . . really do apply either leads to a contradiction among P . . . or a genuine open question that is irresolvable in principle.

3D. Sorites and slippery slopes. The borders of $x$ness can be established only through a foolish consistency of microcriteria.

3E. Empirical challenges: x, were it to exist, would cause certain observed effects. These have been disconfirmed in the lab.

This is a powerful toolbox, and the strategies above lend themselves well to organic combinations. Their deployment places Dennett solidly in the esteemed tradition of constructive skepticism, from Hume to Ryle to Quine. Armed with Dennett's various razors, it is surprising, then, that Dennett frequently ends up with conclusion 5 above, rather than the more restrictive 4. I suspect this is the product of the faculty of Yankee Cognition, or the Mainer Cortex, or maybe just plain Niceness: Occamite New England ontological conservatism *and* a powerful (equally New England) impulse to *preserve appearances*. The opponent should be edified about his or her confusions, not skewered on them.

Preserving appearances is, however, exactly the right initial impulse or "stance" (if I may use the term) in the study of consciousness. It is precisely *appearances* that need to be explained, and so discussion must begin with what seems to be the case. For the really conservative, stubbornly retrograde philosophers—a surly bunch who shall go nameless—discussion must also end with initial appearances. For them, *the ways things seem* are immutable, and anyone who attempts to revise initial appearances is guilty of absurdity *ab initio*.

Dennett, in contrast, holds out the possibility that explanation and rational reconstruction of some appearances can render them as mere apparent appearances, appearing otherwise after the explanation is grasped by the appearee. On the surface, the idea that we can be wrong about what seems to be the case to us seems paradoxical, or it entails an infinite regress of seemings to seem. What seems to me may not be what's real, but that it seems to me is a real mental event that is constituted by the seeming itself—"correction" of this experience by "reality" is impossible. The air of paradox, however, is merely what Dennett calls (in conversation) a "deepity," a claim that appears profound but is in fact a superficial equivocation. (His example of a deepity is "Love is just a four-letter word." It kinda makes you think.) The deepity of unseeming seemings dissolves when one considers the unstated temporal dimension of all judgments, including judgments of appearance and reality. There's real fruit and wax fruit. A wax apple may seem real at time $t1$, and then will seem artificial at time $t2$, about the time you attempt to sink your teeth into it. The discovery of its waxiness alters the way it seems, an alteration of many of its sensory properties. But it will always be true that it seemed real to you *at t1*. That time-indexed seeming is indeed immutable, like any past event, but it would be a confusion of the deepity type to claim that the way an apple seems is immutable *in general*. Every object of perception is subject to change in its appearance, and this is no less true when the "object" in question is a mental episode (like a seeming). The sadness we feel at the end of a two-hankie movie may seem one way today (stirring, noble, magnanimous) and another way tomorrow (sentimental, puerile, foolish).

The deepity about appearances, about states of consciousness as they seem to us and as seemings in themselves, and the ever-shifting current, retrospective, and prospective ways these seemings seem, this deepity would be a relatively minor point were it not subtly enshrined at the foundation of modern philosophy, in Descartes. Descartes raises the famous question, am I dreaming right now? (It's a Dennett sort of question: see strategy 3C above.) Owing to a cognitive accident about dreams, namely, our chronic loss of insight into our own state while dreaming, this question is hard to answer. Dreams seem real as they are dreamed, as does waking reality while it is experienced. Descartes raises the bar a bit by posing the example of the mundane dream ("sitting in front of the fire," etc.). So, at any time, I cannot tell (in principle) whether what seems to be the case really is the case.

Sophomores in Philosophy 101, for whom the natural ontological attitude comes naturally, can be relied on to object strenuously: "Of course I can tell the difference between dreaming and waking," they proclaim. Their account is usually reminiscent of distinctions between dreaming and waking given by Descartes himself in the Sixth Meditation:

> ... for at present I find a very notable difference between the two, inasmuch as our memory can never connect our dreams one with the other, or with the whole course of our lives, as it unites events which happen to us while we are awake. And, as a matter of fact, if someone, while I was awake, quite suddenly appeared to me and disappeared as fast as do the images which I see in sleep, so that I could not know from whence the form came nor whither it went, it would not be without reason that I should deem it a specter or a phantom formed by my brain, rather than a real man. But when I perceive things as to which I know distinctly both the place from which they proceed, and that in which they are, and the time at which they appeared to me; and when, without any interruption, I can connect the perceptions which I have of them with the whole course of my life, I am perfectly assured that these perceptions occur while I am waking and not during sleep. And I ought in no wise to doubt the truth of such matters, if, after having called up all my senses, my memory, and my understanding, to examine them, nothing is brought to evidence by any one of them which is repugnant to what is set forth by the others. (Haldane and Ross 1969, 199)

Case closed. Between the First and the Sixth Meditations Descartes has reassured himself about the reliability of his reason, and thus can appeal to the revisable retrospective judgments of reality and their continuous provisional updating, the regular pragmatics of cognitive life in sophomores and everyone else. But in spite of our everyday confidence, philosophy has overlooked Descartes's pragmatic Sixth while remaining permanently dazed by his First: "[T]here are no certain indications by which we may clearly distinguish wakefulness from sleep. . . . And my astonishment is such that it is almost capable of persuading me that I now dream" (1969, 146). The dream argument, as has often been noted, seems to work too well, succeeding out of proportion with its place as an opening gambit in the method of doubt. But why is that? Descartes's persistent deepity lies in the urgency with which he presents the cognitive risk entailed by his skeptical arguments. The skeptical specter of occurrent error is identified with the risk of real error, the kind that emerges in subsequent correction, with its real effects on the progress of our lives. The Evil Demon amplifies the same deepity. In the demon's thrall, we are deluded about everything, and all the time—a terrible fate, but one whose terrors are only hypothetical, since systematic demonic delusion is without practical consequences. In practice, an uncontradicted delusion is as good as a truth.

The fact that we philosophers share with Descartes the view that his skepticism reveals a genuine epistemic problem indicates that we share a pervasive assumption (an assumption not shared by our wise sophomores). To put this in the most neutral language I can, let us call this the *doctrine of registration*. The doctrine holds that minds model the world, and that from moment to moment the mental model is more or less in registration with the world. In veridical waking perception, the registration is "tight," while in psychosis or dreaming the model ranges far afield. The doctrine of registration assumes several components and specific relations between them: a model, a medium from which the model is formed, a separate world to be modeled, and a mapping relationship between them, which somehow makes sense of both veridical and false modeling. That relationship is our old friend "representation" or "intentionality." It is usually the baby that is preserved as the bathwater of Cartesian dualism is discarded. Because Descartes fills the mind with mental representations that point with intangible but determinate arrows to intentional objects, there is a possibility of widespread occurrent error, error undermining whole continents of cognition. Worse, the error could be covert. We could be unwitting dupes and stooges. In short, with a good dose of Cartesian skepticism, we could experience every intellectual and emotional consequence of error, without ever actually experiencing the pragmatic collision with a contrary world. This is "error lite"; Descartes's freighted weighting of error lite is a splendid deepity and the concomitant creation of the modern mind is an astonishing result.

Had Descartes sprung his deepity on the world in a different time, it might have been less effective. (Indeed, both Augustine and

Montaigne noted the dream problem, but without its modern foundational implications.) He moved at the exact moment when, as Donne put it, "New philosophy calls all in doubt." New cosmology and new physics gave European intelligentsia a galloping case of what we would now call modern science. In a sense, Descartes's worst fantasies were unfolding: What everyone thought to be the case was turning out to be systematically and pervasively false. The forces and laws that governed the physical world were discovered to be quite different from the folk-inspired and Aristotelian theories that had seemed so obvious. And so it goes on to this day: The world-model in one's mind is at best a radical translation of the distal energies of reality.

To borrow a metaphor from Dennett, what Descartes bequeathed the world was the *thought balloon,* a free-floating package of ideas that is *always* distinct from the world of matter (Dennett 1996). The thought balloon of cartoonists, as Dennett notes, typically captures most of the Cartesian legacy. It depicts representation, the mental model of the world. It incidentally depicts unity and sequence, the single stream of consciousness. It implies interiority, popping as it does from the head. It often implies a linguistic basis. It assumes an inner speaker or illustrator, and an inner witness. And its cloudiness suggests its emergence from a nonphysical dimension.

Substance dualism, however, was merely the ontological icing on this epistemic cake. The problems of substance dualism have long been conspicuous and as a result it has been the first Cartesian construct to be deleted from the mix. But that's the easy part. As Dennett has steadily illuminated, what remains after the rejection of dualism is "Cartesian materialism" (including some exotic variants: David Chalmer's quintessentialism; Roger Penrose's quantum dualism; the mysterian philosophies of Thomas Nagel or Colin McGinn). The Cartesian materialist thinks of the brain as a *res cogitans.* But the *res* is now a squishy gray gland, not obviously *cogitans* at all. It is spatially squishy, with elaborate and obscure goings-on all over the place, and it is temporally squishy, with the goings-on going on asynchronously. Where, then, is the thought balloon to be tethered? The Cartesian materialist retreats in space to the pineal frontier, and the surmise that amid the squishy stuff there is a special clearinghouse where the full-blown cogitations gather, and retreats in time to the idea that content crosses a threshold into consciousness. (See, e.g., Baars 1996.)

Dennett summarizes the assumptions of Cartesian materialism in the metaphor of the Cartesian Theater. After many applications of Dennett's wrecking ball, what remains is the Multiple Drafts Model (MDM). It is telling, I think, to examine both what the MDM denies as well as what it tacitly accepts. In *Consciousness Explained,* "the novel feature" of the model is this:

Feature detections or discriminations *only have to be made once.* That is, once a particular "observation" of some feature has been made, by a specialized, localized portion of the brain, the information content thus fixed does not have to be sent somewhere else to be rediscriminated by some "master" discriminator. In other words, discrimination does not lead to a re-presentation of the already discriminated feature of the benefit of the audience in the Cartesian Theater—for there is no Cartesian Theater.

These spatially and temporally distributed content-fixations in the brain are precisely locatable in both space and time, but their onsets do not mark the onset of consciousness of their content. It is always an open question whether any particular content thus discriminated will eventually appear as an element in conscious experience, and it is a confusion, as we shall see, to ask *when it becomes conscious.* These distributed content-discriminations yield, over the course of time, something *rather like* a narrative stream or sequence, which can be thought of as subject to continual editing by many processes distributed around in the brain, and continuing indefinitely into the future. This stream of contents is only rather like a narrative because of its multiplicity; at any point in time there are multiple "drafts" of narrative fragments at various stages of editing in various places in the brain. (1991b, 113)

MDM explicitly denies spatiotemporal pinealism. However, it retains a Cartesian residue in the idea of an "observation" made by "a specialized, localized part of the brain." In another work, Dennett and Kinsbourne (1992, 234) are more explicit about this local "observation":

All the work that was dimly imagined to be done in the Cartesian Theater has to be done somewhere, and no doubt it is distributed around in the brain. This work is largely a matter of responding to the "given" by *taking* it—by responding to it with one interpretive judgment or another. . . . We suggest that the judgmental tasks are fragmented into many distributed moments of microtaking.

Dan Lloyd

Several early respondents to the Multiple Drafts model, myself included, worried that these distributed, yet discrete, microtakings had the effect of replacing the Cartesian Theater with the Cartesian cineplex, a profusion of minicinemas featuring arty films like "I am curious—Yellow" in cine V4, or "North by Northwest" in cine V5 (see the commentaries following Dennett and Kinsbourne 1992). Dennett and Kinsbourne immediately rejected the metaphorical implication that little homunculi took in these shows, but the minicinema objection also highlighted a different problem: If each microtaking is a discrete, determinate neural event, and consciousness was an organized symphony of microtakings, then it might have quite determinate spatial and temporal boundaries after all. Even though there would be no one stream of consciousness, no cardinal microtakings, there would still be a time and place when a content would dribble into the watershed of consciousness. To further complicate things, just about everyone (except me) wanted to insist that many microtakings were unconscious (or preconscious), saddling Dennett and Kinsbourne with the chore of distinguishing when the microtakings emerged from prehistory into consciousness proper. Very theatrical, very Cartesian (Lloyd 1992).

Dennett and Kinsbourne responded to this worry in the midst of a summary of their overall position:

> The creation of conscious experience is not a batch process but a continuous one. The microtakings have to interact. A microtaking, as a sort of judgment or decision, cannot just be inscribed in the brain in isolation; it has to have its consequences—for guiding action and modulating further microjudgments made "in its light," creating larger fragments of what we called narrative. . . . This interaction of microtakings, however it is accomplished in particular cases, has the effect that a modicum of coherence is maintained, with discrepant elements dropping out of contention, and without the assistance of a Master Judge. Because there is no Master Judge, there is no further process of being-appreciated-in-consciousness, so the question of exactly when a particular element was consciously (as opposed to unconsciously) taken admits no nonarbitrary answer. (1992, 235)

The last sentence deploys one of Dennett's sharper razors (3D in the toolbox list). Sharper than intended: If indeed we want to eschew arbitrary boundaries, the cheerful posit of internal "microtakings" is in exactly the same Dennettian hot water. Let's turn up the magnification just a bit. To microtake or simply to judge is, we are told, the job of a specialized part of the brain. For example, in area V4, say, we get the microjudgment we could roughly label "Yellow ho!" Now, does that judgment form just when the V4 yellow neurons fire? How many neurons? Must the spike be fully formed and moving down the axon? But why not consider the microtaking to begin with the presynaptic surge of neurotransmitters that is sufficient to generate the spike train? And why not extend it to all the downstream/ inboard effects of yellow-detection, right on out to the motor response? To insist that any of these questions has a determinate answer is to seek a place "where it all comes together" for the microtaking. It's just like—let's see—the British Empire learning of the end of the War of 1812 (1991b, 146f.). As a distributed entity, the Empire's recognition of world events cannot be precisely dated. But everything material is extended, and no mechanical process is instantaneous. This is true "all the way down." Is an ion channel officially open when its proteins flex, or when the first ion enters, or when it leaves? As for the British Empire, so for this microsystem. Just as there is no nonarbitrary, privileged seat of consciousness overall, when we look more closely, there is no nonarbitrary, privileged seat of the microtakings from which consciousness is built.

But these microtakings are representations, content-bearers, the foundation of cognition; their existence is the central assumption of cognitive science. If they lack identity conditions, then there's trouble ahead. I will hazard two bold generalizations. The first is philosophical: The panoply of antirealist intuition pumps, examples, and arguments deployed against the Cartesian theater and against a host of intentional entities (especially belief) will also afflict the concept of representation overall, whether applied at the micro- or macro scale. The intentional stance might as well be called the representational stance.

Second, we are beginning to see that the empirical project of isolating microtakings—the component tasks of complex behavior—and localizing them in discrete regions of the brain is breaking down.

On this second point, we may make a case study of the current state of the art in functional brain imagery, particularly Positron

Table 9.1

Tabulation of 35 PET experiments (rows) × 38 Brodmann Areas (columns). Significant activation in a Brodmann Area is indicated by "1." Experiments are encoded in three parts: stimulus;task;response. Experiments without stimuli lead with ellipses. Experiments without responses conclude with ellipses. For details, see references.

Stimulus:task:response\B Area	1	2	3	4	5	6	7	8	9	10	11	13	14	17	18	19	20	21	22	24	25	30	31	32	33	35	36	37	38	39	40	41	42	43	44	45	46	47	sum	Reference
...Anxiety...																																							1	(Reiman, 1998)
...Movearm						1																																	2	(Jenkins et al., 1993)
...MoveFingers				1		1			1																														7	(Wessel et al., 1995)
...MoveFingers(0)	1	1	1	1	1	1	1																																6	(Seitz & Roland, 1992)
...Recall15words:speak																	1							1		1	1												4	(Grasby et al., 1993)
...Recall5words:speak																							1			1													5	(Grasby et al., 1993)
...Rigidarm							1			1	1									1				1															3	(Jenkins et al., 1993)
...Sadmemory...											1																											1	4	(Pardo et al., 1993)
...tell"C"words						1			1															1											1			1	3	(Andreasen, 1998)
...tell-memory					1				1															1														1	10	(Andreasen, 1998)
Aud-nouns:silentverbs						1						1					1	1	1									1							1	1			10	(Weiller et al., 1995)
Aud-psuedowords:silentrpt						1						1					1	1	1									1							1	1		1	3	(Weiller et al., 1995)
Aud-tone:liftfings						1						1							1					1				1											8	(Jueptner M, 1998)
Aud-words:saywrongword						1						1							1																			1	5	(Paus et al., 1998)
Aud...RLhandflex	1	1		1	1	1	1																																4	(Fox et al., 1985)
Aud...saccade		1			1	1	1																																2	(Fox et al., 1985)
Aud...saccade		1		1	1	1	1																																2	(Fox et al., 1985)
T:exploreR:Rhandflex		1		1	1	1	1					1																			1								11	(Seitz et al., 1991)
Thand:lifttouchedfinger		1			1	1	1																								1								6	(Paus et al., 1998)
THand:Movefinger-antistim		1			1	1																							1		1								7	(Paus et al., 1998)
Titch-arm...		1				1	1					1							1												1				1	1	1		15	(Hsieh, 1998)
TLhand...		1				1																																	3	(Tempel, 1998)
TLhand...		1				1																									1								3	(Bottini et al., 1995)
Tlips...	1			1		1																											1						4	(Fox et al., 1987)
TLtoe:count...		1		1		1								1	1	1																		1					10	(Jenkins et al., 1993)
TRhand...	1	1		1		1																																	3	(Tempel, 1998)
TRLhand...	1	1	1			1																																	3	(Fox et al., 1987)
TRtoe:count...				1		1															1		1																8	(Pardo et al., 1991)
Ttoe...	1		1			1																																1	3	(Fox et al., 1987)
Vis-words:readaloud	1		1			1					1			1	1				1									1											13	(Fox et al., 1996)

Vis/aud-words:readunison	.	.	1	1	.	1	.	.	.	.	.	1	.	1	1	1	.	.	1	1	.	1	1	.	.	.	.	1	1	.	.	1	1	1	.	.	.	.	16 (Fox et al., 1996)
Vis/Aud...saccade	.	.	.	1	.	1	.	.	.	.	.	.	.	1	.	.	.	.	.	.	.	.	.	.	.	.	.	.	.	.	.	.	.	.	.	.	.	.	3 (Fox et al., 1985)
Vis:attend...	.	.	.	.	.	1	1	.	1	.	.	.	.	.	1	1	.	.	.	.	.	1	.	.	.	.	.	.	.	.	1	.	.	.	.	.	.	.	7 (Pardo et al., 1991)
Vis:saccade-antistim	.	.	.	.	.	1	1	.	.	.	.	.	.	1	1	1	.	.	1	.	.	1	.	1	.	.	.	1	.	.	.	.	1	.	.	.	.	.	10 (Paus et al., 1998)
Vis:saccade-to-stim	.	.	.	1	.	1	1	.	.	.	.	.	.	1	1	1	.	.	.	.	.	.	.	.	.	.	.	.	.	.	.	.	.	.	.	.	.	.	6 (Paus et al., 1998)
5.526315789	3	3	9	15	1	26	7	4	6	3	1	9	1	6	7	7	3	6	12	10	1	4	4	8	2	1	2	3	5	1	7	6	6	3	4	2	3	9	
tasks/BA (mean)																																							
4.757564913																																							
st. deviation																																							
6																																							
BAs/task (mean)																																							

Emission Tomography (PET). The avowed goal of this highly successful research program is the isolation of component tasks of complex cognition, and PET experimental design and interpretation all contribute to this end. Over the last few years, the results of hundreds of experiments have been archived in a database known as Brainmap (ric.uthscsa.edu/projects/brainmap.html). One can ask of each function, each "microtaking," chosen for study, whether it indeed is isolated in a specific component of the brain. To begin with some overview, Brainmap archives 733 distinct experiments (PET, MRI, and EEG), with a total count of local maxima of activation of 7508. That is a mean of 10.24 activation peaks per experiment. It is a rare experiment where all these peaks are located in a single region, suggesting distribution of function. But this in itself is not definitive, since the average experiment might just as well be picking out a dedicated subnetwork of 10 (plus or minus) components. A dedicated processor need not be packed into a single anatomical box.

A more decisive analysis would work through a list of components, asking of each whether it is a locus of activation for specific functions. Perhaps the narrowest anatomical specification of the brain accessible to PET discrimination is the cortical Brodmann area. Brodmann areas are distinct both in their geography and in their cytoarchitecture, two factors that indicated to Brodmann and generations to follow that each of these numbered areas was functionally distinct. Well, are they? As part of a larger project I have tabulated all of the reported areas of activation in thirty-five PET experiments. Thirty-eight Brodmann areas are involved. Table 9.1 compiles the result.

The table shows that each Brodmann area is involved in an average of five tasks out of the thirty-five shown, or 14% of tasks. If all the experiments engaging a particular Brodmann area probed the same function, this observation would be compatible with isolating cognitive specialists, but inspection of table 9.1 reveals that this is not the case. A few areas seem so far to be specialized, but the majority of them light up in scan after scan, and during very different cognitive tasks. Meanwhile, the "specialists" (areas that activate for just one function) are not themselves the sole loci of their dedicated functions. Each specialized area is one part of a pattern involving, on average, nine other activated areas.

The case for distribution suggested by table 9.1 is even stronger if one factors in the many steps of PET study design that favor localist interpretation, the assignment of "microtakings" to regions of the brain. Foremost among these interpretive filters is the "subtraction method." Each image is in fact a difference image, the result of a subtraction of a control condition from a test condition. Often the controls are components of the task. For example, to locate semantic processing the experimenters might use a control scan of subjects reading pseudowords, to isolate just the distinctive components of the task in question. Even after this selective prescreening of the data, however, the table shows distinct multifunctionality for most of the areas. Last but not least, the experiments indexed here are but a tiny slice of all the potential functions of the mind.

Getting (Phenomenally) Real

In homage to Professor Dennett I have turned his razors against the revered foundation of cognitive science, representation, suggesting that it is a Cartesian legacy founded in Descartes's deepity and vulnerable to Dennettian intuition pumps. From the toolbox, I have used a Dennettian analogy between the big fish of intentionality, conscious states, and the small fry, Dennett's "microtakings" (strategy 3B, above); a slippery slope argument about the boundaries of even the tiniest representational state (3D); and an empirical challenge (3E). But it is also in the spirit of Dennett to pick up the pieces, surveying the prospects and future of the field, and from there forge a new worldview (as is often the burden of the intuition pumps, 3A).

How could we even imagine a postcognitive postrepresentational view of the mind or brain? How can we have thoughts without a thought balloon to contain them? Toward this end, I'd like to replace the thought balloon with a trial balloon, a tentative effort to continue along the path Dennett has hewn. How do we turn from Descartes *all the way*? This is what we must abandon, somehow: On the one hand, the world at large is described by science, and concerning it (brains included) we are realists. On the other hand, conscious experience is described by phenomenology, to which is traditionally assigned nasty properties like idiosyncrasy and inescapable subjectivity. The entities of phenomenology do not match the entities of science, and as a result it is common to suppose that "phenomena" are somehow inside our heads. So our scientific realism is married to "phenomenological phenomenalism." As such, we suppose that any examination of phenomenological entities is a special exercise in introspection. However, this inward turn mistakes a fundamental fact about experience (and its phenomenological description), namely, that its domain is also the world, that same real world that science images. Phenomenology simply describes it in very different terms, subject to different epistemic standards. Descartes's legacy emerges primarily in the inward turn for phenomenology (reified, by the way, in the Cartesian Theater) and secondarily in the failure to reconcile phenomenal language with scientific realism. (The impulse to discard either science or phenomenology is accordingly a "reactive Cartesianism," no less presupposing Cartesian metatheory than dualism.) We need, therefore, a more inclusive ontology, which somehow accords equal standing to both electrons and thoughts. I will call this as-yet-undefined ontology *phenomenal realism* (PR).

It's going to be a brain-bender, so in the best Dennettian tradition we must begin with an intuition pump. After scouring the history of modern philosophy, one comes across the following example:

[W]e are shown some alien or antique gadget and asked: what is it for? Is it a needle-making machine or a device for measuring the height of distant objects or a weapon? What can we learn from studying the object? We can determine how the parts mesh, what happens under various conditions, and so forth. We can also look for telltale scars and dents, wear and tear. Once we have compiled these facts we try to imagine a setting in which given these facts it would *excellently* perform some imaginably useful function. If the object would be an equally good sail mender or cherry pitter we won't be able to tell what it *really* is—what it is *for*—without learning where it came from, who made it, and why. Those facts could have vanished without a trace. Such an object's true identity, or essence, could then be utterly undeterminable by us, no matter how assiduously we studied the object.

The author of the passage is Dennett, of course (1987, 155). His purpose here is to get "beyond belief" via the construct of the "notional world," the hypothetical context to which the mystery gizmo would be best suited. Notional worlds (and notional attitudes) were offered as an analysis of "narrow content." That is, notional attitudes offered the richness of real semantics, real meaning, but presupposed no links to the world. Psychology enriched with notional worlds could proceed with its inboard descriptions and laws defined just over mental or neural kinds.

Return to the object that would be an equally good sail mender or cherry pitter, and suppose now we find it in the company of cherries. Cherries and the object pair up in this context, in a special way, expressed in a simple counterfactual: Had cherries been different in some respects—bigger, tougher, cubical—the object, the cherry pitter, would have been different. We can, accordingly, speak of a "functional complex": the cherry pitter *and* the cherries. Though both pitter and cherries are separate entities, the idea of the functional complex underlines a dense network of causal and counterfactual relations between the two. For one to predict the fate of either the cherries or the pitters, their participation in their functional complex is relevant. Moreover, properties emergent from the functional complex may be referred to its components: In a world of pitters, cherries have the property of being pittable. And, among cherries, pitters exhibit the capacity to pit. (Among sails, they exhibit the capacity to mend.)

The idea of functional complexes, exotic as it is, is simply illustrative. We are concerned to dissolve the Cartesian mind-world divide, and to that end let us ponder *phenomenal complexes,* the basic entities of phenomenal realism. In deference to another famous philosopher, the argument for phenomenal realism will be transcendental. That is, it develops from the premise that phenomenal properties are worldly, and asks, what must their ontology be, in order to found this worldliness? We approach via several successive transcendental approximations.

Level the Playing Field

The "realism" of phenomenal realism and scientific realism must be the same realism. Phenomenal properties (P properties) must meet the standards for reality applied to scientific properties (S properties). But how can this be? S properties are the good old primary qualities, defined in part by their existence independent of observers. A rock has mass regardless of who, if anyone, notices. But P properties do not exist in the absence of observers. Hot sauce is hot only if there is some observer to whom its spiciness is noticeable. Does observer-dependence impugn the reality of P properties? It depends on the dependency. If the observation is sufficient for the reality of the P property, then illusory and hallucinatory properties join the real; no ontology can tolerate *that*. On the other hand, if observer-dependence is merely *necessary* for P property realization, there is no problem insofar as *everything* has necessary conditions. What, then, will be necessary *and* sufficient for P property realization? The first approximate answer is simply that P properties are complexes, somehow incorporating both the object exhibiting the P property and the (potential) observer of that property. The whole complex, then, is real in the ordinary sturdy sense.

Real observers and a real object of observation together compose a phenomenal complex. But must the observer really observe and must the object really be observed? It seems to me that the spiciness of hot sauce is a disposition, and as such it need not be manifest in particular observation. That means that as long as there is at least one observer, somewhere, to whom the hot sauce would be hot, then the sauce itself has the P property—even if that observer is forever light years away. (This is analogous to the cherries having the property of being pittable. Only in worlds with cherry pitters of some sort can cherries be pitted. But a pittable cherry need not be pitted.) This further entails that there are many P properties as yet unknown. These would be properties we could notice, should they cross our sensory path. Or, they could be properties noticeable to other sorts of observers—martians who sense gamma rays, for example.

Nonetheless it often happens, as a contingent fact, that P properties *are* observed. We do notice them; and here too the analogy with S properties is exact. Both kinds of properties *can be noticed*. Both often are noticed. But neither must be noticed. There are, therefore, *two* roles for the observer to play in the ontology of P properties. First, essentially, an observer with the capacity to observe the

P property must exist. Second, contingently, it may happen that an observer really does observe a P property, just as it may happen that an observer really does observe an S property. The deepity is the conflation of the essential condition, the capacity, with the contingent realization of the capacity. The confusion arises naturally because it is the experience—the realization or actualization of the capacity—that we are most interested in. (What is it like to be a bat? versus, What sorts of properties might a bat be able to notice, if there were bats?)

So far, the leveling of the playing field between S properties and P properties has exactly paralleled Dennett's treatment of qualia in *Consciousness Explained* (CE) and elsewhere (especially 1988). In CE, he begins with the observation that colors are in no way the intrinsic, unitary properties of objects that they seem to be, but "in reality" are both relational and disjunctive. But he initially resists (as have I) the impulse to reel these unruly secondary properties into the mind. Instead, he explains how it came to be that sensory systems could ever develop an interest in "gerrymandered" properties like color. The answer, suggested to him by Akins (1989), is that many species have coevolved mutually advantageous relations of color display and color detection. Although it is not clear whether an evolutionary story is an essential condition for the existence of phenomenal property types, the main tenet of Dennett's doctrine of qualia grants the reality of gerrymandered qualitative properties, as in phenomenal realism. That is, P properties are dispositional properties of the world that are present when there are potential observers (somewhere, as opposed to observer-dependent properties that presuppose actual observation).[2] An emerald can be green despite being forever buried two miles deep; but it can be owned only if someone actively instantiates the appropriate economic relations toward the gem itself.

Dennett summarizes, with reference to "Otto," his fictional qualophiliac antagonist:

What property does Otto judge something to have when he judges it to be pink? The property he calls pink. And what property is that? It's hard to say, but this should not embarrass us, because we can say why it's hard to say. . . . If someone wants a more informative story about those properties,

Dan Lloyd

there is a large and rather incompressible literature in biology, neuroscience, and psychophysics to consult. And Otto can't say anything more about the property he calls pink by saying "It's *this!*" (taking himself to be pointing "inside" at a private, phenomenal property of his experience). All that move accomplishes (at best) is to point to his own idiosyncratic color-discrimination state. . . . Otto points to his discrimination-device, perhaps, but not to any quale that is exuded by it, or worn by it, or rendered by it, when it does its work. There are no such things. (1991b, 382–383)

Dennett here resists the Lockean shuffle from P properties in the world to P properties in the head. However, just five pages after this congenial statement, Otto's inward turn prevails, and qualia move back inside:

When you say, "*This* is my quale," what you are singling out, or referring to, *whether you realize it or not,* is your idiosyncratic complex of dispositions. . . . That "quale" of yours is a character in good standing in the fictional world of your heterophenomenology, but what it turns out to be in the *real* world in your brain is just a complex of dispositions. (1991b, 389)

With the promotion of qualia from "no such thing" to an inboard something (a complex of dispositions), trouble follows. For example, consider the familiar phi phenomenon.

If a little red light is flashed on a screen in front of you, and then another little red light is flashed on the screen slightly to one side or the other, you will see what appears to be a single moving spot of red light. (Dennett 1996, 11)

In several works, Dennett has developed the case of "color phi," the effect of changing the color of the second light. In that case, one sees the phenomenally moving spot change color in mid-trajectory, at a point that has never been occupied by any stimulus. So we have, in the world, two discrete lights in different locations, one red and one green, flashing in succession. And "in the mind" we have a percept of a red light that moves and changes to green as it shifts. The intermediate loci of the moving light, regardless of color, are all illusory. What is happening? Consistent with his other reconstructions of the path to consciousness, Dennett sets the problem as follows:

Your brain cannot create the content of a mid-trajectory color change . . . until it has received and analyzed the second stimulus. . . . It has to "know" that there's a second light, and it has to know where it is and what color it is, before it can start creating the illusion that we observe in this case. (1996, 11)

Scientific realism offers us two events, red-light-at-location-*L1*-at-time-*t1* and green-light-at-*L2*-at-*t2*. Both must have some effect on the observer's brain. But it requires a special assumption to conclude that each event in the world gives rise to a *corresponding* event in the brain—that there is a specific brain-event that is the microtaking with the content "green light" and that it is taken in every case where a green light is detected. Dennett's discussion admits only the "official" stimuli (denizens of science) into the outbound description of the case. What is seen therefore must be composed of internal states, illusory seemings. It is as if the S properties preempt the P properties. In Dennett's interpretation of color phi, the S properties determine a set of S representations, and the P properties are woven around them.

Phenomenal realism, in contrast, would begin with a phenomenal complex consisting of a light (red or green) and the perceiver's brain state, noting that *there is no registration of green flashes as such,* or simpliciter. That is, a green flash following a red flash gives rise to a different phenomenal complex than a green flash alone, owing to the fact that the initial red flash has specific effects on the observer, and those effects alter the effect of the green flash. Specifically, the observer in the color phi experiment "registers" both the red and green stimuli as a single stimulus, a moving light that changes color in mid-trajectory. The appropriate comparison case in PR is one in which the stimulus is a *genuinely* moving light that changes color in mid-trajectory. The observer would form exactly the same percept following this stimulus as in the illusory, color phi condition. From the point of view of PR, the two indiscernible stimuli both exhibit the same phenomenal property, in spite of their (scientifically) real difference. This phenomenal conflation is the breakout from the Cartesian representationalist scenario: Under PR, *there is no color phi illusion.* That is, there is no inner shadow (of a moving color-changing spot) to be contrasted with the outer "reality." Instead, there is a disjunction of outboard conditions that is accurately (but ambiguously) observed. In discussing another example, Dennett makes what I regard as exactly the right observation:

> The difference between the written words "boat" and "coat" is nothing other than the occurrence of "b" at the head of one and "c" at the head of the other, but it does not follow that particular acts of visual recognition of either word consist of independent acts of "b"-recognition and "c"-recognition and so forth. Often it is only the wider context that permits a perceiver to recognize a dimly or distantly seen word as "boat," *which then enables* the perception of the left-most element *as* a "b," something otherwise quite beyond the perceptual capacity of the recognizer. It is even possible for there to be a "boat"-recognizer who hasn't a clue about—and cannot recognize—the individual letters that are the definitive elements of "boat." (1993, 214)

In short, contextual and global features are often detected prior to components, a point with a distinguished history in phenomenology (especially Merleau-Ponty) and gestalt psychology, and recently celebrated in many connectionist models. Why was the alternate reading not brought to bear on color phi? I suspect it reflects the Cartesian tendency to regard perception as an atemporal yoking of stimulus and inner registration. The fact that there is a color phi effect in itself demonstrates that temporal context changes occurrent perception.

As it might be in the perception of motion, so also in many other phenomenally real cases. For example, a cherry can enter into a phenomenal complex as I notice it. That complex consists of the cherry *and* the inflections of the state of my brain that depend on the cherry. Phenomenal complexes are clearly personal and changeable, owing to the Heraclitean brainstorm of neural inflection. They can be changed at will, by simply attending to other aspects and relations within the phenomenal field. It is natural to try to extract stable elements from phenomenal complexes. The standard method is to develop special new properties that are relatively invariant across observers and times of observation. These are the variables and measurements of science. In other words, scientific realism is a special case of phenomenal realism. In the limiting case, science discovers common factors at the objective pole, enabling one to ignore the subjective pole.

To wrap up the first approximation, note that to see a P property *as a P property*, a higher-order observer must notice the entire phenomenal complex, both the sauce and the taster to whom the sauce would be hot. This will be a complicated epistemic undertaking. In short, the first-order observer experiences the world; the second-order observer experiences a phenomenal world, which he or she can distinguish from the scientific world. Both kinds of observation might occur in a single observer, at different times. Nonetheless, we must carefully distinguish these two forms of experience.

On to the second approximation.

Observers Are Brains

"Observation" and "observers" cannot be reassuring to a recovering Cartesian. The next approximation is to put material brains in for the very vague "observers." This approximation of PR thus holds that P properties are properties that are detectable by brains. So also S properties, although the detection might well be mediated by inference or instrument. Because the brain is itself so complex, the inflection appended to the cherry can be nuanced and detailed. It can embrace everything from my awareness of the cherry's color to my remembrance of cherries past, their similarities and differences, the role of cherries in literature, their role in exciting a food allergy, and so on. Each of these, I would argue, is an inflection in the occurrent experience of particular cherries, as opposed to a distinct further thought. Each is a phenomenal, albeit nonsensory, halo that alters the cherries in our experience. But the halo is real: Connectionists have shown that distributed representations are capable of encoding all these cherry nuances and cherry contexts. The halo of inflection I just described is implemented in a distributed neural representation. It is a real component of the phenomenal complex that binds the cherry to the cherry experience as a single complex entity (Lloyd 1995; 1996).

But the wonderful brain is just a place-holder for undeciphered complexity. Because we have not yet said what it is about the brain that makes it an observer, the door is not yet closed on representational models of consciousness. We have still not cut the Cartesian umbilical cord. On to the third approximation.

Brains Are Detectors

The fundamental divide between S properties and P properties concerns the independence of S properties. Since no event is either uncaused or without consequence, this is a special sense of independence. I suggest that the most minimal sense of independence enjoyed by S properties is that they can exist *undetected*. This means not just that they happen to escape detection (which is also true for P properties) but that they can exist happily in a universe where no appropriate detector exists. That suggests, in turn, that the minimal condition for expelling a property from the paradise of scientific realism is its dependence on a detector.

What might a detector-dependent property be? Let us look again at the simpler S properties. An S property, as part of the map of the scientific image of reality, owes its robust reality to its place in the system of regularities that could be described (but not created) by scientific theory. Its role in the lawful description of nature explains why it need not be paired with a detector to be real—it already has real work to do, regardless of whether notice accrues to the work. (Its straight-ahead engagement in the causal fray is also what makes it so detectable.) A P property, in contrast, does not have a role in the lawful description of reality, *except* insofar as it is detected. A P property might, for example, be a complex disjunction of S properties. Without a detector to make something of it, the disjunction, although each disjunct is perfectly real, does not find expression in any law of nature or scientific theory. The detector changes that, because the event of detection (the change of state of the detector itself) *is* a unitary event and as a result specific lawlike regularities may radiate from there. Detection, in other words, gathers up the disjuncts and makes something of them. But without a detector, there is no gathering up, no bundling of the disjuncts, no property, no "there" there. The kinds of detectors that resonate to P properties, accordingly, are more complex than S detectors, since the properties they detect are complexes. And, as in the earlier approximations, once the world has a P detector in it, the P property can be harnessed. Then, once the detector and the detectee both exist, the phenomenal property exists too.

The idea of detectors and detection, in short, preserves the core intuitions of phenomenal realism: P and S properties are both real, but S properties can endure in worlds without detectors specific to them, whereas P properties cannot. P properties are constituted by devices that detect them (even though those devices might never see action).

Detection Is Not Representation

But what is detection? In "Real Patterns," Dennett invokes a mathematical conception of randomness and its complement, pattern:

A series (of dots or numbers or whatever) is random if and only if the information required to describe (transmit) the series accurately is *incompressible:* nothing shorter than the verbatim bit map will preserve the series. . . . A pattern exists in some data—is real—if *there is* a description of the data that is more efficient than the bit map, whether or not anyone can concoct it. (1991a, 32, 34)

This information-based sense of pattern is appealing if one wants to naturalize representation (as in Ross, this volume; Dretske 1981; Lloyd 1989). The natural representation of a pattern is its compressed description—the description encodes the pattern. But is it the job of detectors to *encode* the stimulus they detect? We, with our view from above, can see the coding relation, but the detector cannot. From the detector's point of view, something happens, and the detector is blind to any "meaning" or "reference" in its state change beyond the brute fact of being in a new state. In particular, nothing about the state change of the detector necessarily indicates the type of property it has detected, P or S. This is true regardless of the complexity of the detector's own state. (It may even be that the detector state in some way resembles a world-state. But that resemblance does no work. That is, the detector will bring about whatever it brings about regardless of whether we interpreters see a resemblance to something else.)

Furthermore, there is no guarantee that the gerrymandered P property supports a compressed representation. That is, it could be random. In that case, a detector would be a template for the random pattern. Still, it detects. Thus, compressed description cannot be an essential condition for detection. In short, we should resist the temptation to say that the detector encodes the stimulus it detects.

These claims greatly enlarge the class of detectors, especially detectors of P properties. The broken glass on the sidewalk, for example, could arise via a disjoint set of possible causes, any one of which may have been the real cause. That disjoint set of causal conditions thus becomes a P property. But, appearances notwithstanding, this is a welcome result. Recall that the stripped-down detectors described here may signal the presence of a P property to us, but that interpretation is lost on the detector itself. To detect a P property *as a P property* requires detection of an entire phenomenal complex. That is, to see the bottle as an indicator of its possible causal conditions requires an explicit apprehension of at least some of those causal conditions. That, however, is just what the phenomenology of the case suggests: The broken glass, and every other object in the world, is shadowed by a story. In the act of seeing we read that story, with all its ambiguities and ellipses. An important part of the constitution of phenomenal objects is exactly their open-ended origins and uncertain destinies. Our awareness of these aspects of objects and events, although it is not sensory awareness, is distinctly part of our ongoing experience of the world.

Is That All There Is?

Since the phenomenal complex is two components, and since both must be real for the P property to exist, to perceive a P property *as* a P property demands the detection of the whole complex by a "meta-detector." As a small consolation to the Cartesian, consider the continuum of P property meta-detectors, lest we underestimate their formidable cognitive and pragmatic abilities. These are no mere thermostats. To do their job, they must not only be accurate but thorough, because to ascertain the existence of a P property one must search hither and yon for its appropriate detector (since the mere existence of that detector suffices to constitute the P property). In a very simple world, consisting, say, of two keys and two locks, such a search might be quite mechanical (although even here a real detector will have to solve most of the hardest questions posed in AI to do its job). But in our world of infinite joints and vast search spaces, the establishment that some property is a P property depends on a massive background of implicit know-how, aided by myriad heuristics. You'd have to have a big brain to pull it off. The bigger the brain, the harder to deny it consciousness.

The meta-detector detects P properties, and distinguishes them from S properties. But does it experience P properties? Or is there some missing link, some extra quintessence that must be superadded to boost our clever detector into the realm of "real" consciousness? In these questions, as in the last reel of a B movie, Descartes rises from his crypt and walks the earth—as a cryptocartesian, if you will. The cryptocartesian is advancing two claims. First, he is claiming that the phenomenal realist has "left something out" of the ontology of consciousness. And that something is *inside,* not outside the mind/ brain. It is a Cartesian worry because it reintroduces exactly the interiority that PR has labored mightily to dissolve. But so be it. Let the cryptocartesian have his way, and join in the search for something special on the "detector side" of the ontology of mind. We'll call this the "detectors-plus" view, or D+ (not to be confused with the grade I might give this move in a term paper). What then can we say about the hypothetical plus-stuff that distinguishes real experience from mere detection? Can the plus-stuff be detected? No, say the cryptocartesians: Plus-stuff need have no observable effects— and thereby the cryptocartesians create an unlikely league of allies, the zombies.

We turn instead to the causal antecedents of plus-states or "experiences." The cryptos *could* claim that plus-states are sui generis, utterly disconnected from any detectable properties, but this would be a weird claim to make. Surely everyone must grant that experience, for all its magic, must somehow fit with some aspects of the observed or detected world. So, whatever lends the plus to D+ must itself correlate with some other property. And everyone also agrees that this property is material.

With this concession, the cryptos yield a critical toehold. For now there is a distinction between a D+ experiencer and a mere detector that can be expressed in terms of a property the D+ device is sensitive to. This is tantamount to enlarging the sphere of properties for the detector to detect. D+ turns out to be a detector after all—at least part of the distinction is in the complexity of the properties it can detect.

The argument from here is inductive. *Every* time the cryptocartesian insists that something is missing, the phenomenal realist can answer by translating the interior, Cartesian position into a realist analogue involving a new detectable property. That property can be phenomenal, in the sense discussed above.

This brings us to the second part of the crypto's claim. These Cartesians not only point to something left out, the plus-stuff, but also make the claim that a materialist theory of consciousness cannot account for this residue. Phenomenal realism accounts for the reality of phenomenal properties, and explains how minds/brains/detectors could be sensitive to phenomenal properties as well as scientific properties. A detector is a functional type, however, so its full explanation would also account for its implementation. Here we drop down to level of structure and material. But this is exactly what good old scientific explanation handles best. In short, PR rebuts the deepity that materialist theories of consciousness "leave out the phenomenal." PR embraces the phenomenal in the only sense a realism could, by reconstruing it as a complex of properties that can be detected by highly specialized devices. PR tells us what these phenomenal detectors have to be able to do, and it expands easily to accommodate the most elaborate demands of the cryptocartesian. Scientific realism handles the rest, the implementation-level description of the phenomenal detectors. The cryptos can offer only two kinds of "something else," a missing phenomenal property or an intrinsic state of the conscious system, and the dynamic merger of phenomenal realism and scientific realism is prepared for either one.

But why carve nature at *these* joints? With the phenomenal complex bundled in this way, there is no additional need to *refer* or *project* the brain-based inflections *onto the world*. That reference or projection is superfluous, a *Cartesian* extravagance. Thus ends the thought balloon. But it is not the end of thoughts. Rather, the human world is reconceived as a *thoughtful world,* in which brains and other entities engage in a fabulous ongoing dance.

Non Sunt Multiplicandi Mundi Praeter Necessitatum

To summarize: Cartesianism split the world in two, creating an inboard model of an outside world. Ever since Descartes, science and philosophy have preserved this fundamental divide. One of Daniel Dennett's enormous contributions to philosophy has been his agile skepticism toward all the shoots and tendrils of the Cartesian mind-world picture. The endless creativity of his persuasions intimates the resolution of the Cartesian rift, and has offered me the incentive to take Dennett to the limit, scuttling even the concept of representation.

If you really want *consciousness* explained, *mental content* is the wrong place to look. Phenomenal realism dumps *all* of the contents of consciousness into the world. Not into an "outer" world, nor into an "inner" one. Just into the one world, in which the brain is just one entity among others. The brain is special only by virtue of the subtlety and idiosyncrasy of its spatiotemporal integrations. To sort the world into S and P properties is subtle indeed, and it takes a big brain to handle the huge set of stimulus energies our sensory neurons transduce.

With content in sight and out of mind, what remains of consciousness itself is simply the complex pattern of neural activity, ever shifting according to its own dynamics and the pushes and pulls of the proximal environment. Our state of mind is simply what we are (or, more precisely, what our brains are). Dennett is right to banish qualia, and should likewise purge "microtakings" and "drafts" and every other intentional or representation item as well from the account of consciousness.[3] But at the same time the world of phenomenal realism is far more lush than the world of science. (The phenomenal realist, accordingly, welcomes Ross's Rainforest Realism, this volume.) This tradeoff could finally cure the hangover from Descartes's deepity.

But backsliding is a continual risk. I'll conclude by offering dual substance abusers—and who among us is really immune?—a five-step program:

1. Renounce dual substance abuse. Instead, acknowledge the higher explanatory power of monism.
2. Renounce Cartesian materialism: first, by acknowledging that it is indeed Cartesian.
3. Renounce pinealism (Cartesian theatricality). Instead, distributed representation.
4. Renounce micropinealism (the Cartesian cineplex). Instead, indeterminate microtakings.
5. Renounce representationalism in all its forms. Instead, phenomenal realism.

Dennett's philosophy elegantly moves us through the first four steps. Here, I've outlined a fifth, possibly final step. But really the essential commitment is in the first step. One must overcome the temptation of Cartesian duality, whether in its full-blown metaphysical form or in all of its stand-ins. One must keep one's gaze steadily on the one world, and resist the multiplication of worlds with the same zeal that one resists the multiplication of entities. As Occam might put it, in response to the Cartesian tradition, do not multiply worlds beyond necessity. There is one world—we live there, entirely within it. We create the problems of intentionality and consciousness at the moment we create an ersatz shadow world, the "mental model." Can we live without this crutch? We'll see, one day at a time.

Notes

1. Many thanks to Dan Dennett, Don Ross, Miller Brown, and Richard Lee for their insight and suggestions, and to Kate Weingartner for her help with the bibliography.

2. In a recent book, Jerry Fodor also comes close to endorsing PR (Fodor 1998, chapter 7), expressed through the example of the reality of doorknobs.

> Since there are minds, the ontological conditions that the mind-dependence of *doorknobhood* imposes on there being doorknobs are ipso facto satisfied. The

mind-dependence of *doorknobhood* is not an argument for there not being door-knobs. (1998, 148)

I agree with Fodor that mind-dependent properties are ontologically kosher. The goal here is to go beyond this allowance to an account of sufficient conditions for the reality of a phenomenal property. (A secondary goal is to discharge the "mind" from the account of the real, without lapsing into behaviorism. See below.)

3. Yet another close approach to phenomenal realism:

> Being "in consciousness" is more like being famous than like being on television, in at least the following regards. Television is a specific medium; fame isn't. The "time of transduction" can be very precise for television, but not for fame. Fame is a relative/competitive phenomenon; television isn't. (Some people can be famous only if others, who lose the competition, remain in oblivion.) And then consider the curious American institution, the Hall of Fame. There's a Baseball Hall of Fame, a Football Hall of Fame, and for all I know, a Candlepin Bowling Hall of Fame. But as many inductees into such edifices must have realized at the time, if you're already famous, then being inducted into the Hall of Fame is a mere formality, acknowledging the undeniable; and if you're not already famous, being inducted into a Hall of Fame doesn't really make you famous. No "quantum leap" or momentous transition in phase space or "catastrophe" occurs when you cross the finish line and enter the Fame module—unless of course that event is famous on its own hook, because of your own current fame or the current fame of the institution. (Dennett 1996)

That television is a representational medium suggests that, in contrast, fame might be a nonrepresentational process or phenomenon. One can take the metaphor in different ways, of course. It usefully directs attention away from individual microtakings—the perceptions of individual members of the public. It doesn't matter what individuals think of the Piltdown man or Eval Knievel, as long as they have *some* take on them. Nonetheless, the collective public apprehension of the famous person or event still seems to exhibit intentionality, and as such preserves that much at least of the Cartesian tradition.

References

Akins, K. (1989). *On Piranhas, Narcissism, and Mental Representation,* unpublished.

Andreasen, N. (1998). Remembering the past: Two facets of episodic memory explored with positron emission tomography. *American Journal of Psychiatry* 152: 1576–1585.

Baars, B. (1996). *In the Theater of Consciousness.* Oxford: Oxford University Press.

Bottini, G., Paulesu, E., Sterzi, R., Warburton, E., Wise, R., Vallar, G., Frackowiak, R., and Frith, C. (1995). Modulation of conscious experience by peripheral sensory stimuli. *Nature* 376: 778–881.

Dennett, D. (1987). Beyond Belief. In *The Intentional Stance.* Cambridge, Mass.: MIT Press. A Bradford Book.

Dennett, D. (1988). Quining Qualia. In *Consciousness in Contemporary Science*, A. Marcel and E. Bisiach (eds.). New York: Oxford University Press.

Dennett, D. (1991a). Real patterns. *Journal of Philosophy* 88: 27–51.

Dennett, D. (1991b). *Consciousness Explained*. Boston: Little, Brown.

Dennett, D. (1993). Back from the drawing board. In *Dennett and His Critics*, B. Dahlbom (ed.). Oxford, UK: Blackwell.

Dennett, D. (1996). Consciousness: More like fame than television (in German translation: *Bewusstsein hat mehr mit Ruhm als mit Fernsehen zu tun*). In *Die Technik auf dem Weg zur Seele*, C. Maar, E. Pöppel, and T. Christaller, Rowohlt (eds.).

Dennett, D., and Kinsbourne, M. (1992). Time and the observer: The where and when of consciousness in the brain. *Behavioral and Brain Sciences* 15: 183–248.

Dretske, F. (1981). *Knowledge and the Flow of Information*. Cambridge, Mass.: MIT Press. A Bradford Book.

Fodor, J. (1998). *Concepts: Where Cognitive Science Went Wrong*. Oxford: Oxford University Press.

Fox, P., Fox, J., Raichle, M., and Burde, R. (1985). The role of cerebral cortex in the generation of voluntary saccades: A positron emission tomographic study. *Journal of Neurophysiology* 54: 348–369.

Fox, P., Burton, H., and Raichle, M. (1987). Mapping human somatosensory cortex with positron emission tomography. *Journal of Neurosurgery* 67: 34–43.

Fox, P., Ingham, R., Ingham, J., Hirsch, T., Downs, J., Martin, C., Jerabek, P., Glass, T., and Lancaster, J. (1996). A PET study of the neural systems of stuttering. *Nature* 382: 158–162.

Grasby, P., Frith, C., Friston, K., Bench, C., Frackowiak, R., and Dolan, R. (1993). Functional mapping of brain areas implicated in auditory-verbal memory function. *Brain* 116: 1–20.

Haldane, E. and Ross, G., trans. (1969). *Philosophical Works of Descartes, Vol. 1*. Cambridge: Cambridge University Press.

Hsieh, J. (1998). Urge to scratch represented in the human cerebral cortex during itch. *Journal of Neurophysiology* 72: 3004–3008.

Jenkins, I., Bain, P., Colebatch, J., Thompson, P., Findley, L., Frackowiak, R., Marsden, C., and Brooks, D. (1993). A positron emission tomography study of essential tremor: Evidence for overactivity of cerebellar connections. *Annals of Neurology* 34: 82–90.

Jueptner, M. (1998). Localization of a cerebellar timing process using PET. *Neurology* 45: 1540–1545.

Lloyd, D. (1989). *Simple Minds*. Cambridge, Mass.: MIT Press. A Bradford Book.

199
Popping the Thought Balloon

Lloyd, D. (1992). Toward an identity theory of consciousness. *Behavioral and Brain Sciences* 15: 215–216.

Lloyd, D. (1995). Consciousness: A connectionist manifesto. *Minds and Machines* 5: 161–185.

Lloyd, D. (1996). Consciousness, connectionism, and cognitive neuroscience: A meeting of the minds. *Philosophical Psychology* 9: 61–81.

Pardo, J., Raichle, M., and Fox, P. (1991b). Localization of a human system for sustained attention by positron emission tomography. *Nature* 349: 61–63.

Pardo, J., Pardo, P., and Raichle, M. (1993). Neural correlates of self-induced dysphoria. *American Journal of Psychiatry* 150: 713–719.

Paus, T., Petrides, M., Evans, A., and Meyer, E. (1998). Role of the human anterior cingulate cortex in the control of oculomotor, manual and speech responses: A positron emission tomography study. *Journal of Neurophysiology* 70: 453–469.

Reiman, E. (1998). Neuroanatomical correlates of anticipatory anxiety. *Science* 243: 1071–1074.

Seitz, R., Roland, P., Bohm, C., Greitz, T., and Stone-Elander, S. (1991). Somatosensory discrimination of shape: Tactile exploration and cerebral activation. *European Journal of Neuroscience* 3: 481–492.

Seitz, R. and Roland, P. (1992). Learning of sequential finger movements in man: A combined kinematic and positron emission tomography (PET) study. *European Journal of Neuroscience* 4: 154–165.

Tempel, L. (1998). Abnormal cortical responses in patients with writer's cramp. *Neurology* 43: 2252–2257.

Weiller, C., Isensee, C., Rijntjes, M., Huber, W., Mueller, S., Bier, D., Dutschka, K., Woods, R., Noth, J., and Diener, H. (1995). Recovery from Wernicke's aphasia: A positron emission tomographic study. *Annals of Neurology* 37: 723–832.

Wessel, K., Zeffiro, T., Lou, J., Toro, C., and Hallett, M. (1995). Regional cerebral blood flow during a self-paced sequential finger opposition task in patients with cerebellar degeneration. *Brain* 118: 379–393.

10

Phenomenology and Heterophenomenology: Husserl and Dennett on Reality and Science

David L. Thompson

Introduction

Dennett's naturalistic philosophy of mind aims at a delicate mean between reductionism and eliminativism, on the one side, and dualism and mysterianism on the other. It is frequently assumed that Husserlian phenomenology should be lumped in with the latter camp; indeed Dennett himself seems to make this assumption. I think, however, that this assumption is only partly right. It is true that Husserl, unlike Dennett, is not a naturalist. Many themes in phenomenology are therefore not consonant with Dennett's project and it is not my intention either to reduce Dennett's work to Husserl's, or to judge Dennett from the standpoint of a "true believer" in phenomenology. In the end, my sympathies lie rather with Dennett's project of naturalizing consciousness. But, despite the provocatively named *Consciousness Explained* (Dennett 1991a), Dennett's proposal is still an unfinished project, and Husserl may be a useful ally in achieving the balance between greedy reductionism and dualism that the book aims at.

My aim in this paper is twofold: First I want to show that Dennett's heterophenomenology is more similar to traditional, Husserlian phenomenology than one might suspect. But this is not a fault; indeed my second aim is to suggest that even further incorporation of Husserlian concepts into Dennett's naturalism might help to resolve some problems in Dennett's account of consciousness. My comments are offered as friendly amendments to Dennett's project, though whether they ultimately support the main motion, naturalism, must be left to the reader's judgment.

First I will outline briefly Husserl's approach, focusing on three of his central concepts: the *epoché*, intentionality, and constitution. Then I will show where these concepts turn up in *Consciousness Explained* but lead to problems. I will indicate directions in which a more thoroughgoing application of phenomenological method has promise for resolving these difficulties.

Husserl

Husserl shares with Dennett a strong belief in science. He is not, however, willing to leave the belief on the level of faith, but wants to find a rigorous foundation for the certainty of science, and especially mathematics. He holds that natural, causal laws of psychology or neurophysiology could never account for the objectivity of logic or mathematics; yet he is also convinced that knowledge originates in subjective experience. The study of what is given to consciousness, that is, phenomenology, is therefore not a subjective, psychological introspection, but an attempt to understand the status of scientific reality and to justify scientific method. Husserl has the empiricist's faith that scientific objectivity, far from being incompatible with subjective experience, is somehow built upon it.[1] Where Dennett's *Consciousness Explained* studies consciousness for its own sake while taking science for granted, Husserl investigates consciousness in order to establish a solid foundation for science.

Husserl's investigation is articulated through three key concepts: *epoché*, intentionality, and constitution. I'll explain each in turn.

Epoché

The kingpin of the phenomenological method is the *epoché*. Husserl claims we should describe consciousness purely as we experience it without prejudging it from the standpoint of any philosophical doctrine, any scientific theory, or even our everyday faith that there are things in the world independent of our experience. To do otherwise would be to presuppose the validity of those theories for which we are attempting to find a foundation. We should take what we are conscious of at face value and not twist our experience into what we believe it should be.

To accomplish this unbiased description, the *epoché* must in particular suspend any reference to the causes of our experiences. If I experience a triangle and describe it as having three sides, the validity of this description is independent of whether the experience was caused by a triangle of marble in a physical world, by a sequence of neural firings in my brain, or even by a Platonic Form. What is experienced, the phenomenon, is what phenomenology sets out to describe.

Husserl's project requires therefore that he avoid taking for granted the laws of physics, the findings of neurophysiology, the theory of evolution, or any belief in the reality of electrons, neurons, or brain representations. Scientific realities are to be validated at the end of his project, not presupposed from the beginning.

Philosophical theories must also be suspended. The Cartesian claim that experience takes place within a substantial mind, closed in upon itself, is not a given. It seems to us that we see a table in the room, not in our heads, and so that is how we should describe the phenomenon. Only someone who allowed their Cartesian bias to override their experience would misinterpret the "table as experienced" as the "representative of the table in my mind." Hence Husserl eschews those who interpret his method as introspection.

Husserl maintains that, once the *epoché* is in effect, our experience is absolutely certain. We may run into secondary difficulties communicating our experience to others in words, but the phenomena experienced are as indubitable to us as Descartes's cogito. As Husserl puts it, in his own inimitable style:

No conceivable theory can make us err with respect to the *principle of all principles: that every originary presentive intuition is a legitimating source of cognition, that everything originarily (so to speak, in its "personal" actuality) offered to us in "intuition" is to be accepted simply as what it is presented as being, but also only within the limits in which it is presented there.* We see indeed that each ⟨theory⟩ can only again draw its truth itself from originary data. Every statement which does no more than confer expression on such data by simple explication and by means of significations precisely conforming to them is, as we said at the beginning of this chapter, actually an *absolute beginning* called upon to serve as a foundation, a *principium* in the genuine sense of the word. (1982, 44)

It is by describing consciousness within the *epoché* that Husserl hopes to build his justification of science.

Intentionality

Applying this method, Husserl claims that his most important finding is the intentionality of consciousness: Consciousness is of or about an object. That is, when we experience something, it is that object itself that we are conscious of, not some intermediary or representative of it.

All agree that objects don't appear before consciousness magically: A process is involved that makes the presence of the object possible. A fundamental mistake occurs, according to Husserl, when, in theorizing about the process, we succumb to the temptation to say that it is the process we are conscious of, rather than the object. We then substitute some part of the process for the object and misunderstand consciousness as consciousness of this representative of the object, rather than of the object itself. The doctrine of intentionality is the rejection of this mistake. Let me call this fundamental mistake *representativism*. (This is my term, not Husserl's.) As Husserl puts it:

It is therefore fundamentally erroneous to believe that perception . . . does not reach the physical thing itself . . . *without any mediation by "appearances."* . . . The spatial physical thing which we see is, with all its transcendence, still something perceived, given "in person" in the manner peculiar to consciousness. It is not the case that, in its stead, a picture or a sign is given. A picture-consciousness or a sign-consciousness must not be substituted for perception. (1982, 92–93)

I'll give two illustrations of the mistake. When we become conscious of mathematical relationships, we do so by manipulating concepts in our minds. Some philosophers, mistaking these psychological concepts, *by means of which* we think mathematically, for the mathematical objects themselves, conclude that the validity of mathematics is derived from psychological laws. It was to combat this "psychologistic" error that Husserl, spurred on by Frege, created phenomenology in the first place (Husserl 1970a, 90–193).

A second illustration: When we visually perceive a chair, we do so by means of a retinal image and possibly some later, higher-level, mental images. Almost no one makes the mistake of claiming that what we are conscious of is the retinal image, but many do hold that it is some mental representative of the chair that we are really conscious of, rather than the chair itself. The most notorious offender, of course, is Descartes, who, in proposing his Theory of Ideas, claims that the mind is never in contact with anything outside itself. The notion is also prevalent in traditional empiricism. Indeed, it is endemic to all of modern philosophy (Husserl 1970b, 83 et seq.).

Husserl insists that it is the object itself that consciousness grasps, and he repudiates all such representativism. Intentionality is not, of course, a claim that there are no representations; the existence of retinal images itself would overthrow such a foolish stand. Rather it is the claim that whatever intermediate entities there may be in the *process* of grasping an object, it is not these representatives that we are conscious *of*, but the object itself.

Constitution

Being conscious of an object is not, however, a mechanical process, for we can only be conscious of something insofar as it has some meaning for us. This brings us to Husserl's third key concept, constitution, by which he means the establishing of meaning within experience, the process by which we come to have a world of meaningful objects. Husserl claims that I can only be conscious of anything insofar as it has a *sense* for me. Intentionality involves constitution: All consciousness *of* is consciousness *as*. How I experience things is how I take them to be.

Like perception, *every* intentive mental process—just this makes up the fundamental part of intentionality—has its "intentional Object," that is, its objective sense. Or, in other words, to have sense or "to intend to" something, is the fundamental characteristic of all consciousness. .... (Husserl 1982, 217)

The most important unity of meaning we constitute is "an object." The notion of a constituted object should be contrasted with the idea of a self-contained substance having an intrinsic essence that defines its being independently of consciousness, an idea that Husserl eventually concludes is incoherent. "Object" does not refer, however, only to physical things; there are many "regions of being" with different forms of unity: melodies, numbers, personalities, theoretical entities such as gravity, and so on (Husserl 1982, 18–22). That is, there are various modes of reality each constituted in its own right. Describing the interrelations between these constituted realities is an important task for phenomenology.

The status of the "constituter" of meaning is a major concern for Husserl. It is not the empirical ego, that is, the self as studied by psychology, for that is a constituted object among other objects. He labels the constituter "transcendental ego," but this title ultimately adds little, for by "transcendental" all Husserl ever means is "concerned with the origination of meaning." In his later works (e.g., 1970b, 262) he talks about transcendental *intersubjectivity* as the constituter and connects constitution with culture and language, thereby preparing the way for Heidegger, Derrida, Rorty, and other postmodernists.

Dennett and Heterophenomenology

This summary of three of Husserl's major concepts does not do justice to the scores of volumes in which Husserl investigates these issues in meticulous, indeed torturous, detail. My main concern, however, is to apply these three concepts to Dennett's work, especially to *Consciousness Explained*. I think Dennett employs the *epoché*, though not perhaps as radically as he might. However, although Dennett at first sight accepts the intentionality of consciousness, I will argue that he ultimately falls into the trap of representativism. I will then suggest a way that Dennett might use Husserl's notion of constitution to resolve an ambiguity about the status of scientific reality.

Dennett's Method: Heterophenomenology and the *Epoché*

In studying consciousness, Dennett adopts a method he calls *heterophenomenology*, which he presents as an alternative to Husserl's phenomenology, or *autophenomenology* as Dennett labels it. By heterophenomenology, Dennett means the process of interpreting the expressions of a speaker as revealing the content of the reporter's heterophenomenological world, as revealing how things seem to the speaker (Dennett 1991a, 72–88). Dennett uses two analogies. First, in fictional worlds created by authors, such as Conan Doyle, what the author says goes. So there are trains in Sherlock Holmes's London, but there are no aircraft. The second analogy is with cultural worlds studied by anthropologists such as the (hypothetical) world of a jungle people who believe in the god Feenoman. An anthropologist must take the natives' word about what things are true in their world. The main point of the two analogies is to grant to the heterophenomenological reporter the same absolute right to say how things are in the heterophenomenological world as authors and natives have about how things are in fictional or cultural worlds. To say that such reporters must be given the last word is to say that no one else, not even a scientific observer of brain states, could ever overrule them. As "fictions" to be taken at face value, theoretical causes of such experiences are irrelevant in these reports. Scientific or commonsense truths about realities have nothing to do with how things may or may not seem to be to the reporter. As Dennett puts it: "you get the last word. . . . You are not authoritative about what is happening in you, but only about what seems to be happening in you" (1991a, 96). By "in you" he means something like "occurring as a real neurological process in your brain."

For example, if we present someone with a red flash of light followed rapidly by a green one to the side of it, she will report seeing a single moving dot that changes color halfway along. Heterophenomenologists accept that that is how it seems to her and do not impose what we know about the scientific reality on her account of her experience.

Despite his tendentious labeling of the moving dots as "theorist's fictions" (Dennett 1991a, 97), in giving the reporter the last word

David L. Thompson

Dennett is practicing a method very similar to Husserl's *epoché*. He is suspending both the natural attitude and scientific theories. Of course he is applying the *epoché* not to the consciousness of his own experience, but to the reporter's text; that's what makes it hetero-phenomenology rather than autophenomenology. Nevertheless, his method has a similar effect to Husserl's: it insulates the heterophe-nomenological world from scientific causes and nonheterophenom-enological realities.

But what about the status of the scientific world itself? Dennett appears to hold that the world science reveals to us is real independently of consciousness. Husserl would hold, however, that there can be no science without scientists. All the paraphernalia of books and articles, of laboratories and instruments, would not qualify as *science* unless there were people to understand and use them. This vast corpus needs to be interpreted in much the same way that a heterophe-nomenological report needs to be interpreted. If we interpret scientific texts, we find them referring to various objects, relations, and theories, that is, to the scientific world. The scientific world is therefore one heterophenomenological world among other worlds. It is a privileged world in a number of ways: It is widely shared; it is subject to reforming criticism; it is frequently exact and based on univocal concepts; and so on. Given these privileges, it is not unreasonable to grant this world the honorific label *real* to distinguish it from *subjective* worlds, worlds proper to individuals. Nevertheless, it remains a heterophenomenological world, and as such it can be accessed only through interpretation, only by grasping what the terms in the heterophenomenological reports mean for the scientists and the scientific language communities involved. Though scientific objects may be labeled real, they are nonetheless inconceivable without reference to a community of meaners for whom the relevant texts mean something. Husserl would claim that the *epoché* has been selectively applied; Dennett has applied it to the reports of the victim of the Phi (or other) experiment, but has failed to apply it to the reports of the cognitive scientist performing the experiment. As Carr puts it, Dennett "seems unwilling to take phenomenology to its limits, namely to turn it back on its own position" (Carr 1998, 338). Husserl, in his radical search for ultimate foundations,

would insist that it be applied evenhandedly to the reports (or experience) of everyone, including the investigator.

Even from Dennett's own point of view, however, the conclusions
of *Consciousness Explained* need to be applied to the nature of science
and to the status of the scientific world. Dennett frequently writes
as if scientists had a god's-eye view of the world, as if they could
know things-in-themselves, things as they are in absolute independence from the meanings that human knowers set up. But his pande-
monic account of the production of speech (or writing), for
example, must apply to scientific discourse as it does to any other
discourse (Dennett 1991a, 227 et seq). *Consciousness Explained* has its
own implications for the nature of science, and a god's-eye view by
scientists is not compatible with them. I think Husserl would correctly see Dennett as adopting an uncritical scientism. Husserl applies the *epoché* to all experience, including scientific experience.
Insofar as *Consciousness Explained* neglects to make the equivalent
move, it leaves science as a kind of skyhook without foundation, to
invert a metaphor.

Dennett and Intentionality

As in the case of the *epoché*, Dennett at first sight also appears to
accept Husserl's notion of intentionality. There are objects to which
heterophenomenological descriptions refer, that is, such descriptions have contents. He insists that "we distinguish representing
from represented, vehicle from content" (Dennett 1991a, 131). He
assigns the representing function to various brain processes and crit-
icizes others for confusing the properties of these processes with the
properties of the objects represented. He disagrees, for instance,
with those who think that, once the brain has analyzed an incoming
signal as a pain originating in the toe, something must then be pro-
jected back into the foot. The pain is *represented* as in the toe; nothing
further has to occur in the *representing* process (Dennett 1991a, 131).

Dennett uses an analogy to make the distinction clear. If someone
receives letters about various events, the order of arrival of the letters
need not be the same as the order of the events reported in them.
Our habit of dating letters when we send them means that readers

have no trouble distinguishing between the time of the representing, that is, the arrival time of the letters, and the time of the events represented in the letters (Dennett 1991a, 146). Similarly, events we are conscious of are represented as occurring at a time and in an order that may not coincide with the time or order of the brain events that make up the process of representing. As Dennett puts it, "[t]he representation of presence is not the same as the presence of representation."

So far, Dennett's dichotomy of vehicle and content, of representing and represented, is consonant with Husserl's point about the intentionality of consciousness. Husserl too wants to distinguish sharply between the process by which we are conscious, which he calls the *noesis,* and the object of which we are conscious, the *noema.* But Dennett now asks another question. Could the objects in a reporter's heterophenomenological world turn out to be brain events? It seems to me that at this point Dennett falls into representativism, which I think he himself would like to avoid. Let me show how I think this happens.

Dennett claims that, in contrast with Husserlian phenomenology, his own heterophenomenology does not commit him to any doctrine that intuition reveals indubitably how things really are "in us." Whether a heterophenomenological report has anything to say about brain realities has to be discovered empirically by objective, neuroscientific investigation. A historian might find evidence to confirm that the fictional trains in Holmes's London actually correspond to real trains. The anthropologist might find an old man in the forest who, except for slight religious exaggerations, is the real Feenoman to which the cultural myth actually refers. By analogy, if a speaker's heterophenomenological world includes a moving light that changes from red to green, as in the Phi experiment, a neuroscientist can investigate whether or not there is any corresponding "real" brain event. There might be; but there might not. As Dennett puts it, "If we were to find real goings-on in people's brains that had *enough* of the 'defining' properties of the items that populate their heterophenomenological worlds, we could reasonably propose that we had discovered what they were *really* talking about—even if they initially resisted the identifications" (1991a, 85).

From a Husserlian perspective, this investigation is confused. The doctrine of intentionality claims that experiences are about the objects experienced, not about the processes that give rise to these experiences. The moving light is seen in the world, alongside the tables and chairs in the room. If the experience is true, it is about a moving light in the room; in the Phi experiment, where scientists are in agreement that there is no such moving light, the experience is not about anything; it only seems to be, as Dennett points out so often. Whether the experience is of something real or not, it is never about a brain event, but always, correctly or incorrectly, about lights *in the world*. The notion of *unwitting* reference is being misused here (Dennett 1991a, 84).

The analogies have misled us. The reason, I think, is that in the analogies we are dealing only with two kinds of things: the objects in the novel or myth and the objects in the external world. In the Dennettian account of consciousness we are dealing with three kinds of things: objects that seem to be in the heterophenomenological world, objects in the "real," that is, scientific, world, but also brain events. Brain events have no counterparts in the fiction and myth analogies.

What has gone wrong? In attacking the Cartesian account of consciousness, Dennett does three things. First, he points out that there is no central theater in the brain in which everything finally comes together to be recognized by a central recognizer. Instead, he proposes to fragment the process of recognition and disperse it throughout the brain. Second, as a result, the recognizer, the formerly unified Cartesian subject, must also be decentralized. Third, Dennett splits the confused Cartesian notion of a unified *idea* and distinguishes the representing process from the represented object.[2]

Nevertheless, Dennett still asks whether an object represen*ted* in a heterophenomenological world might correspond to a brain event, that is, a process of represen*ting*. When the answer is yes, then he implies that the real thing "in us" that a heterophenomenological report is about is the brain event. Dispersed as the experiencer and representings may be, one fundamental Cartesian dogma remains. Descartes believes we are conscious of ideas, conscious of internal objects or events that mediate between ourselves and the

David L. Thompson

world. Dennett appears to cling to this dogma rather than going all the way with intentionality. Husserl's doctrine of intentionality maintains that consciousness is of the objects experienced and does not stop at intermediate events along the way, whether these are on one unified stage or dispersed throughout the brain. It's not just that there is no big screen; there are no little screens either. Brain events are part of the *process,* never the *objects* of experiencing. (An obvious exception, of course, is the case of a neuroscientist for whom brain events are themselves the objects of investigation.)

The status of these heterophenomenological objects may be elucidated by examining an argument offered by David Carr. Carr argues that Dennett misunderstands what it means to label something "fiction." Sherlock Holmes may be a fictional character, and objects in a heterophenomenological world may be labeled "fictions" by analogy. "But presumably the phenomenologist is going to be talking about ordinary experiences like seeing the tree in the garden or meeting a friend on the street. Are the tree and the friend, the intentional objects of these experiences, just fictions?" (Carr 1998, 336). Dennett, in effect, argues that whether they are fictions or not is a matter of empirical fact. If an objective investigation shows that there is a real tree in the garden, then the heterophenomenological tree is not a fiction; otherwise it is. But Carr argues that this is a poor analysis of the fictional status of Holmes.

Suppose, by incredible coincidence, that there really was someone whose description and every action matched all the things Conan Doyle attributed to Sherlock. Would we then reclassify the work in the history section? More likely it would be filed under bizarre, unexplained coincidences. . . . My point is that the fictional or non-fictional status of the central character in a narrative is a function, not of whether it in fact corresponds to something in the "real world," but rather of the sense of the text as it is read or read and understood. (Carr 1998, 343)

Unlike Carr, my concern is not with the relationship of the heterophenomenological world to the "real, everyday, world," but rather with its relationship to the brain. Nevertheless, let me argue in a similar way that what a report of a moving light in the Phi experiment is about is to be determined by what it seems to be about to the reporter. Inaccurate as the report may be, it seems to be about a light *in the world* and not some goings-on in the brain. If a neuroscientist discovers that, at the same time as the report, there is a continuous stream of neural firings leading from the "red" area of the optical lobe to the "green" area, we should file this under curiosities. It might be very interesting that some brain events mirror seemings and it might be of importance for understanding brain processes. But to then conclude that these brain events are what the report is really *about* is a category mistake. The reports would still be about what they seem to be about, namely a purported event in the external, everyday world. "Aboutness," that is, intentionality, is not a real, objective, causal relationship, but an intrinsic feature of consciousness or of the heterophenomenological report. The criterion for determining what a report is about is therefore what it seems to be about, and to invoke external evidence from neuroscience not only violates the methodological restraints of the *epoché*, but misunderstands the nature of intentionality.

One of the reasons for Dennett's misunderstanding, I suspect, is an ambiguity in the notion of representation. In the philosophical tradition from Descartes to Kant, *representation* is a mental object, a unity of which the mind is conscious, and it is in this sense of the term that Husserl attacks representations. In recent cognitive science, *representation* is used in a quite different way to refer to a brain structure that in one way or another tracks something in the world. Although Husserl knew nothing of cognitive science, he was fully aware that the body is involved in perception, so I doubt he would have had any objection to the notion of a representation as a tracking process. He would, however, understand such a tracking-represent*ation* as a part of the represent*ing* process, and so it is not the kind of thing that could ever qualify as an object that a subject could be conscious of. That is the point of his rejection of representativism. Since Dennett's own distinction between the representing and the represented implies that what cognitive scientists call a "representation" falls under representing rather than represented, he should agree with a Husserlian on this point. That he doesn't suggests to me that, though he jettisons much of Descartes's position, Dennett hasn't gone far enough and appears to be stuck with a residual trace of Cartesian representativism.

David L. Thompson

Dennett and Constitution

Representativism may be wrong, but it is a natural enough mistake. Perception can be in error; so if I see, for instance, a moving light when I know there are only two stationary lights in rapid succession, it is natural to describe myself as seeing an illusion, a mirage, which, since it is not there in the world, must be something I see in my head. It is an easy step from there to claim that even when I am not in error, what I am conscious of is in my head: in my mind for Descartes himself, in my brain for Cartesian materialists. I think this way of putting it is a fatal mistake, but it does bring to the fore one essential feature of consciousness: What I am conscious of must be *for-me*. It is this feature of consciousness that Husserl calls *constitution*.

In one way, Dennett's heterophenomenological world captures this Husserlian notion of a world-for-me. Dennett insists that we not misinterpret the heterophenomenological world as a duplicate, as a second world over and beyond the real world. Phenomenal space and time, he says, are neither brain space and time, nor real (mentally real?) seemings; they are just how space and time seem to us (Dennett 1991a, 130–131). The analogy to a fictional world, however, can lead to misunderstandings. The heterophenomenological world is, after all, the world we live in. It is this world of tables and chairs that we see and act in that is being referred to by the heterophenomenological report. The job of my brain is to give me access to the world, not just to a story. It is true, of course, that it is the world-for-me, but that is the point of Husserlian constitution: The world-for-me is the only world that I can be conscious of. That is why Husserl calls himself a *transcendental idealist*.

Now Dennett is not an idealist. He holds that scientific objects are real. Objects in a heterophenomenological world, however, are what they are insofar as they seem that way to the reporter who gets the last word. Dennett is insistent that there are no "real seemings," that is, things that are "in me" without regard to how I take them to be. It is a central feature of heterophenomenological worlds that the objects in them are not "in themselves"; they are no more than what I report them to be. Their being and their characteristics are exhausted by how they seem to me. Dennett is sympathetic to verifi-

cationism, at least to "first-person operationalism," that is, to operationalism as it applies to "the realm of subjectivity" (Dennett 1991a,
132). He dismisses the "bizarre category of the objectively subjective" (Dennett 1991a, 132). Behind the Germanic jargon, however,
this is actually all Husserl means by transcendental idealism:[3] Objects
are only insofar as they are taken to be, only insofar as they are meaningful. With respect to objects in heterophenomenological worlds,
then, Dennett is a transcendental idealist.[4]

Dennett and Husserl nevertheless differ on two points. First, in
the "subjective" realm Husserl maintains that words describe preverbal experience ("phenomena"), a position Dennett vehemently
rejects. Since heterophenomenology is an interpretation of a text,
the method itself would exclude recourse to anything preverbal;
this is the central difference between hetero- and autophenomenology. Behind this very real disagreement, however, lies a central
core of agreement: For Husserl, even preverbally experienced
objects are never real in the sense of being "in-themselves;" their
being is still exhausted by how they are taken, by their meaning for
me. They are never subjectively objective in the sense that we could
apply the reality/appearance distinction to them (Dennett 1991a,
132).

Second, and more important, Husserl consistently applies his notion of constitution to all objects in any interpreted world, including
the scientific. For him, there are many kinds of realities, each constituted in its own fashion. There is not one single spectrum stretching
from irrealism, through mild realism, to industrial strength realism,
but rather qualitatively different modes of being constituted. The
realities of physics, important as they are, are but one constitutive
mode. For Husserl, science is not a project of God, but of humans,
and so the scientific world is a world-for-us. But he also wants to
preserve the privilege of science. The whole of Husserl's phenomenology can be read as his attempt to reconcile the for-itselfness of
consciousness with the universal claims of science, and his notion
of constitution is the key to this attempt. He proceeds by describing
in detail how perceptual worlds and scientific worlds get constituted
and what the relationships between them are (Husserl 1970b, 343–
351).

Adopting the notion that all reality is constituted in this Husserlian sense would not be a complete about-face for Dennett, since it
could be argued that in his theory of different stances he has already
taken some steps in this direction (Dennett 1987, 16–17). Haugeland, in pointing out that "constitutive standards . . . determine the
being of the objects," claims that "Dennett puts the intentional and
the physical exactly on a par: each is understood in terms of a possible stance" (1993, 65). Dennett's original concept of a stance,
however, assumes an underlying realism about the pattern that
the stance recognizes (Dennett 1987, 26). He later qualifies this
realism as "mild" (Dennett 1991b), which narrows the ontological
gap between the physical and the intentional. I am suggesting that
he should apply his even later concept of the heterophenomenological world to the objects of all stances, including the scientific or
physical.

In considering the status of scientific reality, philosophers are
tempted by two extremes. The first is to treat science as divine rather
than as a human project. The second is to reduce it to the biased
illusions of the subject. A thorough application of the *epoché* serves
the methodological function of preserving us from the first temptation of assuming a god's-eye view. Within the *epoché* we must treat
all objects, even scientific objects, as for-us, that is, as objects in a
heterophenomenological world. But equally important is the concept of intentionality, which preserves us from the temptation of
representativism. Intentionality reminds us that objects in a heterophenomenological world are not objects in our heads (whether
minds or brains) but objects in the world, constituted as they may
be. For Husserl, a constitutive approach to scientific reality is valid
only within the contexts of the *epoché* and of intentionality.

I should admit that I believe that Husserl's project to find an absolute, Archimedean point for the foundation for science in a description of consciousness ends in failure. I am very sympathetic to the
approach to consciousness taken in *Consciousness Explained,* but I
think the approach is still incomplete.[5] What is lacking is an account
of how the analysis of consciousness therein can be made consistent
with the naïve scientific realism assumed throughout. Since Husserl's attempts ended in failure, Dennett may fear, with good reason,
that treating scientific objects as constituted realities within a hetero-

phenomenological world may lead him—as it has others—away
from realism toward some kind of Rortyan postmodernism. If so, I
can only repeat Rorty's exhortation to him to be courageous and
finish the task, wherever it may lead (Rorty 1993, 198).

Conclusion

Let me conclude by saying that Dennett's heterophenomenology is
not as far from Husserl's (auto)phenomenology as might first appear, and that heterophenomenology could benefit from some of
the conceptual apparatus that Husserl has worked out. A more rigorous application of the Husserlian notions of *epoché,* intentionality,
and constitution could clarify and advance some of the problems
with which Dennett is struggling, most notably the status of scientific
reality. If such an application were to lead the heterophenomenological approach away from scientistic realism and down the road toward some kind of constitutive realism, we should not be surprised.
In a postmodern world science cannot be exempted from its status
as an evolutionary institution that depends on human consciousness.

Notes

1. "... *We* are the genuine positivists" (Husserl 1982, 39).

2. To be fair, Descartes does distinguish between the formal being (representing?)
and the objective being (represented?) of ideas. See the Third Meditation (Descartes
1988, 90).

3. Let us avoid two red herrings: First, constitution for Husserl is to be found after
the *epoché,* that is, when reliance on causality has been set aside. His claim that consciousness constitutes all worlds, including the perceptual and scientific worlds, is no
more a claim that it causes them than is Dennett's claim that the heterophenomenological report constitutes a heterophenomenological world (Dennett
1991a, 81). Second, the constituter, for Husserl, is not the empirical consciousness
of an individual subject. Constitution is the work of a Transcendental Ego, or Transcendental Intersubjectivity, which I would argue (but won't here) is better understood as a community of meaning, or perhaps even as the meme-sphere, to put it
in Dennett's or Dawkins's terms.

4. Dennett abhors being labeled with "isms," and for very good reasons. I am happy
to withdraw the label immediately. It is used only temporarily to emphasize a similarity that Husserl's use of the term would normally obscure.

5. Dennett makes some attempt to apply the evolutionary approach to science (Dennett 1995, e.g., 380–381).

References

Carr, D. (1998). Phenomenology and fiction in Dennett. *International Journal of Philosophical Studies* 6(3): 331–344.

Dahlbom, B., ed. (1993). *Dennett and His Critics.* Cambridge, Mass.: Blackwell.

Dennett, D. C. (1987). *The Intentional Stance.* Cambridge, Mass.: MIT Press. A Bradford Book.

Dennett, D. C. (1991a). *Consciousness Explained.* Toronto: Little, Brown & Company.

Dennett, D. C. (1991b). Real patterns. *Journal of Philosophy* 88: 27–51.

Dennett, D. C. (1995). *Darwin's Dangerous Idea.* Toronto: Simon and Schuster.

Descartes, R. (1988). *Descartes: Selected Philosophical Writings.* New York: Cambridge University Press.

Haugeland, J. (1993). Pattern and being. In *Dennett and His Critics,* B. Dahlbom (ed.). Cambridge, Mass.: Blackwell.

Husserl, E. (1970a). *Logical Investigations.* Trans. J. N. Findlay. London: Routledge/Kegan Paul.

Husserl, E. (1970b). *The Crisis of European Sciences and Transcendental Phenomenology.* Trans. D. Carr. Evanston, IL: Northwestern University Press.

Husserl, E. (1982). *Ideas Pertaining to a Pure Phenomenology and to a Phenomenological Philosophy.* Trans. F. Kersten. The Hague: Martinus Nijhoff Publishers.

Rorty, R. (1993). Holism, intrinsicality, transcendence. In *Dennett and His Critics,* B. Dahlbom (ed.). Cambridge, Mass.: Blackwell.

11

Judgments and Drafts Eight Years Later

Andrew Brook

Isolating The Task

In *Consciousness Explained* (1991a; hereafter CE),[1] Dennett's most extended treatment of consciousness to date, he lays out an interpretationist approach to what conscious contents *seem* to be like (heterophenomenology), mounts a series of challenges to the idea that some basic questions about conscious experience have determinate answers, sketches what he calls a multiple drafts model of what consciousness is *actually* like, and urges that conscious experiences are judgments, not (what has been understood by terms like) sensible images. In general, he has two main targets: states or events in which something seems to us to be a certain way—seemings in his parlance (i.e., what others call qualia or appearances)—and what is seemed to, the subject (subjects are also meaners and agents).

Now that some years have passed, how does this picture of consciousness look? On the one hand, Dennett's work has vastly expanded the range of options for thinking about conscious experiences and conscious subjects. On the other hand, I suspect that the implications of his picture have been oversold (perhaps more by others than by Dennett himself). The rhetoric in CE is radical in places, but I am not sure that the actual implications for common-sense views of seemings and subjects are nearly as radical.

For thirty years now, Dennett has worked to give an account of content and of consciousness. Dennett's characteristic modus operandi for dealing with content (intentionality) is as follows (1978f, 1987d). First he argues that a target psychological or behavioral phenomenon can be accounted for in terms of the subjects' reasons via an idealization of the subject's instrumental rationality. This mode of explanation goes with a certain metaphysics of mind. The patterns it reveals are real but they are patterns discernible in behavior, not in the head (1991b, p. 98). The phenomenon in question then comes out as another such pattern. Adopting this technique is adopting the intentional stance. Dennett mops up any residual resistance with some vigorous, often verificationist counterarguments. His well-known hostility to qualia (CE, ch. 12) and to even the bare possibility of zombies (Polger, this volume) are two of the best known of these mopping-up operations. ("If it looks like a duck and quacks like a duck, then most probably it is a duck" is the basic move.)

Now, consciousness is a psychological phenomenon. Yet the intentional stance plays little role in CE. Dennett so much as mentions it only about four times, and his longest discussion of it is less than one page (CE, 76–78). The first two-thirds of the book are written in an unabashedly realist idiom—and here I mean the old-fashioned realism of conscious experiences as states in the head, not the special realism of "Real Patterns" (1991b).

So how does the metaphysics of the intentional stance relate to the multiple drafts model of consciousness, and so on? Here is Dennett a few years after CE:

Conscious experiences are real events occurring in the real time and space of the brain. (1994a, 135)

And,

Sensory qualities are nothing other than the dispositional properties of cerebral states to produce certain further effects in the very observers whose states they are. (1994b, 146)

He has consistently denied this about psychological states such as beliefs and desires. If they are to be mapped onto anything real, it is to real patterns in behavior, not real events in the brain. Recall the Jacques, Sherlock, Tom, Boris thought-experiment. The four men all come to believe that Jacques shot his uncle dead in Trafalgar Square, but they acquire this belief in utterly different ways and even via different languages—Jacques by doing it, Sherlock by investigating the deed, Tom by reading about it in the *Guardian,* and Boris by reading about it in *Pravda.* Says Dennett,

> If [theorists] insist [that there is nevertheless] a similarly structured object in each head, this is a gratuitous bit of misplaced concreteness, a regrettable lapse in ideology. (1987b, 55)

How do these two positions hang together?

Well, the intentional stance may not play much of a role in CE but a closely related notion does: heterophenomenology. The intentional stance is a device for arriving at a view of what is moving a subject. Heterophenomenology is a device for arriving at a view, from the point of view of an outsider, of how things *seem* to that subject. (This used to be called empathy before the term was bent out of shape by ramming it together with sympathy. Thus Dennett, one of the most graceful of writers, had to resort to a horrendous neologism.) It is part of the metaphysics of the intentional stance that there need not be (and almost certainly are not) any states in the subject's brain that are the beliefs, desires, and so on, ascribed to her. In apparently the same way, it seems to be part of the metaphysics of what we might call the heterophenomenological stance that there need not be any states in the subject's brain that are or contain the way things seem to her. At any rate, this much is true. Just as the intentional stance is a device for ascribing a pattern of beliefs and motives that fits not just with brain states but also with behavior, history, and environment, heterophenomenology is a device for ascribing a view of how self and world seem to the subject that fits not just with brain states (and information they may contain) but also with the subject's behavior, history, and environment. Thus Dennett has a two-part model:

1. A realist part concerning the events and dispositions that are really in play when people are conscious, things seem a certain way to them, and so on.

2. An interpretationist part concerning how things seem to people.

Can these two parts be reconciled? One wonders. How, for example, can conscious experiences come out as real events, sensory qualities real dispositions, while how things seem to someone might be a mere fiction, no more real than a novel (CE, 98)? Surely "sensory qualities'' is simply a *name* for how something seems to someone. Can sensory qualities both be and not be real events or dispositions in the brain? We need an interpretation that avoids this outcome.

There is a risk of ambiguity in Dennett's treatment of the hetero-phenomenological stance. What is he denying? Merely that we are as we seem to ourselves? Few will quarrel with that, though his *wholesale* jettisoning of the categories of folk psychology goes further than most people (CE, 319). (Most of us think that when we seem to be aware of such basic things as beliefs and desires in ourselves, here at least we are probably right.) But Dennett seems to want to go farther. He seems to want to say that when we seem a certain way to ourselves, there need not be any events or pattern of events in us that *contains or constitutes* that way of seeming (CE, 98). (How much further he wants to go in this direction will occupy a good part of this paper.)

The difference here is the difference between a seeming being accurate and it having a vehicle. If we think again of the novel analogy, it would be the difference between the novel's story being true and the novel being a real object. This is a substantial difference! It may contain a way out of the prima facie contradiction I generated earlier. More generally, I want to explore exactly what metaphysics of mind the analysis of CE supports. In addition, I want to ask whether CE contains any new arguments for this metaphysics, whatever exactly it is, arguments different from those used in earlier works to defend the metaphysics of the intentional stance.

CE has three parts. Part I is introductory, and Part III is mostly aimed at the special preoccupations of philosophers. In Part II Dennett mounts his challenges, aiming to show that conscious experiences are less determinable than we might be inclined to think, and sketches the multiple drafts model. Then in the first two chapters of Part III he gives his theory of conscious experiences as judgments. So Part II and the first chapters of Part III are the crucial sections for our purposes.

Traditional Notions and the Trilevel Approach

It will help frame the question of what metaphysics of consciousness is supported in CE and how if we put the issue into a broader context. For the few hundred years that people have had a stable notion of consciousness at all,[2] folk psychology has ascribed a fairly constant group of features to seemings and to subjects (not necessarily under these names, of course). Clearly, the metaphysics of the intentional stance rejects some aspects of these notions. The holism and externalism of the intentional stance entail not only that "meanings just ain't in the head," in Putnam's memorable (1975) phrase, but that content of any sort "just ain't in the head." All that's in the head is "syntax" (in the wildly inflated sense of the term "syntax" used in contemporary philosophy of mind) (1987b). They also entail that indeterminacies are a central feature of the mental. If so, there is nothing that has some of the central features traditionally ascribed to seemings and subjects.

This is a kind of eliminativism. If the intentional stance is eliminativist about seemings and subjects, what about CE? Is it as eliminativist as the intentional stance? More so? Put the question a bit differently. To what extent does the book argue that seemings and subjects as traditionally conceived do not exist and to what extent does it just want a better model of them? (Modeling something does not challenge its existence.) And whatever the answer to these questions, what does Dennett (in CE) offer by way of new arguments for its position?

Let's try to make the eliminativist issue more precise. Start with that mainstay of cognitive science, the triple of task, procedure, and implementation.[3] Here is an example. Add two numbers. The task is to add the numbers correctly. The procedure is whatever algorithm is used to perform this task. And the implementation is whatever arrangements in a physical system the running of the algorithm happens to consist in on this occasion.

The three notions go with three, nested kinds of description. A single task will usually be an assembly of dozens or even hundreds of units of procedure, units that may vary widely from instance to instance of the same task, and a single procedure may well be an assembly of dozens or even hundreds of implementation units, units that also may vary widely from instance to instance of the same procedure (Marr 1982; Dawson 1998).

Consciousness is more than a repertoire of tasks. This is one of the things that makes it resistant to cognitive science. So we need to broaden the first notion. The following loose concept will do for our purposes: features by which we identify something. Let us call this the F-level (for identifying features).[4] More is almost certainly involved in the middle level of consciousness than algorithmic procedures. Processes of other kinds are also probably involved. So let us call the second level the P-level (for processes of all kinds, not just procedures). Call the third level the I-level (for implementation). We won't have much to say about it.

Now, when Dennett goes after the picture of seemings and the subject of the tradition, is he going after the F-level picture, certain P-level theories developed in the tradition to account for these F-level features, or both? If he denies the existence of something central to either F-level picture, then he is an eliminativist about at least that aspect of consciousness. If he rejects only traditional P-level theories of the processes and procedures that subserve the F-level features, then he is not an eliminativist, he just wants a better theory. Which is it?

Here is a sketch of the F-level features of seemings found in folk psychology:

F-level concept of seemings: Seemings are real states or events of some sort in us in which something appears to be some way, something is like something for us.

In the tradition, most theories of the P-level processes and procedures that realize these F-level features would contain the following elements:

P-level theory of seemings: Seemings are reidentifiable events in the head with clear start and stop points. These events can be identified and reidentified independently of other similar events around them. They present scenarios to something called "the mind." . . .

and so on (the list is not meant to be exhaustive). Again, if Dennett rejects significant aspects of the F-level concept, he is an eliminativist about seemings. If he rejects only the P-level account, he just wants a better P-level theory. Which is it?

Dennett clearly rejects the P-level theory and any theory like it. When he says that we don't have qualia in any way different from those that a CADBLIND system could have (CE, 374), that "I'm denying (that Descartes's real seemings) exist" (CE, 363), he is at least doing that much. However, the fierce rhetoric of CE suggests more than that. The rhetoric suggests that Dennett wants to deny that any states or events have even the *F-level* properties of a seeming, and many people have taken him just this way. Here are some of the things that Dennett says:

[The category of] the way things actually, objectively seem to you [is a] bizarre category. (CE, 132)

There is no such phenomenon as really seeming—over and above the phenomenon of judging in one way or another that something is the case. (CE, 364)

There is no such thing [as] actual phenomenology. (CE, 365)

Yet it is unclear what these statements amount to. The first statement occurs in an attack on an aspect of a P-level theory, namely, Cartesianism (as he sees it), and the second and third in the context of mounting his own P-level alternative. Dennett may not be going after the F-level picture in any of them. OK, so what about things like this:

[A subject's heterophenomenological world is a] theorist's fiction. (CE, 98)

Heterophenomenology exists . . . as novels and other fictions exist. (CE, 98)

These do look strongly eliminativist about seemings, as does the later claim that seemings are, like centers of gravity, mere *abstracta*, postulates useful in some explanatory exercise but not corresponding to any material state or process (CE, 95–96). We will try to sort out exactly what kind of eliminativism and how Dennett argues for it (whatever "it" turns out to be) in the next two sections.

Dennett knows full well that we certainly *seem* to have seemings, of course. Indeed, he insists on the point. But this is just autophenomenology, heterophenomenological interpretation applied to self. How things seem to someone may be totally different from how they are. Put a bit paradoxically, that we seem to have seemings does not entail that we do! (We will pass over the appearance of self-refutation in this sentence, at least for a while.)

Andrew Brook

About the subject, the issue of eliminativism is less complicated. The F-level story of the subject in folk psychology is built around something like list (1):

List 1: F-level concept of the subject. A subject:

operates by forming things like beliefs and desires about objects, events, etc.;

marshals various cognitive resources (beliefs, desires, values, concepts, etc.) to generate an intention to do something and then marshals diverse bodily resources to do it;

is aware of a number of things at once in some way that allows us to relate things to other things;

consciously focuses attention on tasks;

and so on (again the list is not meant to be exhaustive). List (2) spells out the P-level theory developed by the tradition to explain what is going on at the F-level. It is Dennett's main stalking horse.

List 2: Dennett's account of the traditional P-level theory of the subject. A system able to do the things on list (1) would have:

a Cartesian theater;

a central meaner, the shared contents of which are highly integrated and "enter consciousness" as though the mind has a synchronous clock speed;

a class of mental events called, variously, appearances, qualia, and the felt quality of things. These events are viewed as in their own traditional Plevel theory sketched above; for example, as having clear start and stop points.

The list of features in list (2) provide a theory or model of the items in list (1).

Dennett is clearly an eliminativist about the items on list (2) and any other like it. But that is merely to reject certain theories of what is needed to realize the features of subjecthood. It is not to eliminate our F-level concept of the subject. To be an eliminativist about subjects as traditionally conceived, one would have to go after the items on list (1), not just list (2). If Dennett accepts that subjects have at least most of the F-level features ascribed to them in our folk psychology and just denies that it takes anything like the items on list (2) to realize these features, he is not an eliminativist about subjects. He just wants a better theory of them.[5]

Are Indeterminacies of Consciousness a Problem for Seemings?

Seemings first. Dennett's treatment of seemings has three main parts, all of which were mentioned at the beginning of this chapter: the heterophenomenological stance, the series of challenges, and the theory of conscious experiences as judgments. Let's start with the challenges.

Judging by the intentional stance, eliminativism about the F-level notion of seemings could take two forms in Dennett, and it is important to separate them. It could take the form of a claim that there are no states or events in which something is seeming like something, or it could take the form of a claim that, though there are states or events that have that property, they do not have some other crucial feature of seemings of the F-level picture. Here is how the difference plays itself out in Dennett's writings on intentional content (see Viger, this volume). Dennett's more instrumentalist writings take the first route—intentional explanation is merely a device for connecting behavior to various inputs, and the entities it postulates to explain these connections have no more reality than that. Intentional entities are abstracta. More recent writings take the second route— intentional phenomena are real, but they are not in the brain as the traditional F-level picture of them would have it. They are real patterns discernible in behavior (1991b).

Dennett does not take the first route with seemings, not entirely at any rate. Something seeming like something has to involve conscious experience in *some* way, and this closes off the second route, at least partially. As we saw, he says that conscious experiences are "real events . . . in the brain." So if he is an F-level eliminativist about seemings at all, he has to take the second route: insist that these "real events in the brain" lack some central F-level feature ascribed to seemings by the tradition. They cannot lack location in the brain in the way that intentional patterns are said to do, so what they do lack?

The answer to that question is complicated and far from straightforward. Let's start with a simpler one: Do any of Dennett's challenges to the determinateness of conscious states challenge the traditional F-level picture of seemings? Here is a summary of the main challenges:

1. There is often no clear sense to be attached to the idea of a specific point at which something becomes conscious (Stalinesque/Orwellian impasses).

2. The time order that contents of consciousness appear to have is often different from the time order in which we encountered the events originally.

3. Often there is no way to distinguish between an organism misrepresenting one thing and correctly representing another thing.[6]

4. We can carve mental events up in ever finer slices, describe them in boundlessly varied descriptions, and embed descriptions of them in higher- and higher-order attitudes without limit.

5. No sense can be made of the notion of an inverted spectrum.

All these claims have considerable interest in their own right. Do they undermine the F-level notion of seemings? Seemings, recall, are not just something seeming like something—Dennett clearly accepts that that occurs. They are *states or events* of something seeming like something. It is not clear that Dennett's challenges threaten such states or events. My reasons for saying this vary from claim to claim, so we need to examine them individually.

Stalinesque/Orwellian (S/O) Impasses

An S/O impasse is generated when something is misremembered but there is no way to determine whether it was misperceived (the Stalinesque option: history is falsified from the beginning) or perceived correctly but immediately misremembered (the Orwellian option: history is initially recorded correctly but falsified afterward). An example: The Lady Remembered with Glasses.

A short time after seeing a lady who is not wearing glasses, we remember seeing her with glasses. And the question is, where did the mistake occur? It seems that there are two possibilities: The lady in question might have been misperceived with glasses (the Stalinesque option) or she might have been perceived correctly but, owing to a later revision, immediately misremembered (the Orwellian option). Dennett argues that no possible information could adjudicate between these options, so they are not really options and there is no fact of the matter about when the error began (1991a, 125).

Why might S/O impasses be a problem for the existence of seemings? Well, if such elementary impasses as these cannot be resolved, then it would seem that there is nothing that meets the most basic requirements for being a real seeming: there being a clear point at which one ends and the next one begins, a way of determining when we are encountering the same one again, when we are encountering another one of the same kind, and so on.

Are all S/O impasses merely apparent, distinctions that correspond to no difference? The answer is not obviously yes. Consider pain and pain tolerance (1978b, 222–224). A person has suffered some mild bang, yet complains he cannot work, the pain is so bad. Does this person feel unusually intense pain for such a mild injury or does he have the usual modest pain but a very low threshold at which pain becomes seriously debilitating?[7] On the other hand, we see a Freud soldiering on even though cancer of the jaw has rotted his whole cheek away and left a great gaping hole. Does he have severe pain but astonishing pain tolerance or does he just happen to feel less pain from this lesion than others would feel? These examples generate S/O impasses, but the difference between levels of pain and levels of pain tolerance seems to be perfectly real, certainly in many cases. (Pain creates problems for Dennett in other ways, too, as we will see.)

In fact, it is not so clear that S/O impasses are irresolvable in principle. One option is the "outside in" approach. Start from cases where everything is clear: A foot is mashed to a pulp and the person is screaming; a woman was perceived and remembered correctly for a time but then an error crept in. Next correlate the conscious contents with whatever one can find, perhaps even brain states (though

Dennett thinks it unlikely that we will ever do that). Then apply the correlates to the cases where the short time-scale, etc., generates an impasse. Dennett himself uses this strategy to great effect in 1978b and touches on it in 1988 and a number of times in CE (85, 96, 326 fn., and 396). His reasons for viewing it as inevitably inconclusive in certain key cases are not clear.[8]

But suppose that some S/O impasses are genuinely irresolvable? Would seemings then be in trouble? I think not. The process of generating conscious experiences may contain more indeterminacies than we imagined but we still get to a stable state at the end: a clearly misremembered lady, a pain of a particular intensity, and so on. Maybe getting there is less than half the fun but we still get there. If so, there is no problem here for the existence of seemings.

Real and Apparent Time-Order

An example: the phi phenomenon. The phi phenomenon is very simple. A red dot is flashed on a screen. A short time later and an appropriate number of degrees of arc away, a green dot is flashed on the screen. Everyone sees the red dot *moving* and *changing into* the green dot—and everyone sees the one changing into the other before the green dot appears. This, of course, is impossible—the brain must be reconstructing the apparent time-order after the actual sequence of events in their actual time-order is completed.[9]

Does the phi phenomenon pose a problem for seemings? No, only for certain theories of seemings. There is a perfectly good state of how things *seem* to be unfolding—that is, a perfectly good seeming. We can even date it—the latter half of the state giving us how things seem (the part from the point at which the dot begins to appear to change color) cannot begin until after the green dot has actually been perceived.

Misrepresentation

The classic example of misrepresentation is the frog flicking out its tongue at an object that is in fact a black BB thrown across its visual field. Does it misperceive the BB as a fly, or correctly perceive it as a black object?

The putative problem for the existence of seemings is that if there is no way to answer this question, it is natural to conclude that there is no fact of the matter about what the frog sees. I think that this conclusion would be a mistake, and that there is no problem for the existence of seemings here. However, the story is trickier than it was in the earlier cases.

First we need to distinguish between the state of something *appearing* and what that thing appears to be *like*. In the case of the frog and most or all other cases like it, there is a quite determinate state of *something appearing*. It simply cannot be resolved what the thing appears to be like—not by us and, we can perfectly well allow, not by the organism either. What makes this possible? To be aware not just *of* something appearing but of what the thing appears to be *like*, we need not one thing, information about something, but two— information about something plus application of apparatus for de- termining what the thing appears to be like. Whatever the truth of Dennett's claim that all seemings *are* judgings, perception clearly *requires* judgings. We must both be presented with something and characterize it in some way (one of Kant's most basic claims: 1781, A51–B74).[10] Where characterization is needed, we can have a deter- minate presentation even though our view of what precisely is being presented is undetermined (a point that will become significant later). If so, misrepresentation is no threat to the existence of seemings.

It may appear that I am begging the question against Dennett's theory that seemings simply are judgings. I don't think I am. On Dennett's theory, the distinction I am after would come out as some- thing like this: The judgment *that* something is appearing is different from judgments about *what* the thing appears to be like. The first judgment yields a perfectly determinate seeming even if determinate judgments of the second kind cannot be made.

Boundless Descriptions

Dennett holds that an intentional object can be embedded in propo- sitional attitudes in endless ways, carved up into ever finer represen- tational states, and so on. This phenomenon gives rise to two problems. First, it creates a risk of an "explosion of distinct 'representational states'" (CE, 316). Second, since one of the places where it shows up is in memory, it is a new venue for S/O impasses. We have dealt with S/O impasses; what about the representational explosion? Well, let's suppose that there is some indeterminateness in the range and extent of the attitudes we can take to some represented content, that *here* things seem to be more determinate in folk psychology than they are. Would that show that the content itself could not be a state or event in which something seems like something? No.

Inverted Spectra

Supposed example: Where you see red, I could see green, even though all my speech and behavioral dispositions and therefore all my behavior, including all my statements about color, are the same as yours. I entirely agree with Dennett that no good sense can be made of the idea of an inverted spectrum or of inverted qualia, absent qualia, or any similar product of credulous faith in the power of thought-experiments to reveal genuine possibilities. Dennett suggests that inverted qualia, etc., require real seemings; no real seemings, no possibility of inverted qualia, etc. (CE, 393), and again I am happy to follow him. But how about the other way around? Would the incoherence of inverted qualia rule out real seemings? I am not sure whether Dennett wants to go *from* the incoherence of the idea of inverted qualia *to* the impossibility of real seemings (see CE, chapter 12, especially sections 4 and 5). For my part, I do not see how such an inference could go through. How would the impossibility of inverted qualia rule out seemings? That colors as they appear to us cannot be inverted seems entirely neutral with respect to whether those appearances are real events and if so what kind of event.[11]

The five challenges to traditional ideas about the determinateness of various aspects of conscious experience that we have just examined certainly open up new ways of thinking about conscious experience. They just happen not to give reasons to reject the traditional F-level notion of a seeming. Dennett has another argument against seemings. What is really going on when people seem to be having seemings, he says, is—judgings! "There is no such phenomenon as really seeming—over and above the phenomenon of judging" (CE, 364). Let's turn to that argument.

A Theory

Here are some claims that illustrate the central idea behind the theory. When we seem to be surveying an already existing "field," what we are in fact doing is judging that the field is filled in (Dennett 1996). Often when we seem to be reporting something "presented" to us, what we are actually doing is making a judgment about the thing. Indeed, often it is hard to apply the perception/inference distinction to experience at all. This rejection of presentations in favor of judgments goes with another idea. Often when we think our "mind" is showing us something, it is in fact telling us about it— the thing is not appearing in an image or anything imagelike; rather, we are describing it in some code.

The famous Warhol room of Marilyn Monroe posters is an example. All the Marilyn posters in the room seem to be alike. We think that we perceive this. However, a poster off to the left actually has Mickey Mouse ears and a Hitler mustache. We do not notice this. The reason is that we can perceive items clearly only through six degrees of arc or so. We are actually *judging* that all the posters are alike. We do not *find out* what is in the rest of our visual field, we *fill it in*. Filling in is a process of judgment, not anything imagelike.

What can be said for this theory and the inference that Dennett draws from it? The theory is empirical and stands or falls on the evidence, which I cannot summarize here. It is probably at least partly right. On the other hand, even in the Marilyn Monroe room there is still a lot of real seeing going on—thanks to rapid eye movement, much, much more than our six degrees of focal vision would give us.[12] In at least one case, moreover, the theory seems plain wrong: the case of pain (of which more later). And it does give rise to a question about Dennett's real target.

By "seemings," I have so far meant simply states or events in which something seems like something. All sorts of mental states are seemings: judgments, thoughts, and desires, as much as perceptions and sensations. Even abstract concepts and ideas appear to us in a certain way.[13] This broad view is Kant's view, and it is also Dennett's official view: "Seeming is simply 'the way things look to us' " (CE, 373; see also 58, 319, and others). But his examples often take a narrower view, one more like the notion of seemings in the empiricist tradition. Here seemings are thought of in terms of images, that is, states fully formed prior to cognitive processing. Think for example of the importance he attaches to getting representation in images out of his CADBLIND system. Think too of Dennett's general iconophobia, as he called it, throughout the 1970s (1978a, 1978e, for example). The answer, I think, is that Dennett is after *both:* both the idea that mental images are central to seemings and something about seemings as such. The distinction, however, is important for the scope of the theory.

Now suppose not just that seemings are not images (as I and many others would grant) but that Dennett's whole theory is right: Seemings are simply judgings. Would that entail that seemings in the F-level sense do not exist? Certainly not. *Judgings are themselves seemings!* When I judge, both what I am judging and the act of making the judgment *appear* to me, are like something for me. More than once Dennett says that "there is nothing more to phenomenology" than judgment (CE, 366; see also 364). This is a peculiar thing to say. Judgings themselves *have* phenomenology—full, rich, robust folk-psychological phenomenology. There is no argument against the existence of seemings here.

So what is going on? It seems to me that the theory of phenomenology as judgings is aimed at a certain *theory* of what seemings are like: passive presentations of already stable and well-formed material about how something seems. When Dennett says that there is no more to phenomenology than judgment, what he means is that all states having phenomenology are judgments. That is to say, he is offering a P-level theory of what seemings consist in. I don't know if this has been noticed before but Dennett's pronouncements against seemings in this part of the book all have a *theory* of seemings as their target, the theory that Dennett calls Cartesian materialism, not the idea that seemings are real states of some kind. Recall the claim that the category of the objectively subjective is bizarre. This claim is aimed at the notion that there are states that carry a certain phenomenology around with them "intrinsically." (This has to be false. How something seems in some representation is a relational matter affected by, for example, how the state or event is taken by the cognitive system in which it occurs.) Equally, when Dennett urges that there are not two stages, a presentation stage and a stage of judging the presentation, but only one, he is also after a theory of seemings, not the idea that there are such things.

To sum up: In the theory of seemings as judgings, Dennett is offering a theory of what the real P-level processes realizing seemings are like. This theory might support other aspects of the metaphysics of the intentional stance, for example, the idea that individual seeming states cannot be identified and reidentified independently of other such states, but it provides no independent support for the idea that there are no seemings.

We can imagine how this new theory of seemings as judgings might begin to work itself out in connection with perception. We could investigate how information about an object is coded in the visual cortex and, from the structure of this coding, make precise inferences about how the perceiver will judge the object to appear. "From the fact that this edge is coded as covered, this corner is coded as having a 60° angle, the organism will seem to be seeing the object from underneath and in front." Or whatever. This analysis could be very precise. What we would have been doing is exploring the specific states and events in the brain that a certain seeming is based on.[14] Dennett would accept all this without any qualms. When he urges that "there is nothing more to phenomenology" than judgings, among the things that judgings consist in are "various events of content-fixation" (CE, 366, 365), that is to say, events exactly like the ones we just sketched for perception.

By now unease will be growing. "While you have been pulling this realist story out of the hat," I can imagine someone objecting, "haven't you rather ignored the 'theorist's fictions' of heterophenomenology? Surely in the latter at least Dennett is flatly denying that seemings exist. In your introductory section, you yourself said that the doctrine of heterophenomenology is where the hard objections to the reality of seemings are found." Many people have read

Dennett this way (including me) but it is at least a partial misreading (as Dennett has prodded me into seeing). When Dennett talks about a theorist's fiction, he is talking about the *content* of a seeming—the way something seems to someone. *This* could be a fiction, even if the person is seeming a certain way to him- or herself. But this is not to deny that there are vehicles of seemings. There are indeed vehicles of seemings: judgings.

He does not say straight out that he accepts that there are vehicles for seemings (in CE) but he is a realist about processes of content-fixation:

Conscious experiences are real events occurring in the real time and space of the brain. (1994a, 135),

and the only candidate for content-fixers in his theory is judgments. (Dennett develops the theory of the whole middle section of CE in an entirely realist vocabulary.) He clearly accepted the reality of vehicles in (1978a), the paper for which he invented the story of Feenoman and the Feenomanologists so central to *Consciousness Explained,* and he has expressed the same view again recently (private communication). Folk psychology may well oversimplify seemings, as Dennett says (CE, 320), but it is not wrong when it takes them at least to exist.

So what is Dennett after when he says that the contents of seemings are abstracta, that the heterophenomenological world is a theorist's fiction (CE, 95, 98)? One thing is the *truth* of the *contents* of a seeming (as opposed to the *existence* of a *vehicle* of seemings). In the same way that the world need not be as it appears to us, we need not be as we appear to ourselves, not even when we appear to have basic things like seemings and beliefs and desires (CE, 319). Another is that in heterophenomenology, we devise sense-making interpretations; we do not "read off" preexisting patterns. Dennett does not say a lot about how this aspect of heterophenomenology relates to the reality of seemings (CE, 319 illustrates the gap), but here is how the story would go if told under the constraints of the intentional stance.

When a bit of content is fixed in the brain by a microjudgment, that gives us some organized information to use. However, it is a long way from this information to a fully developed seeming.[15] History, environment, knowledge of the subject's psychology, how the subject is using the content, causal connections running from the content-bearing state to the world, and so on, all enter into both the subject's first-person and our third-person judgments about how things seem based on this information. How these factors will seem when bound together is not "built into" them; it is how we judge them to be.[16] If so, states or events of things seeming like something are very unlikely to correspond to an aspect of judging events or events of any other kind in that person's brain, in exactly the same way that there is unlikely to be any "similarly structured" events underlying the shared belief of Tom and Sherlock and Jacques and Boris. Even a token-wise mapping is unlikely.

None of this is to deny the existence of real vehicles for seemings; the judgment about how things seem is the vehicle. It is instead to argue two things. First and obviously, the business of settling how something seems is vastly more complex than dreamt of in Descartes's philosophy. (Kant came closer to getting it right, or so I have argued, Brook 1994). Second and less obviously, the "how things seem" aspect of the judgment has a special reality-status. (This is often called the "content" of the judgment, but this very term begs the question in favor of a stronger brand of realism than Dennett would accept. Though he uses the term himself, he tends to restrict his use of it to the information "locked in" by microjudgment. There it is OK.)

We can now fit the realism about context-fixation and the interpretationism about hetero- (and auto-) phenomenology together. Put in the jargon of "syntax" in the inflated sense mentioned earlier, what Dennett calls the "conscious experiences" in the passage quoted earlier would have to be the syntax, the physical structure on which a seeming is based. It might be the acts of content-fixing judgments, the content thus fixed, or both. The "how things seem" of a seeming would then be free to float off into the world of "Real Patterns" or something even less brain-state real than that. Surely, it will be objected, this has to be wrong. Surely when a subject judges that so-and-so is such-and-such, the "so-and-so is such-and-such" part has to be something real, some proposition-like structure just as real as the judgment that arrived at it. But that is not so. Here's the question to ask: How do we—how does anybody—fix this aspect of judging, generate something determinate to ascribe to the judgment?

It can happen in two ways: in autophenomenology and in heterophenomenology. In autophenomenology, it has already been done: When the subject arrives at a judgment about how something is (that is, how it seems to her), she has also arrived at a judgment about what that "seeming to her" is like, namely, how that thing seems to her.[17] This is *an interpretation* of how things seem to her. This interpretation will be constrained, to be sure, in various ways (by information available not to her but in the system that is her), history, and so on, but it is not clear what it would mean to say that there is something more than the interpretation, something outside the interpretation for it to correspond or fail to correspond to.

Well, what about the interpretation itself? Do you mean the act of interpreting or the interpretation achieved? There is no problem with the reality of the act of interpreting—and the interpretation achieved is merely how something seems to her. In autophenomenology, we never shake free of interpretation to reach something that is being interpreted. The interpretation and the interpretation of the interpretation are all merely the interpretation of how something seems to us. The "content" of a judgment is merely how something is being interpreted as being; there is no "what the interpretation actually is" (over and above the vehicle of the interpretation—the vehicle is more than how something is interpreted).

The heterophenomenological story is similar and much more straightforward. Here someone else is interpreting how things seem to the subject. This is an interpretation of the same thing, namely, how something seems to her, but from the standpoint of another. And again there is nothing that the interpretation itself *is*. If I on the outside want to know what my interpretation itself is, there is nothing I can do but go auto—and the story we just told for the subject will now unfold for me. All I have to work with is my interpretation of how something seems—in this case, how something seems to me about how something seems to her. And if I want to know what this interpretation is really like, all I can do is "interpret my interpretation," that is, pay attention once more to how things about her seem to me. Again, all I have is the interpretation itself, that is, how something seems to me (in this case, about how something seems to her). Again we do not get beyond interpretations to something being interpreted. In fact, interpretations of how things seem have less reality than intentional stance patterns on Dennett's more recent view of them. The latter can at least be discerned in behavior. How something seems need not even have any expression in behavior. (When he treats heterophenomenology as about behavior, Dennett might seem to be denying this. I don't think he is. He certainly does not have to. By definition, heterophenomenology is limited to behavior—what else could it use?—and therefore is possible of zombies [CE, 95], but the same is not true of autophenomenology.)

Earlier we left two threads dangling: the air of self-refutation of "that we seem to have seemings does not entail that we do" and the question of what to do with seemings lacking brain-state realism. It turns out that the same point ties up both threads: The "how things seem" aspect of a judgment is merely an interpretation of something, and the only awareness we have of it is exactly the same interpretation. This *could* be called "self-interpretation" but it would be misleading to do so; it would suggest that there is something there both to do the interpreting and be interpreted. All that is there is *action*. It interprets the world—which is also an interpretation of what is being interpreted (see Dretske 1995, 56). To sum up, there are only interpretations and constraints on interpretations. These interpretations are not also things to be interpreted—which removes the air of self-refutation and explains what to do with seemings that lack brain-state realism.

Can auto- and hetero-interpretations come apart? If they can and if there could also be reason to favor the hetero-interpretation (we usually favor third-person interpretations over first-person ones), this would threaten first-person authority. Dennett says that we could do heterophenomenology on zombies (CE, 95), so it seems he would hold that heterophenomenology can override autophenomenology and that there is no special first-person authority. In fact, this is the very opposite of his position.

When we put you in the phenomenologist's clutches, *you get the last word.*
. . . We are giving you total, dictatorial authority over the account of how
it seems to you, about *what it is like to be you.* (CE, 96, his emphases)

When there is a first-person point of view (autophenomenology),
it trumps the third person one. First-person authority, as Dennett
interprets it (CE, 77, 81), is the idea that I am the best authority
about how things seem to me. And there does seem to be something
to this idea. I can be wrong about a lot of things but how could I be
wrong about how things *seem* to me? This would require a distinction
between how things *seem* to seem and how they *really* seem. So the
question is: Can we keep heterophenomenology and first-person authority, too?

I think we can, but first we need to understand first-person authority a bit better. Why is it that although we can distinguish between
how something is presented to someone, how it *ought* to seem to
them, and how it does seem to them, we cannot distinguish between
how it seems to them and how it seems to seem to them? In the
literature, it is now common to attribute the impossibility of the latter to the conditions of the agent's words having the meaning they
do (Davidson 1986), or the conditions of holding one another morally responsible (Bilgrami 1998), or some other social factor. I don't
think first-person authority has anything to do with social factors.
We are authoritative with respect to how things seem to us because,
roughly, how things seem to us is simply and always the *first stage in
conscious belief acquisition.* How things seem to us is—how things seem
to us. There is no room, not even a concept of room, for anything
to intervene between how things seem to us and how they seem.
Anything intervening would *by that intervention* immediately replace
the old state and itself become how things seem to us. For this reason, first-person authority is inviolable.

Of course, we can learn more about how something seems to us,
for example, by acquiring better concepts for thinking about things
of that kind. But this would be for something new to intervene, for
how the things seem to change. Notice that as I've characterized it,
this first stage is completely content-neutral. It is also neutral with
respect to whether a given seeming has a clear starting point or is

smeared out temporally as underlying bits of information fight to shape it.

Blindsight and other pathologies of consciousness are no counterexample. A blindsight patient *seems* not to being seeing anything in the scotoma and is authoritative about this. What makes their case special is that what they seem to themselves to be seeing and what they have some measure of informational access (Flanagan) or access consciousness (Block) to diverge more widely than they do in the normal case.

This may protect first-person authority but at the cost of raising another question: If the subject is authoritative about how things seem to her, what is left for heterophenomenology to do? Surely all a third party has to do and even can do is ask the subject. Well, perhaps; but we also have to understand the answer. Even if the subject is authoritative on how things seem to her, she is not authoritative about her *descriptions* of these seemings. When she describes how things seem to her, she is using public language and every element of the description requires interpretation. This makes room for heterophenomenology.

Some commentators have wondered if the realism of CE and Dennett's more recent writings on consciousness can be reconciled with the interpretationist metaphysics of mind of the intentional and heterophenomenological stances (Sedivy 1995, e.g.). To be sure, by using words like "experience" to describe the processes in the brain, Dennett himself muddies the waters, but they can be. We merely have to take *both* the realism *and* the interpretationism seriously.

So far we have examined how much and what kind of hostility to seemings is built into Dennett's picture of consciousness, and how the two sides of that picture, the realist side and the interpretationist side, hang together. Does CE offer arguments for the interpretationism about heterophenomenological content not found in earlier works? The claim that seemings are judgments is new, the interpretationism of heterophenomenology is not. Dennett's way of arguing for the seemings-as-judgments view is largely to urge its merits as a problem-solver as against any of the alternatives.[18] The theory faces a problem.

Judgments and Pains

The problem is this. In at least one case, the theory of seemings as judgings appears to be wrong. Dennett does not shrink from hard cases and the hardest case for his kind of theory is pain. Here is a passage on its close companion, suffering:

> Suffering is not a matter of being visited by some ineffable but intrinsically awful state, but of having one's life hopes, life plans, life projects blighted by circumstances imposed on one's desires, thwarting one's intentions. . . . The idea of suffering being somehow explicable as the presence of some intrinsic property is as hopeless as the idea of amusement being somehow explicable as the presence of intrinsic hilarity. (CE, 449)

I don't know about the awfulness of suffering being ineffable or intrinsic—indeed, I am not even sure what these terms mean—but the idea that suffering is merely a matter of judgment does not seem right. However, let us grant it. Dennett distinguishes suffering and pain rather sharply (1995, 352). Let us grant this, too. Now, what about pain? What does Dennett have to say about it?

No theory of *pain* as thwarted projects is going to do. If I hit my thumb with a hammer, what I feel will not be a gloomy sense of a reversal in my life fortunes. Indeed, a short, sharp pain like that will probably have no implications for my life fortunes (beyond the five minutes it takes the pain to fade). Yet it still hurts. Dennett himself offers an exactly parallel example (1995, 352). So what does he want to say about it?

The only positive account of pain that he has given puts pain squarely on the interpretation side of the interpretation/physical realization split.

> Are pains real? They are as real as haircuts and dollars and opportunities and persons, and centers of gravity. . . . (CE, 460)

A motley collection but (almost) all matters of interpretation—remember how Dennett views the reality of persons (I am not sure what haircuts are doing here). He seems to push the pain-as-judgment line in (1995), too, even thought he explicitly talks about short, sharp pains there.

The case of morphine suggests that no such account will work. As Dennett himself has articulated very nicely (1978b), morphine acts against pain in a peculiar way. Subjects claim that it does not remove the sensation of pain—but the pain no longer hurts. (Subjects say things like, "I still have the pain but it no longer hurts!") That is to say, it seems to the subject that the pain is still there—but a feeling-state characteristic of pain is not, namely, the hurting, the awfulness. This example would seem to cut against any reduction of pain to judgment decisively. Yet like the short, sharp pain, again it is Dennett's own example.

Dennett's approach to this example (private correspondence) is to suggest that how things seem to a subject is not definitive (except for how things seem to the subject). Moreover, there *is* a difference of judgment before and after: As we just saw, the subject *judges* her situation after the morphine to be different from her situation before. All true—and important. There is more judgment involved in even sharp, emotionally uncomplicated pain than many have thought. But! First, if even a difference as large as the difference between what I judge a feeling to be like and whether it hurts does not count, if even excruciating sensations come out as judgments, what is the force of the claim that all phenomenology is judgment? There is a risk in an "all" claim like this. Is Dennett reducing phenomenology to judgment—or merely bending the notion of judgment out of shape, expanding it so that it just becomes another name for phenomenology? What is being denied? What would a conscious state that was not a judgment *be like?* (This move should appeal to Dennett.)

I don't think that that this worry is real. The claim that all phenomenology is judgment includes, for example, a claim that there is always description or other encoding involved. If so, Dennett is not simply redefining "judgment." But there is a weaker worry. What is it about some judgments, descriptions, in virtue of which they hurt, whereas others don't? Absent an answer to this question, we have not made much progress with pain (or, mutatis mutandis, any other sensation).

In general, Dennett offers a pretty bloodless account of sensations (and also, I think, affects). Or worse. At one point in his long campaign to wean us away from the traditional theory of seemings, Dennett suggests that the traditional notion needs something like pseudo-pigment, an illusory substance that he calls figment (CE, 346). I am inclined to turn this move around. Dennett attempts to give us an account of pains but what he ends up with seem to be—fains.[19] Fains may make us act like they're pains and even thwart our intentions like they're pains (to the extent that pains do thwart our intentions), but they're not awful to have, so they're not pains. (This is one place where looking like us and "quacking" like us is *not* enough for being like us.)

Dennett is perfectly well aware of what pain is like, of course. Early in CE (1991a 25, 60–64) and in more recent writings (1998, 174, 280), he speaks very eloquently about it. Part of the problem may be a nasty lurking dilemma. As Dennett says, any account of what the awfulness of pain consists in must, in some way, break it down into elements that are not themselves awful to have. If your analysis merely breaks it into elements that are themselves awful, you haven't analyzed the awfulness (CE, 64). (Compare Fodor on propositional content: "if it is something, then it is something else" [1985, 9]). This creates a prima facie dilemma: If you keep the awfulness, it will be at the cost of giving no analysis of it; but if you analyze the awfulness, it will be at the cost of losing "the thing itself . . . the pain in all its awfulness," as Dennett has his alter ego put it (p. 64). Over the years, Dennett has gone both ways. In (1978b), the awfulness is essentially unanalyzed, and Dennett, in a fine application of what I earlier called the "outside in" strategy, focuses on how the awfulness and whatever it is that we are aware of as pain could be connected to the brain. In CE, he tries to say something about what pain, including its awfulness, might consist in—and loses the awfulness. Nasty.

Can we rescue Dennett on pain? (Not that he thinks that he needs any rescuing.) Notice that he treats pain as an intentional phenomenon. If it is, it has to be handled like belief and perception and seeming, and that is how Dennett handles it. Instead of treating pain as intentional and forcing it into the metaphysics of the intentional stance, why not view it as like processes of content-fixation, that is, as real events occurring in the brain? On this, I think more plausible view, certain brain processes would simply *be* sensations that are awful to have—sensations that obliterate concentration, cause nausea, disappear with analgesics, and so on. Most pains are not intentional, that is, about anything, and treating them as real brain events seems preferable to treating them as having the reality of blighted hopes, dollars, centers of gravity, and so on.[20]

There is a lot to commend this view. Moreover, we can accept it and still keep everything Dennett would (should?) want to say about heterophenomenology and pain. Exact what kind of pain one has and what implications it has for one's life could still be a matter of judgment, as lacking in brain-state reality as the result of any other heterophenomenological judgment. (A pain can be awful, indeed truly horrendous, without our having any precise view of what kind of pain it is.) In fact, we would end up exactly where morphine patients say they are: "I still have the pain" (heterophenomenological judgment) "but it no longer hurts" (the awful-feeling brain state has been altered). And we retain both blighted hopes and short, sharp pains.

Subjects

We turn now to Dennett's theory of the subject and the multiple drafts model. Is Dennett an eliminativist about subjects? Recall our F-level list of features of the subject:

List 1: F-level concept of the subject. A subject:

operates by forming things like beliefs and desires about objects, events, etc.;

marshals various cognitive resources (beliefs, desires, values, concepts, etc.) to generate an intention to do something and then marshals diverse bodily resources to do it;

is aware of a number of things at once in some way that allows him to relate things to other things;

consciously focuses attention on tasks; and so on.

Dennett is clearly hostile to the first item on this list as anything more than an explanatory abstracta of the intentional stance and states that we seem to ourselves to have. However, this is not new to CE, being fully present in the metaphysics of the intentional stance. Dennett carries it over (CE, 319, e.g.) but does not offer new arguments for it. So what about the rest of the list?

A notion of mental unity is at work in all three items. Now, if Dennett's multiple drafts model is hostile to anything in the traditional F-level notion of the subject, it would seem to be the idea of mental unity. So mental unity is a good test case. Six kinds of mental unity can be distinguished:

Cognitive Unity

Cognitive unity consists in our ability to bring an extremely wide range of cognitive resources to bear: what we want; what we believe; our attitudes to self, situation, and context; input from each sense; information of all kinds; language; memory of various kinds; bodily sensations; our skills; and so on. And we bring all these elements to bear in a highly integrated way. In this regard, Dennett himself mentions binding of textures, shapes, etc., into representations of constant objects (CE, 47, 258).

Unity of Consciousness

In addition to cognitive unity, consciousness displays unities of various kinds and in various places. Let's give them separate names: *unity of simple consciousness; unity of focus; unified consciousness of one's psychological states;* and *unified consciousness of self.*

i. Unity of Simple Consciousness
Unity of simple consciousness starts from the intuitive idea that we are aware of a great many things at once. Here is a better definition:

The unity of consciousness = *df.* a representing in which a number of items as represented are combined in such a way that to be aware of any of these items is also to be aware of other represented items as connected to it and of the whole as a single complex represented "world."

ii. Unified Consciousness of One's Conscious States
All the other unities of consciousness can be thought of as special instances of unified simple consciousness. The second is unified consciousness of our own conscious states. As well as having unified consciousness of situations and events not themselves conscious, we are able to be aware of seeing them, having feelings, thinking things, remembering things, and so on.

iii. Unity of Focus
The third instance of unified consciousness worth distinguishing is unity of focus. In unity of focus, some items from unified simple consciousness are selected in a specially focused kind of consciousness, and we are able to focus a number of considerations at the same time on these items—desires, beliefs, situations in the world, probabilities, and so on. Focal attention comes up once (CE, 397).

iv. Unified Consciousness of Self
The fourth and final form of unified consciousness that I will distinguish is unified consciousness of self. In unified consciousness of self, each of us is aware of him- or herself as him- or herself and as apparently the single subject and agent of the representations giving us unified simple consciousness of the "world," the single "common subject" of one's mental states, as Kant put it (1781, A350).

Consciousness of one's psychological states and oneself is different from consciousness of the world. All animals are conscious of the world, or almost all, but it is at least debatable whether any animal other than *Homo sapiens* is conscious of self.[21] Unified consciousness of one's own psychological states and of oneself as the single "common subject" of one's mental states figures centrally in Kant (1781/1787, A350; see Brook 1994, chapter 3). Dennett goes both ways on the unity of consciousness in general. On the one hand, he treats it as merely how we seem to ourselves (CE, 74, 108; 1994a, 134). On the other hand, he discusses pathologies of unified consciousness a number of times (CE, 326, 358, 419–425) and pathologies are breakdowns, hence require something that has broken down. Consciousness of self in particular is a theme throughout (e.g., CE, 67, 77, chapter 10).

Unity of Behavior

Finally, our behavior is highly unified. In doing what we do, we coordinate our limbs, eyes, bodily attitude, and so on, in ways the precision and complexity of which would be difficult to exaggerate. Think, for example, of a concert pianist performing a complicated concerto. Or Dennett sitting in his rocking chair, rocking, reading, listening, and looking all at the same time.

Focused, deliberate, integrated reflection and action require all the items on list (1) except (if Dennett is right) the first one. Dennett would accept that the rest of the list refers to something real. What about the mental unities? As will be clear from the views I have just summarized, he is at least not deeply hostile to them.

He is quite hostile to a lot that has been said about them, of course. Indeed, one of the main objectives of CE is to show that the P-level system realizing any such unities (and everything else to do with consciousness) could be and most probably is very different from anything conceived of in the tradition.[22] According to the multiple drafts model, all mental unities and all F-level features of conscious subjects could be realized in a system having the following P-level properties:

content-fixing processes (particularly judgments) that do not generate clearly discrete contentful states;

multiple drafts of various contents generated by the processes;

procedures for selecting some drafts, deselecting others, and tying some of the selected drafts together in a variety of usually loose, sometimes tight and well-integrated ways;

storage in memory ("criterial for consciousness" [CE, 132]);

implementation in a Pandemonium architecture.

The whole of this model has come to be known as the multiple drafts model, even though a specific provision concerning multiple competing drafts is just one part of it. (The model has important implications for the nature of individual conscious experiences, too, so my tying it so closely to Dennett's views on the subject is a bit artificial.) As far as I know, it is at least as likely to be true as any other model of the conscious subject and more likely than most. At any rate, I won't question it here. Among the most interesting claims Dennett makes based on it are that:

many temporal issues in connection with consciousness are by no means as straightforward as they might appear (S/O impasses and the others we examined earlier are only some of them); and

auto-stimulation by probes is a basis of, perhaps *the* basis of, consciousness of self.

On the multiple drafts model, the P-level procedures and structures that realize consciousness are *very* different from what the mental unities might lead us to expect. Dennett also urges that unified consciousness has been overrated. Indeed, he wants to downsize the role of mental unities in consciousness quite radically (see, e.g., his comments that conscious practical reasoning is relatively rare and that it is dangerous to take such rare occurrences to be a guide to the whole [CE, 252]). But none of this is to deny that mental unities or the subject exists. In his view, we are focused, unified, able to coordinate rich cognitive resources, and able to report with all the subtlety of the intentional stance on the results of many of these goings-on in us. It would seem, then, that Dennett is not an eliminativist about anything in the traditional list of F-level features of the subject except the first item, which the metaphysics of the intentional stance had already attacked. Nor is he an eliminativist about the mental unities closely associated with that list.[23] He just wants a better P-level theory of all these things. The one he comes up with is radically different from anything in the tradition but it is still a theory to explain these features, not an argument that nothing has such features.

More generally, if we accept that the traditional subject exists, we must not prejudge what it might be like (a point already made by Kant and, more recently, by van Gulick 1988). Who knows what kind of structures and procedures could result in or go with being a subject? What we observe in ourselves and others are cognitive states and activities tied together in various ways. It is an open question what the procedural and neural "substrates" of these representations and activities might be like, to use Kant's word (1781/7, A350). In particular, the substrate may well be processes of content-fixation generating multiple drafts of narrative fragments, just as Dennett says. Accepting that something exists answering to list (1) and the sketched unities does not commit us to any P-level conception of the subject, traditional or contemporary. In particular, the traditional F-level conception of the subject does not commit us to such postulated P-level entities as homunculi, Cartesian theaters, or any of the other weird and wonderful things that Dennett looks upon with such deep suspicion.

Dennett has made important suggestions about what can and cannot appear in an acceptable P-level account in other works, too. In particular, he has been urging for decades that there can be no undischarged homunculi, no exempt agents, in such an account (1978c, 102; 1978d, 124). He has also made a suggestion for how we can discharge the homunculus without abandoning the subject of list (1). Following Fodor (1975, 74fn.), he offers the idea of representations that can represent to themselves as a possible way out (1978c, 101–102). Again, however, this is a recommendation for P-level theory, not an attack on the existence of the F-level subject. Dennett's notion of the virtual captain (CE, 228) is a theory of what a unified subject consists in, not an argument that unified subjects do not exist.[24]

To conclude: Dennett's multiple drafts model does not pose a threat to the F-level subject of folk psychology, though it is a massive rejection of most previous P-level theories of it.

Two Last Issues

I will close with a brief look at one interesting implication of Dennett's model and one omission. The implication arises out of this question: What are we doing when we attribute the items on list (1) and the attendant mental unities to someone? We are not just describing how people seem to themselves, so we are not just doing heterophenomenology. Indeed, if the person in question is not "psychologically minded," he might very well not *seem* to himself to have these features at all. Anyway, the consciousness in question is not merely a matter of how subjects seem to themselves. Not just consciousness but unified, focused consciousness makes a difference to performance, so it is more than merely how we seem to ourselves (performance is generally worse when conscious attention is absent, distracted, split between two tasks, etc.). Think of the work of theorists such as Baars (1988 and many other works). If so, what are we doing? At minimum, we are attributing properties that *explain* what the person is and does, not merely how he seems to himself. This sounds more like the intentional stance. But we are not doing that, either.

Intentional stance attributions are governed by considerations of the appropriateness of beliefs and desires and the practical rationality of actions. But the unity of consciousness, unified focus, and so on, are not *reasons for action*. Thus, when we ascribe them, we are doing something more than and different from adopting the intentional stance. When they ascribe consciousness to some subjects, lack of consciousness to others, they are not postulating states and processes that rationalize behavior. In short, attributions of consciousness use neither heterophenomenology nor the intentional stance.

What *is* going on, then? Something more like inference to the best explanation. In Dennett's jargon, attributions of consciousness are done from something more like the design stance or even the physical stance than the intentional stance.[25] Inference to the best explanation, however, is held by many theorists to be entirely compatible with many kinds of realism about the inferred states and processes—which returns us to a point noted a couple of times already: the traditional realism of the vocabulary of much of *Consciousness Explained*. Of course, even if inferences to the best explanation are compatible with traditional realism, it does not follow that they require it. But Dennett has always been a traditional realist about the physical stance and, in a way and at times, about the design stance, too (see, e.g., 1987c, 39). If so, Dennett should be a traditional realist about consciousness. And, as we saw, he is, at any rate about conscious experiences and sensory qualities (though not, of course, about how things seem in them). From where I sit, that is all to the good. The more realism, the better. All that is left for the intentional and heterophenomenological stances is intentional content and judgments about how things seem.

That's the implication. Here's the omission. If the subject is unified, it is unified both at a time and over time. The most significant element in unifying the subject over time is autobiographical memory, specifically, memory of having experiences and doing actions (Kant 1781/1787; Parfit 1984). Whatever the implications of such memory for "personal identity" (being one person over time), it is central to personal unity over time. Indeed, it is so central that, as Parfit (1970, 15) has put it, if I remember doing something done by an earlier person or feeling something felt by an earlier person, I will automatically assume that that person was me. Dennett discusses memory a number of times in CE (as we saw, he even calls it criterial for consciousness). Indeed, semantic memory, both short- and long-term, has been central to his model of consciousness since at least 1978e. Yet there is hardly a mention of autobiographical memory in the work.

Summary box score: 1. Dennett has no quarrel with the existence of vehicles of seemings; he does not even question the idea. His target is a certain theory of seemings. 2. Likewise with subjects. The multiple drafts model is aimed at the traditional theory of the subject, not at the idea that subjects exist at all. 3. Dennett's theory of seemings as judgments and the multiple drafts model are generative and suggestive. 4. The account faces some problems. Nothing I have said undermines Dennett's account but I may have domesticated it a bit. It has been thought to have very radical implications. I am not sure that it does.[26]

Notes

1. Page references without a date of publication will be to this work.

2. See Wilkes (1988) for my reasons for limiting the claim to the last few hundred years.

3. Another version of the triple, one associated with Newell, is the trio of knowledge, physical symbol procedure, and system implementation. Dennett claims that his tri-

ple of intentional, design, and physical stances is closely related (1991a, 276) but his notion of the intentional is different from the original notions of task or knowledge level in some respects (note 25 gives my reasons for saying this).

4. Sellars's (1963) manifest image is a rough parallel. A host of issues about lexical semantics, defining characteristics, essences, and so on, arises here. I am going to duck them all.

5. What if there is no clear breakpoint between list (1) and list (2)? Perhaps folk psychology is itself infected with theory. That would be no surprise. My question would then become: Starting with the most general, least theoretic features, how far down does Dennett want to go before he starts to urge outright elimination? Short answer: maybe a little distance for seemings, quite a long way for subjects.

6. Dennett does not advance this claim in CE but he makes it in (1987a).

7. The recently advanced view of some pain specialists that pain can arise in the brain entirely endogenously gives this question some urgency.

8. Flanagan (1992, 81–85) has an excellent discussion of the "outside in" strategy so I will not pursue it further here. In a response to Flanagan in his wrap-up paper for the volume on his work in *Philosophical Topics,* Dennett give this as his reasons for holding that there is no resolution of S/O and the other impasses: "tremendous progress is made by assuming that there isn't" (1994c, 532). Thus, his reason is pragmatic, not principled. He says that simplification is what generates the progress. But is the simplification based on falsehood? *That* would not be progress. As I said, I won't pursue the issue here.

9. As Dennett notes (p. 139), Kant was already aware that the time order in which events are presented to us can be different from the time order in which we experience them (Kant, 1781/7, fn. to A37=B54).

10. As Kant saw, the same is true of our awareness of our own self. We are aware of ourselves only as we appear to ourselves, not as we are; and appearance of self requires characterization just as much as appearance of anything else does. Dennett of course agrees (CE, 67).

11. As Palmer (1999) and others have pointed out, the possibilities for inverting qualia of color are in fact quite limited.

12. I owe this point to Zoltan Jakab.

13. Flanagan makes this observation in (1992, 67–68). My Kantian/empiricist distinction is similar to his distinction between the wide and the narrow senses of "qualia."

14. What we are doing here is closely related to the old project of figuring out the "existential status" of intentional objects—and may be a first step toward a solution (Dennett 1978a, 181). More recently, Dennett has said that attributions of how things would seem to the perceiver here are done from the intentional stance, and so presumably have all the holism and indeterminacy that goes with this stance. Given the realist presentation of the whole idea of content-fixation in CE, this comes as a surprise. The text of CE suggests exactly the opposite. But, he says, it is his view (1994c, 528).

15. Even though, according to Dennett (1994c), p. 528, the determination of *what* content has been fixed even by a microjudgment itself requires the intentional stance. As I said in note 14, this claim is a surprise. We would expect the intentional stance to kick in only about when autophenomenology kicks in: when we start to judge how things are (i.e., how they seem to *us*).

16. I mean to be using a concept of binding broader than the one found in contemporary vision theory here, one more like Kant's notion of synthesis.

17. Harman 1990, 1996 and Dretske 1995 both emphasize the idea that when we are aware of a seeming, as we would put it, what we are aware of are the properties of what is represented in it. So long as the idea is not overgeneralized to our awareness of the vehicles of seemings, too, it seems right.

18. There is an argument that I have not considered: Dennett's repeated invitation to ask whether there could be anything in the brain that has the properties of how Santa Claus or some other intentional object seems to us (CE, 96; see also 85, 134). Two problems. (1) Distinguish the *referent* of a phenomenological item from the *vehicle* of that item and this argument disappears. What we want to investigate are the brain events (if any) that a phenomenological item *consists in,* not the events that *it represents* (brain events or otherwise; they are rarely brain events, of course). Who thinks that the way we seem to ourselves *is* apt to be anything like what we actually are? (2) It isn't a new argument. Dennett has been using it since (1978a).

19. I owe this lovely neologism to Chris Viger.

20. In a roundabout way, I owe this view to Don Ross—roundabout because it came to me when he was once trying to put pain firmly on the other side of the intentional/context-fixing divide.

21. With respect to distinguishing consciousness of the world from consciousness of self, Dennett has gone both ways in different writings. In (1987e), he carefully distinguishes them. In CE, he never does so explicitly, though he toys with the distinction in a few places (e.g., 45).

22. Here I am treating the unities as F-level phenomena. They are so integral to, indeed so close to being simply a redescription of, the items on list (1) that it is hard to see how we could have one without the other. Plus, treating them as P-level would complicate the telling of the story I want to tell without changing anything but the telling.

23. One of the interesting implications of what I have just been saying is that unified conscious subjects and any belief/desire structuring of cognitive processing turn out to be quite independent of one another. Robust, conscious subjects could exist even if belief/desire psychology turns out to be false.

24. I have been known to suggest that Dennett's notion of the virtual captain is a perfectly good P-level sketch of what Kant's transcendental unity of apperception might consist in (Brook, 1994, 229)! I meant to be provocative but I also endorse the idea. I also argue in ch. 9 of that book that a Kantian spin on the idea of a self-representing representation can take us a long way.

25. As I noted earlier, Dennett (CE, 76) claims that the intentional stance is quite closely related to the task- or knowledge-level of Newell and company. Since

attributions of consciousness are often F-level—i.e., task-level—attributions, we can now see why I said earlier that the intentional stance seems quite different from the task- or knowledge-level of Newell and others.

26. I would like to thank Pamela Goold, Don Ross, Robert Stainton, and especially Zoltan Jakab for probing and helpful questions and suggestions. I owe a special debt to Dan Dennett for correcting a mistake in a most generative way.

References

Akins, K., ed. (1996). *Perception*. Vancouver Studies in Cognitive Science, 5. Oxford: Oxford University Press.

Baars, B. (1988). *A Cognitive Theory of Consciousness*. Cambridge: Cambridge University Press.

Bilgrami, A. (1998). Self-knowledge and resentment. In Wright, Smith, and MacDonald (1988).

Brook, A. (1994). *Kant and the Mind*. New York: Cambridge University Press.

Davidson, D. (1986). Knowing one's own mind. *Proceedings and Addresses of the American Philosophical Association* 60: 441–458.

Dawson, M. (1998). *Understanding Cognitive Science*. Oxford: Blackwell Publishers.

Dennett, D. C. (1978a). Two approaches to mental images. Reprinted in Dennett 1978f.

Dennett, D. C. (1978b). Why you can't make a computer that can feel pain. Reprinted in Dennett 1978f.

Dennett, D. C. (1978c). A cure for the common code. Reprinted in Dennett 1978f.

Dennett, D. C. (1978d). Artificial intelligence as philosophy and psychology. Reprinted in Dennett 1978f.

Dennett, D. C. (1978e). A cognitive theory of consciousness. Reprinted in Dennett 1978f.

Dennett, D. C. (1978f). *Brainstorms*. Montgomery, Vt.: Bradford Books.

Dennett, D. C. (1987a). Evolution, error and intentionality. Reprinted in Dennett 1987d.

Dennett, D. C. (1987b). Three kinds of intentional psychology. Reprinted in Dennett 1987d.

Dennett, D. C. (1987c). Real patterns, deeper facts, and empty questions. In Dennett 1987d.

Dennett, D. C. (1987d). *The Intentional Stance*. Cambridge, Mass.: MIT Press. A Bradford Book.

Dennett, D. C. (1987e). Consciousness. In *The Oxford Companion to the Mind*, R. Gregory (ed.). Oxford: Oxford University Press.

Dennett, D. C. (1988). Quining qualia. In Marcel and Bisiach (1988), 42–87.

Dennett, D. C. (1991a). *Consciousness Explained*. Boston: Little Brown and Company.

Dennett, D. C. (1991b). Real patterns. Reprinted in Dennett 1998.

Dennett, D. C. (1994a). Real consciousness. Reprinted in Dennett 1998.

Dennett, D. C. (1994b). Instead of qualia. Reprinted in Dennett 1998.

Dennett, D. C. (1994c). Get real. *Philosophical Topics* 22: 505–568.

Dennett, D. C. (1995). Animal consciousness: What matters and why. Reprinted in Dennett 1998.

Dennett, D. C. (1996). Seeing is believing. . . . In Akins (1996).

Dennett, D. C. (1998). *Brainchildren*. Cambridge, Mass.: MIT Press. A Bradford Book.

Dretske, F. (1995). *Naturalizing the Mind*. Cambridge, Mass.: MIT Press. A Bradford Book.

Flanagan, O. (1992). *Consciousness Reconsidered*. Cambridge, Mass.: MIT Press. A Bradford Book.

Fodor, J. (1975). *The Language of Thought*. New York: Thomas Y. Crowell.

Fodor, J. (1985). Fodor's guide to mental representation. Reprinted in Fodor 1990.

Fodor, J. (1990). *A Theory of Content and Other Essays*. Cambridge, Mass.: MIT Press. A Bradford Book.

Harman, G. (1990). The intrinsic quality of experience. In *Philosophical Perspectives* 4, J. Tomberlin (ed.). Atascadero: Ridgeview, 31–52.

Harman, G. (1996). Explaining objective color in terms of subjective reactions. In *Philosophical Issues*, E. Villanueva (ed.). Atascadero: Ridgeview, pp. 1–18.

Kant, I. 1781/7. *Critique of Pure Reason* (1781 and 1787). Trans. Norman Kemp Smith as: *Immanuel Kant's Critique of Pure Reason*. London: Macmillan, 1963.

Marcel, A., and Bisiach, E., eds. (1988). *Consciousness in Contemporary Science*. New York: Oxford University Press.

Marr, D. (1982). *Vision: A Computational Investigation into the Human Representation and Processing of Visual Information*. New York: W. H. Freeman.

Palmer, S. (1999). Color, consciousness, and the isomorphism constraint. *Behavioral and Brain Sciences* 22, 6: 923–943.

Parfit, Derek. (1970). Personal identity. *Philosophical Review* 80: 3–27.

Parfit, Derek. (1984). *Reasons and Persons.* Oxford: Oxford University Press.

Putnam, H. (1975). The meaning of "Meaning." In his *Mind, Language, and Reality.* Cambridge: Cambridge University Press, 215–271.

Sedivy, S. (1995). Critical notice of D. Dennett, *Consciousness Explained. Canadian Journal of Philosophy* 25, 3: 455–483.

Sellars, W. (1963). Philosophy and the scientific image of man. In *Science, Perception, and Reality.* London: Routledge and Kegan Paul.

van Gulick, R. (1988). Consciousness, intrinsic intentionality, and self-understanding machines. In Marcel and Bisiach (1988).

Wilkes, K. V. (1988). __, yishi, duh, um, and consciousness. In Marcel and Bisiach (1988).

Wright, C., Smith, B., MacDonald, C., eds. (1988). *Knowing Our Own Minds.* Oxford: Oxford University Press.

12

Zombies Explained

Thomas W. Polger

Dennett's Challenge[1]

Zombies are imaginary creatures that are stipulated to lack consciousness despite being otherwise identical in one way or another to human beings or other conscious creatures. In an essay titled "The Unimagined Preposterousness of Zombies," Daniel Dennett laments the sad state of philosophy in which there is serious debate over whether or not this fictional kind of being is possible:

> Sometimes philosophers clutch an insupportable hypothesis to their bosoms and run headlong over the cliff edge. Then, like cartoon characters, they hang there in mid-air, until they notice what they have done and gravity takes over. Just such a boon is the philosophers' concept of a zombie, a strangely attractive notion that sums up, in one leaden lump, almost everything that I think is wrong with current thinking about consciousness. (1995, 322)

The precipitant of Dennett's distress was an essay by Owen Flanagan and myself in which we critiqued a zombie thought experiment created by Todd Moody (Flanagan and Polger 1995; Moody 1994). Moody argues that it is impossible for a planet of zombies to evolve, because zombies could never originate mentalistic vocabulary. Flanagan and I thought that Moody's analysis missed the mark (and Dennett agreed). But we tried to use the notion of a zombie world to press questions about the evolution and function of consciousness. Dennett saw us as thereby legitimizing the zombie construct.

To that charge we plead guilty. We *do* think that zombies are a useful fiction.

The reprinting of Dennett's essay in his recent anthology, *Brainchildren* (1998), provides an occasion to revisit the question of zombies. Dennett set down a challenge: "If the philosophical concept of zombies is so important, so useful, some philosopher ought to be able to say why in nonquestion-begging terms. I'll be curious to see if anybody can mount such a defense, but I won't be holding my breath" (1995, 326). Here it is.

Zombies: A Taxonomy

Zombies are stipulated to be creatures identical in some way to human beings, but which lack consciousness. They are stipulated to be at least behaviorally identical to human beings or other conscious creatures. They may also be identical in other ways, as we shall see. The main question about zombies is whether they are possible.

The zombie problem, like the problems of absent, inverted, alien, and dancing qualia, is just one way of pushing questions about consciousness (cf. Block 1980a, Shoemaker 1982, Chalmers 1996). These thought experiments, and many others, serve the function of putting questions about the nature and causal efficacy of consciousness in a particularly salient form. By facing us with entities that exemplify our theories, thought experiments force us to think carefully about proposed explanations of mind and consciousness.

Of course no thought experiment is to be conducted in a vacuum. The purpose of such considerations is to draw out the commitments, conditions, and caveats of various theories about mind and consciousness. Are zombies possible? The answer depends on the details of how the zombies are stipulated, what kind of possibility is in question, and what sort of theory of consciousness you hold. As Güven Güzeldere writes, "playing with the idea of zombies could turn into playing with philosophical fire. But precisely for that reason, it is important to pay attention to the *particulars* in using zombies as a tool of imagination in thought experiments" (1995, 327).

Güzeldere's (1995) essay, intended to reconcile partially Flanagan's and my view with Dennett's view, provides a taxonomy of zom-

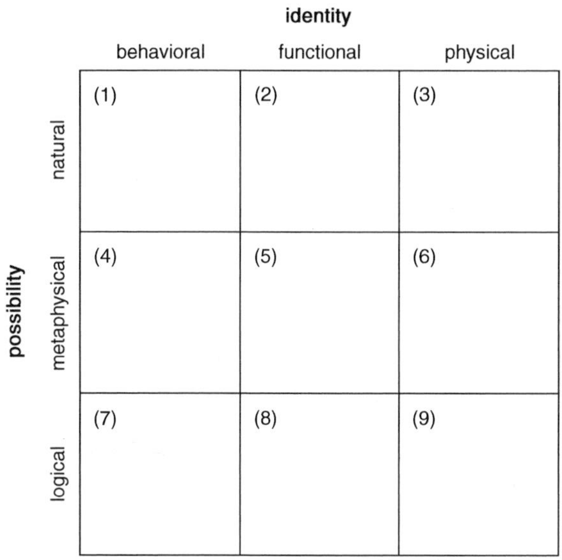

Zombies Explained

identity

Figure 12.1
Zombie Scorecard

bies based on the question of how zombies are identical to conscious creatures: Are they supposed to be behaviorally, functionally, or physically[2] identical to conscious beings? Flanagan and I drew a modal distinction regarding zombies: Are zombies logically, metaphysically, or naturally possible?[3] Taken together these two distinctions form the axes of the Zombie Scorecard (figure 12.1).

The Zombie Scorecard is a way of organizing nine different questions about zombies:

(Q1) Is it naturally possible that there be zombies that are behaviorally identical to human beings?

(Q2) Is it naturally possible that there be zombies that are functionally identical to human beings?

(Q3) Is it naturally possible that there be zombies that are physically identical to human beings?

(Q4) Is it metaphysically possible that there be zombies that are behaviorally identical to human beings?

(Q5) Is it metaphysically possible that there be zombies that are functionally identical to human beings?

(Q6) Is it metaphysically possible that there be zombies that are physically identical to human beings?

(Q7) Is it logically possible that there be zombies that are behaviorally identical to human beings?

(Q8) Is it logically possible that there be zombies that are functionally identical to human beings?

(Q9) Is it logically possible that there be zombies that are physically identical to human beings?[4]

Logically possible just means *not contradictory*. There is some question about whether there is an even weaker sort of possibility, something like conceivability (Horgan 1987) or epistemic possibility (Kripke 1972), but let us ignore that in the present discussion. *Naturally possible* I take to be something like *compatible with all and only the actual substances and laws of nature.*[5] There is no general agreement about what metaphysical possibility is. Whether or not metaphysical possibility is connected to conceivability is a point of contention; although there is de facto (if grudging) consensus that conceivability is our best guide to metaphysical possibility.[6] The lack of agreement about metaphysical possibility makes it difficult to fill in the middle row of the Zombie Scorecard.

Behaviorally identical zombies make all the overt movements and utterances that conscious creatures do, but they may have any internal structure and may be composed of whatever material. Behaviorally identical zombies needn't be hollow shells; they could be quite sophisticated. However, in considering behaviorally identical zombies their internal organization is left unspecified. Functionally identical zombies not only make the movements that conscious creatures do, they also have the same internal organization that conscious creatures do. Physically identical zombies are identical to conscious creatures cell for cell, molecule for molecule, or atom for atom (see note 2).

These three ways in which zombies could be stipulated as identical to conscious creatures parallel three families of theories: behaviorism, functionalism, and identity theory. For the present purposes behaviorism, functionalism, and identity theories are considered as theories of consciousness. Although functionalism, for example, is often held as a theory of mind (cognition and intentionality, say) but not of consciousness (see, e.g., Ned Block 1980a), what is at stake here are just those functionalist theories that are intended to explain consciousness (see, e.g., William Lycan 1987, 1996).

Robert Kirk's original zombies—the logical possibility of physically identical zombies—were introduced as a problem for materialism (1974). The strongest claim represented in the Zombie Scorecard is of the natural possibility of physically identical zombies. The weakest claim is of the logical possibility of behaviorally identical zombies—the kind that Flanagan and I defended against Moody's thought experiment (1995).

If the zombie questions are asked in the form, "Is it y-ly possible that there be creatures that are x-ly identical to human beings but which lack consciousness?" (where y is a mode of possibility and x is a degree or kind of identity) then someone might object that this begs the question as to whether human beings are conscious. I happen to think that human beings are conscious, as does Dennett. But to avoid any appearance of impropriety, the questions should be rephrased, "Is it y-ly possible that there be two creatures that are x-ly identical to one another but differ in that one is conscious and the other is not?"

This formulation has the additional advantage of making transparent how the form of the zombie construct is related to absent, inverted, alien, and dancing qualia thought experiments:[7]

Zombies and absent qualia: Is it y-ly possible that there be two creatures that are x-ly identical to one another but differ in that one is conscious and the other is not? (Cf. Kirk 1974, Block 1980a).

Inverted qualia: Is it y-ly possible that there be two creatures that are x-ly identical to one another but differ in that one's consciousness is "inverted" with respect to the other's? (Cf. Shoemaker 1982.)

Alien qualia: Is it y-ly possible that there be two creatures that are x-ly identical to one another but differ in that one has consciousness that is entirely different in quality from those had by the other? (Cf. Lewis 1980.)

Dancing qualia: Is it *y*-ly possible that there be two creatures that are *x*-ly identical to one another but differ in that one is always conscious and the other sometimes has the same sort of consciousness as the first and other times has a different sort of consciousness (inverted or alien) or none at all (absent)? (Cf. Chalmers 1996.)

Zombies are just one among many thought experiments designed to explore our theories of consciousness.

This brief sample of the wrangling over formulations serves as a reminder that, when it comes to zombies, the details matter. After all, zombies are stipulated, not discovered. Imagining zombies is just a vivid way of forcing ourselves to face the consequences of views that we already hold. Some of the consequences of a view, or the caveats necessary to maintain it, may not be palatable to all philosophers. But those consequences and caveats don't come from the notion of a zombie; they are merely highlighted by asking the zombie questions. As Güzeldere writes,

Belief in zombies has become a litmus test for intuitions in recent philosophy of mind. . . . The set of answers one chooses to give to questions of this sort is usually a good indicator of where one stands with respect to a variety of issues regarding consciousness—its ontology, nature, function, evolutionary role, and so on. (1995, 326–327)

But this is precisely what Dennett will have none of.

Dennett says the burden on the zombie defender is:

One must show that there is a difference between conscious beings and zombies, *and* one must show that one's demonstration of this difference doesn't depend on underestimating in the well-nigh standard way the powers of zombies. (1995, 325)

The disagreement between Dennett and zombie defenders concerns the natural possibility of functionally identical zombies (Güzeldere 1995). If that is right, then the above statement of the challenge makes it look as though the burden on the zombie defender is to show that functionally identical zombies are naturally possible—that is, to show that functionalism is false. Now that's a tall order!

But Dennett's summary statement overstates the burden. Elsewhere he puts the point differently, fretting that, "the philosophers' *concept of a zombie,* a strangely attractive notion . . . sums up, in one leaden lump, almost everything that I think is wrong with current thinking about consciousness" (1995, 322; emphasis added) and writing, "I have never seen an argument in support of *the zombie distinction* that doesn't make a mistake of imagination. . . ." (1995, 325; emphasis added). With these statements Dennett makes a more modest demand: that someone defend the *concept* of zombies.

I'm not going to argue that functionally identical zombies are naturally possible. To show that functionally identical zombies are naturally possible I would have to provide, for example, an argument for type-identity theory or dualism (either of which allow for the natural possibility of functionally identical zombies) or an argument against functionalism (which entails the natural impossibility of functionally identical zombies).

Dennett's challenge is to meet the modest demand, to show that the concept of zombies is not incoherent. To answer this challenge I do not have to show that functionally identical zombies are naturally possible; I can leave the question of the natural possibility of functionally identical zombies open. It will be more than enough if I show that functionally identical zombies can be conceived in a way that is not self-contradictory, is useful, and is not question-begging.

One might think that how functionally identical zombies are conceived depends very much on what notion of functional identity (notoriously, there are many) is invoked. In particular, functional specifications come in coarser (or higher-level) varieties and finer (or lower-level) varieties. The coarsest sorts of functional identity come close to being behavioral identities; the finest sorts of functional identity come close to being complete physical identities. Indeed there are arguments that exploit these facts to show that functional identity really is either behavioral or physical identity (e.g., Lycan 1987, Hill 1991). So one might think that it matters a great deal whether the functionally identical zombies are fine or coarse functional duplicates.[8] This, I take it, is part of Dennett's point in reminding us about his modified, complex zombies, the *zimboes* (1991, 1995).

Zombies and Zimboes

Given uncompromising remarks such as, "It's hard for me to keep a straight face through all this, but since some very serious philosophers take the zombie problem seriously, I feel obliged to reciprocate" (1991, 95) and "I confess that try as I might, I cannot summon up conviction for any other verdict: Zombies are ridiculous!" (1994, 540), it would be understandable if one thought Dennett's position on zombies was clear and simple. On closer inspection, his view is neither clear nor simple.

Dennett argues that all extant discussions of zombies depend on "underestimating in the well-nigh standard way the powers of zombies" (1995, 325). Let us begin with a passage in which he himself appears to make exactly this mistake.

First Dennett reminds us of his functionally sophisticated kind of zombie, the zimbo: "In [*Consciousness Explained*] I introduced the category of a *zimbo,* by definition a zombie equipped for higher-order reflective informational states" (1995, 322). Zimboes are zombies that are functionally complex. Dennett then goes on to say,

As I pointed out when I introduced the term, zombies behaviorally indistinguishable from us are zimboes, capable of all the higher-order reflections we are capable of, because they are competent, *ex hypothesi,* to execute all the behaviors that, when we perform them, manifestly depend on our higher-order reflections. Only zimboes could pass a demanding Turing Test, for instance, since the judge can ask as many questions as you like about what it was like answering the previous question, what it is like thinking about how to answer this question, and so forth. (1995, 323)

But zombies that are behaviorally indistinguishable from us are . . . zombies! Zimboes don't *behave* any differently (neither better nor worse) than their functionally less sophisticated cousins, the behaviorally identical zombies. Zimboes are zombies, and all zombies are at least behaviorally identical to conscious creatures. As Dennett himself notes only paragraphs before, "If, *ex hypothesi,* zombies are behaviorally indistinguishable from us normal folk, then they are really behaviorally indistinguishable!'' (1995, 322). The Turing Test is an entirely behavioral test, so it could not be used to distinguish between zombies and zimboes. It's simply not the case that only zimboes (functionally sophisticated zombies) could pass the Turing Test—*any* zombie could pass that test.

It looks as though Dennett has underestimated the powers of zombies. Since he raises these points in the context of arguing that the zombie concept is irreparably confused, some might expect Dennett to respond, in Wittgensteinian fashion, that he was showing us what he could not say with an argument, namely, that the concept of zombies is self-contradictory. But there is a better explanation: Dennett believes that simple behaviorally identical zombies are not naturally possible, so *any* zombie is *at least* functionally sophisticated—is at least a zimbo. I'll explain.

Dennett holds that it is a fact about human beings that nothing could be behaviorally identical to us without also having a high degree of functional sophistication, without "higher-order reflective informational states" (1995, 322). For example, he responds to Flanagan's and my suggestion that conscious pain is not necessary for injury avoidance, writing,

In creatures as cognitively complex as us (with our roughly inexhaustible capacity for meta-reflections and higher-order competitions between policies, meta-policies, etc.), the "blood-is-about-to-be-lost sensors" and their kin cannot *simply* be "hooked-up to the right action paths" as Flanagan and Polger put it. (1995, 323)[9]

For Dennett, behaviorally identical zombies—that are not also functionally sophisticated—are not naturally possible. That is why Dennett claims that only functionally sophisticated zombies (zimboes) could pass the Turing Test. But Dennett is certainly not making the Cartesian point that there are fundamental limits on the mechanical powers of organized bits of matter; and he is not arguing that the concept of a behavioral duplicate is ipso facto the concept of a conscious thing (as analytical behaviorism would have it). Rather, Dennett is making the straightforward engineering point that performing sophisticated behaviors requires sophisticated mechanisms. Imagining a behavioral duplicate that is a hollow shell is an exercise in fantasy.

If I am correct, Dennett would probably respond that examples of behaviorally identical zombies are only possible if we imagine them to have complex control mechanisms. Dennett is not arguing that consciousness is *constituted* by behavior. He is arguing that the sorts of mechanisms responsible for consciousness are also required to perform certain behaviors. If a future George Lucas or Steven Spielberg or Rodney Brooks is going to design a perfect behavioral duplicate, it is going to have to be *complicated*.

Suppose Dennett is right that the degree of functional complexity that is a prerequisite of behavioral identity is also sufficient for consciousness. In that case there could be no merely behaviorally identical zombies. Even so, it would not be *because* the behavioral duplicates are behaviorally identical that they are conscious, but *because* the duplicates are functionally sophisticated. In virtue of their complex functional organization they are conscious, not in virtue of their behavioral identity *simpliciter*.

Clarifying Dennett's claims about zombies and zimboes is sufficient to dissolve the prima facie tension in his remarks. For Dennett, behavior is a reliable indicator of consciousness. Dennett's reliance on zimboes, and his conviction that behaviorally identical entities must also be functionally sophisticated, reinforce the claim that what is at stake in Dennett's arguments is the natural possibility of functionally identical zombies. Let us agree that behavioral identity, if we are not to be dabbling with spirits, or gremlins, or élan vital, requires complex mechanisms. What zimboes have that zombies do not is a sophisticated internal mechanism—they are functionally complex.

But what is in question with zombies is functional identity, not just functional sophistication; so it must be that Dennett intends the zimboes to count as functionally identical. And I see no reason to suppose that those mechanisms necessary for behavioral identity must be functionally *identical* to our own mechanisms, unless to produce the same overt behavior and utterances is ipso facto to be functionally identical. And even if behavioral identity requires functional *identity*—as opposed to functional sophistication—one needn't accept that every mechanism functionally identical to consciousness is thereby a conscious mechanism. This last point is (or is part of) a response that Dennett compares to vitalism and derides as, "too puny to weigh against the account of life presented by contemporary biology" (Dennett 1991, 281–282). But the response is not puny.

What is Dennett's argument for the conclusion that there are limits on nonconscious mechanisms? If—and this is the reading that I have been *discouraging*—Dennett is maintaining that it is a logical truth that all mechanisms functionally identical to consciousness are conscious mechanisms, then he has provided no argument for that claim. If—as I have suggested—Dennett is making a claim about the natural limits of nonconscious mechanisms, he has provided no constructive argument for that claim, either. The single reason Dennett provides for holding this view is that the alternative (the possibility that functionally equivalent mechanisms may differ in that some are conscious and some are not) leads to epiphenomenalism and "pernicious nonsense."

If Dennett is right, those consequences would indeed worry most defenders of zombies. (Whether it would be enough to compel one to accept his conclusion is not altogether clear.) But the question is moot because Dennett's reasoning is faulty.

Zombies and Epiphenomenalism

What was difficult to discern in the discussion of zombies and zimboes in *Consciousness Explained* is that Dennett is presenting the zombie defender with a dilemma. He makes the point directly in "The Unimagined Preposterousness of Zombies":

[The point of introducing zimboes] was to make a distinction within the imaginary category of zombies that would have to be granted by believers in zombies, and that could do all the work they imputed to consciousness, thereby showing either that their concept was subtly self-contradictory, since some zombies—zimboes—were conscious after all, or that their concept of consciousness was not tied to anything familiar and hence amounted to an illicit contrast: consciousness as a "player to be named later" or an undeclared wild-card. (1995, 322–323)

So the purpose of introducing a distinction between zombies and zimboes—between behaviorally and functionally identical zombies—is to set up a dilemma: Either all the differences between the conscious and unconscious are functional differences (remember, Dennett holds that there are certain things that only a functionally complex zimbo can do), or else the alleged difference is "not tied to anything familiar" and is thus consciousness "in the systematically mysterious way that supports such doctrines as epiphenomenalism" (1991, 406).

The shape of Dennett's challenge is now clear. Either the concept of a functionally identical zombie is self-contradictory, or else it involves a conception of consciousness as epiphenomenal.[10] There can be little doubt about the first horn of the dilemma. On Dennett's conception of consciousness, zombies are incoherent. So to answer Dennett's challenge, one must address the second horn of the dilemma—one must show that a conception of consciousness that allows for the possibility of functionally identical zombies does not entail epiphenomenalism.

Dennett defines philosophers' notion of epiphenomenalism as follows: " 'x is epiphenomenal' means 'x is an effect but itself has no effects in the physical world whatever' " (1991, 402). This is what Dennett is referring to as epiphenomenal "in the ridiculous sense." I call this kind of epiphenomenalism *strict metaphysical epiphenomenalism* (Polger and Flanagan, in press).

In contrast, Dennett writes, Huxley's sense of epiphenomenalism is that of a "*nonfunctional* property or by-product." He continues, "Huxley used the term in his discussion of the evolution of consciousness and his claim that epiphenomenal properties (like the 'whistle of the steam engine') could not be explained by natural selection" (1991, 402). Dennett's explication of Huxley's notion leaves room for confusion. There is a concept of epiphenomena as *not having been selected for by natural selection*. Traits that are epiphenomenal in this sense are free riders or, if they are nevertheless useful, spandrels (Gould and Lewontin 1978). I call this notion *etiological epiphenomenalism* because it denies that a trait has an etiological (selected for, as by natural selection) function (Polger and Flanagan, in press). Flanagan, for example, argues that dreams are etiological epiphenomena (1995, 1996, 2000; see also Polger and Flanagan 1999, in press).

But etiological epiphenomenalism is not what Huxley had in mind (even though he was discussing natural selection), and it is *not* what Dennett refers to in discussing Huxley. Huxley's notion is that some physical effects of mechanisms are not themselves part of the operation of the mechanism (the steam of the locomotive to the engine, the bell to the clock in a clock tower). The sounds of whistling steam and ringing bells are physical effects (therefore *not* systematically mysterious), but they are not parts of some particular mechanistic systems. I call this *causal-role epiphenomenalism* (after Cummins's 1975 notion of causal-role function) because it denies that a trait has a role in a causal mechanism (Polger and Flanagan, in press). Causal-role epiphenomenalism is what Dennett calls epiphenomenalism "in Huxley's sense."

Why does Dennett think the mere possibility of functionally identical zombies entails a "systematically mysterious" epiphenomenal concept of consciousness? The argument is contained in a dense paragraph in *Consciousness Explained* that pursues two lines of reasoning from the possibility of some kind of zombies to some sort of epiphenomenalism. The first part reasons from the "in principle" indistinguishability of zombies to epiphenomenalism "in the ridiculous sense," strict metaphysical epiphenomenalism. The second part reasons from the functional (but not physical) indistinguishability of zombies to the claim that consciousness is epiphenomenal "in the Huxley sense," causal-role epiphenomenalism.

Indistinguishability and Epiphenomenalism

Dennett first argues that the "in principle" indistinguishability of zombies entails epiphenomenalism in the ridiculous sense:

A philosopher's zombie, you will recall, is behaviorally indistinguishable from a normal human being, but is not conscious. There is nothing it is like to be a zombie; it just seems that way to observers (including itself, as we saw in the previous chapter). Now this can be given a strong or weak interpretation, depending on how we treat this indistinguishability to observers. If we declare that *in principle,* a zombie is indistinguishable from a conscious person, then we would be saying that genuine consciousness is epiphenomenal *in the ridiculous sense.* That is just silly. (1991, 405; emphasis original)

Thomas W. Polger

How does the "in principle" modifier operate in this argument?

We already know that behaviorally indistinguishable zombies are, for Dennett, also functionally sophisticated. Perhaps it's not just that the functionally identical zombies are indistinguishable in practice, but rather that they are *really* functionally indistinguishable—they are functionally identical. So "in principle" is contrasted with "in practice." If this is what Dennett has in mind, then the first argument parallels the second argument (that the possibility of functionally identical zombies entails that consciousness is epiphenomenal only in the Huxley sense) except that it vies for the stronger conclusion, that consciousness is epiphenomenal in the ridiculous sense.

A better interpretation is that "in principle" works to modify the indistinguishability of the zombies. So when Dennett talks about zombies that are "in principle" indistinguishable, he has in mind zombies that are identical in every way to conscious creatures, that is, physically identical zombies. The argument, then, is that if physically identical zombies are naturally possible, then consciousness is epiphenomenal in the ridiculous sense. On this reading, the first argument is a change of target for Dennett, since he is otherwise primarily concerned with functionally identical zombies.

If the debate is constrained to broadly naturalistic views (leaving aside considerations of dualism) then it is correct to say that the natural possibility of physically identical zombies entails that consciousness is epiphenomenal in a mysterious sense.[11] Almost none of Dennett's opponents dispute this point; most naturalists deny the natural possibility of physically identical zombies.[12]

Dismissing the "in principle" indistinguishable zombies, Dennett sets into an alternative interpretation of the zombie defender's claim. Dennett's second argument is that the natural possibility of functionally identical zombies entails that consciousness is epiphenomenal merely in the Huxley sense:

So we could say instead that consciousness might be epiphenomenal in the Huxley sense: although there was some way of distinguishing zombies from real people (who knows, maybe zombies have green brains), the difference doesn't show up as a functional difference *to observers*. Equivalently, human bodies with green brains don't harbor observers, while other human bodies do. (1991, 405)

Earlier Dennett says that if qualia are epiphenomenal in the Huxley sense of epiphenomenalism, then they "*are* physical effects and *have* physical effects; they just aren't functional. Any materialist would be happy to admit that this hypothesis is true" (1991, 404). He continues, "That cannot be what epiphenomenalists have in mind, can it? If it is, then qualia as epiphenomena are no challenge to materialism" (1991, 405). Dennett is concerned to make the point that the Huxley sort of epiphenomenalism cannot be, specifically, what Frank Jackson is defending in his "Epiphenomenal Qualia" (1982). But the point is perfectly general: If consciousness is epiphenomenal in the Huxley sense then it is no problem for materialism; it is not systematically mysterious.

Given this recognition, it is puzzling that Dennett proceeds to argue that the possibility of zombies entails that consciousness is epiphenomenal in the Huxley sense—and therefore that,

It is time to recognize the idea of the possibility of zombies for what it is: not a serious philosophical idea but a preposterous and ignoble relic of ancient prejudices. . . . What pernicious nonsense. (1991, 405–406)

Two questions arise: Why does Dennett think that the possibility of zombies entails epiphenomenalism in the Huxley sense? And even if zombies do have that consequence—I will argue they don't—what is so pernicious about a possibility that is no threat to materialism?

For Dennett, if two creatures are functionally identical but differ with respect to their consciousness, then whatever consciousness is ("a 'player to be named later' or an undeclared wild-card") it does not occupy a causal-mechanical role in the system that has it. Thus it is an epiphenomenon in the Huxley sense.

Escaping Dennett's Zombie Dilemma

Let us begin by constructing an argument that has the same structure as Dennett's argument that the possibility of functionally identical zombies entails that consciousness is a causal role epiphenomenon:

We could say that carburetors might be epiphenomenal in the Huxley sense: although there was some way of distinguishing cars with carburetors from "zombie" cars that don't have carburetors (who knows, maybe zombie cars have electric pumps), the difference doesn't show up as a functional difference to observers.

Of course some cars do not have carburetors, and they in fact have something like electric pumps—they have fuel injectors. From the fact that a car might have a carburetor or might have a (functionally identical) fuel injector, it does not follow that carburetors are causal-role epiphenomena.[13] On the contrary, carburetors are crucial mechanisms in the cars that have them, just as fuel injectors are crucial mechanisms in the cars that have them. It is a mistake to think that because some mechanism is not required, because it is inessential, that it is epiphenomenal.[14]

Because there might be two possible mechanisms that could accomplish a function, Dennett's logic would have us conclude that *neither* of them is a causal mechanism—that they are both epiphenomenal in the Huxley sense. Now *that* is ridiculous.[15]

If I gave a possible explanation of how your car worked—one that, say, posited a super-strong super-fast platypus turning the drive shaft—you would not think that I had threatened your previously held beliefs about automobile engines. So why should it give philosophers even a moment's pause if someone claims that it is possible (logically, metaphysically, or naturally) for some creature (real or imagined) to accomplish nonconsciously all the things (behaviors, movements, utterances) that we human beings accomplish with consciousness? When it comes to giving causal-mechanical explanations, possible explanations won't do the trick. It's not enough that it be possible that an abstract car be describable in terms of an organization that allows that a platypus is the source of locomotion. Explanations of particular cars must describe the actual workings of their actual parts. Often more than one part could have been used; the right explanations tell us which of those possible parts were actually used. The explanations had best involve, in the case of my car, a combustion engine rather than a platypus and a fuel injector rather than a carburetor.

Of course Dennett does not encourage us to think of alternate mechanisms that could have the same effects, but rather alternate brain colors. The example of green brains is supposed to make us think that it is silly to believe that some factor other than functional equivalence could make a difference, for example, to whether something is a conscious brain or is a carburetor. I could make my zombie car story have more of Dennett's rhetorical panache ("maybe zombie cars have little magic silver boxes"), but the argument would still be a fallacy. By inviting us to think of a difference that we do not assess as important to whether a creature is conscious (surface color of the brain material), Dennett distracts us from considering the relevant alternative—differences in mechanism.

Functionalism, Mechanism, and Epiphenomenalism

The zombie defender is free to think of conscious states, or processes, or events as mechanisms that have certain properties, among which that they are conscious. Those mechanisms have causal powers, but they are replaceable with functionally equivalent mechanisms that have some distinctive properties. Some mechanisms are conscious, others are not. Both have causal powers—they are not epiphenomenal.

A 230-horsepower platypus and fuel injectors that masquerade as carburetors may not be the best examples of alternate mechanisms. Consider instead the plumbing in a house. A functional account or explanation of the plumbing in the house will include the following sorts of information: the water pressure entering the house, the water pressure exiting from various points (faucets, sewer, etc.), the overall capacity of the system in volume and pressure, required water temperature at various points (water heater, faucets, etc.), and so forth. Let us call this functional specification or explanation of the house the Pipe Theory, Π for short.

Π will mention many of the characteristics of the parts of the plumbing system that transport water from one location to another at certain pressures, temperatures, volumes, and so on. But Π will not include such details as the exact routing of the pipes (kitchen before bathroom, bathroom before kitchen), the cross-section shape of the pipes (oval, circular, square), or even whether they are pipes (rather than hoses or aqueducts). And Π will not specify whether the pipes, or hoses, or aqueducts are made of aluminum or plastic. (They don't all have to be the same, either. There could be some aluminum pipes, some plastic hoses, some cement aqueducts. But it will be simpler to assume that the whole house is built one way or another.)

Let us say that the house has pipes, and the pipes are made of aluminum. It is entirely consistent with Π that the house had plastic hoses. If there were plastic hoses instead then they might have to run a different route, be a different shape, or some such. But those characteristics of the system were not part of Π to begin with. So the aluminum pipes and plastic hoses are both entirely consistent with Π; they make no difference to the functional explanation of the plumbing.

Does it follow that either the aluminum pipes or the plastic hoses are epiphenomenal to the plumbing of the house? No. Π, being a functional theory or explanation, is multiply realizable. Π may apply to a house that has aluminum pipes, in which case aluminum pipes are what play the causal-role of water-carrier in that system. Those aluminum pipes are not causal-role epiphenomena; they are what carries the water. Π may also apply to a house that has plastic hoses, in which case plastic hoses play the causal role of water-carrier in that system.

Π is an abstract description of one or more possible systems. Π picks out parts of the system by their causal roles, by their functions. A part would never even be picked out or specified by Π unless it had a causal-role. So how could someone think that a part specified by Π could be epiphenomenal in the Huxley sense?

The trouble lies in thinking that it is the roles, rather than the occupants of the roles, that have the causal powers. Π may include claims such as ". . . and the water-carrier bears the water to the water-heater. . . ." But *water-carrier* is a role. It is not a thing that has causal powers; it is a variable, a way of picking out any number of things in terms of their causal powers.[16] Π is an abstraction; only when it is instantiated do any of its parts have causal powers. Aluminum pipes can have those powers; plastic hoses can have those powers. Neither Π nor any part of it has any causal powers. Realizations of Π—aluminum pipes and plastic hoses—have causal powers. Aluminum pipes are not epiphenomenal in the Huxley sense; they are parts of a causal-mechanical system that realizes Π.

This is why a physical difference (aluminum pipe or plastic hose) without a functional difference (both are described by Π) does not entail that the different physical parts are causal-role epiphenomena. Exactly the same reasoning can be applied to consciousness. To an identity theorist, for example, the brain is a complicated sort of plumbing.[17] According to identity theory consciousness is a pipe—it is a realizer that may occupy a role. Suppose, for the sake of argument, that there is a theory or description that is a functional description of human cognitive capacities. This theory or description, ψ, will specify many aspects of human cognition, many functional parts. Some of these functional parts are states, processes, or properties that are, in us, conscious states, processes, or properties. That is, some brain states, processes, or properties that realize parts of ψ are in human beings conscious states, processes, or properties.

But ψ could also apply to another kind of creature, a zombie, for which those roles that are occupied in us by conscious states, processes, or properties are, in it, occupied by nonconscious states, processes, or properties. This zombie would be functionally identical to human beings (for ψ applies to it) but would lack consciousness. It does not follow that consciousness is epiphenomenal in the Huxley sense, for conscious states, processes, or properties realize causal roles in our system. Likewise, some other things occupy those roles in the zombie; and whatever occupies those roles is not epiphenomenal in the zombie.[18]

Why should we care whether consciousness is part of our system? Functional specification is interest-relative. One might care about the nonfunctional (relative to water-carrying) details of one's plumbing if, for example, one was inclined toward postindustrial interior design, or if one was concerned about how easy it is to access the pipes for repair. (Dennett 1971 points out that we often care about the physical specification of things when they break.) Likewise, the interests of psychology are not the only human interests. We might care about the physical details of our system that are not specified by ψ for a variety of reasons, such as aesthetic or moral reasons. Conscious states may be replaceable with respect to our bodies carrying-on their cognitive duties, but we value having them.

Metaphysical questions about consciousness are directly related to what we think—morally, for example—about animals, infants, fetuses, people with brain damage, sleeping people, people on drugs, computers, thermostats, aliens, and rocks or buckets of water whose molecular motion temporarily mimics a finite state machine. This is why zombies are important. We care about bizarre, extreme, imaginary cases of creatures that are physically different from but behaviorally and functionally identical to us, precisely because we care about how they reveal our intuitions about the less bizarre, less extreme, and all too real cases of creatures that are *both* physically different—because of their nature, age, or injury—*and* functionally or behaviorally different from us. Dennett calls zombies "pernicious" because he thinks that the defender of zombies is committed to saying that these important considerations rest on whether or not a subject has some epiphenomenal quality. That would indeed be troubling. But I have argued that the possibility of functionally identical zombies does not depend on consciousness being epiphenomenal, so Dennett's worry is unfounded.

The explanation that I've given for why Dennett is wrong to think that consciousness would have to be epiphenomenal in order for functionally identical zombies to be nomologically possible is just like that used by Block (1980b) against a similar argument from Shoemaker (1975) regarding absent qualia.[19] Block took Shoemaker to be arguing that creatures with absent qualia, zombies, are not possible on the grounds that their consciousness would have to be epiphenomenal (and thus, on a causal theory of knowledge, that they would violate the self-evident fact that we have knowledge of our conscious states). Accordingly, Block was arguing that Shoemaker fails to show that absent qualia are impossible, on the grounds that absent qualia do not entail epiphenomenalism. Let us suppose that was the debate. Dennett would be right to point out that Block's defense depends on the denial of functionalism. Likewise, my version of Block's argument depends on the denial of functionalism with respect to consciousness.

But my dispute with Dennett differs from Block's debate with Shoemaker in an important way. Dennett's challenge does not require me to show that functionally identical zombies are possible (as Block was trying to show that absent qualia are possible). Rather, Dennett's challenge is to show that there is a coherent way of construing zombies that does not entail that consciousness is epiphenomenal. And that I have done.

Dennett, remember, presents the zombie defender with a dilemma: Either the concept of a functionally identical zombie is self-contradictory, or else it involves a conception of consciousness as epiphenomenal. I have not disputed the first horn of the dilemma. If consciousness is a functional role, as Dennett seems to hold, then the notion of functional zombie—a thing functionally identical to you or me but lacking consciousness—is indeed incoherent. It is surely this combination that rightly elicits such strong reactions from Dennett. But, to borrow a phrase, those are not the zombies I am looking for.

My purpose has been to attack the second horn of the zombie dilemma. On that horn, Dennett argues that a notion of consciousness that permits functionally identical zombies (that is, a conception on which functionally identical zombie are *not* incoherent) is epiphenomenalist. I have argued, following Block, that functionally identical zombies can be coherently conceived, such that their natural possibility does not entail that consciousness is epiphenomenal in the Huxley sense—it is a causal-role epiphenomenon. To do so I have adopted a different metaphysical stance than Dennett's. I now need to show that this move does not constitute question-begging with respect to Dennett's zombie challenge.

Consciousness: Occupant or Role?

How a functional role is instantiated, what the mechanism is (carburetor or fuel injector, engine or platypus), is important if consciousness is a state, property, process, or event. But this is exactly the view that Dennett is rejecting. So against my defense of functionally identical zombies it may be objected that consciousness on Dennett's view is not an occupant, it is a role. If consciousness is a functional role, then it makes no sense to talk about two creatures that are functionally identical (i.e., their systems are explained identically in terms of functional roles) but which differ in consciousness (i.e., one or more of the functional roles). Thus one might argue that by treating consciousness as an occupant in my defense of zombies, I am missing the point of Dennett's overall argument and begging the question.

I agree that if consciousness is taken to be a functional role, then functionally identical zombies are not just naturally impossible, they are logically impossible. This is the first horn of the dilemma. It would be a contradiction in terms to claim that there could be a functionally identical zombie, something whose functional explanation both has and lacks a certain functional role. On this interpretation the possibility of functionally identical zombies does, trivially, entail that consciousness is epiphenomenal in the Huxley sense— but it also entails that consciousness is causally efficacious, and that the moon is made of cheese.

The claim that consciousness is a functional role is central to the current debates over the nature of consciousness—it is the claim of functionalist theories with respect to consciousness. Whether consciousness is to be explained in terms of states, properties, processes, events, or in terms of functional roles is a core question about the metaphysics of consciousness. All of the positions are controversial.

Moreover, I agree that Dennett is arguing that consciousness is a functional role. His argument is as follows: First, he provides a sophisticated hypothesis about the mechanisms of our cognitive capacities—the multiple drafts model. Then he asserts that the multiple drafts model is a theory of consciousness: "I hereby declare that YES, my theory is a theory of consciousness. Anyone or anything that has such a virtual machine as its control system is conscious in the fullest sense, and is conscious *because* it has such a virtual machine" (1991, 281). Finally, Dennett provides a negative argument that the alternative view entails epiphenomenalism, namely, the two-part argument examined above. Dennett's overall strategy thus depends on whether the negative argument goes through. This is why Dennett is such a vigorous critic of zombies. The challenge he sets for the zombie defender, the dilemma, is in fact crucial to his whole argument for the multiple drafts model in *Consciousness Explained*. Recall the dilemma. Either Dennett's view is right—in which case functionally identical zombies are incoherent; or else functionally identical zombies are possible—in which case consciousness is epiphenomenal. The first horn I have stipulated to. It is with the second horn of the dilemma that Dennett depends on the possibility of functionally identical zombies entailing epiphenomenalism. The claim is that any view that *allows* for functionally identical zombies is to be rejected because it will entail that consciousness is epiphenomenal in the Huxley sense. That is, it is on the *opposing* view—the one that does *not* treat functionally identical zombies as internally incoherent—that the possibility of functionally identical zombies is supposed to entail that consciousness is epiphenomenal. Therefore, for the purposes of this horn of the dilemma *the consequences of Dennett's own functional role view are irrelevant*. Dennett's argument depends on the claim that *nonfunctional-role* views of consciousness that allow for functionally identical zombies entail that consciousness is epiphenomenal. And that is what I have shown to be false. Specifically, identity theory allows for the possibility of functionally identical zombies without entailing that consciousness is a causal-role epiphenomenon ("the Huxley sense"), much less that it is a strict metaphysical epiphenomenon ("the ridiculous sense").

Conclusion

Dennett's challenge is best put when he writes, "If the philosophical concept of zombies is so important, so useful, some philosopher ought to be able to say why in nonquestion-begging terms" (Dennett 1995, 326).

I have defended the concept of functionally identical zombies. Dennett's zombie challenge is a dilemma. To meet the challenge one must examine both horns of the dilemma: Either zombies are incoherent or else they involve an epiphenomenal conception of consciousness. The first horn is straightforward: On Dennett's view zombies are self-contradictory. The second horn of the dilemma depends on the claim that the alternative to Dennett's view (the nonfunctionalist view) permits the possibility of functionally identical zombies—it does!—and thereby entails that consciousness is epiphenomenal—it does not! Considering this horn of the dilemma *requires* one to consider the consequences of a nonfunctionalist view. Therefore it is not question-begging for this purpose to assume a nonfunctionalist stance in arguing that the possibility of functionally identical zombies does not entail epiphenomenalism.

I've shown that there is a way to conceive of zombies in which functionally identical zombies are coherent and consciousness is not epiphenomenal. That is the burden set by the arguments in *Consciousness Explained* (1991). That is the demand made explicit with the zombie dilemma in "The Unimagined Preposterousness of Zombies" (1995).

I conclude that I have met Dennett's zombie challenge.

Notes

1. Thanks to Owen Flanagan, Güven Güzeldere, Steve Geisz, and Brook Sadler for discussing with me several drafts of this chapter. I am greatly indebted to Valerie Hardcastle for her extensive comments, and particularly for drawing my attention to the relevance to my argument of the exchange between Ned Block and Sydney Shoemaker over absent qualia. William Lycan, Michael Lynch, and David Chalmers also provided helpful suggestions.

2. Güzeldere actually considers behavioral, functional, and *physiological* zombies. I shall consider zombies that are physically identical to any arbitrary degree of specificity. The purpose of stipulating zombies in this way is to ensure that if the distinction between the physical and the functional can be maintained at all (and several have argued that it cannot; e.g., Lycan 1987, Hill 1991) then physically identical zombies are a distinct construct from functionally identical zombies. Specifically, the distinction holds even if the biological (physiological) structure of organisms is essentially functional in nature (as per Millikan 1989, 1993; Lycan 1987, 1996; Neander 1991).

3. David Chalmers, in *The Conscious Mind* (1996), introduces a similar framework of distinctions.

4. Güzeldere suggests that an equivalent, and more convenient, way of talking about the ways that zombies could be identical is by considering them as distinct kinds of zombies: behavioral zombies, functional zombies, and physical zombies (1995). I will sometimes use this way of talking. So when I ask, say, whether behaviorally identical zombies are naturally possible, this is shorthand for question (Q1), "Is it naturally possible that there be zombies that are behaviorally identical to human beings?"

5. This is what Terence Horgan calls *physical possibility*, which he distinguishes from a slightly weaker *nomological possibility* (1987).

6. It is sometimes joked that what is metaphysically possible is what Saul Kripke says is metaphysically possible. David Lewis says that he does not know how to prove that something is possible (1980). Appeals to possible worlds explain to what statements of metaphysical possibility refer, but they do little to tell us *which* worlds are metaphysically possible.

7. These questions are all phrased in terms of interpersonal comparisons. If you think that the interpersonal cases are always or sometimes ill defined (what Shoemaker 1982 calls the Frege-Schlick view), you can still ask all of these questions in their intrapersonal form. To do so, simply consider the two creatures in the above formulations as two creature-stages; that is, "Is it y-ly possible that a creature at time t_2 be x-ly identical to the same creature at t_1 but differ in that . . . ?" It is a short step from the intrapersonal form to the first-person form, "Is it y-ly possible that I at time t_2 be x-ly identical to myself at t_1 but differ in that . . . ?"

8. I am not suggesting that there is a single level that is *the* functional level, nor that a theory must be in terms of only one level. Distinguishing finer and coarser varieties of functional specification does not in itself involve the mistake that Lycan (1987) calls "Two-Levelism."

9. But the matter is not simple. Dennett tells Michael Gazzaniga, regarding an extremely sophisticated robot, Cog, designed to model some human capacities, "Achieving human-level hand-eye coordination is a central goal, but before that can be addressed, we have to ensure that Cog won't poke its eyes out with inadvertent motions of its arms! So a pain system, and innately 'hard-wired' (actually software-controlled, of course) avoidance of such mischief is a high priority" (quoted in Gazzaniga 1997).

10. To be precise: epiphenomenal or otherwise "systematically mysterious." But the only sense of ungrounded mystery that Dennett provides is epiphenomenalism.

11. Since Dennett's opponent in ch. 12, sec. 5 of *Consciousness Explained* is Frank Jackson (1982), his argument is in part against nonphysicalist claims about consciousness and qualia. Eliminating dualism from consideration would not be allowable if we were trying to settle the matter between Jackson and Dennett. But my goal is to defend the notion of zombies on naturalist terms.

12. But not all. Dretske's (1995) wide-content view of consciousness may permit physically identical zombies.

13. Dan Ryder has cautioned me that it could be objected that carburetors and fuel injectors are not functionally equivalent on the grounds that fuel injectors have performance characteristics that carburetors do not. The response to this is as follows: First, although one *can* construct a fuel injector to have better (e.g., more fuel efficient) operation than any carburetor, one does not *have* to. That is, it is possible to construct a fuel injector with the same performance characteristics as a carburetor. I see no reason that this duplication could not be so complete as to also match the counterfactual cases (such as those outside the range of any carburetor). Specifically, the fuel injector would be designed to break under certain conditions, viz., those under which the carburetor would break.

14. Dennett is not the only philosopher who falls victim to this sort of thinking. David Chalmers's (1995, 1996) argument for the incompleteness of physical theory

vis à vis consciousness seems to rely on the following reasoning: it is always possible to provide an explanation for mental phenomena in functional or mechanistic terms that do not mention or entail facts about consciousness; therefore consciousness must not be explainable functionally or mechanistically.

15. Bruce Mangan calls this the *Fallacy of Functional Exclusion* (1998). Mangan and I independently arrived at similar ideas about a mistake being made in the debate about the function and efficacy of consciousness, and came to similar diagnoses of the origin of the problem (viz., in early, computational versions of functionalism). I developed the point as having to do with the structure of the debate over functionalism and the invocation of possible explanations (Polger 1998), whereas Mangan concentrates on exposing the fallacy, locating the problem in philosophers' failure to think of consciousness in biological terms (Mangan 1998).

16. If Π is applied to a system of pipes, then *the water-carrier* is a bound variable, with the value *pipe*. What could be less mysterious?

17. I have in mind *type*-identity theories.

18. From this possibility it does, however, follow that either psychology is not entirely functional (ψ is not a psychology) or else consciousness is not essential to psychology.

19. See also Shoemaker's reply (1981), and Valerie Hardcastle's (1995, chapter 7) discussion of the exchange.

References

Block, N., ed. (1980a). *Readings in Philosophy of Psychology*, vol. 1. Cambridge, Mass.: Harvard University Press.

Block, N. (1980b). Are absent qualia impossible? *The Philosophical Review* 89, 2: 257–274.

Block, N., Flanagan, O. and G. Güzeldere, eds. (1997). *The Nature of Consciousness: Philosophical Debates*. Cambridge, Mass.: MIT Press. A Bradford Book.

Chalmers, D. (1995). Facing up to the problem of consciousness. *Journal of Consciousness Studies* 2, 3: 200–219.

Chalmers, D. (1996). *The Conscious Mind: In Search of a Fundamental Theory*. New York: Oxford University Press.

Cummins, R. (1975). Functional analysis. *Journal of Philosophy* 72, 20: 741–865.

Dennett, D. C. (1971). Intentional systems. *Journal of Philosophy* 68: 87–106.

Dennett, D. C. (1991). *Consciousness Explained*. Boston: Little, Brown, and Co.

Dennett, D. C. (1994). Get real. *Philosophical Topics* 22, 1 and 2: 505–568.

Dennett, D. C. (1995). The unimagined preposterousness of zombies. *Journal of Consciousness Studies* 2, 4: 322–326. Reprinted in Dennett 1998.

285

Zombies Explained

Dennett, D. C. (1998). *Brainchildren*. Cambridge, Mass.: MIT Press. A Bradford Book.

Dretske, F. (1995). *Naturalizing the Mind*. Cambridge, Mass.: MIT Press. A Bradford Book.

Flanagan, O. (1995). Deconstructing dreams: The spandrels of sleep. *Journal of Philosophy* 5, 27. Reprinted with modifications in Flanagan 1996.

Flanagan, O. (1996). *Self Expressions: Mind, Morals, and the Meaning of Life*. New York: Oxford University Press.

Flanagan, O. (2000). *Dreaming Souls: Sleep, Dreams and the Evolution of the Conscious Mind*. New York: Oxford University Press.

Flanagan, O., and T. Polger. (1995). Zombies and the function of consciousness. *Journal of Consciousness Studies* 2, 4: 313–321.

Gazzaniga, M. (1997). *Conversations in the Cognitive Neurosciences*. Cambridge, Mass.: MIT Press. A Bradford Book.

Gould, S. J. and R. Lewontin. (1978). The spandrels of San Marco and the Panglossian paradigm: A critique of the adaptationist program. *Proceedings of the Royal Society, London* 205: 581–598.

Guttenplan, S., ed. (1994). *A Companion to the Philosophy of Mind*. Oxford: Blackwell Publishers.

Güzeldere, G. (1995). Varieties of zombiehood. *Journal of Consciousness Studies* 2, 4: 326–333.

Hardcastle, V. (1995). *Locating Consciousness*. Amsterdam: John Benjamins.

Hardcastle, V., ed. (1999). *Where Biology Meets Psychology: Philosophical Essays*. Cambridge, Mass.: MIT Press. A Bradford Book.

Hill, C. (1991). *Sensations: A Defense of Type Materialism*. Cambridge: Cambridge University Press.

Horgan, T. (1987). Supervenient qualia. *Philosophical Review* 96: 491–520.

Jackson, F. (1982). Epiphenomenal qualia. *The Philosophical Quarterly* 32, 127: 127–136.

Kirk, R. (1974). Zombies v. materialists. *Proceedings of the Aristotelian Society* 48: 135–152.

Kripke, S. (1972). *Naming and Necessity*. New York: Cambridge University Press.

Lewis, D. (1980). Mad pain and Martian pain. In Block (1980a).

Lycan, W. G. (1987). *Consciousness*. Cambridge, Mass.: MIT Press. A Bradford Book.

Lycan, W. G. (1996). *Consciousness and Experience*. Cambridge, Mass.: MIT Press. A Bradford Book.

Mangan, B. (1998). Consciousness, biological systems, and the fallacy of functional exclusion. Presented at *Toward a Science of Consciousness* (Tucson III), Tucson, Az.

Millikan, R. (1989). In defense of proper functions. *Philosophy of Science* 56: 288–302. Reprinted in Millikan 1993.

Millikan, R. (1993). *White Queen Psychology and Other Essays for Alice*. Cambridge, Mass.: MIT Press. A Bradford Book.

Moody, T. (1994). Conversations with Zombies. *Journal of Consciousness Studies* 1, 2: 196–200.

Neander, K. (1991). Functions as selected effects: The conceptual analyst's defense. *Philosophy of Science* 58: 168–184.

Polger, T. (1998). Escaping the epiphenomenal trap. Presented at the Southern Society for Philosophy and Psychology, New Orleans, La.

Polger, T. and O. Flanagan. (1999). Natural answers to natural questions. In V. Hardcastle (ed.), 1999.

Polger, T. and O. Flanagan. In press. Consciousness, adaptation, and epiphenomenalism. In *Consciousness Evolving*, J. Fetzer and G. Mulhauser (eds.). Amsterdam: John Benjamins.

Shoemaker, S. (1975). Functionalism and qualia. *Philosophical Studies* 27: 291–315. Reprinted in Block 1980a.

Shoemaker, S. (1981). Absent qualia are impossible—A reply to Block. *Philosophical Review* 90, 4: 581–599.

Shoemaker, S. (1982). The inverted spectrum. *Journal of Philosophy* 79: 357–381. Reprinted in Block, Flanagan, and Güzeldere 1997.

13

Content, Interpretation, and Consciousness

David M. Rosenthal

First-Person Operationalism and Higher-Order Thoughts

We are all familiar with situations in which memory distorts some current experience. I may see a person I don't know at all, but my memory of an old friend causes me to misperceive that person as my friend; the conscious experience that results is of seeing the friend. Perhaps, for example, my friend wears glasses and the person now before me doesn't. Although I see a person without glasses, my memory of the friend intrudes and I seem, so far as consciousness is concerned, to see a person wearing glasses.

Folk psychology accommodates two distinct explanations of such cases. My memory of the earlier experience might contaminate the current visual information before it even reaches consciousness; if so, I in effect hallucinate the glasses. But perhaps, instead, I begin by consciously seeing the person as having no glasses, but the memory then immediately revises the experience by adding the glasses and also overwrites any current memory of the new visual experience without glasses.

These are the two scenarios that Dan Dennett and Marcel Kinsbourne labeled Stalinesque and Orwellian, respectively, famously arguing that the distinction between them is spurious. When it comes to consciousness, they urge, we cannot distinguish between appearance and reality. So, if the two scenarios are indistinguishable to consciousness, they are indistinguishable in reality, as well. Since consciousness cannot fix the time of contamination as being before or after the new visual information reaches consciousness, the two hypotheses differ only verbally. Folk psychology, by allowing for distinct scenarios, misleads us into thinking that this kind of case can occur in two different ways. (Dennett and Kinsbourne 1992a,b; Dennett 1991).

As Dennett puts their view, "there is no reality of consciousness independent of the effects of various vehicles of content on subsequent action [and hence, of course, on memory]" (1991, 132). So "there are no fixed facts about the stream of consciousness independent of particular probes" (1991, 138; cf. 275). Dennett usefully calls this view *first-person operationalism* (1991, 132), since it holds that the facts about consciousness are wholly fixed by the effects consciousness has on other things.

Because theory outstrips observation, a satisfactory theory can often settle questions that won't yield to observation alone. So even if the Stalinesque and Orwellian scenarios are indistinguishable to consciousness itself, perhaps a reasonable theory of consciousness will, in principle at least, show us how to tell which scenario any particular case conforms to.

I have argued elsewhere (1993a, 1995a, 1995b) that we can do just this on a theory according to which a mental state is conscious just in case it is accompanied by a higher-order thought (HOT) to the effect that one is in that state. We do not regard as conscious any mental state of which we are wholly unaware. So we must in some way be conscious of every conscious state, and having a thought about a state is one way of being conscious of it. Intuitively, it seems that the way we are conscious of our conscious states is direct. We can explain this intuition by hypothesizing that we remain unaware of any inferences or other antecedent factors that might lead to HOTs or explain their occurrence; HOTs seem to arise spontaneously.[1] Indeed, HOTs need not themselves be conscious, and typically won't be.[2]

On this theory, a mental state becomes conscious at the onset of the relevant HOT. So whether my unrevised visual sensation reaches consciousness depends solely on whether the contamination occurs before or after the onset of some HOT. Since HOTs are determinate states, their exact moment of occurrence is determinate, whether or not we can discover it in practice.

At the same time, however, the HOT model explains why we should feel a certain reluctance to classify particular cases as being Stalinesque or Orwellian. Suppose a sensation occurs and very quickly becomes conscious. But then, almost immediately, the sensation changes, and a moment after that one becomes conscious of the change. Is this revision Stalinesque or Orwellian? That depends on whether we focus on the sensation in its original or changed form. The case is Stalinesque relative to the changed sensation, since that change occurred before the sensation became conscious in its new form. But relative to its original form the case is Orwellian, since the sensation was conscious in that original form before it changed. The case looks Stalinesque if we regard the revised sensation as a new, distinct state, and Orwellian if we see the revised sensation as just a latter stage of the original state.

But the choice between these two descriptions is in most cases unprincipled, since it will typically rely on artificially precise identity conditions for mental states. Whether such a case is Stalinesque or Orwellian hinges on arbitrary questions about taxonomizing our mental states themselves. Still, this does not show that it's not determinate when states with specific content properties become conscious, nor that the facts about when revision occurs and when states become conscious are exhausted by how things appear to consciousness.

Thinking, Speech, and Probes

"(T)here are," according to Dennett, "no fixed facts about the stream of consciousness independent of particular probes" (1991, 113). One of the most intriguing applications of this challenging claim has to do with the connection between thinking and speech.

When we speak, we express the thoughts we have. Our speech acts, moreover, reflect the content of those intentional states. It is natural to hold that this correspondence of content is exact; whenever we say anything, the speaker's meaning of our speech act is the same as the content of the intentional state we express.

We all have experienced how putting our thoughts into words can appear to tighten up those very thoughts. It's usually assumed that this happens because the process of finding suitable words for one's thoughts clarifies the thoughts themselves. On that account, the clarifying speech act does not actually outstrip, in respect of content, the antecedent intentional state it expresses. It's just that fixing on the right words results in a new intentional state, whose content is more fine grained than one's original thought. So goes our ordinary, folk-psychological description of these cases, and so it seems to us from a first-person point of view. We have a robust first-person sense that our speech acts exactly match in content the antecedent intentional states they express. Whether or not the match is exact, it seems that way to us.

We will see below that folk psychology and our first-person sense of things overestimate the exactness of this match of content. But it is worth considering certain ostensible counterexamples to the idea that our first-person impression is always that an exact match obtains. We do sometimes discover as we say something that what we're saying does not really reflect our thoughts after all. We may have changed our mind, or even find that we never actually thought that thing at all, but said it only conversationally or from habit. But when this type of thing happens, our first-person sense is not of really saying the thing in question, but something like "as if" saying. We don't sense ourselves saying the thing with full illocutionary force, but simply producing the relevant utterance. In Wilfrid Sellars's apt metaphor,[3] the utterance is produced parrotingly, as with mere recitations, from causes that are tangential to what one thinks. We do sense in these cases a divergence between our speech and what we think, but the speech productions do not seem to us, from a first-person point of view, to be full-fledged illocutionary acts.[4]

As we saw, an exact match in content between full-fledged illocutionary acts and the thoughts they express can accommodate cases in which our speaking seems to clarify our thoughts. But these cases seem to fit equally well with another interpretation, which itself lends support to Dennett's first-person operationalism. Perhaps putting our thoughts into words clarifies our thinking not because it results in our having clearer thoughts, but because speech acts themselves actually fix the content our thoughts have. Speech acts, on this view, are one sort of probe that determines the facts of consciousness. This is the "pandemonium model" of speech production that Dennett develops in chapter 8 of *Consciousness Explained*,[5] on which there are no determinate intentional states prior to the occurrence of verbal expressions. It is not simply that our choice of words often influences the content of our thoughts.[6] Rather, many forces occur in the intentional arena and compete for expression. The speech act that ultimately wins out in effect results from the vector product of those forces, rather than from some single, antecedently existing state with the relevant determinate content.

The folk-psychological view that speech acts always mirror the content of the intentional states they express reflects our subjective impression of these situations. It always seems, from a first-person point of view, that what we say exactly matches the content of some intentional state we are in. But Dennett's pandemonium model also does justice to this subjective impression. After all, if speech acts do fix the content of the intentional states they express, we will sense a perfect fit between them.

In addition to squaring with our subjective impressions, these two models both capture important aspects of the connection between thinking and speech. But the aspects they capture are different. One aspect has to do with what it is for a speech act to be meaningful. Two things are needed. One is that the sentence uttered have semantic meaning. But even so, no utterance is meaningful if it's a mere recitation without underlying thought, if, as Sellars put it, it is produced parrotingly. We can, of course, distinguish tolerably well between meaningful and parroting speech production, independent of any appeal to theory. But if we want to explain what that difference consists in, we must appeal to the idea that meaningful speech acts express intentional states, whereas parroting utterances do not.

The folk-psychological picture of the relation between speech and thought reflects this explanation. Nonparroting speech productions express antecedent intentional states, and expressing an intentional state means that the semantic meaning of the speech act matches to some suitable degree the content of that intentional state. Such an explanation is unavailable on the pandemonium model. If speech acts fix the content of our intentional states, it cannot be that expressing an antecedent intentional state with roughly the same content is what makes a speech act nonparroting.

One might reply that the pandemonium model can, after all, explain the difference between parroting and nonparroting speech productions. Speech is nonparroting if it results from the forces competing in the intentional arena for expression; otherwise it is parroting.[7] Whether this reply works depends on just what those intentional forces are that the pandemonium model posits. If they are merely subpersonal events that resist folk-psychological taxonomy as full-fledged intentional states, the reply fails, since parroting utterances also result from the interaction of subpersonal events that resist folk-psychological taxonomy.

But perhaps the pandemonium model actually posits full-fledged intentional states operating in the intentional arena. Speech acts, then, simply settle which of these states wins out in the competition for expression, rather than converting subpersonal events of content fixation[8] into genuine intentional states. Then the model can explain speech as nonparroting if it results from such intentional states. But the pandemonium model so construed does not differ relevantly from the folk-psychological picture, which also posits antecedent intentional states, and regards nonparroting speech as that which results from such states. Any satisfactory explanation of how parroting and nonparroting utterances differ must invoke the intentional states posited by the folk-psychological model.

There is good reason, in any case, to construe Dennett's pandemonium model as positing only subpersonal events of content fixation, rather than full-fledged intentional states. Thus he writes:

We replace the division into discrete contentful *states*—beliefs, meta-beliefs, and so forth—with a *process* that serves, over time, to ensure a good fit between an entity's internal information-bearing events and the entity's capacity to express (some of) the information in those events in speech. (1991, 319, his emphasis; compare 1993, 930–931)

The forces whose interaction results in speech acts are properly speaking proto-intentional, and precipitate into intentional states only when they issue in speech acts or in reactions to some relevant probe. Moreover, just which speech acts and intentional states these subpersonal forces issue in depends to some extent on factors irrelevant to the intentional content at hand. Events of content fixation determine speech performances more in the manner of instructions in aleatory music than fully developed scores.

Nonetheless, the folk-psychological model arguably exaggerates the match in content between speech act and intentional state, and the pandemonium model provides a useful corrective. If the content of an intentional state corresponds exactly to the semantic meaning of the speech act that expresses it, thinking must itself exhibit a language-like structure; perhaps thinking even takes place in a language of thought whose syntax and semantics echo those of overt natural language.[9] Such a picture, however, arguably underestimates the extent to which what we think and how we think it are affected by the way we express our thoughts in speech. The pandemonium model seeks to capture the effect our putting words to our thoughts has on the thoughts themselves.

Is there a view that preserves the virtues of both models, allowing us to explain the difference between parroting and nonparroting speech without tempting us to adopt an unqualified language of thought? Arguably yes. Perhaps meaningful, nonparroting speech acts always express intentional states with antecedently fixed content, but the speech acts are nonetheless often richer and more fine grained in content than the intentional states expressed. The content of the speech acts rules out more possibilities and invokes more distinctions than the less refined content of the intentional states those speech acts express.

How would this work? Which speech acts we perform is of course largely determined by the intentional states they express. But speech acts express those states in words that have, to some extent, an independent semantic life.[10] So, although the content of speech acts derives mainly from the intentional states expressed, the words used in expressing that content often go beyond it, making for speech acts whose semantic meaning is correspondingly enriched and refined.

Our thoughts, by contrast, seldom need to respect the fine-grained semantic distinctions inherent in natural language. Any intentional state can typically be expressed equally well by a range of speech acts whose semantic meanings are not exactly the same. So it's reasonable to regard the content of our intentional states as neutral among the distinct semantic meanings of those various possible speech acts. Any particular choice of words, then, produces a speech act with semantic meaning more fine grained than the content of the corresponding intentional state. Some match of content is required for a speech act to count as expressing an intentional state, but the match need not be exact.

What words we choose to express an intentional state may itself sometimes be due to some other intentional state. In these cases we might regard the resulting speech act as expressing both intentional states: that which led to some such speech act's being performed and also that which influenced the particular choice of words. The speech act would be more fine grained in content than either intentional state, but might not outstrip the two combined. But choices of words are doubtless often arbitrary, resulting from no mental factor at all. Mere habit or word pattern might determine what words we use; indeed, it is likely that this is what typically happens. In such cases, our speech act does outstrip in content any relevant antecedent intentional states. And, since the content of intentional states can be less fine grained than the meaning of the speech acts that express those states, there is less temptation on this view to suppose that thinking fully mirrors the syntactic and semantic properties of natural language.

Indeed, it may sometimes be difficult to capture our more coarse-grained thoughts in words, especially with the intentional states we ascribe to nonlinguistic animals. Dennett therefore concludes that the "'thought' (of such an animal) might be inexpressible (in human language) for the simple reason that expression in a human language *cuts too fine.*" But Dennett concedes that "we may nevertheless exhaustively describe what we can't express" (Dennett 1996, 42; see also 1997, 219–235). But if we can exhaustively describe the content of a thought, we can use those very words to frame a sentence that would, however awkwardly, express that thought. If the content of some thought elides various distinctions inherent in human language, suitable disjunctions can provide neutrality in respect of those distinctions. Even when no straightforward sentence could express the content of thought, some complex compound should succeed.[11]

A speech act expresses an intentional state only if its content matches that of the intentional state, but the match need not be exact. How close must that match be? No precise answer is possible, but neither should we expect precision. For one thing, it is unclear just how finely we can differentiate intentional states and speech acts in respect of content. In addition, the distinction between parroting and nonparroting speech productions itself doubtless admits of an intermediate gray area. Nor, finally, should we expect to be able to specify with precision just which speech acts express which intentional states. Some reasonably close match of content is required even though the precise degree of correspondence eludes specification. It is an advantage of the present model that it does not aim for such precision.

Consciousness and Verbally Expressing Our Thoughts

Let's call this third picture of the relation between thinking and speech the *refinement model.* Arguably, it avoids the disadvantages of both the folk-psychological and pandemonium models, by allowing us to explain the difference between parroting and nonparroting speech performances while circumventing the temptation to hypothesize a full-fledged language of thought. The refinement model shares with the pandemonium model the recognition that speech often outstrips our thoughts in content. But unlike the pandemonium model, the refinement model preserves both our folk-psychological taxonomy and the traditional view that speech acts express antecedent intentional states.

Nonetheless, the refinement model appears to face a difficulty that both the pandemonium and folk-psychological models avoid. As noted earlier, whenever we express our thoughts in words, our subjective impression is that what we say exactly matches the content of the intentional state we express. It never seems, from a first-person point of view, that our speech act is richer or more fine grained in content than our antecedent intentional state. The folk-psychological and pandemonium models both reflect this, since both posit an exact correspondence of content between speech act and intentional state, differing only about whether the intentional state fixes the content of the speech act or the other way around. Either way we would seem to sense a perfect fit between them.

Folk psychology generally trades, of course, on such conformity to our subjective impressions. And in this case the pandemonium model follows suit. Can we defend the refinement model despite its departure from our subjective impressions about thinking and speech?

A slight detour here will be useful. As noted earlier, putting our thoughts into words sometimes seems to clarify those very thoughts. By itself, however, the clarifying effect of verbally expressing our thoughts does not tell against an exact match of content between thought and speech. It could simply be that the process of finding words to express our thoughts forces us to clarify those very thoughts. As we mentally hear ourselves say what it is that we think, we find it confused or unclear, and so revise on the fly what we think. But by adjusting our words as we go, we get the right thought out. The content of the resulting speech act could still match exactly that of the suitably revised thought.

There is, however, another way in which putting words to our thoughts might have a clarifying effect on those thoughts. Rather than leading us to clarify the thoughts themselves, it could result instead in our becoming clearer about just what those thoughts are. We would know better, having spoken, just what it was that we had been thinking all along. We discover what we think only as we say it.

Dennett takes this kind of case to support the pandemonium model, on which the content of our thoughts is fixed only when we speak (1991, 245); hence his striking epigram from E. M. Forster: "How do I know what I think until I see what I say?" (Dennett 1991, 193). But our discovering what we think only as we say it does not, by itself, support the pandemonium model, since it does not show that our thoughts lacked fixed content until we spoke. It could instead simply be that our thoughts often are not conscious in the relevant way until we express them in words. Even if the speech act results from an antecedent intentional state whose content exactly matches that of the speech act, perhaps it's only as we speak that we become conscious of the intentional state *as having that content*.

These considerations help with the problem the refinement model faced. On that model, our speech acts often outstrip the intentional states they express in respect of content. But that is never how it seems from a first-person point of view. Our subjective impression is always that our speech acts exactly match in content the intentional states they express.

But these first-person impressions may not accurately reveal the content of our intentional states. It could be that our speech acts do often outstrip our intentional states in content, but that we are nonetheless conscious of those intentional states *as having the richer content*. We might subjectively sense an exact match in content not because such a match obtains, but because that is how we are conscious of our verbally expressed thoughts. Because we are conscious of such a thought as expressed by a particular speech act, we in effect read back the content of the speech act onto the intentional state it expresses. We interpret the intentional state as having the content exhibited by the speech act.

The idea that we interpret our thoughts in the light of our speech acts fits well with the spirit of Dennett's pandemonium model. To some extent at least, we rely on the same considerations others do in determining what we think. As Dennett notes, in cases when we discover what we think only as we say it, "we are . . . in the same boat as our external . . . interpreters, encountering a bit of text and putting the best reading on it that we can find" (1991, 245). Hence Dennett's heterophenomenological method, on which our theorizing about mind seeks to do justice to the verbal reports people make about their mental states (Dennett 1991, 72–85; 1978, 174–189).

The pandemonium model, however, takes these self-interpretations to be the last word about the content of our thoughts.[12] This squares with Dennett's first-person operationalism, which rejects the idea that there can be a difference between how things seem and how they seem to seem (1991, 132). Intentional states are subjective states; they are a matter of how things seem to us. And how things seem to us in virtue of our being in some intentional state is a matter of the content that state has. So there is no difference, on first-person operationalism, between the content one's intentional states seem to one to have and the content they actually have. If it seems to one that an intentional state has a certain content, that's the content it has.

This approach saves an explanatory step. Why, if our speech acts outstrip in content the intentional states they express, do the intentional states subjectively seem to us to have the richer content of the speech acts? The pandemonium model avoids having to answer that question by positing that the intentional states really do have that richer content.

But even if the content of our speech acts does outstrip that of the thoughts they express, we can readily explain why those thoughts and speech acts seem, subjectively, to have the same content. As remarked earlier, a speech act counts as expressing a thought only if it has roughly the same content.[13] But we also sometimes convey our thoughts by actually reporting them—by saying literally that we have those thoughts. Suppose I think that it's raining. I verbally express that thought by saying, simply, that it's raining, whereas I report that very same thought by saying, instead, that I think that it's raining.

Indisputably, two such speech acts differ semantically, since they have distinct truth conditions. Still, they are easily conflated, since, with minor qualifications about degree of conviction that won't matter here, we can appropriately say one thing whenever we can appropriately say the other. This equivalence of performance conditions, moreover, is second nature for us; any time I actually do say it's raining, I might as easily have said that I think that it's raining, and conversely.

Suppose, then, I think that p and I express my thought with the somewhat richer, more refined statement that p'. The richer statement that p' is, then, performance-conditionally equivalent to the statement that I think that p'. And because this equivalence is second nature, I might as easily have said that I think that p'. But if I had made the higher-order remark that I think that p', my statement would have expressed a thought that has roughly the same content;

it would have been the HOT that I think that p'. And, since I might just as easily have made that statement, I must have had the HOT that the statement would have expressed.

The upshot is that, whenever I say that p', I have a HOT that I think that p'. And that HOT determines how I am conscious of the thought my speech act expresses. So, whatever the actual content of my thought, I am conscious of that thought *as having the content; that p'*. We can explain why, even though my speech act may be somewhat richer and more refined in content than the thought it expresses, I am conscious of the thought *as having* the richer, more refined content.[14]

But a difficulty looms for this explanation. If first-order conscious thoughts can be less fine grained than the speech acts that express them, why can't the same happen with HOTs as well?[15] And if our verbal report of a first-order thought might outstrip in content the HOT that report expresses, the HOT need not, after all, reflect the richer content of that report. And then we wouldn't be conscious of the first-order thought as having that richer content.

Perhaps this is all so. But recall that we are not trying to show that speech acts invariably have more fine-grained content than the thoughts they express, but only that this may sometimes happen, despite our subjective sense that it never does. And we have no reason to think it ever does actually happen with HOTs.

Indeed, it is highly unlikely that it ever happens there. We think that first-order thoughts have less fine-grained content than their verbal expressions because it seems clear that what we think could have been expressed equally well by distinct, semantically nonequivalent speech acts. But that's not the case with the HOTs that accompany our verbally expressed intentional states. Suppose I verbally express my first-order thought that p by the more fine-grained remark that p'. How I express my HOT about my less fine-grained, first-order thought that p is now dictated by the performance-conditional equivalence between saying the more fine-grained p' and saying that I think that p'. So I will now express that HOT only by saying that I think that p'. Verbally expressing my thoughts constrains the way I am conscious of them.[16]

David M. Rosenthal

The Refinement Model and First-Person Operationalism

On the refinement model, speech acts often outstrip in content the intentional states they express. To explain how this squares with our subjective impressions, we must distinguish the content those states have from the content they seem to us to have. But the content of intentional states is a matter of how things seem to us. So this explanation conflicts with Dennett's first-person operationalism, which denies any difference between things' seeming a certain way and their seeming to seem a certain way.[17]

But there is reason to reject that denial. Consider the game Dennett describes of "Hide the Thimble," which dramatizes how we can look straight at an object we're trying to find and yet fail consciously to register it (1991, 334). This kind of case invites us to distinguish our seeing something consciously from our seeing it without being conscious of seeing it; things may seem a certain way even though they don't consciously seem that way.

The striking and subjectively surprising limits on parafoveal resolution that Dennett cites take us even farther. Parafoveal vision can produce only low-resolution sensations of most of the Warhol Marilyns (Dennett 1991, 354),[18] but it seems subjectively that we are aware of them all in a clear and focused way. What it's like for one to have a particular conscious sensation is a function of how one is conscious of that sensation. So the best explanation of this case is that we have blurry parafoveal sensations of most Marilyns, but the way we are aware of those blurry sensations represents them as having high resolution.[19] What our sensations of the Marilyns is like for us is a function of how we're conscious of those sensations.[20] And, if the way we're conscious of our sensations sometimes goes beyond their mental properties by in effect refining them or touching them up, it is highly likely that the same happens with our intentional states, as well.[21]

On the pandemonium model, our intentional states come to have determinate content only when expressed by a speech act, or fixed by some other sort of probe. This applies equally, Dennett argues, to the higher-order states in virtue of which we are conscious of our conscious states; those higher-order states themselves "(come) to be *created* by the very process of framing the report."[22] Such "hetero-phenomenological reports" are the verbal pronouncements people make about their own mental states, to which Dennett's heterophe-nomenological method seeks to do justice. Since framing those re-ports fixes the higher-order content, Dennett holds that sincere heterophenomenological reports are constitutive of what it's like for the subject at that time and, hence, constitutive of that subject's con-sciousness. It is those heterophenomenological reports, rather than any antecedently occurring intentional states, that fix the contents of consciousness.

This conclusion might seem tempting because we are seldom con-scious of the higher-order states in virtue of which we are, in turn, conscious of our conscious mental states. So our first-person impres-sion will be that heterophenomenological reports alone determine how we are conscious of those states. But this first-person appear-ance is unreliable. We are in many intentional states of which we are not conscious, and we should expect that we typically remain unaware of the HOTs in virtue of which we are conscious of our conscious states. Such HOTs would be conscious only if we had third-order thoughts about them, and we can safely assume that that seldom happens.

Moreover, we are occasionally conscious of our HOTs, wholly in-dependently of whether we express them in heterophenomenologi-cal reports. Focusing introspectively on some particular state makes us aware not only of that state but also of the reflective, higher-order state of being aware of the lower-order target. The only reason to hold that heterophenomenological reports, rather than the HOTs they express, fix the contents of consciousness is Dennett's rejection of the folk-psychological model, on which speech acts generally ex-press antecedent intentional states.

HOTs not only determine what it's like for us to be in various mental states; they also are, in effect, subjectively spontaneous in-terpretations of the mental states we are in.[23] Indeed, there is an important connection between consciousness and our seemingly spontaneous self-interpretations. When we spontaneously interpret ourselves as being in certain states, we are conscious of ourselves *as being in those states*. What it's like for us to be in particular states is a function of how we spontaneously interpret those states. In the absence of any such spontaneous self-interpretations, our mental states simply aren't conscious; there is nothing it's like for us to be in them.

First-person operationalism is also interpretationist, but it imposes a special constraint all its own. Mental states are conscious, on first-person operationalism, only when accompanied by intersubjectively accessible probes. Because we have no access to the mental states of others apart from these probes, such probes provide our sole basis for interpreting what states others are in. So tying the consciousness of mental states to the occurrence of probes means that mental states are conscious only when they are available for interpretation by others. First-person operationalism holds that the consciousness of mental states is a function of interpretation, but only third-person interpretations matter.[24]

But this third-person constraint is gratuitous. The self-interpretations that HOTs provide are by themselves sufficient for one's mental states to be conscious. Indeed, one might well wonder how third-person interpretations could have any bearing at all on the consciousness of mental states. The key is the denial by first-person operationalism of any difference between mental states and their being conscious—between how things seem and how they seem to seem. Given that denial, an interpretation of somebody as being in a particular state serves indifferently as reason to think that the person is in that state and that the state is conscious. First-person operationalism restricts itself to third-person interpretations because it denies the distinction between mental states and their being conscious.

Rejecting first-person operationalism allows us to distinguish being conscious of our mental states from the states we are conscious of. And that opens the way to explaining the consciousness of mental states along lines different from those invoked in explaining other mental properties. In particular, it may well be that mental states have determinate content even though the way we are conscious of those states is a function of the subjectively spontaneous self-interpretations embodied in HOTs. So, too, for the HOTs themselves; what it's like for us to be in various mental states is just a matter of the self-interpretations our HOTs embody, but those HOTs can themselves be determinate in content.[25] Interpretationism can be true about what it's like for us to be in mental states without thereby holding for their content or other mental properties.[26]

Notes

1. Though HOTs are noninferential from a first-person point of view, they might still result sometimes from inferences we are unaware of. We need not suppose that the way we are conscious of our conscious states actually is unmediated to explain our intuitive sense that it is.

2. They will be conscious only when we are conscious of target states in the deliberate, attentive way we call introspection. A development of the HOT model is avaliable. (See Rosenthal 1986b, 329–359; 1993b, 197–223; 1993c, 355–363; 1997, 729–753.)

3. First used in a published letter to Roderick Chisholm: Chisholm and Sellars (1958), 524.

4. Insincere speech and the speech productions of actors' playing a part are also like this. (See Rosenthal 1986a, 151–184.) Thus J. L. Austin notes that if I insincerely say "I promise," I don't strictly speaking promise, but only say I do (Austin 1970, 101–103). Similarly, Frege remarks that "stage assertion is only sham assertion" (Frege 1977, 8).

5. Esp. 245 and 247; see also chapter 10, section 5, especially 315.

6. Which Dennett suggests also happens (Dennett 1991, 247).

7. I owe this idea to Tim Kenyon, in conversation.

8. Dennett speaks (1991) of such nonconscious, subpersonal events that subserve mental states taxonomized folk psychologically. Because they occur nonconsciously, "their onsets do *not* mark the onset of consciousness of their content" (1991, 113, emphasis Dennett's). And he holds that, unlike mental states taxonomized folk psychologically, "content-fixations . . . are (each) precisely locatable in both space and time" (1991, 113).

9. Most forcefully and impressively defended by Jerry A. Fodor (1975; 1978, 501–523; 1987; 1990; 1994).

10. Partly for reasons developed in compelling detail by Tyler Burge (1986, 3–45, and elsewhere).

11. It is possible that many human thoughts have content that makes them better suited to being expressed by specific nonverbal actions than by speech; doubtless

this is true of the thoughts of nonlinguistic animals. One might have a thought, for example, that is expressed by one's getting in out of the rain. Deliberate cases of such an action are not merely automatic; some intentional state with suitable content are among their causes. It may not be clear in these cases just what that content is—whether it is, for example, to get out of the rain, to seek shelter, to stop getting wet, or what. But it would be surprising if that content could not be captured, in some gerrymandered way, in human language.

12. The heterophenomenological method relies on the reports people make of their mental states; such reports in effect constitute self-interpretations. Dennett also regards cases in which we learn what we think by seeing what we say as involving a kind of self-interpretation (1991, 245). But there self-interpretation occurs by way of speech acts that verbally express our intentional states, rather than explicitly reporting them. Seeing verbal expressions of intentional states as self-interpretations as well as reports suggests that Dennett may be tacitly assimilating reports to verbal expressions. And that, in turn, may help explain why he regards self-interpretation as the last word about the content of our thoughts. Even if speech acts can differ in content somewhat from the intentional states they express, one might plausibly regard such expressions as better than any other evidence could be about the content of those states. So, assimilating reports of intentional states to their verbal expressions will make such self-interpreting reports themselves seem to be decisive about the content of the states those reports are about. Assimilating the reporting of intentional states to their verbal expression also encourages the idea that mental states are all conscious, since the content of every mental state would itself then affirm, as reports do, that one is in that state. This idea may, moreover, be implicit in first-person operationalism, on which a state's mental properties are determined by how that state appears to consciousness.

13. It is arguable that, in addition, the intentional state must be causally implicated in producing the speech act. (See Rosenthal 1986a, 151–184.)

14. These considerations explain, more generally, why it is that all verbally expressed cognitive intentional states are conscious. Whenever I express my thought that p by saying that p, I could as easily have said that I think that p. So I must have had the HOT I think that p, and on the HOT model my thought that p will accordingly be conscious. It is unlikely that any other model can explain why verbally expressed cognitive states are conscious. For more, see Rosenthal, "Why Are Verbally Expressed Thoughts Conscious?" (in prep., *Consciousness and Mind*). In "Consciousness and its Expression" (1998). I show how these considerations also explain why affective states, unlike cognitive states, are often verbally expressed without being conscious.

15. This echoes a challenge Dennett raises for the HOT model, that the pandemonium model should apply at higher levels as well; "the second-order state," he claims, "comes to be *created* by the very process of framing the report" (1991, 315, his emphasis). Also: "The emergence of the (verbal) expression (of a higher-order thought) is precisely what creates or fixes the content of higher-order thought expressed" (Dennett 1991, 315).

16. Dennett notes with approval Elizabeth Anscombe's argument that it is "wrong to claim that we *know* what our intentions are; rather we just *can say* what our intentions are" (Dennett 1991, 315, n. 10; Anscombe 1963). The present explanation reflects this primacy of verbal expressions. On that explanation, the verbal expres-

sion of a thought constrains, by the performance-conditional equivalence, the content of our HOT about the target first-order thought, and hence how we are conscious of that target thought.

17. The hierarchy of levels ends up, he claims, in our "having to postulate differences that are systematically undiscoverable by any means, from the inside or the outside," distinctions that are "systematically indiscernible in nature" (Dennett 1991, 319).

18. A striking illustration is available of the limits on parafoveal vision in attempting to discern the color of playing cards seen parafoveally at arm's length. (See Dennett 1991, 53–54.)

19. Similarly, in the thimble case; there is a conscious sensation in our visual field corresponding to the location of the thimble, since no subjective gap occurs there, but we are not conscious of that sensation *as* a sensation of a thimble. We may also be conscious of sensations in ways that leave out aspects of their qualitative character, as when a throbbing pain is conscious only as painful and not as throbbing, or a sensation of red is conscious as red but not in respect of any particular shade. So, even though visual sensations appear to us to be "ultimately homogeneous," in Wilfrid Sellars's useful phrase (1962, 36), it may well be that their sensory qualities are actually composed of many pixels representing specific characteristics; their ultimately homogeneous appearance may be due only to the way our HOTs represent collections of such pixels. We are conscious of our sensations in a way that smooths them out, so to speak, and elides the details of their particulate, bit-map nature. For more on sensations' diverging from the way we are conscious of them and the way HOTs function in that connection, see "State Consciousness and What It's Like" (in prep., *Consciousness and Mind*, Oxford: Clarendon Press), and "Consciousness and Metacognition" (forthcoming, *Metarepresentation: Proceedings of the Tenth Vancouver Cognitive Science Conference*, New York: Oxford University Press).

20. Consider the striking results John Grimes reports, in which subjects fail consciously to notice dramatic changes of color and shape in a salient object if the change occurs during a saccade (Grimes 1996, 89–110). Our subjective sense that conscious experience is continuously responsive to changes in what we see outstrips the extent to which we actually track changes in our visual sensations. This lends support to the conclusion, argued for by Dennett (1991, chapter 11), that our subjective sense of great detail throughout our visual field is also illusory. The way we are conscious of our sensations goes beyond those sensations themselves.

21. Because what it's like to be in conscious states is sometimes informationally richer than the states themselves and that additional informational content is occurrent, we must posit occurrent states of higher-order awareness of the states, and not just dispositions to be aware of them.

22. Dennett (1991), 315. Also: "The emergence of the (verbal) expression is precisely what creates or fixes the content of higher-order thought expressed" (1991, 315).

23. Subjectively spontaneous because we are unaware of any antecedent factor that might explain their occurrence. Because HOTs are not themselves typically conscious, we will seldom be explicitly aware of engaging in the self-interpretations these HOTs embody.

24. And such third-person interpretations cannot distinguish between a state's never coming to be conscious and its coming to be conscious too briefly to affect memory.

25. As well as determinate as to time of occurrence, which makes it determinate when our mental states come to be conscious. The HOT model may sometimes count a state as conscious even though there is nothing it's like for one to be in that state, for example, in some cases where we find it hard to decide between Stalinesque and Orwellian explanations. The occurrence of a HOT would be decisive in any event, regardless of first-person impressions; it is standard for well-established theories to resolve problem cases when the empirical input, including first-person impressions, does not suffice.

26. Work on this paper began at the Center for Interdisciplinary Research (ZiF), University of Bielefeld, Germany. I am grateful to the Center for congenial and stimulating surroundings and to a PSC-CUNY Research Award for supporting my stay there. I am also grateful for helpful reactions to an earlier draft from the participants in the November 1998 Memorial University of Newfoundland Conference on Dennett and from members of the CUNY Cognitive Science Symposium.

References

Anscombe, G. E. M. (1963). *Intention,* 2nd ed. Oxford: Basil Blackwell.

Austin, J. L. (1970). Other minds. In *Philosophical Papers.* 3rd ed. Oxford: Oxford University Press.

Burge, T. (1979). Individualism and the mental. *Midwest Studies in Philosophy* 4: 73–121.

Burge, T. (1986). Individualism and Psychology. *The Philosophical Review* 95, 1: 3–45.

Chisholm, R. M. and Sellars, W. (1958). Intentionality and the mental. In *Minnesota Studies in the Philosophy of Science* II, Feigl, H., Scriven, M., and Maxwell, G. (eds.). Minneapolis: University of Minnesota Press.

Dennett, D. (1978). Two approaches to mental images. In Dennett, *Brainstorms.* Cambridge, Mass.: MIT Press. A Bradford Book.

Dennett, D. (1991). *Consciousness Explained.* Boston: Little, Brown and Company.

Dennett, D. (1993). The message is: There is no *medium. Philosophy and Phenomenological Research* 53, 4: 919–931.

Dennett, D. (1996). *Kinds of Minds: Toward an Understanding of Consciousness.* New York: Basic Books.

Dennett, D. (1997). How to do other things with words. In *Thought and Language,* J. Preston (ed.). Cambridge: Cambridge University Press.

Dennett, D. and Kinsbourne, M. (1992a). Escape from the Cartesian Theater. *The Behavioral and Brain Sciences* 15: 234–247.

Dennett, D. and Kinsbourne, M. (1992b). Time and the observer: The where and when of consciousness in the brain. *The Behavioral and Brain Sciences* 15: 183–201, 201–234.

Fodor, J. A. (1975). *The Language of Thought.* New York: Thomas Y. Crowell.

Fodor, J. A. (1978) Propositional attitudes. *The Monist* 61, 4: 501–523.

Fodor, J. A. (1987). Why there still has to be a language of thought. Appendix, *Psychosemantics: The Problem of Meaning in the Philosophy of Mind.* Cambridge, Mass.: MIT Press. A Bradford Book.

Fodor. J. A. (1990). A theory of content. In *A Theory of Content and Other Essays.* Cambridge, Mass.: MIT Press. A Bradford Book.

Fodor, J. A. (1994). *The Elm and the Expert: Mentalese and Its Semantics.* Cambridge, Mass.: MIT Press. A Bradford Book.

Frege, G. (1977). Thoughts. In *Logical Investigations,* tr. P. T. Geach and R. H. Stoothoff. New Haven: Yale University Press.

Grimes, J. (1996). On the failure to detect changes in scenes across saccades. In *Perception,* Akins, K. (ed.). New York: Oxford University Press.

Rosenthal, D. (1986a). Intentionality. *Midwest Studies in Philosophy* 10: 151–184, sec. 5.

Rosenthal, D. (1986b). Two concepts of consciousness. *Philosophical Studies* 49, 3: 329–359.

Rosenthal, D. (1993a). Multiple drafts and higher-order thoughts. *Philosophy and Phenomenological Research* 53, 4: 911–918.

Rosenthal, D. (1993b). Thinking that one thinks. In *Consciousness: Psychological and Philosophical Essays,* Davies, M. and Humphreys, G. W. (eds.). Oxford: Basil Blackwell.

Rosenthal, D. (1993c). State consciousness and transitive consciousness. *Consciousness and Cognition* 2, 4: 355–363.

Rosenthal, D. (1995a). First-person operationalism and mental taxonomy. *Philosophical Topics* 22, 1 and 2: 319–349.

Rosenthal, D. (1995b). Multiple drafts and facts of the matter. In *Conscious Experience,* Metzinger, T. (ed.). Exeter, UK: Imprint Academic, 1995.

Rosenthal, D. (1997). A theory of consciousness. In *The Nature of Consciousness: Philosophical Debates,* Block, N., Flanagan, O., and Güzeldere, G. (eds.). Cambridge, Mass.: MIT Press. A Bradford Book.

David M. Rosenthal

Rosenthal, D. (1998). Consciousness and its expression. *Midwest Studies in Philosophy* 22: 294–309.

Rosenthal, D. (in prep.) Why are verbally expressed thoughts conscious? *Consciousness and Mind.* Oxford: Clarendon Press.

Rosenthal, D. (in prep.) State consciousness and what it's like. *Consciousness and Mind.* Oxford: Clarendon Press.

Rosenthal, D. (forthcoming.) Consciousness and metacognition. *Metarepresentation: Proceedings of the Tenth Vancouver Cognitive Science Conference,* Sperber, D. (ed.). New York: Oxford University Press.

Sellars, W. (1962). Philosophy and the scientific image of man. In *Frontiers of Science and Philosophy,* Colodny, R. G. (ed.). Pittsburgh: University of Pittsburgh Press.

14

Dennett on Ethics: Fitting the Facts against Greed for the Good

T. Brian Mooney

In his "The Moral First Aid Manual" (1998, 121–242) and *Darwin's Dangerous Idea* (1995), Dan Dennett has applied the implications of his radical naturalism to the field of ethics. The ethical positions he outlines raise a number of very practical concerns for ethical theory. In particular there is a strident rejection of forms of greedy ethical reductionism together with a pragmatically oriented critique of rule fetishism and a firm appreciation of the importance of actual time constraints on ethical decision making. Indeed it is the latter that provides the impetus for the practical judgments delivered in "The Moral First Aid Manual."

In this paper I would like to pursue some of Dennett's ideas by expanding on the bases for his critiques of deontology and utilitarianism. In particular I will argue that we ought not to reject just greedy reductionism but also its motivational opposite—it might be termed greedy or pleonexic[1] maximization. This should provide further reasons for the rejection of rule fetishism on the grounds that it does not fit the facts, and for rehabilitating the notion that ethical time constraints and "computational intractability" are vitally important in determining both moral deliberation and what sort of ethical system we should adhere to. It will, I hope, also lead us to a deeper appreciation of Dennett's preference for plural values.[2] Finally I would like to suggest that there is a whole field of ethical discourse that coheres with the naturalistic impulses of Dennett's work, in particular, with evolutionary theory. This field of discourse is virtue ethics.

One of the fundamental arguments that motivates the creation of the moral first aid manual is the notion that there are objective time constraints on ethical decision making together with the idea that the sorts of computational intractability that effect idealizing moral theories amounts to a real charge against their value. Dennett puts it as follows:

> No remotely compelling system of ethics has ever been made computationally tractable, even indirectly, for real-world moral problems. So, even though there has been no dearth of utilitarian (and Kantian, and contractarian, etc.) arguments in favor of particular policies, institutions, practices, and acts, these have been heavily hedged with ceteris paribus clauses and plausibility claims about their idealizing assumptions. These hedges are designed to overcome the combinatorial explosion of calculation that threatens if one actually attempts—as theory says one must—to consider all things. (1995, 500)

This is undoubtedly true, as was widely recognized in the ancient and mediaeval worlds. But it is equally widely and conveniently forgotten in contemporary deontological and utilitarian speculation. What is even more important, however, is the lack of appreciation of the ideas of equilibrium and balance that affects these two moral theories. Dennett's presentation of the moral first aid manual implicitly recognizes that balance is a crucial element of actual moral situations where objective time constraints and computational intractability come into play. One of his preferred strategies to deal with these is what he calls "conversation stoppers." (1995, 506) This, however, is a structural solution to the time constraints and computational intractabilty issues. I, on the other hand, think that there are prior moral considerations which justify the moral first aid policy but provide a richer subtext from which the individual moral agents can rationally adopt the first aid agenda with all the appropriate moral motivations.

What is at stake here is the opposite side of the coin to greedy ethical reductionism. Contemporary deontologists and utilitarians are essentially value maximizers in ways that do not fit the facts and particulars of moral situations. Or, to use the terminology of Plato, they are motivationally pleonexic. Pleonexia is Plato's term for the kind of motivation that refuses to deal with objective limitations. Although widely used in the Platonic corpus, the issue is most focused in the *Politeia* and the *Philebus*.

In discussing the nature of justice in the *Politeia*, Plato argues that all human crafts are responses to objective needs in human endeavors and that moral qualities resemble crafts in this respect. The mark of the just person is that his or her desires are harmonized with what is necessary—the right amount—and not with some form of excess. Plato first broaches this issue in Socrates' discussion with Polemarchus.[3] Polemarchus has just advanced a position that is essentially a civic conception of justice. On this view justice is delivered institutionally or structurally once one knows *impartially* how it is one should treat those designated as friends or enemies. (In this respect it has much in common with many contemporary theories of justice.) Such knowledge is, according to Polemarchus, delivered by the social context. Duties and obligations are imposed by knowing what the social expectations are for dealing with friends, enemies, physicians, mothers, fathers, and so on.

It is in this context that Plato delivers his version of the Sermon on the Mount. Socrates argues that it can never be the function of justice to harm anyone. Justice is primarily something an agent brings to situations, rather than some external sets of constraints imposed upon them. He is essentially saying that the excellence of justice must always have in view the goal that it promotes. This provides an interesting gloss to Dennett's discussion because it suggests that ethical considerations are exercises of human powers or capacities—virtues—and that what marks out the characteristics of the just person is a specific form of knowledgeable activity that deals with the issue of what is appropriate given the vagaries of everyday complexity. Although Dennett is well aware of everyday exigencies and the subsequent limitations on moral deliberation, he appears to think that structural solutions are the answer, of the sort he puts forward as moral first aid. He does not take the extra step, which locates the proper exercise of rational and moral deliberation in the exercise of specific human powers or virtues.

Socrates is attempting to show us that for any given craft there will be a subject matter that delimits the field of activity, and there will be goals that are internal to the nature of the craft. Thus justice conceived of as a craft is the product of a human power or excellence and the exercise of this power is determined by the goals that the skill promotes in harmony with knowledgeable activity. The goodness that justice conceived of as a craft promotes cannot be judged by external values but only in respect to the "product" itself, namely, whether or not justice, and more generally, the good, is in fact promoted. A shoemaker may engage in his craft in order to make money, but whether qua shoemaker he makes good shoes is judged by the goals of shoemaking, the exercise of his knowledgeable activity and by his overcoming or meeting the needs demanded by his craft.

The importance of these considerations is that part and parcel of what constitutes knowledgeable activity is the understanding of objective limits on human action and deliberation. Socrates' craft analogies illustrate that the kind of intelligence required in any field is related to knowing what is required and in not wanting to have more. Thrasymachus is in the *Politeia* the chief exponent of pleonexia—the desire to have more than what meets an objective need in any given context. Knowledge, for Plato, ultimately is anti-pleonexic and this is as true for the moral sphere as it is for the crafts.

But this is precisely where deontology and utilitarianism let us down. Both theories are value maximizers and idealizers in ways that tell against practical intelligence, balance, and motivational correctness. In what follows I would like to show that there are both conceptual and evaluative problems with value maximization and moral idealization.[4] This, in its turn, will open the way for providing the background to the structural positions of the moral first aid manual. As well, it will show that an account of the virtues provides the soundest basis in evolutionary theory for why we need moral first aid in the first place and for maintaining that there is nothing irrational in desiring it.

David Wiggins is a maximizer who thinks that maximization holds for purely conceptual reasons. In his essay "Weakness of Will, Commensurability, and the Objects of Deliberation and Desire"[5] he argues that "if nothing else besides F-ness counts positively for anything, there is nothing to commend any other course of action over the one that is most F." (1980, 255). Purely hedonistic maximization is, of course, comparatively rare, but the point is brought out most starkly with hedonism. If pleasure is the object of my concerns then I must, according to the maximizing position, care most for most pleasure. Certain caveats may be appended. For example, it may be said that what is cared for is a particular thing or kind of thing. Thus I might enjoy a good meal without that meal being made better by the addition of extra ingredients or courses. This leads to the idea that what is cared for in respect of particulars are things or kinds of things viewed contextually, that is, in respect of other things that are cared for. If I am right this begins to weaken the original maximization claim. I will return to this presently.

Donald Davidson has provided another basis for making maximization claims. In "How is Weakness of the Will Possible?" (1969) he seems to suggest that in order to understand acting and deciding on reasons we need to hold to a maximizing schema. Davidson couches his arguments in terms of explanation. If I go to the pub to get a pint of Guinness because Guinness is my favorite tipple then it is reasonable to assume that going to the pub is most conducive to achieving my ends, where the pleasure of drinking the pint is my value or what is cared for. The kind of maximization under discussion here is rationality maximization. Schematically, given that I desire X and believe $Bi, Bii, Biii \ldots$ the most rational thing for me to do would be A. Supposedly this explains why I do A. Thus it would appear that if one denies maximization then it becomes difficult to either explain or interpret decisions and actions based on reasons. The notion is that choosing what is nonmaximal must be reduced to, and explained by, external considerations such as my not having enough money for the pint.

Yet there is something very fishy here. Nonmaximizing care seems to me to be a standard and noncontroversial aspect of many people's lives. And this fact does not seem to throw our intuitions about decision making or action into chaos. It seems perfectly consistent for me to say that I do not want too much pleasure, study, Guinness, and so on. The maximizers, and moral theories more generally, thus must have something to say about nonmaximal care. For to argue, and I must point out again that we are dealing with conceptual claims here, that we must care most for most *F*, just doesn't hold water.

Maximizers at this point tend to invoke the idea that in order for there to be nonmaximal care for *F*, some other value or values must come into play. Where less *F* is better, it is better only in respect of some other relevant feature or object of care. But this is counterintuitive because it fails to deal with what maximization sets out to explain, namely, that more *F* is better than less *F*. There need not be any other features as the example of the good meal shows.

Another possible line of maximizing recalcitrance might be that attendant features, which count against what is maximally cared for, mitigate the maximization of *F*. This is precisely the issue that Plato and Aristotle saw in their nonmaximizing moral theories. Aristotle was only too well aware that good fortune could become an excess when drawn up with eudaimonia.[6] And Plato saw that maximal care for somatic pleasures was unjustified because of long-term and intense somatic distresses.

The point of such reasoning is to show that there are indeed plural objects of care, and as a result, nonmaximal care is a rationally sound strategy. Moreover, such plural objects of care may even be hierarchized, with pleasure, for example, falling somewhere below wisdom. But this does not yet definitively refute maximization since the maximizer will argue that it is precisely this "mix" of values that is to be maximized. My response is that such a reply fails to understand how a mix works and the kinds of equilibrium that are required. For one thing it is very difficult to know how to compare different kinds of values. I am not saying that one cannot rationally judge the relative characteristics of several instances of, say, pleasure. One might rank listening to a good philosophy paper higher than drinking a fine pint of Guinness (but even here the matter is not without its difficulties, of time, mood, and so on.)

Rather, I am suggesting that it is very difficult to rationally assess the comparability of certain kinds of value mixes when the values are values such as love and justice, which at least apparently on occasion come apart. Again, the point is that where the maximizer claims that what is cared for is "some F" as part of a greater package of value maximization, the initially plausible maximizing claim is rendered vacuous since it no longer provides adequate explanations of how to discriminate and rank options.

Now, clearly, both utilitarianism and deontology amount to greedy pleonexic maximizations of value. Utilitarianism is so because it maximizes either the greatest happiness of the greatest number or the preference satisfactions of the greatest number, and so on. Deontology does so because it requires that duty be done no matter what are the competing morally relevant considerations. Deontology also falls short in wanting too much, because, as Dennett astutely points out:

> What, though, do the Kantians put in the place of the unworkable consequentialist calculations? Maxim-following (often derided as rule worship) of one sort or another, such as that invoked in one of Kant's (1785) formulations of the Categorical Imperative: Act only on that maxim through which you can at the same time will that it should become a universal law. Kantian decision-making typically reveals rather different idealizations—departures from reality in other directions—doing all the work. For instance, unless some deus ex machina is standing by, a handy master of ceremonies to whisper suggestions in your ear, it is far from clear just how you are supposed to figure out how to limit the scope of the "maxims" of your contemplated actions before putting them to the litmus test of the Categorical Imperative. There seems to be an inexhaustible supply of maxim candidates. (1995, 499–500)

Moreover, the good must be done even where in situations of conflicts of duties one of a number of possible alternatives may not be in itself obligatory. Kant, in particular, finds it difficult to provide any mechanisms with respect to which we can prioritize or rank competing duties in conflict situations. A deontologist maximizer such as John Rawls, for example, wants to maximize value throughout a whole society along welfarist sorts of lines (1973).

Rawls himself is aware, however, of at least one version of a problem for maximization. In his discussion of the nature of fairness maximization in terms of just distribution, the issue arises that maximization of such distribution is unfair. Rawls attempts to get out of this problem with the now familiar strategy of plural values.

T. Brian Mooney

Fairness may be the central value, but there are others, and it is the "mix" that is important.[7] But conceptually this is difficult because, as I have pointed out, it is no easy task to be able to say one form of "mix" is better than another. How does one *measure* one "mix" that has more love than justice and another that has more justice than love?

My claim is not that one cannot make comparative judgments but that certain kinds of plural value comparisons are so intractable that they are pragmatically not useful. To take a structurally similar issue, consider comparative judgments in aesthetics. We certainly can talk of loud or unattractive colors, or of preferring the sound of the Irish flute to the concert flute. But in such judgments we readily evoke notions of taste or preferences. It is likely that aesthetic appreciation of material properties does no more than indicate the effect of certain kinds of perceptual traits and traditions upon our capacity to take pleasure in certain kinds of sensations. Such, I suspect, is also the case for judgments of the comparative values in value "mixes." (And indeed this is the basis for some of the communitarian critiques of Rawls. The values adopted behind the veil of ignorance are precisely the values that one brought up with liberal democratic convictions would have.) A good act is better than an evil one but not clearly better than a rose, just as a loving act is better than a hateful one but not clearly better than a just one.

A further pleonexic side to deontology is its rigid application of rules. The objections to this side of deontology are well known. But as with certain evaluative problems, which I will present shortly with maximization, deontology finds it difficult to accommodate the virtues of friendship and love in its moral schema. Plato too often is taken as a sort of moral maximizer, but he is certainly no rule fetishist. Even when developing a series of concrete rules for an actual state as he does in the *Laws,* he is at pains to develop long and elaborate preambles because he recognizes that rules and laws are subject to interpretation and that they, no matter how detailed, cannot be made to fit the polymorphism of the moral life.[8] Even in the *Politeia* it is clear that the vision of the Agathon does not yield any concrete moral codes or rules. Indeed, the Platonic metaphysics assures us that we can say nothing whatsoever about the nature of the Good—

it is *epekeina tes ousias,* completely beyond being. Rather the vision of the good moulds the soul by giving it a direction, but not a material rule of conduct.[9] Plato's particular vision with its insistence on the importance of *paideia,* good teachers and a good society, is summed up in the Benedictine dictum that the monk lives *sub regulum vel abbate.* The rule requires the experienced and wise interpreter to meet the demands of the particulars of a moral situation.

Aristotle is even more forthright. He writes in the *Nicomachaean Ethics:*

Now questions of conduct and expedience have as little fixity about them as questions of what is healthful; and if this is true of the general rule, it is still more true that its application to particular problems admits of no precision. For they do not fall under any art or professional tradition, but the agents are compelled at every step to think out for themselves what the circumstances demand, just as happens in the arts of medicine and navigation. (1103b–1104a)

To which he adds somewhat later:

When we are discussing actions, although general statements have a wider application, particular statements are closer to the truth. This is because actions are concerned with particular facts, and theories must be brought into harmony with them. (1107a)

Perhaps more than anything else we can see the differences between the consensus of the ancient world and Kantianism in the above quotations. Kant's elaboration of the a priori dictates of reason— the Categorical Imperative—and his derivations of moral rules from these as well as his articulation of the good will come apart with the facts and particularities of moral experience.[10] Even if Kant himself can be extricated from this criticism, many other deontologists and Kantians cannot. In Plato's terms, he wants too much, more than what is needed or required by the facts.

Returning to the question of deciding whether it is conceptually possible to evaluate the maximization of plural "mixes," Michael Stocker has made the following instructive criticisms. Stocker argues that

we cannot find out which course of action is best by finding out which mix has the most and the greatest goods; . . . instead we have to find out which mix is best—and perhaps also which has the greatest goods—by finding out directly which mix is best. (1990, 295) [11]

Stocker's point, put rather cryptically here, is that understanding what is good is often enough determined by judgments about what is better. He pushes this singularly Platonic point very clearly when he suggests that

> we construct the good from the better, rather than the better from the good. To the extent that the better is prior to the good, maximisations that tell us to do what is best are parasitic on other evaluations. (1990, 301)

The point is that when we are dealing with a mix such as a good life, it is obvious that in far too many instances the addition of further goods, or good maximization, does not produce a greater good. As Plato's Philebus shows so clearly in respect to hedonist maximization, too much pleasure is not pleasurable. And both Plato and Aristotle recognize that a good life requires plural values and their proper balance. Adding a good to the balance may actually destroy the balance, and this is true whether it involves the adding of a new good or more of the same good. Moreover, understanding the goodness of the good life is itself part of the good life and therefore part of the balance. So conceptually maximization fails.

But maximization fails concretely in terms of actual moral lives. Against the Kantian requirement that duty must be done though the heavens fall, we all recognize that we need not always pursue what duty requires or what is best. (Kant, of course, does distinguish between the morally obligatory and what is good but not obligatory, but his puritanical side more often than not is paramount, pushing us in the direction of heroic moral sainthood.) One might want to become both an accomplished musician and an excellent philosopher but time requirements as well as a million contingent factors in ordinary lives force, to some extent, degrees of specialization. One may well recognize the desire that both accomplishments be fulfilled but there need be no moral requirement that both must be. Indeed in terms of a good life it may well be that being a *good enough* musician and philosopher produces the more fulfilled life. It is an ordinary and, I believe, noncontroversial aspect of phenomenological experience that we knowingly and intentionally choose what is less than optimal. This need not be akratic—it may bear no connection whatsoever with weakness of will or incontinence.

The issue is brought home yet again when we look at instances of self-regarding and other-regarding virtues, and most starkly in discussions of moral saints and altruism. Put schematically, it involves the notion that one must achieve the right kind of balance between supererogation and self-regarding virtues. This tells against maximizers in a very serious sort of way, because the sort of balance that is required is not a computational or mathematical one. What is required, I suggest, in a complex and ordinary human life is the development of phronesis. As I understand this term in the later Plato and Aristotle, it is not just practical wisdom and judgment based on considerations of particulars and their relations to universal considerations, but more importantly, the cultivation of certain dispositions that undergird practical deliberation.

Plato addresses the issue most vigorously in the *Gorgias*. The problem is however a very contemporary one even in the manner of Plato's presentation. What does one do in a situation where a philosophical opponent does not even understand the words that one uses?—where what I mean by justice is an alien concept to the other, and her conception is alien to me? Plato in a deeply pregnant passage argues that the problem is massive but not insurmountable. He suggests that we need to return to the pathemata. The pathemata are the etiological causes and experiences a person undergoes that create the conditions for beliefs of radically different sorts. The pathemata are what can unite a shared vision because when touched they can reawaken the sense of our commonality with others.

One of the central forms of pathemata for Plato is the experience of eros. But in the Gorgias, experiences such as eros are the preconditions for genuine communication. To paraphrase Plato's argument, or rather appeal—when the soul is well balanced, it is capable of entering into real communion with others (*Gorgias*, 507e ff). But the existence of the pathemata is only a precondition for such communion. What is required is that eros or love be oriented in the direction of the good and the disturbing passions restrained by *sophrosyne*. If the lusts are unrestrained, a person cannot engage in communion with either the gods or his fellows because without the experience of love and commonality one is incapable of friendship. And it is the establishing of love and friendship that enables us to take on the difficult tasks of moral and political elucidation. If Plato is right then philosophy begins in love and friendship, and these are, as it were, dispositions, and I might add dispositions that evolution has opened to us.

Yet another concrete reason for rejecting maximization follows from the last points. Love and friendship relationships are essentially nonmaximizing. A central problem in these areas involves what it is that is loved when we love another person. Many reflective people when asked this question point to qualities of the beloved. I love her for her wit, charm, beauty, *joie de vivre*, and so on. To which the objection runs, well if you love a person for these qualities, it is precisely the qualities that are loved and not the person. Therefore if someone holds the loveable qualities to a higher degree then one should swap beloveds. Clearly this runs counter to many of our deepest intuitions about love and friendship. Thus, to adulterate something of Brentlinger's (1970, 159–60) analysis, we might argue that I love a pint of Guinness and in attempting to say what it is about Guinness that I love, I can point to certain qualities of the pint. I enjoy and love the manner in which it is pulled, its taste, its aroma, and its colorful blend of dark and cream. When describing my love of a pint of Guinness this way, it is not at all clear that I am saying that I love these properties/attributes/qualities, and that the pint of Guinness is a means to achieving these ends.

But in making these claims about what I love I am doing no such thing; these are things about the pint of Guinness that I love, they are not separable from the pint of Guinness. While I might also love a pint of bitter, also for its taste, its color, its aroma, these qualities as instantiated are different to those in the pint of Guinness and thus in no way substitutable. In part my love for the pint of Guinness is attributable to historic/cultural circumstances peculiar to my own identity.[12]

Roger Scruton (1986) suggests that there is a difference between an emotional reaction to universals and one to particulars. He is no doubt correct. One can, for example, love a universal like justice, caring about it passionately, as an ideal and working tirelessly to achieve justice in one's own life and in the world around one. One also loves a particular person and the kind of attachment one has to that person does indeed seem different. Robert Brown appeals to this distinction in his platonizing conception of love in his book *Analysing Love* (1987, 106–107). Brown thinks that love of individuals is to be understood in terms of characteristics or qualities. He argues that we love a particular person because that person exhibits certain qualities in a unique manner. Moreover, this concatenation of qualities, including potential ones, is part of an open-ended commitment to the bearer of these qualities, and thus leaves open the possibility that there may be development of new or different qualities. The universals (the qualities) are loved, then, as they are exhibited by the subject. In other words, there is a symbiotic relationship between the universal qualities, which both attract and are loved, and the subject within which these qualities inhere.

Now this sort of appeal seems to work quite well for the Platonic theory of *eros*. By arguing that what is loved in another person is not just qualities but the qualities as exhibited and instantiated in the beloved, one appears to avoid the difficulty that love is nonpersonal. If the symbiotic relationship between qualities and the subject that instantiates them is maintained, one thereby explains the fact that one does love qualities but also persons. Moreover, by appealing to the manner of instantiation, it also accounts for the historical features that contribute to the development of a love relationship, as well as highlights the uniqueness and irreplaceability of the particular instantiation. More in matters of love is not always or even usually better. It is precisely the notion that in real love relationships the beloved is in some sense unique and irreplaceable that pushes us to reject maximization.

The points about love and friendship are also immune to the satisficing maximizers. For here we are talking not about satisficing a "mix" but of internal features of loving a person. The sorts of commitments, trust, and loyalty that are structurally built in to a love or friendship relation, while they do require balance with other elements of a good life, are nevertheless largely independent of maximizing evaluations. The fact that ethical theories like utilitarianism and deontology find it so difficult to accommodate love and friendship in their moral systems is a damning criticism. After all, love and friendship are two fundamental elements of a good human life and to live a life bereft of them would be to live a morally truncated life.

Much of what I have argued to this point involves the notion that we seek to achieve a balance in our complex moral lives that tells against value maximization and idealizing moral theories. I will now show that this antimaximization thrust is both morally and rationally correct and that it is best looked for in virtue theory. A good life is not dissimilar to Sartre's conception of *le projet*. The good life is a kind of orientation, and we judge what is moral and rational in respect to this larger orientation or goal. Whether we attribute goodness to any projects or even to the means to fulfill the projects is determined by the manner in which the action, desire, emotion, and so on, serves this greater whole. The whole in question need not be what is best, nor even the best option.

For example, it may be that in loving another person I am engaging in a long-term and open-ended project that conduces to my well-being. (I use this kind of language hesitantly since it does not capture the essence of a loving relation. Nevertheless, it suffices for the sake of this particular argument.) As in most cases, the sorts of structural commitments that attend to loving another person mean that there will be gains and losses. My love for the other tells against the time that needs to be put in to become a great philosopher, musician, or football player. Nevertheless, since I have a deep sense of moral integrity, I am *already* engaged in a project, and even though this structural commitment together with a sense of personal integrity tells against other deep seated values I have, I am still committed to my beloved. In other words, I have settled for, knowingly, a less than maximally optimizing life.

Indeed I may even come in time to believe that my life would be better without my beloved but still deem that my life is good enough. All sorts of indexical rankings of values might come into play, where I may think that the opportunities afforded to me by rejecting my beloved would open up all sorts of value possibilities, yet they must be presented in the context of disvalues counting against my love and its moral requirements of trust, care, and so on. A utilitarian calculus of the Benthamite type, or indeed of any type, is practically useless. Again we have need of moral first aid.

Dennett has argued correctly, I believe, that we must build our moral viewpoints upon what it is to be a human person. This is the decisive implication of naturalism. The naturalistic fallacy, that one cannot derive an ought from an is, smacks of a kind of arid intellectualism. The fact that I promise to go to the movies with my beloved does have moral force and provides an example of an ordinary situation where the very fact of a promise yields a moral ought. It may amount to no more than sophistry, but it tells us much about the complexity of ordinary lives.

The implications of my arguments with respect to nonmaximization in ordinary moral lives are that a good life, which implies moral diversity and pluralism, is a question of finding the right kinds of balances in a world that is complex. Not just the balances between self- and other-regarding virtues, but between public and private morality and the inner constitution of the soul, to mention just a few. The processes of deliberation are themselves part of this process of evaluation and balance. Moreover, the actual time constraints and a myriad of competing contingent exigencies make this balance precarious. My rejection of maximization, however, together with my phenomenological appeal to actual experiences raise the vista of a process of paideia, which elaborates the dispositions required both to engage in moral discourse in the first place and to make moral decisions in the second.

I have suggested that the development of certain kinds of perceptual traits that "see" the particularity of a given ethical situation provide the basis for rational judgment. No doubt these need to be balanced with an account of general principles, but it is already a good start to know that what is at issue is the question of balance. The development of these perceptual traits in their turn leads to an elaboration of dispositions, virtues, and powers that enable the moral agent to act well in a complex world. It might be further argued that these dispositions are the result of evolutionary possibilities grounded in finding a balance between the complex exigencies of the world and our capacities to live well within it. One of the advantages of such a view is that it reconciles the irreconcilable, Plato's qualities of the bestial and the peaceful. It would help us understand how and why the virtue of warlikeness, a possibility inherent in the human condition, is a virtue in a time of war but not one in a time of peace.

It would also help us reconcile ourselves to faults in our rational processes dealing with moral issues. The friend who comes to us for advice may need admonishment more than caring attention. We may get the response wrong but still know that we have acted well, with the right motivations, to the right level for the right amount of time, and so on. We may also have the appropriate regrets, and indeed this is a mark of the balanced moral agent in a less than optimal world. We may also refuse to give the bequest to any of the 250,000 legal entrants, or arbitrarily cut the number of applicants by random selection, or any other strategy that may be adopted, without thereby having acted badly (see Dennett 1995, 501–505). We may employ conversation stoppers, but throughout, we will have proceeded in real moral situations in a way that does not destroy our capacities to act at all, and in a way that is consistent with the proper balances in a good life. We may have acted rationally, emotionally, and evaluatively well without an external good having been produced. Moreover, by way of appeal, we have opened up a line of discourse and moral behavior capable of touching the pathemata of the recalcitrant evil doer. The fact that we have certain dispositions may not tell against such recalcitrance, but the story we tell about how a good life is enabling and good might. In a less than optimal world perhaps this is as much as we should expect and hope.[13]

Notes

1. Pleonexia is Plato's term for a type of motivation that refuses to acknowledge objective limitations. See *Republic*, Book I.

2. Although Dennett does not discuss plural values as such, I take it that much of the thrust of *Darwin's Dangerous Idea* is deeply indebted to pluralism. And in particular his recommendations about the sorts of plural interests one wants in philosophical colleagues in "The Moral First Aid Manual" warrant this assumption.

3. See Plato, *Politeia*, 331c–336a.

Dennett on Ethics

4. Throughout this paper I use the term maximization to engage in a debate initiated by Michael Stocker (1990) and related to standard issues in this field dealt with by, for example, Griffin (1986) and Hardin (1987).

5. Wiggins makes purely conceptual points in his paper. My subsequent remarks are not intended to label him as a hedonistic maximizer.

6. See Aristotle, *Nicomachaean Ethics*, 7, 13: 1153b.

7. In fact, for Rawls, fairness specifies all obligations and nothing overrides obligation. This means that the other values have no real force. Read in this way Rawls seems to be a more pure maximizer than I have attributed to him above. (See, in particular, Rawls 1973, 112.)

8. Plato, *Laws*, 722c ff.

9. On this issue, see the excellent commentary in Voegelin (1995), 112–117.

10. The best examples of the ways in which Kantian thinking comes apart from the facts and our moral intuitions is when dealing with the virtues of love and friendship. (See, in particular, Annas 1984, 15–31.)

11. I am deeply indebted in my discussion of maximization to Stocker's work and to long conversations with him on these issues. As a doctoral student of Stocker's, I used to come to his office armed with reams of my own work and Stocker would invariably speak about the relationship between what I was saying and his own research. At the time it was disconcerting but I am now thankful for his direction.

12. It might be thought, however, that this argument does not do the work it needs to do in the case of loving another person, because although (for the most part) one pint of Guinness is substitutable for any other pint of Guinness, our intuitions about loving other persons do not allow for such easy replaceability. In "Loving Persons" (unpublished), I show that there are other factical aspects to a love relation with another person that escape this difficulty. Nevertheless, for the moment it suffices to argue that the Platonic theory is not incompatible with the idea that the instantiation of qualities requires an attachment not just to the qualities but also to the objects within which they inhere.

13. I would like to thank my colleagues in the philosophy program at Edith Cowan University, Alan Tapper and Damian Cox, for invaluable comments on early drafts of this paper. I have also drawn considerably on discussions with two of my doctoral supervisors, Michael Stocker and Kimon Lycos.

References

Annas, J. (1984). Personal love and Kantian ethics in Effi Briest. *Philosophy and Literature* 8, 1: 15–31.

Brown, R. (1987). *Analyzing Love*. Cambridge, Cambridge University Press.

Davidson, D. (1969). How is weakness of will possible? In *Moral Concepts*, J. Feinberg (ed.). Oxford: Oxford University Press.

Dennett, D. C. (1995). *Darwin's Dangerous Idea: Evolution and the Meanings of Life.* London: Penguin Books.

Dennett, D. C. (1998). The moral first aid manual. In *The Tanner Lectures on Human Values.* Cambridge: Cambridge University Press.

Brentlinger, J. (1970). *The Symposium of Plato.* New Haven, Conn.: University of Massachusetts Press.

Griffin, J. (1986). *Well-Being.* Oxford, Oxford University Press.

Hardin, R. (1987). Rational choice theories. In *Idioms of Inquiry,* T. Ball (ed.). Albany: State University of New York Press.

Rawls, J. (1973). *A Theory of Justice.* Oxford: Oxford University Press.

Scruton, R. (1986). *Sexual Desire.* London: Weidenfeld and Nicolson.

Stocker, M. (1990). *Plural and Conflicting Values.* Oxford: Clarendon Press.

Voegelin, E. (1995). *Order and History,* vol. 3, Baton Rouge, Louisiana: Louisiana State University Press.

Wiggins, D. (1980). Weakness of will, commensurability, and the objects of deliberation and desire. In *Essays on Aristotle's Ethics,* A. O. Rorty (ed.). Berkeley and Los Angeles: University of California Press.

15
With a Little Help from My Friends

Daniel C. Dennett

With a Little Help from My Friends

Tom Sawyer's trick of getting his friends to vie for the privilege of helping him whitewash the fence made a big impression on me when I was a boy, and I have had great luck emulating Tom over the years. Nobody could afford to hire the talent that has labored on improving my theories and fixing my arguments, and never has my sense of this been stronger than at the St. John's, Newfoundland conference. Philosophy is often done in an atmosphere of one-upmanship and triumphant refutation, and nothing about our discipline damages its reputation in neighboring fields more. But here is a collection of essays that are often deeply skeptical of my positions, and boldly critical of my arguments, but always presented with an eye on how to get the weaknesses replaced by strengths, the problems repaired. They go beyond what I have said, beyond what I have tried to say, beyond what I understand even now, after reading and rereading the essays and writing and rewriting this commentary.

I have come to grips with some of their proposals and arguments quite well, I think. I have seen what was up and what to make of it. Sometimes I agree; sometimes I don't, and say why. But there is a convergence of attention by several authors on ontological questions—on realism of one sort or another—that I have still not been able to sort out, not because I think they are all wrong, but because I am tantalized by them all. This is the major shortcoming (I'm pretty sure) of this commentary. I ought to have been able to digest and put into a single perspective the various constructive suggestions regarding ontology coming from (in alphabetical order) Kenyon, Lloyd, Ross, Seager, Thompson, and Viger, but I can't get such a consilience to settle down yet. I can only list the points of convergence and invite the readers of this book to propose further unifications.

The order of my commentaries is based on an obvious principle of building: Wherever the comments on one essay seemed to me to benefit from following the comments of another, I put them in that order, until all were in a single string. Not surprisingly, the one essay by a nonphilosopher is the one that seemed to need the least philosophical wind-up before I could comfortably deliver.

Evolution: Crowe and Dumouchel

Timothy Crowe shows that the problems of communication among evolutionary theorists continue to be severe, and that my own interventions have not achieved the clarifications I had sought. This is frustrating, but let's just try to fix it, locating the points of misunderstanding and ignoring the issue of who's to blame. Crowe characterizes my overall aim in *Darwin's Dangerous Idea* (DDI henceforth) as the attempt to show that "Natural selection . . . plays an essential role in the understanding of every biological event at every hierarchical level, from the creation of self-replicating macromolecules to evolutionary lineages." It all depends on what you are trying to understand about a biological event, of course, but yes, I do think that natural selection plays an essential role—some role or other—at every scale, though in different ways at different scales. But once we get down to cases and ways, I rather doubt that Crowe would disagree with me, since mine is not, I think, an extreme view.

Crowe breaks down his interpretation of my position into three aims, and argues that I don't achieve two of them. Batting .333 is fine in baseball, but I aspire for better. He accepts (1) my characterization of skyhook-free evolutionary explanation, but thinks I fail (2) "to show that natural selection equals biological engineering driven by a foolproof, gradual, step-by-step, substrate-neutral, algorithmic design process." He uses his own research with African guineafowl as a telling example for showing where, by his lights, I've gone wrong on this second quest. He also finds fault with my attempt (3) "to prove that natural selection is a 'universal acid' that has effects and applications well beyond biology," including the development of human culture, but since his remarks on this score are so brief, I will have little to say about them.

I'm interested that the one success he grants me, defending a skyhook-free vision of evolution, he sees as uncontroversial, perhaps because he diminishes it from the outset: "I know of no evolutionary biologist, including Gould, who disputes the central importance of natural selection and its various cranes in the process of adaptation." My claim, however, is not the bland truism that cranes are "of central importance" but that *there are no skyhooks,* and to this day Gould has declined a number of invitations to acknowledge this point, perhaps because he is still uncertain just what a skyhook is. This surprised me, by the way. I had thought when I introduced the skyhook/crane distinction to Gould, some years before DDI came out, that he would grant me that point, and then go on to articulate his objections to (his version of) neo-Darwinism on that shared foundation. But he resisted. So Crowe's welcome attempt at ecumenical agreement on this first point doesn't quite get the job done. But leaving that issue aside, let's turn to the main topic of Crowe's essay.

First let me break down (2) into its constituents. Natural selection is

(a) Biological engineering;

(b) Algorithmic;

(c) Gradual, step-by-step;

(d) A substrate-neutral design process.

These are, I think, distinct claims that do not have to stand and fall together, though I will defend them all against his criticisms.

Biological Engineering

Here there has been a miscommunication of my aim, since I agree with the points he makes about the process of natural selection. In particular, I agree, indeed insist, that natural selection does *not* involve forward-thinking, goal-directed R&D, but I claim that that does not mean that it does not involve R&D. I can see why one may naturally assume that R&D is *by definition* forward-looking and goal-directed, but it is precisely my aim to resist this definition and insist that the process of natural selection is importantly *like* human R&D *in spite of* not being forward looking and goal-directed. Perhaps, then, we are just differing on the aptness of the R&D or engineering label, as he surmises. But I would still disagree with a point of contrast he urges on us: "The cranes of natural selection lift the fitness of individual organisms, demes, and populations, *rather than* [my emphasis] developing biological design-features that are in reality effects of that upliftment." I don't understand the "rather than"; I would replace those words by the word "by." What is the issue, then? I am not at all sure. Perhaps it is this. Do we view the long-term survival of the eagle (individual lineage, demes, populations) as a by-product of the natural selection of its excellent eyesight and wings (among other adaptations), or do we view the emergence of its excellent eyesight and wings (and other adaptations), as a by-product of the long-term survival of the eagle (demes, populations, etc.)? Shouldn't we view both as the emergent effects of a long history of natural selection? I think this is a nonissue, and I have certainly not claimed that there is any foresighted design project of creating better wings *so that* eagle lineages might prosper.

Algorithmicity

So much for (a); let's consider (b), algorithmicity. Crowe takes his research on guineafowl evolution to demonstrate that I am wrong about the algorithmicity of natural selection. He argues that the diversity of phenotypes among the subspecies of mutually cross-fertile guinea-hen varieties is due to

an incidental, accidental, indirect, even maladaptive consequence of normal adaptation, a process that falls squarely within the realm of historical contingency. Furthermore, contrary to Dennett, such situations show that natural selection does not time and again produce the guaranteed results generated by an algorithmic process.

But I see nothing in his account of the guineafowl that challenges my view of evolution. Evolution by natural selection is often a noise-amplifier, an exploiter of "frozen accidents," a tolerator of drift, not only in the case of Kimura-style accumulation of random mutations that are not expressed phenotypically, but also of phenotypic don't-cares, features that may vary even into maladaptive regions at least for a while. Crowe's misunderstanding here is particularly frustrating, since I anticipated just this misreading in DDI, and went to some lengths to forestall it with a variety of examples (52–60). I noted that the elimination tournament algorithm, as a sorting algorithm, is much more akin to the algorithms of natural selection than, say, long division is, and then I gave several examples of tournament algorithms that involved mixtures of chance—massive contingency, luck—and skill. My coin-tossing tournament is unadulterated 100% contingency, and yet it *is* an algorithm, after all, guaranteed to produce a winner, every time. Or consider the tennis tournament supplemented by Russian roulette: The winner in each round puts a revolver to his head, spins the chamber and pulls the trigger. If he's lucky, he advances to the next round; if not, his just-defeated opponent advances instead. Again, this algorithm is guaranteed to produce a winner, but it is also a contingency amplifier; it doesn't guarantee at all who (or what) will win. This contrast between "selective determinism" and "historical contingency" (to use Crowe's terms) is a remarkably persistent red herring—and I hasten to add that he is far from being alone in resisting the many corrections Dawkins and I (among others) have issued on this score. For some reason, it doesn't matter how many times you say "there is no conflict between algorithmicity and contingency" or how many ways you illustrate the point; some people are determined (!) to interpret algorithmicity as "selective determinism." Maybe there's a gene for it! (Joke) Seriously, I would like to know what Crowe makes of the fact that I cheerfully embrace his research as grist for my mill. This must come as a surprise to him. What in my writing led him to think otherwise?

So far as I can see, Crowe's research on guineafowl exemplifies circumspect adaptationist theory at its best—and he himself welcomes that prospect in his penultimate paragraph. The role of "dynamic creation and reconnection of habitat islands" in creating geographical isolates, together with drift within the isolates, may suffice to explain the differences in the absence of any more direct or powerful adaptational forces, favoring the different arrangements. But then he offers a further argument, which I am dubious about:

Because of their central importance to successful interbreeding, the components of SMRSs [specific mate recognition systems] should be under extremely strong stabilizing selection to "resist" change.

I don't think so. I would think that this is precisely the circumstance in which the positive feedback mechanism of "runaway" sexual selection can be amplified, in which a minute and functionless bias in female preference (which can be presumed to vary in the population) can swiftly lead to morphological change in SMRSs, rather than stabilizing selection. What is crucial, if breeding is to occur, is not that SMRSs stay the same, but that SMRSs track each other in male and female. Once the female bias is amplified to nonnegligible relative frequency in a subpopulation (which is ensured by the bottleneck), there is every adaptationist reason for the genes for the male response to that bias to track that bias—even at the cost of "cutting itself off from the fullest spectrum of potential mates," a cost invisible to myopic local selection in any case. Sexual selection is a real and important phenomenon. It is triumphantly part of, not a challenge to, adaptationism—as highlighted in the role of the peacock in Helena Cronin's (1991) title. So I'm delighted with Crowe's "just so story" about guineafowls, which I see as exemplifying the sort of good adaptationism I defend.

Gradualism

Now to gradualism, (c): As I noted in DDI, gradualism must be distinguished from what Dawkins calls "constant-speedism." One can maintain that evolution sometimes runs very fast, and sometimes very slow, but still is gradual, even when it is running very fast. The denial of *this* doctrine is one version or another of saltationism, positing leaps rather than steps, and here one must tread cautiously. Everybody agrees that several different kinds of isolated leaps are possible: A small, indeed, single step in mutation space can be a rather large step in phenotype space, for instance, adding a whole, well-formed digit, or changing the color of the whole organism, or—to take the truly monstrous cases—building a leg where an eye should be, or creating an extra head. It is even possible, indeed frequent, that single, small mutations can virtually ensure speciation, by disrupting the SMRSs that are, as Paterson vividly puts it, the glue that binds species together. Another way species can become distinct in the absence of the imposition of geographical barriers is a slight change in behavior. If some members slightly prefer (for no good reason at all) to mate at night, and others during the day, this assortative mating can swiftly lead to reproductively isolated subpopulations living together in the same region. Such events create quite abrupt macroscopic changes in the selective environment, and hence in the organisms that thrive in them, but do not count as saltations of the sort denied by gradualists. So, as Crowe says, speciation can be an incidental, accidental effect of adaptation. This does not go counter to anything any adaptationist wants to maintain, so far as I can see, but readily becomes one sort of event that typically occurs in the cascade of small steps that mount up to make for eventual large differences—like the differences between a cow and a whale. Speciation is not itself an adaptation, but it creates an important ratchet or one-way-valve, preventing the random walks of recombination and mutation from returning to the point of departure, and hence forcing further developments to wander down distinct paths. So far, Crowe and I are in complete agreement.

I appreciate his diplomatic attempt at a rapprochement with Gould and his camp, encouraging me to "admit the secondary importance of possible rapid nonselective and/or macromutational change, especially coincident with speciation." But I already did so. As I noted in DDI (294–298), the creation of speciation bottlenecks is indeed a major ratchet in evolution, but it is the bottleneck, not the speciation, that does the work. I also note that a single mutation-event can be a transposition or doubling or other single-step event (287), rather than a single base mutation; and that molecular evolution in unexpressed DNA can accumulate gradually over time in an undirected way, but then come to be expressed, with dramatic (but usually fatal) results (288). In short, in DDI, I think I acknowledged and even highlighted all the points that Crowe urges me now to acknowledge. And since Gould himself has been most insistent that he never intended his view to be read as a defense even of macromutation ("Punctuated equilibrium is not a theory of macromutation," 1982, 340, quoted in DDI, 289), I think he would cringe at Crowe's claim that he has defended the view that "evolutionary change, especially during speciation, can occur in large, effectively saltatory, steps." In his *New York Review of Books* attack on me, Gould's greatest wrath (which is saying a lot) was concentrated on my claim that he had once flown a saltationist trial balloon. My friendly advice to Crowe: don't use the word "saltatory" within earshot of Professor Gould.

Substrate-neutrality

What about (d), substrate-neutrality? Crowe takes up this feature in his discussion of my third aim, my defense of memes as Darwinian analogues in cultural evolution of genes in biological evolution. He asserts that natural selection cannot be a substrate-neutral process, but since the grounds he gives for this don't seem to me to be relevant, I surmise that once again we have a failure of communication on my part. Of course any particular instantiation of an algorithmic process is not substrate-neutral—you can't run Mac software on a PC, for instance—but the power of the algorithm (bubble sorting, or word-processing, or morphing or whatever) is independent of the substrate of any particular instantiation. Crowe is not the only biologist who has arrived at this misreading of my point. Orr's similar claims (1996) also land wide of the mark, as I have explained (Dennett 1996).

Crowe's discussion of cultural evolution is so compressed—a single paragraph incorporating many claims with scant support—that any useful response from me would first have to extrapolate boldly from his few remarks, and then (guessing that I had captured his intent) compose rebuttals to these views of my own devising. Not likely to be convincing to anybody. So let me do the next best thing by including a generic response (from Dennett, unpublished) to what may or may not be two of Crowe's points. (*Seager* also has doubts about memes, which I will discuss briefly in the context of my other comments on his essay.)

One often hears it said that the ways in which cultural entities evolve are profoundly un-Darwinian. Two claims, in particular, are often presented as if they carried the day: Cultural evolution, unlike Darwinian evolution, is "Lamarckian," and cultural evolution, unlike Darwinian evolution, is replete with "horizontal transmission"—that is to say, design elements can hop freely from lineage to lineage, not bound by the requirements of heredity. Once reptiles and mammals have gone their separate ways, reptile innovations cannot jump to mammals, but only to descendant reptiles, but this restriction does not exist in cultural evolution. I have sometimes wondered why we don't hear more about a third disanalogy: cultural ideas don't reproduce sexually—mama and papa ideas getting it on to make little baby ideas of both genders. Probably we don't hear it because it would wear its disingenuousness on its sleeve—a lazy (or desperate) stab at something that would excuse one from having to think further about the prospects of a Darwinian account of culture. *Sexual* reproduction is not, after all, an obligatory element of Darwinian evolution; surely 99% of all the Darwinian evolution that has ever occurred on this planet was among asexually reproducing replicators, and however large sexuality looms now, it is itself an evolved feature, not a precondition for Darwinian evolution. So the absence of sexual reproduction in the memosphere is no challenge to neo-Darwinian explanation. But exactly the same point can be made about the purported disanalogies of Lamarckianism and horizontal transmission or anastomosis (lineage joining).

Let's consider Lamarckianism first. Neo-Darwinian orthodoxy, since Weissman, declares that characteristics acquired through use cannot be transmitted genetically to one's progeny. Darwin himself, notoriously, was quite happy to countenance this feature of Lamarckianism, but he has long been deemed in error. Weissman's distinction between germ line—roughly, eggs and sperm—and somatic line cells—all the rest—has proven itself over and over, and the doctrine that there are no avenues by which somatic line innovations could enter the germ line is indeed a textbook verity, although various exotic possibilities have been seriously discussed in the literature, and arguably exist in some restricted quarters. But notice that this, the orthodox, way of identifying Lamarckian phenomena (as things that don't happen) applies crisply only to multicellular organisms. What counts as a Lamarckian phenomenon in the world of bacteria, archaea, or in the world of viruses? In the case of a virus, which I have described as just a string of DNA with attitude, the line between soma and germ line is nonexistent. Something that changes the structure of an individual virus string can be called a genotypic change—a mutation—if it is passed on in replication, and otherwise a mere phenotypic change. It is not that such a line can't be drawn, but it becomes a line that prohibits nothing. The claim that Lamarckianism has been vindicated in the world of viral evolution would thus be Pickwickian. And since memes are no more multicellular than they are sexual, the fact that there is no clear way—no "principled" way, as they used to say at MIT—of distinguishing mutations from phenotypic acquisitions hardly shows that they are disqualified from a neo-Darwinian treatment. Most—much more than 99%—of the life forms on this planet have evolved under just such a regime, and neo-Darwinism certainly covers their evolution handily.

The same verdict applies to anastomosis, although this is a recent and ill-appreciated discovery: There is lots of horizontal transmission in protist and bacterial evolution—a fact that plays hob with attempts to define separate bacterial lineages in a "principled" way—and once again, the bulk of the evolution on the planet has been among just such tiny bits. Once we shift our focus away from our own multicellular, sexually reproducing lineages to the more numerous lineages on the planet, these standard objections lose much if not all their force. Memes are indeed not very much like elephant genomes, but so what?

Paul Dumouchel wonders if all Good Tricks are Forced Moves. I have one perhaps trivial difficulty with this very interesting paper, which I must expose at the outset. Whether or not Dumouchel's understanding of a Good Trick and a Forced Move is itself a good trick, it is not quite my trick. I meant slightly different things by these terms, and I found myself going cross-eyed trying to do the requisite translations when reading his essay. So I may not have understood him, but rather some artifact of my own reconstruction. Briefly, I claim that a Good Trick has a wide basin of attraction (or Mt. Fuji of attraction) in Design Space, so that many paths lead to it, from many different starting points. A Forced Move is when your options are reduced to a few; all but one of which is fatal. It is the best move, trivially, but hardly the sort of move one would want to have to choose on a regular basis. As the Godfather would say, you have been made an offer you couldn't refuse. That reverberating phrase, by the way, nicely captures one of the ideas at the heart of Dumouchel's paper. Might it not be true that the more you know about the world, the more *all* your choices come to be seen to be Forced Moves, since the apparent alternatives are either not really available at all, or turn out, on further examination, to be dominated by a Forced Move after all? Consider the home of the Forced Move, the chessboard, and recognize that against perfect opposition, you may be lucky to have *any* move that isn't part of some supersized mating net. In the unfeasible but imaginable algorithm for playing perfect chess, you look at the total decision tree of the game and, if you are white, see if any of the sixteen available first moves is colored white (meaning that there is an unbeatable path to victory by staying on the white moves, one of which will always be available). If there is not, then you must choose a gray move (stalemate guaranteed)—any one you like, if any are available. If there is no gray move, you must choose a black move and pray that at some time your opponent slips up and lets you find a gray or white move. Any such move is a forced move, of course, since it is the only escape from the mating net that began when you agreed to play chess. But for Dumouchel, Forced Moves are forced "because they are all there is."

Stuart Kaufmann has toyed with the idea that all evolution is a set of Forced Moves (in Dumouchel's sense), but it is Brian Goodwin, his sometime Santa Fe colleague, who is the exponent of the view that there really isn't any—or much—optionality in evolution; there only appears to be. The *apparently* available alternatives are not really available at all. Actualism threatens, Dumouchel notes, but so does an evaporation of our explanation (or is it only the illusion of an explanation?) of biological design. Selecting the best out of a field with only one candidate is no different from selecting the worst, so it can't explain why there seem to be such *excellent* designs in the world. If so, then natural selection could not explain the good design in nature, since it would all be just a charade that it had grown out of a genuine exploratory process of R&D. It is like the jungle boat ride in Disneyland, running on underwater railway tracks and presenting us with phony choice point after phony choice point. The destination, and all the narrow escapes, have been foreplanned and designed as a single path.

Dumouchel notes that this view—Goodwin's or maybe Kauffman's—parallels one of our old friends from the free will literature: "could *evolution* have done otherwise?" Observe, with Dumouchel, that the issue is divorced from classical determinism, both here and in the free will debate (or at least so I have claimed). The alternative to Goodwin's frankly mysterian view is not that evolution proceeds by *genuinely indeterministic* exploration of Design Space, but just that it proceeds by a quite probably deterministic but nonetheless pseudo-random or chaotic canvassing of actual possibilities. (Jacques Monod made the mistake of supposing that unless mutation in natural selection was genuinely random—quantum random, you might say—the theory could not explain the evolution of design. Do we know that this is a mistake? I submit that we do, and that a host of successful demonstrations of evolution by artificial life programs reinforce the theoretical conviction that pseudo-random generation of diversity is quite sufficient.) As Dumouchel says, it is probability that comes to the rescue to salvage the needed distinction between fitness and survival. Many with good designs succumb and many with bad designs flourish, but *over the long haul* and *over the whole population* the good designs will rise like cream to the top, where they can be retrospectively crowned, as the good ideas we may or may not have thought them to be.

I am pleased that Dumouchel has taken this opportunity to introduce Polya's Urn into philosophical discussion. It is a multi-use example of considerable power. Not only is it true, as he says, that the eventual value of the ratio of white to black balls in the urn is a function of nothing but the history of sampling, but it is also true that there is no telltale feature of the sampling histories themselves that could be used to distinguish Polya's urn from a standard urn, which begins with a determinate number of white and black balls and is sampled repeatedly (without doubling the sample). But I think Dumouchel slightly misspeaks when he says "once a particular value has been 'chosen,' it will always come to fixation after a period of fluctuations." It is rather that as the population in the urn grows, the effect of any further drawing has a diminishing effect on the overall proportion. But at no time is a particular value "chosen." The value always evolves, just slower and slower and slower. So I like the example but I am not quite sure what point he wants to make with it.

I have recently concocted a new example of my own; drawing once again on my favorite topic of chess-playing computers, to illustrate a point this is at least close to Dumouchel's. Install two different chess-playing programs on your computer, and yoke them together with a little supervisory program that pits them against each other, game after game, in a giant tournament, and let some arbitrary function—readily available from the pseudo-random number generator bundled with the computer—adjust the starting state of each program at the outset of each match. (I'm not supposing these programs are learning programs—I just want to get "rewinding the tape of life" into the picture so these two programs don't just play the same game over and over and over again. I want them to play a huge variety of games from their implied competencies.) Now sit back and look for patterns. Perhaps A always beats B; perhaps not. I don't care for the moment about that pattern. I want to focus on the standard patterns of chess strategy, on such facts as the near inevitability of B's loss in any game where B falls a rook behind, as the fact that when A's time is running out, A searches less deeply in the remaining nodes of the game tree than it does when in the same local position with more time remaining, and so forth. There is a cornucopia of regularities of this sort to detect, and they have the effect of highlighting moments in the unfolding of this deterministic pageant that otherwise would be all the same. After all, the two programs yoked together in "combat" under conditions determined by the next few digits of the pseudo-random number generator form a single utterly deterministic automaton unfolding in the only way it can, with no "real" forks or branches in its future; all the "choices" made by A and B are already determined.

If you look down in the computer's engine room, the CPU, all you find are fetch-execute cycles, and they're all alike; each one causes the next. At a higher level or perspective, you get chess moves—white's failure to detect the sacrifice-opportunity at move 5 caused white to terminate search earlier than otherwise, which in turn caused black to have less time to ponder without the clock running, which caused black to miss the deep continuation. . . . That led black to make the dumb move that caused white to win. So white's earlier failure led "inexorably" to white's eventual victory. It would happen again and again—*if* white and black were placed in *exactly* the same state. Of course white's initial "failure" to detect the sacrifice-opportunity was in turn caused by each earlier state of the system, and so forth. It is only when we gather data from lots of runs—when we "wiggle the events" as David Lewis has put it—that we can see the higher-level patterns that in one sense justify our conviction that not all fetch-execute cycles are created equal. Some of them are "pivotal." In what sense? In the sense that they, and not others, appear again and again in varied reruns of the tape of life. There are patterns that emerge from multiple runs that tell us something about what is "important."

As Hume showed, we cannot rationally defend our assumption that the future will be like the past. It is interesting, nevertheless, that Mother Nature, or evolution, proceeds *as if* it was assuming that the future will be like the past. It cannot help doing this, of course, just as we cannot, as Hume notes. It is not rationally defensible, but there is something to be said for it, if only in the form of a rhetorical question. Recall the proposed campaign slogan when the notoriously dim-witted Gerald Ford was running for president. "If I'm so stupid, how come I'm President?"

Dumouchel and I are on the same trajectory so far, I think, but then I lose him when he says: "If Good tricks and Forced Moves can be pried apart, it would in principle be possible to show that it is because certain moves are good that they were selected, rather than conclude that it is because they were selected that they are good." I am not sure I understand what Dumouchel calls his "naturalized

Kantianism"; he says both that we need to answer the question—
Are all Good Tricks Forced Moves?—and that we cannot. Moreover,
he says that this fact "indirectly supports the claim that our intentionality and reason are products of natural selection." I'm not sure
why. Dumouchel's claims about the implications of this for evolutionary ethics are a topic that I am hoping to survey more carefully
in the near future, but it is too complicated to address here. (I offer
a few opening suggestions in my comments on *Mooney* below.)

Evolution and Intentionality: Millikan, Kenyon, Seager

Ruth Millikan's essay addresses both topics, and hence serves as the
perfect segue, especially since her views and mine on these topics
have been so closely intertwined over the years. She wonders
whether the residual differences between our views on intentionality
and indeterminacy can be made to evaporate, and toward that end
she identifies several apparent points of contention. (1) I take the
intentional stance to be "more basic" whereas she takes the design
stance to be more basic. (2) I recommend adopting the intentional
stance toward natural selection itself (Mother Nature) and she finds
this otiose. Finally, (3), I think indeterminacy is a "holist" and presumably global phenomenon, whereas she thinks it is local, and
not such a big deal. I do think we can close the gap, thanks to her
efforts and those of Kenyon (and the others, in the discussions in
Newfoundland).

First, I agree with her that the design stance is more basic, in the
sense she defends. Not all animals display "real rationality patterns,"
she claims; tortoises, for instance. I agree that there is a huge difference in the versatility and richness of the perceptuo-behavioral tal-
ents of different species, and I wouldn't be all that surprised if there
were some theoretically meaningful way of identifying a subset of
them as those whose rationality patterns deserved to be called real,
but I haven't yet seen such a scheme that can persuade me that my
more open-ended way of identifying intentional systems (which includes not just the tortoise but the thermostat, after all) is a tactical
error. Millikan doesn't tell us what convinces *her* that a species is one
of those designed to have real rationality patterns, and there are in

Daniel C. Dennett

fact lots of vexing penumbral cases in between the tortoises and us—supposing with her that tortoises really do fall on the low side of some important divide. Filling in the gaps here is a philosophically significant chore, by the way, as Seager's essay makes clear. If we are the only species on the happy side of the "real rationality patterns" divide, we will have to make sure that our evolutionary story doesn't stop short of reaching *us*. (Curiously enough, in these days at the turn of the millennium, there are still philosophers and even scientists who harbor hunches about how the gap between *Homo sapiens* and all other animals needs a skyhook to be closed.) Millikan is right in any case that it is no accident that the entities that succumb to the intentional stance *projectibly* must have been designed to do so. "From enough apparently rational behavior one can infer design for rationality, just as one can infer design for seeing from good sight. . . . An intentional system *is* a designed system." Since this is what she means by saying that the design stance is more basic, and since I accept it, I can go along with her gladly on this point, but doing this then obliges me to confront (2): Since the process of natural selection is not itself a designed thing (though it is a designing thing), it cannot be an intentional system, can it? Yes it can, because it meets (or evades) the design requirement in a unique way.

Use of the intentional stance in biology—the Mother Nature stance, you might say—is at least a convenient compactor of messy (and largely unknown) details into a useful interpretation-label. It is *as if* Mother Nature had this or that "in mind"—and Millikan herself lapses into just this usage at one point. Free-floating rationales abound in biology. Evolutionary game theory exploits them in a big way. When an organism's environment is largely unpredictable (to whom?—to the process of natural selection, really), evolution wisely installs learning mechanisms instead of rigid tropisms, etc. But Millikan asserts with as much plausibility as emphasis: "*There is nothing in Nature analogous to beliefs and nothing that so much as reminds one of inference.*" What gives? Surely Millikan is right that the process of natural selection is not a designed, structured, representing system like a brain, but all the same, I think she is wrong, in a very interesting way, when she claims that "nothing so much as reminds one of inference." As Sherlock Holmes, the patron saint of inference, famously said, once you have eliminated all other possibilities, the one that remains, however improbable, must be the truth. Is that not an inference? Does not Mother Nature eliminate all other possibilities, on a vast (not actually Vast) scale, thereby "inferring" the best design? When Deep Blue eliminates a few billion legal moves and comes to rest on one brilliant continuation, it surely reminds Kasparov of inference! Natural selection, like a clever stage magician, hides almost all her trials, giving rise to the illusion of a miracle. She accomplishes by brute force (plus the utterly indispensable ratchet of selective accumulation of local progress) what otherwise would require foresight and intuition and brilliance. Deep Blue was designed to eliminate huge haystacks, thereby finding needles. Natural selection was not originally designed; it was a fortuitously emergent process of replicator-sorting. But, unlike Deep Blue, it happens to be a self-improving, self-redesigning phenomenon: It has made crane after crane after crane, becoming ever more efficient, even to the point of creating foresight—in us— so that it has bootstrapped *thoughtful* design into existence. Deep Blue is an intentional system—even for Millikan, if I understand her aright. Compared to Deep Blue, what natural selection lacks in pedigree—it is not *from the outset* the product of an R&D history of intentional design—it makes up for in forward-looking versatility and the capacity to "learn": It is getting "smarter and smarter" in its subparts.

Millikan also challenges what I have said about the varieties of indeterminacy that can arise in those histories of natural selection that parallels the history of R&D by engineers. She sees these indeterminacies as "temporary and uninteresting," two flexible and perspectival adjectives just begging to be the ground of a rapprochement. I myself find these indeterminacies, which she describes well, deeply interesting, precisely because all the "accidental junk thrown up by mutation" that comes along for the ride doesn't just sully the purity of the "definite" way that the animal has been designed to operate; it is the indispensable seed bed out of which improvement (or just revision) can emerge (DDI, 407–408). Fortunately, it is ubiquitous (and so, like taxes, both temporary and permanent at the same time). Since Millikan notes that "what counts as the correct causal explanation [of what the frog's eye tells the frog's brain] is vague in a way that probably cannot be eliminated in any principled way," I'm hoping to get her now to agree with me that these indeterminacies are not quite so temporary or uninteresting as she has made out. So, having clarified my grounds, thanks to Millikan's good challenge, I remain unrepentant in my usage here, though I do pay a price: witness *Crowe's* all too widely shared interpretation of my engineering claim.

That leaves her claim that they are "local, not holistic," and this brings us to (3), which I will discuss in the context of belief-attribution, not evolution. We are actually close to agreement here, too, I am happy to say, since she agrees with me that the "strong realist" should *not* claim that there is a fact of the matter in those cases where there is, by her lights as well as mine, indeterminacy. The question is: How much indeterminacy is there, really, and what is its importance? *Kenyon* expresses parallel doubts, differently cast, about my line on indeterminacy, and I think my Quinean crossword puzzle may be just the tool needed here to jimmy us all into agreement.

Is 1 down, the retentive membrane, "web" or "sac"? Aha! The puzzle as a whole has two solutions. (It is not, I grant, a thing of beauty; but devising a puzzle with two solutions that are "tied for first place" took some serious fussing on my part. It was an instructive exercise; anybody who thinks that indeterminacy of radical translation is bound to be a common and stable phenomenon in the real world will come to see how remarkably powerful the constraints of even such a simple task as this are.) Whatever its aesthetic shortcomings—and I invite all readers to rise to the challenge and send me something more elegant to use—it instantiates a few key claims.

1. Anybody who asks, "Which word is 1 down *really?*' stands convicted of a certain sort of overreaching realism. *There is no fact of the matter.* I deliberately set it up so there wouldn't be a fact of the matter. For instance, I didn't compose the puzzle with one set of answers (the historically first or original answers and "hence" the *real* answers) and then cast about for another set. I worked out the two

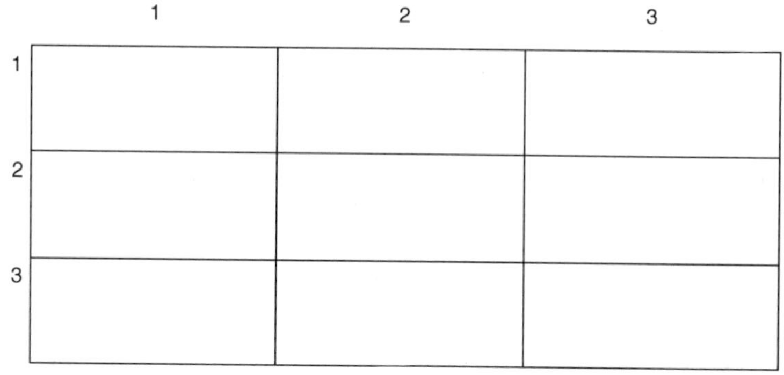

Across

1. Suck the resources out of

2. Epoch

3. Sleep furniture

Down

1. Retentive membrane

2. Earlier

3. For some kids, a best friend

Figure 15.1
Dennett's Quinean Crossword Puzzle

solutions together, drawing from a list of pairs of short words I'd drawn up that had similar meanings.

2. The reason it is possible to construct such a puzzle is that there are norms for definitions that admit some flexibility. Both solutions include words that just barely fit their definitions, but the conspiracy of the surrounding fit (the holism, to give away the punch line) pulls the words into two quite stable configurations. And I daresay everybody will agree that there is not going to be a third solution that competes with either of these. In general, the cryptographer's constraint holds: If you can find *one* solution to a puzzle, you've found *the only* solution to the puzzle. Only special circumstances permit as many as two solutions, but such cases show us that this is not a metaphysical necessity, but just a hugely powerful constraint.

Now people are much more complicated than either crossword puzzles or computers. They have squishy brains full of neuromodulators, and these brains are attached to bodies that are deeply entwined with the world, and they have both an evolutionary and personal history that has embedded them in the world much more invasively. So I agree with Millikan that given the nature of design constraints, it is unlikely in the extreme that there could be different ways of skinning the cat that left two radically different, globally indeterminate, tied-for-first-place interpretations. Indeterminacy of radical translation is truly negligible in practice. Still, the principle survives. The reason we don't have indeterminacy of radical translation is *not* because, as a matter of metaphysical fact, there are real meanings in there (Quine's "museum myth"), but because the cryptographer's constraint just makes it a vanishingly small worry. When indeterminacy threatens in the real world, it is always just more "behavioral" or "dispositional" facts—more of the same—that save the day for a determinate reading, not some mysterian "causal power" or "intrinsic semanticity." Intentional interpretation almost always asymptotes in the limit at a *single* interpretation, but in the imaginable catastrophic case in which dual interpretations survived all tests, there would be no *deeper* facts to settle which was "right." Facts do settle interpretations, but it is always "shallow" facts that do the job. That is all that Quine and Davidson and I have ever wanted to hold out for, I think. It is all that I have wanted, in any case. And so far as I can see, this brings me right alongside Millikan; we agree that design features, which are the crucial "shallow" constraints, leave no room for doubt in general.

I remain skeptical, however, about Millikan's optimism about how the indeterminacy always stays local. The rationality generalization is of course both the joy and the bane of AI and expert systems researchers. When people confront expert systems, they naturally, ineluctably, infer more rationality than is there. Consider Douglas

Lenat's (Lenat and Guha 1990) CYC—a system designed to be rational, designed to have "beliefs" that are both globally and locally rational. What happens when CYC exhibits "local" irrationality? Let's say it "believes" that lawyers are adult human beings that engage in various activities, but it might not notice the anomaly of a proposition that asserted, or presupposed, that a lawyer appeared in court in bathing costume, or had an IQ of 50. Would such "local" failures of rationality indict the whole system of CYC, showing that it was an impostor, not a believer at all? Do local indeterminacies mount up to global disqualification? What *is* the content (if any) of CYC's lawyer-data-structures? Are these cases in which the system's mechanisms are well designed, but "laboring under conditions that fail to support them properly"? I am not convinced that Millikan can make this distinction, on which her case depends. I'm also not convinced that she can't. (I have recently come to think that Dan Sperber, "Apparently Irrational Beliefs," 1985, offers a wealth of novel insights on this family of issues. See especially his suggestions about "semi-propositional representations.")

Before leaving Millikan's rich paper, I want to applaud her point about how utterly unlikely an *exaptation* for rationality would be (cf. *Seager's* discussion of Chomsky). I also want to agree with her note 5, that there is no one perfect ideal of rationality, and to acknowledge as well her excellent examples of William and James, whose belief-relevant dispositions do not have a pure intentional explanation. Add these examples to the case of a belief causing someone to blush (see my discussion of *Viger*) and the case of the computer that thinks it should get its queen out early and we have a panoply of different phenomena filling in the penumbral territory between the purest intentional stance and a design stance that uses intentional characterizations simply as labels for the design elements under discussion. Which of these have "legitimate intentional explanations"? I see a gradualistic ramp of cases, but am open to arguments showing that there are important thresholds to be marked.

Tim Kenyon points out that Chomsky's challenge to Quine—"why suppose that the under-determination of content ascription is more exotic than that found everywhere?"—was never answered (but just rebuffed) by Quine, and suggests that I might be invited to make good on my mentor's promissory note. My Quinean crossword puzzle is the downpayment; here's the rest.

Way back in *Brainstorms,* I developed an example that highlights the difference between physical stance and design (or intentional) stance disagreements:

Suppose Jones and Smith come across a particular bit of machinery churning away on a paper tape. They both study the machine, they each compile a history of its activity, they take it apart and put it back together again, and arrive at their pronouncements. What sorts of disagreements might there be between Jones and Smith?

First we might find them disagreeing only on the interpretation of the input and output symbols, and hence on the purpose or function of the Turing machine, so that, for instance, Jones treats the symbol-features as numbers (base two or base ten or what have you) and then "discovers" that he can characterize the Turing machine as determining the prime factors of the input numbers, while Smith interprets the symbol features as the terms and operators of some language, and has the Turing machine proving theorems using the input to generate candidates for proof sequences. This would not be a disagreement over which Turing machine had been realized, for this is a purely semantic disagreement; a Turing machine specification is in terms of syntactic relationships and functions only, and ex hypothesi Jones and Smith agree on which features are symbols and on the rules governing the production of the output strings. In principle a particular Turing machine could thus serve many purposes, depending on how its users chose to interpret the symbols.

More interesting and radical disagreements are also possible, however. Jones may announce that his device is TM_j, that its input and output are expressions of binary arithmetic, and that its function is to extract square roots. However, let us suppose, he proves mathematically (that is, on the basis of the machine table he assigns it and not the details of the engineering) that the program is faulty, giving good answers for inputs less than a hundred but failing periodically for larger numbers. He adds that the engineering is not all that sound either, since if you tip the machine on its side the tape reader often misreads the punched holes. Smith disagrees. He says the thing is TM_s, designed to detect certain sorts of symmetries in the input sequences of holes, and whose output can be read (in a variation of Morse code) as a finite vocabulary of English words describing these symmetries. He goes on to say that tipping the machine on its side amounts to a shift in input, to which the machine responds quite properly by adjusting its state-switching function. The only defect he sees is that there is one cog in the works that is supposed to be bent at right angles and is not; this causes the machine to miscompute in certain states, with the result that certain symmetries are misdescribed. Here there is disagreement not only about the purpose of the machine, or the semantics of the language it uses, but also about the syntax and alphabet. . . . The two may still agree on the nature of the mechanism, however, although they disagree on what in the mechanism is deliberate design and what is sloppiness. That is, given a description of the physical state of the machine and the environment, and a physical description of the tape to be fed in, they will give the same prediction of its subsequent *motions*, but they will disagree on which features of this biography are to be called malfunctions, and on which parts of the machine's emissions count as symbols. ("The Abilities of Men and Machines," 258–259).

A saying in the world of software development expresses the crux of such disagreements rather well: "it's not a bug, it's a feature." The reliance on one or another ideal of *excellence* (or *rationality* in the case of cognitive excellence) opens up the space for further indeterminacy once we move above the physical stance. (I *think* this is what Kenyon means, in the end, by his proposed principle: "The truth conditions for content ascription cannot be purely physical, on pain of its being possible that there are psychological truths that are unverifiable in principle." An unremarked difference between the physical stance and the design stance is that no oxygen atom is "defective" or subpar in any way. They are all "perfect." If they weren't, there would have to be a physical design stance of sorts, and it would be vulnerable to all the caveats and fallings-short that arise in the world of design. In fact, even design stance attributions go through quite determinately as long as design elements are sufficiently robust, sufficiently close to their "specs." In practice no problem arises about how good a resistor or capacitor has to be to count as a resistor or capacitor, and designs composed of such elements don't have to be massively redundant in order to cope with the inevitability of ubiquitous imperfection. If we were not products of natural selection, if we were all Model Z3J Electronic Believers, doing our thing (not things) in a standard environment (so that the prospect of evaluating CYC in *our* multifariously convoluted human environment didn't arise), hermeneutics would be child's play. As it is, hermeneutics is a haven for indeterminacies of the sort that thrive on the inevitable fact that one programmer's bug is another programmer's feature.

Kenyon is dubious about my efforts to get philosophers to lighten up about such traditional issues as ontology and truth:

Those uneasy with the suggestion that our theory of psychological explanation implicitly incorporates a theory of voices or a theory of salt will react sharply to Ryle's and Dennett's maneuver. The obvious objection is that we already have a word that means "true with a grain of salt" or "true in one logical tone of voice." That word is "false."

Yes, that is the way philosophers are apt to think. And Kenyon is right that neither Ryle nor I go to the lengths we would be obliged to go to satisfy those uneasy folks. But we do what we can to add to their unease, by showing them that the very verdict they are so tempted to declare about our cases will also have to be rendered for less controversial endeavors they might regret abandoning. Their bracing allegiance to the true-false dichotomy is not quite so comfortable to live with as one might think, and Kenyon is helping to see what the issues are by holding the tradition he was trained in at arm's length, throughout his essay.

In contemporary philosophy of mind, emphasizing the central epistemic role of behavior is rather like admitting to being a liberal in American politics: You must immediately backtrack, qualify your position, and distance yourself from everyone else who ever said anything similar. But the idea is really quite benign.

So true. I also endorse Kenyon's argument about color and subvening bases (*modulo* some sophistications that Kathleen Akins would rightly insist on. See also my comments on *Lloyd,* below). I'm glad to have a more patient defense of this than I have undertaken. I also applaud Kenyon's lengthy note (don't miss it) on Fodor on Stich's Mrs. T. He has seen exactly what is untenable in Fodor's response. And his comments on Crispin Wright and Michael Dummett persuade me that I have been underestimating a literature that has more to show me than I had thought. The one point where I feel the need to issue a (minor) correction is Kenyon's opening overstatement of my view about misrepresentation (by the frog's eye): I do not *maintain* that "misrepresentation can always be dissolved in this [disjunctive] manner"; I am issuing a challenge to those who find this claim a reductio: Figure out, then, how to block that deflation-by-disjunction.

William Seager's essay covers so much ground, running from evolution to intentionality to consciousness to ontology, that I have had trouble finding a good place for it in the marching order. I find so much to admire in his analysis of the issues that I feel churlish refusing to go the last step, abandoning the Scientific Picture of the World for Surface Metaphysics. I do have my reasons, though, and Seager comes within a whisper of articulating them. But first, let me show how far Seager leads me before I resist.

Consider his master stroke: his contrast between the demands of naturalization in chemistry and psychology. In the case of chemistry, you don't *have* to have a prior understanding of the higher level (the chemistry-level concept of valence) in order to understand, from the bottom up, as it were, the lower level: "someone could (albeit inefficiently) learn what valence is without bothering about developing a prior acquaintance with chemistry—there is no need to understand chemistry in order to understand the physics of valence." But *some* prior understanding is required, however; in such a case, he notes that "no one could understand the physical account of valence without already understanding what explanation is supposed to be." This is no threat to naturalization of chemistry since the mentalistic or intentional concept of explanation is not itself a chemical notion. But when we try to make the same move in psychology we unavoidably step on our own toes:

> You can't understand what a mind is unless you already know what a mind is, since you can't understand mentality without understanding the intentional stance, which requires you to already understand a host of essentially mentalistic concepts.

Is this really a problem? It certainly seems to be a problem, and this is a fine way of expressing a background fear that has haunted many a move in the philosophy of mind. Now that it is so well exposed, we can confront it. (Another version of this fear is the unease people often feel with my account of heterophenomenology. It seems to some of them [but not to *Thompson*, see below] that I *must* be doing something viciously circular in giving pride of place to the third-person perspective over the first-person perspective.) Seager's is a better setting in which to consider the issue, I think, since it abstracts away from the overheated topics of qualia and zombies and presents itself as a minimalist demand on *explanation:* If a purported naturalizing *explanation* of minds as phenomena in the world presupposes that the *explainee* (the one to whom the explanation is supposed to be illuminating) already understands mentality, this will be an unacceptable surrender to what Seager aptly calls Plato's problem. And as he notes, this shows us how to make good use of Davidson's claim that "discovering the neural 'correlates' of mental states does not *explain* the physicality of the mind."

Seager sees, correctly, that I have tried to articulate an alternative naturalism that "must forsake rule bound naturalization." (This is a point upon which there seems to be a convergence of agreement, from *Ross, Lloyd,* and *Viger,* at least. I find this heartening.) And it proceeds, as he says, with the help of Darwin. Exactly right. Nobody has articulated better than Seager the underlying rationale of my Darwinism, especially in this context. Let me underline what he has said to make sure we secure this key point once and for all.

In a world without perspectives, without minds, without errors, a process of replication and competition initiates itself. This process inevitably yields lineages of *(proto-)wanters*—competitors for the resources needed for replication—that achieve efficiency by evolving sense organs that provide them with *(proto-)beliefs* about those resources and the means to secure them. If you're going to move, you're going to need reconnaissance, and so informavores, pattern-detectors, hemi-semi-demi-minds are, as Seager puts it, "a fat evolutionary target." For the reasons he enunciates, there is a large—maximally large, I would say—basin of attraction for this Good Trick.

But Seager sees problems with my project of extending this explanatory account all the way up to us. There is a big gap to be traversed—including, perhaps, the notorious "explanatory gap" of consciousness itself—between, on the one hand, the proto-minds of bacteria and other thermostat-like strivers for reproduction, and, on the other hand, our indefinitely complex and versatile minds. If this gap is filled with mere "accident or spandrel" we are right back to a mysterian acquiescence in brute fact. (Seager is deliciously on target when he points out that Flanagan is indeed a mysterian *malgré lui* when he blandly announces that "some patterns of neural activity result in phenomenological experience; other patterns do not.") And that explains why I have devoted so much attention to filling that gap with solid adaptationist extensions of the Darwinian reasoning that gets us rather uncontroversially to the simplest kinds of minds.

Seager thinks, however, that I fail to bridge this gap, even sketchily. He sees that there is *hope* for a "quasi-naturalist" filling of this gap by evolutionary psychology, but thinks the task is largely undone. "It leaves behind an outstanding debt to the scientific worldview, which can be only partially repaid by an evolutionary account of the genesis of the behavior patterns that are the targets of the intentional stance." Why only *partially* repaid? Because of the prospect of "accidents or spandrels," apparently. But we don't know that this is a problem. In fact, I think it is not, but let's leave that issue aside, since I want to argue that Seager's "methodological mysterianism, which is general and unavoidable" is not the embarrassment it appears to be in any case. I say there is nothing viciously circular about our inability to explain minds without presupposing an understanding of minds. For that reason, I don't really like calling it mysterianism—though I approve of the way the term dramatizes the issue—since there doesn't seem to me to be anything puzzling left over, anything to wonder about.

The lack of a neutral Archimedean point from which to start is a curiosity, I think, not a puzzle. One way of deflating its importance might be to imitate Descartes's tactic, in *Le Monde,* of describing "a new world" in loving detail and then, in the punch line, revealing that *that* fictional world is our world. They are us.[1] So imagine that we survey the biota of Planet X, elaborating a Darwinian account of the growing sophistication of the minds (or *schminds,* if you insist) of the Xian fauna, thanks to the various arms races of competition among the clever locomotors there, until we have explained—in good bottom-up, no-skyhooks fashion—the eventual emergence of critters on Planet X with language, with open-ended recursive reflexivity, with cultural sharing of cognitive tools and resources, ... Hmm. They look a lot like us. Don't they? Perhaps what explains *them* explains *us*. Why not? I submit that we can chip away at the limit on inquiry that Seager has identified for us, moving from valence to Planet X zoology, to Planet X psychology, always presupposing *our* intelligence, of course (no use trying to engage a potted palm in scientific inquiry, is there?) but scrupulously restricting our attention to things other than us. To the objection that we are *imposing* our psychology on them, we can blandly reply that if our imposition doesn't work, we will be punished by the falsehood of our predications, and if it does work, we'll have good reason—the best—to conclude that our "imposition" was trivial. Similarly, we may opportunistically "impose" our biology on the (so-called!) fauna and flora of Planet X. If our spade is turned, we will learn something about the limits of our biology; and also about the absence of such limits, if our spade isn't turned.

What limits, if any are there, then, to our simply discovering that we have inadvertently been looking in a mirror? I do not see any, and these considerations suggest to me that methodological mysterianism, once brought into the open, proves to be a bogeyman of no serious concern. (See also my comments on *Thompson* below.) But Seager has performed a very useful service in articulating this subliminal deflector of theory.

Now back to Seager's worry about the only "partial" success of my Darwinian reconstruction of mind. He sees that my account really needs something like memes, and he is as skeptical as *Crowe* is. He gives no more grounds for his doubts than Crowe does, so this is not really the place for a full-fledged defense of memes. It is, however, a place for laying down signposts and promissory notes to just such a defense: Dennett, unpublished a, unpublished b, and various works in progress. (Two international workshops on cultural evolution in 1999, one at Cambridge University in June, and one in Paris in November, should clarify many of these issues.) For the time being, I will provide only one brief rejoinder to Seager's claim that "Memes are products and inhabitants of minds *as such*." I don't think so. The basic phenomenon of memetic transmission and evolution can be built up from a *very* slender base: Mere imitation will perhaps do the trick (see Blackmore 1999, and Dennett, unpublished b), and although imitation is a more sophisticated behavior than running or digging holes, it isn't rocket science. Quite mindless beings could "in principle" harbor memes—teenagers, for instance. (Joke)

Seager helps us think about the scientific picture of the world and the relations that are deemed to hold there by introducing an excellent thought experiment, the massive bottom-up computer simulation of physics. (This is close kin to my use of Conway's Life World in 1991b and 1995, but has its own additional virtues.) The main conclusion Seager wants us to see drawn from this thought experiment is that "the world has no use for" the higher-level patterns that are visible in the simulation: "the *only* role they have in the world is to help organize the experience of those conscious beings who invent them and then think in terms of them." Not quite, I think, but this way of putting the point focuses our attention on the role of *pattern-detectors* in the world, a topic also central to the essays by *Lloyd,* and *Ross.* The Coriolus *force* is non-existent, Seager notes, but the *pattern* of the Coriolus force is as real as can be. Are the patterns "metaphysically otiose"? What does that mean? *Ross,* after all, offers to define existence itself in terms of such patterns. And what does it take to be a pattern-detector? Consciousness, Seager suggests, but this strikes me as backsliding. "Precisely where the changeover from nonmind to mind occurs is a vexed question (even allowing that the distinction will be fuzzy), but what matters is the point that *patterns* have no role to play in the world unless and until they are taken up in understanding by minds." I disagree. All those simpler, thermostat-like minds are responsive to patterns; they digitize (in the sense of Dretske 1981) part of their interaction with the world, willy-nilly creating encodings of those patterns (whether or not the encodings are *for them*). In Seager's opinion, "Mind cannot be 'just another' pattern." Why not? Perhaps I have missed his point.

Aside from this claim of his on which I have just demurred, I find Seager's analysis of different varieties of emergence right and valuable (see also Holland 1995, 1998 for excellent discussions of what Seager calls "benign emergence"). I also like Seager's whimsical sketch of a "spandrel" vision of consciousness, which supposes it to be a surd by-product of the blood-cooling machinery of the human brain. He vividly brings out the dilemma that faces Gould: Either he must mean something so attenuated by his spandrel claim that it doesn't do any work—all adaptations were once spandrels (or exaptations—see Preston 1998 and Dennett 1998c)—or he ends up with an utterly preposterous hypothesis. See *Millikan*'s chapter for a similar argument against Gould.

Finally, I don't want to convey the impression that I think Seager's surface metaphysics is out of the question. I take under advisement the recommendation of van Fraassen's constructive empiricism. I get the point, I think, but don't yet feel the itch. My ontological convictions are now in happy disarray, and I simply have no clear sense of how to put together Seager's proposals with the various ideas of *Ross, Viger, Lloyd, Thompson,* and others, but perhaps my reactions along the way will create a pattern that another mind can detect and understand better than I can. I hope so.

Intentionality and Realism: Viger, Ross

Christopher Viger concentrates on the problems I've created for myself by adopting the abstracta-illata distinction I lifted from Reichenbach (see also *Ross*'s chapter, and below). As Viger suggests, people persist in reading as an (extravagant) *ontological* thesis what I took to be a thesis about different explanatory practices in science and their requirements. It is clear that I have underestimated the sources of confusion that Viger usefully sorts out, and I am grateful for his generally lucid and accurate portrayal of my position, but I see one area in which he exaggerates (perhaps for simplicity) my position on the relationships between (folk) psychology and physics: "When distinct explanatory practices are cross-applied," he says, "hybrid monsters result." I don't think all such hybrids are monsters. After all, I'm quite happy to countenance "Her belief that John knew her secret caused her to blush" (1987, 56), and this is a hybrid, part intentional stance (identifying her state via the content of her belief) and part physical (or, arguably, low-level design) stance. The problem arises from . . . thinking that this is a problem! Apparently, many philosophers have convinced themselves that they cannot countenance such causal claims without going through the Procrustean mills of warring doctrines of supervenience and token identity theories. It is deemed that there is a problem of "overdetermination" along these lines:

Some complex neural state caused the capillary enlargement that is token-identical to her blushing. Either her belief is *token-identical* to that neural state, or it isn't. If it isn't, then it can't have caused her blushing (that's one cause too many) so it must be *epiphenomenal*. Instrumentalism, by denying the token-identity theory, removes abstracta from the realm of causation, and is scarcely distinguishable from epiphenomenalism.

I have encountered the same blockade in reactions to my thought experiment about the Two Black Boxes (DDI, 412–422). How could it be that the *truth* (or believed-truth, or other intentionally characterized property) of the impulse patterns *causes* the red light to go on when we already have a perfectly complete physical-level account of all the microcausation of each state of the two systems?

But the main point of the example of the Two Black Boxes is to demonstrate the *need* for a concept of causation that is (1) cordial to higher-level causal understanding distinct from an understanding of the microcausal story, and (2) ordinary enough in any case, especially in scientific contexts. With regard to (1), let me reemphasize the key feature of the example: The scientists can explain each and every instance with no residual mystery at all; but there is a generalization of obviously causal import that they are utterly baffled by until they hit upon the right higher-level perspective. (In Seager's fine terms, this is an example of "explanatory emergence"; "complexity does outrun the *explanatory resources* provided by an *understanding* of the simple.") With regard to (2), the contrived example of Two Black Boxes is only artificially clearer than a host of familiar cases having the same logic—uncontroversial cases that philosophers have tended to overlook. An earlier example of mine (in Dahlbom 1993, 216) is the center of gravity of a sailboat, which is manifestly an abstractum and just as manifestly implicated in important *causal* generalizations. I didn't bother to spell it all out before, but since this claim has met with skepticism, I will now do so. What did Connor do overnight to *cause* his boat to be so much faster? He lowered its center of gravity. Of course he did this by moving gear, or adding lead ingots to the bilge, or replacing the mast with a lighter mast, or something—but what *caused* the boat's improvement was lowering its center of gravity. This is not just casual shorthand; it is the generalization that *explains* why any of these various changes (and a zillion others one could describe) would *likewise* cause an improvement in performance. Differences in the location of a center of gravity cause projectible differences in performance. It is a kind of cause that can be readily isolated by the Millian method of differences, and any philosophical doctrine that denies that this is a good clear case of causation is in trouble. Manifestly, one doesn't need to be a token identity theorist about those centers of gravity to cite them in such contexts. Selection pressure in evolutionary theory, inflation in economics, and a host of other high-level, diffuse (from the mole's-eye perspective of these philosophers) phenomena are perfectly fine causes. That beliefs can cause blushing is just as uncontroversial. Viger is thus somewhat off-target when has me holding the following:

It is only through the filter of rationality considerations that intentional patterns are visible, and it is for this reason that beliefs and desires have no place in physical explanations.

What is right about it is that it is only via the rationality considerations that one can identify or single out the beliefs and desires, and this forces the theorist to adopt a higher level than the physical level of explanation on its own. This level crossing is not peculiar to the intentional stance. It is the life-blood of science. If a blush can be used as an embarrassment-detector, other effects can be monitored in a lie detector. Pregnancy can be the cause of triggering a positive result in a pregnancy test, and a history of hepatitis can cause telltale effects.

Aside from this point of modification, I find much that is helpful and right in Viger's essay, especially its way of illuminating the fact that ontology, for me, has always been the caboose, not the engine. As Ramberg (1999) puts it, "Such questions, the philosopher's questions of ontology, are for Dennett, as they are for Rorty—and as they were for Dewey, James, Nietzsche and perhaps for Hegel—questions that get settled after hours, after the real work is done." He suggests that I ought to countenance an "instrumentalist" abstractum becoming (or coming to be recognized as) a "realist" illatum in the fullness of time, or vice versa. The difference I illustrate by contrasting a center of gravity and an atom may be dissoluble on closer inspection. I am tempted. After all, in the history of science, items that began their careers as convenient fictions or instrumentalist abstracta have been promoted (if that is the right word) to the company of illata more than once, and the reverse fate is not unknown, though often with some pushing and shoving and Whig history in the aftermath. Atoms, famously, were but a useful fiction to some of their earliest advocates, and Mendel's genes now have to face banishment to the limbo of instrumentalist idealizations of population geneticists now that more robust (if often less tractable) versions of genes are being manipulated by the microbiologists. Are genes real? This is the Age of Genes. How could they not be real? Well, one of the findings in the Age of Genes is that nothing in nature *quite* fits any of the "classical" definitions of a gene. So should we be eliminativists or instrumentalists or realists about genes? I still think these ontological questions are the *last* questions we need to answer—and their answers will not be very interesting or useful once we've got the science in place, with its various levels of explanation.

Don Ross offers to help me with the metaphysics, and I am tempted to follow his lead. I go round and round on this paper, seeing his points and then watching his points evaporate (for me). In the end, discretion wins over valor. What *ontological* lesson should we draw from my various intuition pumps? I don't know. I *still* don't know. I'm not confident about metaphysical judgments, so why risk taking on baggage I don't deeply understand and am not sure I need? Besides, if Ross is right and there is metaphysical gold in them thar hills, I expect he can mine it and refine it better than I can.

In addition to the welcome support he gives my brusque dismissal of the "merely logically possible" worlds in which various famous thought experiments live, Ross comes up with some other new ideas that I like. I particularly like his minimal way of relocating the asymmetry between the special sciences and physics: "the generalizations of the special sciences must not contradict those of physics, whereas no symmetrical limitation holds in the opposite direction." And I find his ingenious way of using my idea of informational compression as the touchstone of ontology both novel and plausible. But I see a problem: I can't figure out how to fold into Ross's recipe what programmers call "*lossy* compression." Like Viger, Ross thinks I should abandon the abstracta-illata distinction. In "Real Patterns," I drew attention to the existence of patterns that were "imperfect," patterns that would have highly compressed descriptions if it weren't for the noise, the defects or blemishes. Idealized descriptions of those patterns describe *nothing*, strictly speaking, since they *over*simplify. But they impose a useful abstraction on messy reality: lossy compression of noisy data yields an abstractum. Or at least so it seems best to me to say. Those patterns, I claimed, are real, without being perfect, and the abstractum, a cognitive crutch of sorts, helps us see them. *We* see them, in spite of the noise, and so they are real for us—which threatens to lead to anthropocentrism. But so what? *Some* instrumentalist posits might indeed be of only local interest, if any. (Even I am not interested, really, in Dennett's lost sock center.) There couldn't be anything wrong with positing a few anthropocentric crutches. We *anthropoi* can make whatever crutches please us, creating *intentional* objects *ad lib*. Those that catch on, communally, create patterns that, although anthropocentric in origin, are in principle *visible* (even if baffling) to other beholders; they are patterns such that if "Martians" missed them, they would be missing out.

Two Black Boxes purports to describe just such a pattern. If you don't find an intentional stance explanation (there are several stylistic variants to choose from, depending on whether you are comfortable attributing mentalistic—not "just" semantic—properties to computers), you will be baffled by the near-perfect generalization that is visible to Martian and earthling alike: Pressing the α button causes the red light to go on and pressing the β button causes the green light to go on. Likewise (see the discussion of *Viger* above) lowering the center of gravity of the sailboat causes it to go faster. Some may want to say that strictly speaking it is not—could not be— the downward motion of the center of gravity (which is not to be token-identified with any particle) that actually causes anything, that we shouldn't confuse what we talk about in causal explanations with what we take to be actual causes. I don't find this persuasive. To me, what count as actual causes are whatever we cite in explanations.

Ross has pointed out to me (in his editorial role for this volume) that even Dennett's lost sock center *could* play a causal role not so different from that of the sailboat's center of gravity. Suppose people need an arbitrary and neutral (in effect, pseudo-random) variable for some political purpose (e.g., deciding the order in which precincts shall get to vote) and hit upon using the wanderings of Dennett's lost sock center as their pseudo-random walk-fixer. Then if political factions ever figure out some political advantage to be gained by manipulating the order of voting, they can cause the order to change by causing Dennett's lost sock center to move (by causing me, in one way or another, to lose a few more socks in various locations). " 'Twas the northerly motion of Dennett's lost sock center, you see, that caused the northern precinct polls to open first, and that caused the landslide." (Fill in the details as you like—I've given just the skeleton of Ross's imagined case.) Notice that what permits Dennett's lost sock center to make a causal difference, unlike the center of gravity of the sailboat, is its becoming an intentional object of communal note (like the gold in Fort Knox); causation does indeed run through the actual location of the lost sock center, but only if (and because) people are good at tracking its actual location so that their shared *beliefs* about its location exert the reliable effect at the next phase. This doesn't make its motion any less of a cause. Some causes produce their effects via beliefs; some don't.

Now is it conceivable that the pattern we *anthropoi* articulate in terms of beliefs could be described even more perspicuously in some currently unimagined Churchlandish terms? I *do* think that Churchland is right to *try* to find a better pattern than that found by the intentional stance (and we should try to find a simpler, better physics, too, while we're at it); I just don't think his hunch that he's going to succeed is remotely plausible. But if he succeeded, I guess I'd agree with him that it had turned out that all things considered, we should say (this is the diplomatic decision) that there really weren't beliefs and desires after all. The intentional stance could, I guess, come to be discarded as a myth, superannuated by the patterns created by its very articulation. In the same way it could turn out, I suppose that there wasn't *ever* any gold in Fort Knox; it was all a hoax.

Rainforest Realism, if I understand it correctly, is my kind of realism indeed; it rules out only silly, unmotivated ontologies, but is otherwise remarkably pluralistic, tolerant of multiple "unreduced" levels of being, what Ryle was trying to get at with his different "logical tones of voice," so long as they can pay for themselves as patterns.

Realism and Consciousness: Thompson, Brook, Lloyd, Rosenthal, and Polger

Dan Lloyd's essay continues and expands on some the ontological themes of the previous section, but I have found it easier to lay the groundwork for a discussion of Lloyd's views by first looking at some of the other essays on consciousness. *David Thompson*'s comparison between Husserl's phenomenology and my heterophenomenology is illuminating in a number of ways, and perhaps I should add that this is no accident. My own philosophical training included a deeply influential dose of Husserl from Dagfinn Føllesdal when I was an undergraduate, and I have always had Husserl in mind—though more distantly remembered than assiduously reread—when working on my own version of phenomenology. Thompson exactly captures the main point of methodological disagreement between us: "Where Dennett's *Consciousness Explained* studies consciousness for its own sake while taking science for granted, Husserl investigates consciousness in order to establish a solid foundation for science." Note that *ideally* the two projects should converge on a common theory or set of answers—on anybody's view. I should expect that whatever assumptions about science I take on unexamined are innocent—they shouldn't require wholesale revision in the light of whatever theory of consciousness I arrive at, and they shouldn't blind me to important truths inaccessible from that vantage point—and Husserl should assume that his Cartesian starting point doesn't somehow start him off on the wrong foot and lead him to a distorted vision of science from which he can't recover. I, however, *suspect* that all Cartesian or "first-person perspective" starting points lure the theorist into inflated and distorted catalogues of the phenomena of consciousness, creating whole genres of bogus *data* for the theorist to stumble over. Like Quine in *Word and Object,* I prefer starting with ordinary things and the science we can make of *them* and then extending the grasp of that vantage point upward (it *seems* to be inward) to such extraordinary things as conscious beings. Symmetry suggests a similar suspicion should run the other way, and so it does: the hue and cry over whether I'm "leaving something out" in my campaigns against qualia and the like, and Thompson's more useful observation that I risk leaving science "as a kind of skyhook without foundation."

Suspicions are not proofs, however. The way to vindicate Thompson's skyhook suspicion is to demonstrate that when, as Carr recommends, I "take phenomenology to its limits, namely to turn it back on its own position," I confound myself with contradictions. I have yet to see the case made in any particularity. Subject the scientists' own heterophenomenology as they conduct their experiments with color phi to the most painstaking analysis. Does it collapse? I don't think so. Hetero-heterophenomenology and its further offspring must avoid incoherence if my view is to be sustained, but I don't see any problems—yet. And, continuing the symmetry, I must say that if *any* Cartesian starting point manages to avoid the pitfalls of positing a *me*dium, it is Husserl's, because, as Thompson points out, Husserl anticipated—indeed helped to shape—my suspicion about the spurious ontology-fountains of Cartesianism. We are kindred spirits, and the *epoché* is our point of closest agreement, from either side of our first-person/third-person starting points. My "discreet charm of the anthropologist" is indeed the studied neutrality of Husserl's *epoché,* and I agree wholeheartedly with Husserl that, as Thompson says, "whatever intermediate entities there may be in the *process* of grasping an object, it is not these representatives that we are conscious *of,* but the object itself."

Thompson thinks, however, that I backslide into "representativism" in spite of this agreement. (Here he and *Lloyd* share a suspicion, but from different perspectives.) "Whether the experience is of something real or not, it is never about a brain event. . . . The notion of 'unwitting reference' is being misused here." I want to defend the notion of unwitting reference, for it is not quite the simple idea—the simple mistaken idea—that Thompson supposes. It may be mistaken, but his objection misses the mark. Consider Peter Bieri's recent novel, *Perlmanns Schweigen* (written under the *nom de plume* Pascal Mercier). Since it is a fiction, a novel, it is not in any way about me, of course. I am not the intentional object constituted by any of its sentences. However, I have been told (not by Bieri, so this may not be true—I haven't checked), that there is a character in the novel who is modeled on me. The sentences about this fictional character do not *refer* to me, even if they may bear a noncoincidental, informationally rich, dependent relation to me. This is not reference, but it is the model for "unwitting reference" that I mean to exploit. Similarly, if some prankster in the jungle is the source of most or all of the beliefs about the feats of Feenoman, it is not strictly true that the Feenomanists' assertions expressing their creed *refer* to this man. Not quite. But almost. Similarly, it may turn out that when I claim to rotate a mental image in my mind's eye, there is something happening in my brain that is the source of most of the details I recount in my heterophenomenological narrative. Manifestly, I am not conscious of these brain processes, however imagistic they may be. Thompson says that Husserl would probably have no trouble countenancing such "brain-representations" and that's a good thing, since then Husserl and I can still be in agreement. These brain-images (if such there were) are part of the *hyletic phase,* part of the causal, material goings-on that make consciousness possible (on my amateur reading of Husserl). But just as the anthropologist may have a scientific interest in determining what is causally responsible for producing the curious contents expressed by Feenomanists, the neuroscientist may have a scientific interest in determining what is causally responsible for producing the curious contents of my "mind's eye imaginings." Notice that when there is, say, a table in front of me, *its* properties handily account for the content of my heterophenomenological declarations about my table-experiences, but when there is no table, when I am, say, hallucinating a table, the question arises of what, if anything, has properties that account for the content of these declarations. It might be something in the brain. It might not. There need not be anything, anywhere that has *just* those properties, but rather some conspiracy

of disparate causes, otherwise unrelated features of things and processes. And in any case, I agree with Thompson (and Husserl) that
my intentional object in such a case of hallucination—what my experience is *about*—is *never* a brain process, however noncoincidentally
the properties of some brain process may be linked to the details of
my hallucination. (See *Lloyd* on this issue, and my comments above,
as well.)

So when Thompson says "Brain events have no counterparts in
the fiction and myth analogies," I think he overstates the case. Some
(but not all) fictional characters have strikingly similar sources in
the world; some (but not all) religious myths have real live sources
in the world. These are not intentional objects, to be sure; but they
are what I had in mind as the things to which "unwitting reference"
was made. No doubt that is a poor term, in retrospect, but the point
of calling it *unwitting* reference was to underscore the fact that it is
not transparent to the experiencer (or the religionist, or maybe even
the novelist) that there is such a source. We have no first-person
authority, as Husserl and I both say, to the causes of our experience;
that's why the epoché is such a good way of isolating the contents
of experience from the contaminations of eager theorizing.

Andrew Brook, like many other philosophers, feels the seductive
tug of seemings, and also of dichotomies that I have tried to dissolve, but unlike most, he doesn't just give in to his gut feelings and
declare my view mistaken or crazy; he is circumspect in his allegiance, and his wary approach to my views is just what is needed. It
exposes the problems. (Levine 1995, is another admirably forthright
confrontation by someone whose bones tell him I must be wrong.)

(First, let me correct two misapprehensions that might be engendered by this mostly exemplary expression of my views. In the matter
of S-O impasses, Brook oversimplifies my account. I grant that there
are [large-scale] cases in which we *can* make a clear and principled
distinction between Stalinesque and Orwellian. My point is that
when you squeeze out the grounds for making these distinctions by
reducing the time frame down to milliseconds, you squeeze out the
only grounds for making these distinctions. He also uses the terms
"filling in" and "finding out" in a way almost opposite to the way
I would recommend. I would prefer to say that we don't bother

filling in our visual fields; we find out some of what's out there to be seen and more or less ignore the rest.)

Brook's analogy of the novel continues the themes of *Thompson's* comparison between Husserl's view and mine. A novel is a real physical object, made of paper and ink and such; there is *not* also a set of real but nonphysical objects "in between" the novel and the (partly factual, partly fictional) world it portrays—a world of phantasms created by the novelist's words. My position with regard to seemings is parallel: There are real physical bodies and real physical events in their brains that serve (in various roundabout ways) to project a fictional world, and there is *not* also a set of real seemings in between the brain events and the (fictional or real) world they depict. See also *Lloyd's* chapter on other ways of handling this temptation.

Brook discusses a contrast between eliminativism with regard to some category of putative things and "wanting a better model" of those things. This contrast is attractive to philosophers, for obvious programmatic reasons, but it is not anywhere near as crisp and clean as Brook *starts* presenting it (in due course he notes the problems—see note 5, which is excellent). How surprising does the "better model" have to be for us to declare that really, there are no such things after all? This has been a theme of mine since the example of fatigues in the Introduction to *Brainstorms* (xix–xx). The issue is political or expository, not factual. In the case of Brook's useful trio, the F level, the P level and the I level, the problem is that the F level is far from "pure"; it gets contaminated by the inadvertent self-theorizing we all do, introducing P level intrusions. Thus, consider what the F level is for framing a mental image: "I form an image in my mind [OK so far, but let's see how this image-talk gets unpacked]; it's a sort of picture [Oh? Where? How big? Is something looking at it?] or at any rate it's like vision somehow [Better; it's hard to fault *that* minimal claim; mental images do come in modalities—visual, auditory, tactile, and so forth] and it's more or less in my control, but there's only so much I can hold in my mind's eye at a time."

The F-level account of the concept of a subject illustrates this tug from the P-level, since to say a subject "operates by forming things like beliefs" is biased toward what we might call the hammer and tongs view of belief formation. Compare it to "A subject is a locus of beliefs and desires." And "consciously focuses attention on tasks" suggests a captain, an agent deciding where to aim the searchlight next. Contrast it with "is constituted by the sequence of tasks in focal attention." Now there is nothing wrong with this F level stress on the voluntary agency of the subject—that *is* the idea of a subject—a central meaner, the Boss. But when we then look to the P-level theory, we must bracket that bias. (See *Thompson*'s chapter on whether Husserl goes this far with me; we may part company right here.) I say we must get rid of the subject (and the seemings) in the P-level theory. As Brook says, there seems to be a nasty dilemma. Only a theory of consciousness as the workings of a vacant automated factory—not a subject in sight—could be successful theory. If there is still a role for a subject, still tasks for a subject to perform, still a need for the subject as witness, then the theory is bankrupt from the start. And the same must be said of any leftover seemings. Seemings *to whom?* Seemings, as Colin McGinn tells us Frege insisted, have to be *somebody's* seemings, but if so, then we have to engineer seemings out of the picture as well. How? Not by denying the undeniable. Not by pretending that the phenomenology is other than it is, but by taking these two *persona non grata* and wedding them—you might call it dice-and-meld. First, the given must be broken up into lots of little microgivens, and the taking (by the subject) has to be broken up into lots of little microtakings of those microgivens. Then when you look at the model, you don't see any subject, and you don't see any single place where the given is taken; instead, all that work is parceled out into many little moments of content-fixation, and although these moments of content-fixation can feed others and so on indefinitely, we must not see them as preliminaries for some master taking yet to happen. (See below in the discussion of *Lloyd* on "is that all there is?" for a further set of moves that needs to be made before we can rest.)

"The difference between levels of pain and levels of pain tolerance seems to be perfectly real, certainly in many instances." Yes, in many instances. But let's not use that fact to support a metaphysical view that goes well beyond it. Compare it to the following issue. Is economic value real? Of course it is. Are things more expensive

now, or is it just inflation? (This parallel: Does it hurt him more now
or is he just less tolerant of *that much* pain?) Yes, sometimes, when
the background conditions can be held constant or tracked in ways
we understand ("in 1960 dollars"), we can make perfectly good
sense of this question, and answer it. Sometimes, however, the circumstances have changed so much that there is just no principled
way of settling what would count as the correct answer. Does a live
goat cost more or less today than it did in Julius Caesar's Rome?
("What is that in real money?" is a classic expression of naive realism
about economic value. "What is that in real hurting?" is naive realism about pain.) Economic value doesn't have to be "intrinsic" or
"absolute" to be real; neither does pain. But that means that a func-
tionalistic, relativistic, nonintrinsic theory of pain does *not* leave out
the ouch!

"In the case of the frog and most or all other cases like it, there
is a quite determinate state of *something appearing*. It simply cannot
be resolved what the thing appears to be like—not by us and, we
can perfectly well allow, not by the organism either." I wonder if
Brook would be as confident of this if we were to extend the range
of his claim to *mechanical* frogs. Do things appear to them? I would
be happy to work with such a concept of appearing, but I doubt it
is what Brook thinks he is talking about here. In the end, I think
Brook still refuses to join me in my rite of exorcism of the seemings
that would *be* over and above the events that could happen even in
a suitably sensitive and discriminating mechanical frog.[2]

Brook asks "What is it about some judgments, descriptions, in virtue of which they hurt, whereas others don't?" A good question. Let
me try to answer it indirectly with a little story.

Once upon a time there was a guy named Dooley who com-
plained about a judgment he kept making—it would only occur
to him when he blinked, by the way. It was a judgment to the effect that somewhere at that very moment a dog was dying. That
was certainly not a pleasant judgment, what with all the further
reflections that invariably came in its wake, but it was not, you
might insist, a *painful* mental event in itself. Well, wait till you've
heard more about it. This judgment didn't just occur to him once

in a while. It occurred obsessively, for uninterrupted periods of several hours a day, whenever, during those periods, he blinked. While this judgment occupied his attention, all other thoughts were banished. It prevented him from concentrating at work and at play. It spoiled his mealtimes, and the very anticipation of the next bout of obtrusive judgment was itself enough to spoil his waking hours. And, of course, it released floods of neuromodulators and hormones, depressing his bodily functions, etc. Drinking helped. He found that when he was mildly drunk, the judgment that somewhere a dog was dying didn't seem to matter all that much. To hell with dogs—that was his usual drunken reaction. Not surprisingly, Dooley developed a drinking problem.

Question: Do these obsessive judgments *hurt* Dooley? I suppose not. But they certainly make him suffer. One would also suffer if one was given local (not general) anesthesia before being tortured, but nothing would *hurt* you during the torture. What is missing in both these cases, but present in the case of somebody who has just been kicked in the unanaesthetized shin, is a variety of *further* neuromodulator releases and neural firings that are apt to provoke/enable (1) identificatory judgments about a location of a particular feeling (these judgments can be wildly inaccurate guides to the location of any trauma, by the way), (2) intensified involuntary muscular spasms (though flinching in reaction to judgments might also be a feature of Dooley's predicament, and would be likely in the case of the anaesthetized torture victim unless blindfolded). I do not know whether local anesthesia diminishes the strength of torture as either a tongue-loosener or long-term behavior modifier. Needless to say, we are not likely to find out the answer to this empirical question, but we mustn't jump to conclusions. Anyway, that's what the difference is, I think, between cognitive events that hurt and those that don't.

Am I an eliminativist? I'm a *deflationist*. The idea is to chip the phenomenon of mind down to size, undoing the work of those inflationists who actively desire to impress upon themselves and everybody else just how supercalifragilisticexpialidocious consciousness is, so that they can maintain, with a straight face, their favorite doctrine:

the Mind is a Mystery Beyond all Understanding. They might be called hype-noetists. A lot of the work in *Consciousness Explained* (henceforth, CE) is just designed to undo the hype so that the job looks more do-able. And I note that in this task the book has rung up some significant victories. Not a few philosophers have been dumbfounded to learn that they were not conscious of as much as they thought, and that consciousness is not always an aid.

One of Brook's interesting questions is what the difference is between my account of the intentional stance and my account of consciousness. How do I explain the greater interest in real processes in the case of consciousness? Thus: A theory of consciousness, even a folk theory of consciousness, is already descending into the P-level, considering not just what it is rational for an agent to do given what it knows, etc., but taking the bolder tack of trying to figure out something about the actual processes involved, so that such tactics as *distracting attention* can come into play. As Brook notes, "focused consciousness makes a difference to performance." The tennis coach knows roughly what you, as an intentional system, believe and desire, but he appreciates that the wrong beliefs and desires are typically *influential* when you swing at the ball, so he devises stratagems for manipulating your consciousness. As Brook says, "performance is generally worse when conscious attention . . . is distracted, split between two tasks, etc." Generally, but not always. Sometimes consciousness gets in the way, and not just on the tennis court. I recently discussed this issue with Gary Burton, the jazz vibraphonist, who confirmed in his own case what I had often noted about my own jazz improvization: when soloing, "the main thing is for me to get out of the way"—by which he means that he *doesn't* focus consciousness on the notes he is playing, let alone what his hands are doing with the mallets. He may think instead, he says, about where he's going for supper, or whether the audience is hip enough for a certain sort of move, or whether he knows that man sitting in the corner.

Finally, Brook is right that I slight autobiographical (or episodic) memory in CE. I am setting out to repair that gap. The first installment is Westbury and Dennett, 2000.

Dan Lloyd wants to egg me on into anti-Cartesian territory I've skirted, and I am happy to follow his lead *part of the way*. But I do have my limits. We all hate to give up our own oversimplifications, I guess. I think Lloyd may have given me some insight into how Jerry Fodor must feel when he reads some of my stuff: "Oh, no! Do I *have* to give up the Language of Thought? The alternative you sketch would make life ever so much more complicated!" Do I *have* to give up microtakings? I'm not sure that's such a good idea, and I am not persuaded by Lloyd's use of my own tool 3D, the slippery slope, against the boundary conditions for them. Powerful tools must be used with discretion, and my point about the temporal boundaries of events in consciousness was not that they don't have *some* boundaries (inevitably blurred if you look closely enough), but that they manifestly didn't have boundaries *within an order of magnitude* of the scale that some theories (or tacit background assumptions) would require. Yes, you *can* date the British Empire's becoming cognizant of the end of the War of 1812, but only to "the winter of 1814–15" or some such conveniently vague phrase. So I am not perturbed by his rhetorical questions about *just* when and where the microtakings have their onsets, since my theory doesn't demand microsecond timing or micrometer location for them.

Before getting down to the details, let me take this occasion to clarify and expand somewhat on his introduction into print of my private term "deepity." The etymological source was Joseph Weizenbaum, the computer scientist who created the Eliza program. Many years ago he told me about a remark his irrepressible thirteen-year-old daughter had made at the supper table the previous evening. He had delivered himself rather roundly of a philosophical reflection, to which she had responded: "Wow. Dad said a deepity!" I delighted in the coinage, but went on to define it for my own purposes (in introductory philosophy classes) as an apparently profound observation that depends for this appearance on a subtle ill-formedness that lets it hover between a trivial truth and a whopping falsehood. What comes through to the unsuspecting is the illusory conjunction of truth and whoppingness. "Love is just a four-letter word" serves handily, since " 'love' is just a four-letter word" is as true and trivial as " 'salt' is just a four-letter word," while anybody who managed to think that love is a *word*, as opposed to an emotional state or an interpersonal relation, or whatever it is, would indeed suffer from heroic misinformation and need most desperately to be set straight. I do commend the term to your use. There are deepities aplenty on the lips of our students, and Descartes is the progenitor (or godfather) of more than a few.

Now back to Lloyd's teetotaling campaign against representations. As a social drinker, I find a healthy place in my life for alcohol, and as a social thinker, I find a healthy place in my life for representations, and I think Lloyd is overlooking a benign home for mental representations after all—but I want to stress that I now think the only way to get there is by first endorsing Lloyd's abstemious resistance to *premature* representationalism. "Early" representations—posited, for instance, in *animal* cognition and in most human *perception*—is as dangerous an abuse as underaged drinking. Representations are, in effect, an adult preoccupation into which one is only gradually initiated. (My thinking on this has also been strongly influenced by John Haugeland's recent book, *Having Thought*, 1998, which builds social thinking on a representation-free base of the sort Lloyd is trying to develop. And see *Thompson* on Husserl on representativeness, a criticism with many points of similarity to Lloyd's.)

The great obstacle to such a view of the mind is, as Lloyd so vividly expresses, the hulking ghost of Descartes, and we have to put in place something like his *phenomenal realism* in order to keep the interiority of Cartesianism at bay as long as possible. (For a helpful alternative—but, I think, harmonious—perspective on this idea, see *Thompson*'s chapter for a discussion of Husserl's concept of *constitution*.) The idea of a "phenomenal complex" seems to me to do the trick, leveling the playing field, as Lloyd says. I have one misgiving to express, but I do so gingerly, since my ontological scruples are in disarray. I don't see why he insists on defining P-properties in such a way that their existence depends not on their being detected but on the brute presence somewhere "in the universe"—but even outside the lightcone, I gather—of P-detectors. This is an intensification—unwarranted, so far as I can see—of my not quite parallel distinction between *suspect* and *lovely* properties (Dennett 1991b):

We do have a need, as Rosenthal shows, for properties of discriminative states that are in one sense independent of consciousness, and that can be for that very reason informatively cited in explanations of particular contents of our consciousness. These properties are partially, but not entirely, independent of consciousness. We may call such properties *lovely* properties as contrasted with *suspect* properties. Someone could be lovely who had never yet, as it happened, been observed by any observer of the sort who would find her lovely, but she could not—as a matter of logic—be a suspect until someone actually suspected her of something. Particular instances of lovely qualities (such as the quality of loveliness) can be said to exist as Lockean dispositions prior to the moment (if any) where they exercise their power over an observer, producing the defining effect therein. Thus some unseen woman (self-raised on a desert island, I guess) could be genuinely lovely, having the dispositional power to affect normal observers of a certain class in a certain way, in spite of never having the opportunity to do so. But lovely qualities cannot be defined independently of the proclivities, susceptibilities, or dispositions of a class of observers. Actually, that is a bit too strong. Lovely qualities *would* not be defined—there would be no point in defining *them*, in contrast to all the other logically possible gerrymandered properties—independently of such a class of observers. So while it might be logically possible ("in retrospect" one might say) to gather color property instances together by something like brute force enumeration, the reasons for singling out such properties (for instance, in order to explain certain causal regularities in a set of curiously complicated objects) depend on the existence of the class of observers. . . .

On the other hand, suspect qualities (such as the property of being a suspect) are understood in such a way as to presuppose that any instance of the property has already had its defining effect on at least one observer. You may be eminently worthy of suspicion—you may even be obviously guilty—but you can't be a suspect until someone actually suspects you. The tradition that Rosenthal is denying would have it that "sensory qualities" are suspect properties—their *esse* is in every instance *percipi*. Just as an unsuspected suspect is no suspect at all, so an unfelt pain is supposedly no pain at all. But, for the reasons Rosenthal adduces, this is exactly as unreasonable as the claim that an unseen object cannot be colored. He claims, in effect, that sensory qualities should rather be considered lovely properties—like Lockean secondary qualities generally. Our intuition that the as-yet-unobserved emerald in the middle of the clump of ore is *already* green does not have to be denied, even though its being green is not a property it can be said to have "intrinsically." This is easier to accept for some secondary qualities than for others. That the sulphurous fumes spewed forth by primordial volcanoes were yellow seems somehow more objective than that they stank, but so long as what we mean by "yellow" is what *we* mean by "yellow," the claims are parallel. For suppose some primordial earthquake cast up a cliff face exposing the stripes of hundreds of chemically different layers to the atmosphere. Were those stripes *visible?* We must ask to whom. Perhaps some of them would be visible to us and to others not. Perhaps some of the invisible stripes would be visible to pigeons (with their tetrachromat color vision), or to creatures who saw in the infrared or ultraviolet part of the electromagnetic spectrum. For the same reason one cannot meaningfully ask whether the difference between emeralds and rubies is a visible difference without specifying the vision system in question. (1991b, 40–42)

I think Lloyd should drop the insistence that P-detectors must *actually* exist for specific P-properties to exist. Why can't we just accept that there are a kazillion P-properties that exist but are of no interest to us at all, our having no reason to suspect that any P-detectors exist anywhere to bundle them disjunctively into potent generalization-precipitators? It seems to me that my lost sock center (Dennett 1991a) exists alongside the center of mass of the moon; ontology isn't always important; importance is important (*pace* J. L. Austin). That qualm aside, I think Lloyd's account of P-properties and P-detectors is wonderfully illuminating, and just what we need to start fending off the dread question from the crypto-Cartesians: *Is that all there is?* Yes, it's hard to get your head around this point—Lloyd points to a few lapses of my own—and there are certainly those who very vehemently don't want even to try to get their heads around it. Even those who, like *Brook,* are willing to give it the old college try find it an alien and uninviting prospect. So Lloyd's staged withdrawal program makes good sense. First, let me take Brook from qualia to judgments, but then quickly from judgments to microtakings (for the reasons I discuss above). Then let's have phenomenal complexes, but I don't see why microtakings can't be the left-hand side—even the "inboard" side—of phenomenal complexes, once we see what they *aren't*—namely, representations in any Cartesian sense. I am happy to rechristen microtakings as eddies[3] in Lloyd's "Heraclitan brainstorm of neural inflection," if this helps.

Anyway, Lloyd and I are agreed that these eddies are not enough *like* pictures, maps, symbols, sentences, and other uncontroversial representations to be called representations, in spite of their own sort of intentionality. But I think there are other phenomena that really are, in quite a strong sense, mental representations. If I do long division in my head, there are representations of the numbers just as surely as there are if I do it on the blackboard. If I conjure up the visual appearance of my late neighbor Basil Turner, there is something briefly in the world that *is* like a photograph of him. (When I do this, normally, the intentional object of my mental activity is Basil Turner, not my "image" of Basil Turner—this is Husserl's point, as *Thompson* emphasizes.) These special cases are terrible models to inspire us when thinking of the basic elements of perception and cognition generally, but they are real enough, for all that. Our capacity, as Gregorian creatures (Dennett 1995), to *use* such representations, as tools for thinking (Dennett, forthcoming), is, I think, one of the features that distinguish most sharply our minds from simpler minds. Descartes was right about *something*, and not just about the relation between algebra and geometry!

David Rosenthal shows that his higher-order thought or HOT theory of consciousness "explains why we should feel a certain reluctance to classify particular cases [of timing in consciousness] as being Stalinesque or Orwellian," but I think it does not go far enough, and this obliges him to bite several bullets that are extremely dubious (to me). Here, then, is my latest installment in the continuing constructive back-and-forth that Rosenthal and I have been conducting for about a decade. (My earlier rounds are CE itself, and 1991b, 1993, 1994.)

The basic idea of my multiple drafts model or pandemonium model (more recently recast as the "fame in the brain" model in Dennett 1996b, 1998b) is that consciousness is more like fame than television; it is *not* a special "medium of representation" in the brain into which content-bearing events must be "transduced" in order to become conscious. It is rather a matter of content-bearing events in the brain achieving something a bit like fame in competition with other fame-seeking (or at any rate potentially fame-finding) events. But of course consciousness couldn't be *fame*, exactly, in the brain, since to be famous is to be a shared intentional object *in the consciousnesses* of many folk, and although the brain is usefully seen as composed of hordes of homunculi, imagining them to be *au courant* in just the way they would need to be to elevate some of their brethren to cerebral celebrity is going a bit too far—to say nothing of the problem that it would install a patent infinite regress in my theory of consciousness. The looming infinite regress can be stopped the way such threats are often happily stopped, not by abandoning the basic idea but by softening it. As long as your homunculi are more stupid and ignorant than the intelligent agent they compose, the nesting of homunculi within homunculi can be finite, bottoming out, eventually, with agents so unimpressive that they can be replaced by machines. So consciousness is not so much *fame*, then, as *influence*—a species of relative "political" power in the opponent processes that eventuate in ongoing control of the body.

The main difference between Rosenthal's HOT theory and mine, then, is that in his theory, being conscious is not like being famous; it's like being *known by the King*. In some oligarchies, perhaps, the only way to achieve political power is to be known by the King, dispenser of all powers and privileges. Our brains are more democratic, indeed anarchic. In the brain there is no King, no Official Viewer of the State Television Program, no Cartesian Theater, but there are still plenty of *quite* sharp differences in political power exercised by contents over time. What a theory of consciousness needs to explain is how some relatively few contents become elevated to this political power, while most others evaporate into oblivion after doing their modest deeds in the ongoing projects of the brain. (Why is *this* the task of a theory of consciousness? Because that is what conscious events *do*. They hang around, monopolizing time "in the limelight"—but we need to explain *away* this seductive metaphor, and its kin, the searchlight of attention, by explaining the *functional* powers of attention-*grabbing* without presupposing a single attention-*giving* source.)

Fame is not like television, not a medium of representation at all. Consider the following tale. Jim has written a remarkable first novel that has been enthusiastically read by some of the *cognoscenti*. His picture is all set to go on the cover of *Time* magazine, and Oprah has lined him up for her television show. A national book tour is planned and Hollywood has already expressed interest in his book. That's all true on Tuesday. Wednesday morning San Francisco is destroyed in an earthquake, and the world's attention can hold nothing else for a month. Is Jim famous? He would have been, if it weren't for that darn earthquake. Maybe next month, if things return to normal, he'll *become* famous for deeds done earlier. But fame eluded him this week, in spite of the fact that the *Time* cover story had been typeset and sent to the printer, to be yanked at the last moment, and in spite of the fact that his name was already in *TV Guide* as Oprah's guest, and in spite of the fact that stacks of his novels could be found in the windows of Borders and Barnes and Noble. All the *dispositional properties* normally sufficient for fame were in place, but their normal effects didn't get triggered, so no fame resulted. The same, I hold, is true of consciousness. It is a mistake (though a very tempting mistake) to think of consciousness as a medium of representation in the brain, such that getting represented in that medium, for however short a time, counts as being in consciousness, whether or not the representation therein leads to the normal *sequelae* of reaction and influence. Of course you can impose such a definition of consciousness by fiat, if you like, but if you do take this course, you will find the costs prohibitive.[4] You will not be able to give an account of the role of consciousness in memory, or in guiding behavior, and you won't be able to explain the difference between unconscious and conscious mental activities or states except by positing some mysterious extra property of the medium of representation you choose.

Ned Block recently[5] objected to this aspect of my view of consciousness, plausibly claiming that if I am a good Rylean—and I like to think I am—I should embrace just such a dispositional analysis of consciousness *so that* I can handle momentary but historically inert flashes of consciousness. Ryle would insist that, say, a cooling glass goblet on the glassblower's pipe might become brittle for a fraction of a second before being rewarmed in the kiln; there is nothing to stand in the way of momentary unactualized dispositions. Just so, but my claim is that consciousness is *not* like that! I venture the diagnosis, moreover, that Block's supposition that what he calls access consciousness *is* like that might be what seduces him into wanting more: creating the gratuitous category of "phenomenal" consciousness to cover for the disappointment one might feel in enjoying a merely dispositional kind of consciousness. Similarly, poor Jim might complain to his agent: "You call that *fame?* That might be a sort of *access* fame–Oprah and all that—but it sure didn't feel like fame to me! I want *phenomenal* fame!'' Jim was disposed to be, as one says, a phenom, but he didn't quite make it.

The strength of the fame-in-the-brain view comes out quite clearly, I think, if we raise certain tough questions for Rosenthal's alternative, the HOT theory of consciousness. Can you have two HOTs simultaneously? A hundred? If not, why not? Is there a bottleneck, a single higher-order-thought-thinker in there, with lower-order thoughts waiting in the antechamber for admission to the throne room? And if you can have many HOTs at once, what if one is much more influential than all the others? Are the contained thoughts all equally conscious, or is there one brand or strain or lineage of HOTS that is the real you? Rosenthal wants to distinguish parroting from nonparroting speech acts, and he claims that on my pandemonium model this is difficult whereas for his it poses no problem. Is that not because he has quietly posited a central meaner to do the meaning? I think that he underestimates the power of the pandemonium model to underwrite whatever distinction we need between parroting and nonparroting speech. The competition in the pandemonium model is far from "aleatory"; it is a competition of skill and relevance in which unity is approached.

A word that stands out like a sore thumb in (my reading of) Rosenthal's essay is the pronoun "we." For instance "As we mentally hear ourselves say what it is that we think, we find it confused or unclear, and so revise on the fly what we think. But by adjusting our words as we go, we get the right thought out." As I noted in my commentary on *Brook*, any theory of consciousness with such a subject still in the picture has a hostage; until it is discharged, we can't tell if there has been any real progress. Contrast the quotations from Rosenthal above with this from the novelist (and excellent phenomenologist) Nicholson Baker:

Our opinions, gently nudged by circumstance, revise themselves under cover of inattention. We tell them, in a steady voice, No, I'm not interested in a change at present. But there is no stopping opinion. They don't care about whether we want to hold them or not; they do what they have to do. (Baker 1996, 4)

Rosenthal's subject is in charge, judging and editing and endorsing, the last functionary to sign off before public relations issues the press release. Baker's subject is an ironic observer, swept along by influential opinions. Baker's "we," just as much as Rosenthal's, has to be dissolved into the uninhabited machinery in the brain's factory, but Rosenthal's is still apparently doing a lot of work. And it is work that needn't be done, in my opinion. I don't find myself agreeing at all with his claim that "our subjective impression is always that our speech acts exactly match in content the intentional state they express." Back in *Content and Consciousness* (1969), I enshrined just such an idea in my ill-considered "awareness line," but came to see that this was a mistake. (Nobody is more critical than a reformed sinner.)

These are not the only points at which I now see that I have misled Rosenthal, and he is not alone. It is my own mode of expression that is often the culprit. I have misled everybody, myself included, on "probes," for instance, and I don't know how to repair the damage, so I warn all to avoid the generous assumption that there is a coherent doctrine there to be teased out. (Note that I have avoided the topic of probes altogether since 1991, hoping to find a better way of making the points that still seem to me to reside there. Some of these points have found alternative expression in the interim; others may lurk in the murk, but don't hold your breath waiting for me to reveal them.) In the meantime, let me just say that I do *not* intend the probe distinction to be what Rosenthal calls a third-person constraint. After all, Robinson Crusoe on his desert island was conscious of myriad things, but nobody *else* needed to react to them. It is internal fame, not external fame that matters. At another point, Rosenthal says, "The key is the denial by first-person operationalism of any difference between mental states and their being conscious—between how things seem and how they seem to seem." These are two different distinctions, on my view. And I do say, as he quotes, that actually framing a report can create conscious content, but this isn't the only way that conscious content gets created. Finally, I was nonplussed by Rosenthal's suggestion that my view might be that speech acts "simply settle which of these states wins out in the competition for expression, rather than converting subpersonal events of content fixation into genuine intentional states." I do not see that any such conversion is possible or necessary, since I don't see the distinction. This is related to something else I don't see in Rosenthal's essay.

Throughout, he adopts without defense a supposition of a sort of content realism that I think needs defense (and can't get it). It would take a separate essay to do justice to my hunch (and his meticulous presentation of the view I am so dubious about), so all I can do at this point is wave a caution flag.

Thomas Polger rises bravely to my challenge to philosophers to defend zombies as a topic of adult discussion, and in so doing clarifies the issue for all of us, a contribution no matter who "wins." It is fair to say that I had simply not imagined some of the subtleties of zombie-doctrine that Polger exposes, which goes a long way to explaining the failure of my campaign to achieve victory—yet. His difficulty locating my position in his taxonomy of varieties of zombism is itself an interesting datum. I say that the concept of zombies is ridiculous, and he doesn't find this either clear or simple. But eventually he clarifies the task before him: "So to answer Dennett's challenge . . . one must show that a conception of consciousness that allows for the possibility of *functionally* identical zombies does not entail epiphenomenalism." This is epiphenomenalism in the Huxley sense, since I gather that Polger concedes that I am right about what he calls the "metaphysically strict" sense of that term: It *is* ridiculous.

I must begin by clearing up a confusion about Huxley epiphenomenalism engendered by Polger's discussion. Suppose for the sake of argument that the difference between a car with a carburetor and a car with a fuel injector is not *functional*—they accelerate the same, are equally fuel-efficient, etc. Polger says that I make a mistake in declaring in such circumstances that carburetors are causal-role (or Huxley) epiphenomena. As he says, carburetors are crucial functional mechanisms in the cars that have them, and fuel injectors are likewise. But this misses the point of Huxley epiphenomena. If the *difference* between having one of these and having the other is not functional, then it—the difference—is epiphenomenal in Huxley's sense. It is not a difference that makes a functional difference, but it is a difference that makes a causal difference. Just look under the hood: One reflects light entirely different from the light reflected by the other (and—to harken to Huxley's case—if you listen really carefully, one gives off a whistle that the other doesn't).

The zombie defender is free to think of conscious states, or processes, or events as mechanisms that have certain properties, among which that they are conscious. Those mechanisms have causal powers, but they are replaceable with functionally equivalent mechanisms that have some distinctive properties. Some mechanisms are conscious, others are not. Both have causal powers—they are not epiphenomenal.

But they *are* epiphenomenal in Huxley's sense—since ex hypothesi their differences in causal powers don't make a functional difference. Setting aside the term, though, I agree that the zombie defender is free to make this move, but he does so at the cost of removing consciousness from the sphere of human interest it currently (and rightfully, if understood correctly) occupies. Polger himself gets close to seeing the problem: "Why should we care whether consciousness is part of our system?" And he answers that there are "a variety of reasons, such as aesthetic or moral reasons. Conscious states may be replaceable with respect to our bodies carrying-on their cognitive duties, but we value having them." But *why* do we value them? The one feature of my challenge that Polger overlooks here is one that I thought he was promising to address: that the zombie-concept is *useful.* If the difference between being conscious and being a zombie is like the difference between having aluminum or plastic plumbing, why should it make a moral difference which one you have? Why should it be immoral to dismantle a conscious person without permission (and without anesthesia) but not immoral to dismantle a zombie without "permission"?

"Dennett calls zombies 'pernicious' because he thinks that the defender of zombies is committed to saying that these important considerations rest on whether or not a subject has some epiphenomenal quality. That would indeed be troubling." Right. I don't see that Polger has made any progress on dispelling that concern, whether we call it epiphenomenalism or not. Given his concept of consciousness, we plastic-brained folks have no moral standing (we're zombies), while our aluminum-brained cousins have the morally important causal property—even though there is no difference in capacity, talent, prowess, or susceptibility to suffering between us. (They suffer, we zombies just suffer$_z$—which doesn't count, for reasons not addressed.) Pernicious indeed.

But the philosophical challenge to the zombie defenders is more basic than this, and need not be put in terms of the moral embarrassments of the view. For suppose, with Polger, that we have two sorts of beings in front of us, of which we know the following (I guess God told us): The type A beings are conscious; they are equipped with "mechanisms that have certain properties, among which that they are conscious. Those mechanisms have causal powers, but they are replaceable with functionally equivalent mechanisms that have some distinctive properties. Some mechanisms are conscious, others are not." The type B beings are equipped with these latter, nonconscious but functionally identical mechanisms. There is no difficulty telling types A and B apart; half the beings have green brains that sworl to the left and make heavy use of acetylcholine, and half have red brains that sworl to the right and make heavy use of serotonin, etc. The trouble is that the labels, "A" and "B," have been removed from our samples and mixed up. Our only task is to examine the samples and determine which are type A and which are type B. What do we look for? What is it about *any* nonfunctional causal difference you care to describe that could *motivate* us to decide that it is the difference that goes with consciousness rather than with unconsciousness? Notice that I am not playing verificationism here. I am not demanding "criteria"; I am asking for the minimum: something, anything, that would give somebody the slightest good reason for preferring the hypothesis that causal property *k* goes with consciousness, not unconsciousness. It will not do, of course, to see which set of nonfunctional causal properties most closely matches *us*, because we are not at this point entitled to any assumptions about how widespread consciousness might be among normal *H. sapiens*.

Evolution and Ethics: Mooney

Brian Mooney proposes virtue ethics as a safe haven for my somewhat inchoate views on ethics. In particular, my distrust of the rule-bound "perfectionism" of both consequentialist and Kantian ethical theories finds an ally in Plato, he says, who condemns "pleonexic maximization" and endorses a "craft" vision of justice. This is a timely contribution since I'd been wondering what I ought to make of virtue ethics, and now I have a much better idea of the prospects, thanks to Mooney's usefully maverick rendition of the issues.

Mooney also hopes to persuade me to go further than heretofore in accepting a pluralism of values: "A good act is better than an evil one but not clearly better than a rose, just as a loving act is better than a hateful one but not clearly better than a just one." We should not bother trying to calibrate all values on a single scale—even though in the real world we must often make decisions that require us to adjudicate conflicts between them. Craft, phronesis, will do the trick.

Virtue ethics, thus seen, challenges rule-fetishism much the same way embodied cognition and situated robotics challenge GOFAI or High Church Computationalism (Dennett 1986, reprinted in 1998d): You don't need representations of rules in your physical symbol system, presided over by a theorem-proving deducer; you just need know-how, embodied skill, talent. The motto of the virtue ethicists, in competition with Bentham's rhyming rules or Kant's Categorical Imperative, might be: "You're good! Fly by the seat of your pants." But then virtue ethics, like embodied cognition, for all its attractions is still just a negative view with a largely unfulfilled promise and a few tempting examples. Not as bad as "Listen to the Force," but not a *whole* lot better either, so far as I can see. What are virtues made of? How is the thinking of a wise person organized, structured, and implemented? These are real questions that consequentialists and Kantians have forthrightly if implausibly answered. Their answers have their problems, but at least they have something on offer. We still need from virtue ethicists a theory of what structures and processes make for virtue in the individual agent. Mooney recognizes this: "it is not just practical wisdom and judgment based on considerations of particulars, and their relations to universal considerations, but more importantly, the *cultivation of certain dispositions that undergird practical deliberation* [emphasis added]." What are these dispositions, and how are they to be cultivated? Even good aviators must be schooled before they can fly by the seat of their pants, and what they learn in flying school, like what children learn in the course of their moral education, is a set of habits of thought, ways of framing issues, *practice* in imagining situations soundly, and these can be seen as tools or instruments of moral decision-making.

Just as you cannot do very much carpentry with your bare hands, there is not much thinking you can do with your bare brain. (Bo Dahlbom and Lars-Erik Janlert, unpublished)

Rules are for fools. You don't really have to understand them (and you certainly don't have to understand their rationale); you just have to be able to follow them doggedly (Dennett 1983). The rule fetishist thinks *all* competence comes from assiduous application of rules— the fundamental assumption of GOFAI as well—and the virtue ethicist thinks at least some competence is more native, more biological, less intellectual. And surely this is right, but it is not clear to me what *ethical* consequences Mooney wants us to draw (some day) from such a realization. We are not born moral, and some of us are more brave, caring, morally imaginative, sensitive, stubborn, than others. These differences give some a head start toward becoming proper moral agents. What supplements do we provide for those less well endowed by nature?

Furthermore, parts of our native endowment, however traditional and emotionally attractive, may stand in need of reconstruction. As Nietzsche and others have wisely reminded us, that something is natural is only prima facie grounds for supposing we should endorse it. Mooney emphasizes the importance of "commitment" to a "beloved" (or to a cause, in the form of loyalty), and we need to recognize that the varieties of commitment that come naturally to us may not all be morally unproblematic in the end, however valuable they are to us as conversation-stoppers when we are confronted with tempting opportunities to defect. Robert Frank (1988) has hypothesized that the evolutionary rationale for our falling "madly" in love, establishing a *commitment* beyond the dictates of sound economic reason ("Honey, you're the healthiest, smartest, prettiest member of the opposite sex who has paid attention to me *so far,* and time is running out; let's get married"), is an abridgment of reason by passion that protects both parties. (See Pinker 1997, 417–419 for a brief exposition.) This hard-boiled justification makes biological sense, and there are certainly some contexts in which it makes moral and political sense—resistance to betrayal and blind obedience do indeed have their times as virtues—but they are also the apparent source of much of the world's worst evil. There is no all-purpose path from either ancient tradition or the biologically natural to the ethically defensible, so virtue ethics is, at best, a part of what we need at the outset of a long project.

Notes

1. Descartes extends this pretext of fiction to his *Treatise on Man.* (See footnote 1, Cottingham, Stoothoff, and Murdoch 1985, 99.)

2. In his *Kant on the Mind,* Brook (1994) attempts to answer the question I raise in *Kinds of Minds* (65–66, 93–98): What do we need to add to (mere) sensitivity to get *sentience* (which I take to be a synonym or at least close cousin to what Brook calls *simple awareness*)? I claim that "we shouldn't assume there is a good answer" to this question, and it is instructive to see that Brook himself is acutely aware of the problems associated with his own attempt to provide an answer. He starts with my old *awareness2* notion from *Content and Consciousness:*

> A is aware2 that p at time t if and only if p is the content of an internal event in A at time t that is effective in directing current behavior.

He adds "memory, other dispositions, and nonpropositional objects" to his account, but in fact my definition already includes all these under its umbrella of "internal events effective in directing current behavior," and then he adds "sensible manifolds" but this is simply declaring the events also sentient without further ado. My "conservative hypothesis" in *Kinds of Minds* about the problem of sentience is that "there is no such *extra* phenomenon. 'Sentience' comes in every imaginable grade or intensity, from the simplest and most 'robotic' to the most exquisitely sensitive, hyper-reactive, 'human'" (97). In short, adding "sensible manifolds" is piling on the *figment* to no good end.

3. I gave a talk in Stockholm some years ago entitled "Eddies in the Stream of Consciousness," about the "temporal anomalies" of color phi, metacontrast, and Libet's effects. When it was published in Swedish translation, the title had become "Regissörer i medvetandets strömmar" (Dennett 1992). I asked the translator about the meaning of the word "regissörer" and he replied that the word "eddies" was unknown to him, and he had just assumed that it was a neologism of mine, a diminutive of "editor," so in his version, my multiple drafts model was implemented in the brain by hordes of *eddies* or *editorunculi.* (I wish I'd said that! You will, Oscar, you will—in Swedish!)

4. Rosenthal's note 29 claims that my view can't distinguish between not being conscious of something and "its coming to be conscious too briefly to affect memory time." He is right, but this isn't a bug, it's a feature.

5. In discussion of my presentation to the King's College London conference on consciousness, April, 1999.

References

Baker, N. (1996). *The Size of Thoughts*. New York: Random House.

Blackmore, S. (1999). *The Meme Machine*. Oxford: Oxford University Press.

Brook, A. (1994). *Kant and the Mind*. New York: Cambridge University Press.

Cottingham, J., Stoothoff, R., and Murdoch, D., trans. and eds. (1985). *The Philosophical Writings of Descartes* (in two volumes). Cambridge: Cambridge University Press.

Cronin, H. (1991). *The Ant and the Peacock*. Oxford: Oxford University Press.

Dalhbom, B. (ed.). (1993). *Dennett and His Critics*. Oxford: Blackwell.

Dahlbom, B. and Janlert, L-E. (unpublished). *Computer Future*.

Dennett, D. (1969). *Content and Consciousness*. London: Routledge, Kegal Paul.

Dennett, D. (1978). *Brainstorms*. Montgomery, Vermont: Bradford Books.

Dennett, D. (1983). Styles of mental representation. *Proceedings of the Aristotelian Society, New Series*, 83, 213–226, 1982/83. Reprinted in Dennett (1987).

Dennett, D. (1986). Cognitive wheels: The frame problem of AI. In Dennett (1998d).

Dennett, D. (1987). *The Intentional Stance*. Cambridge, Mass.: MIT Press. A Bradford Book.

Dennett, D. (1991a). Real patterns. *Journal of Philosophy* 88: 27–51. Reprinted in Dennett (1998d).

Dennett, D. (1991b). Lovely and suspect qualities (commentary on Rosenthal, The independence of consciousness and sensory quality). In *Consciousness* (SOFIA Conference, Buenos Aires), E. Villanueva (ed.), 37–43. Atascadero, Cal.: Ridgeview.

Dennett, D. (1991c). *Consciousness Explained*. Boston: Little, Brown and Company.

Dennett, D. (1992). Regissörer i medvetandets strömmar. *Framtider*, 11: 21–22, Institutet för Framtidsstudier, Stockholm. (Also published as: Eddies in the stream of consciousness, *Future Studies*, Stockholm, 1993.)

Dennett, D. (1993). The Message is: There is no *medium* (reply to Jackson, Rosenthal, Shoemaker, and Tye). *Philosophy & Phenomenological Research* 53 (4): 889–931.

Dennett, D. (1994). Get real. Reply to 14 essays. *Philosophical Topics* 22 (1, 2): 505–568.

Dennett, D. (1995). *Darwin's Dangerous Idea: Evolution and the Meanings of Life*. New York: Simon & Schuster.

Dennett, D. (1996). The scope of natural selection (reply to Orr 1996). *Boston Review* 21 (5).

Dennett, D. (1996b). Consciousness: More like fame than television (in German translation: *Bewusstsein hat mehr mit Ruhm als mit Fernsehen zu tun*). In *Die Technik auf dem Weg zur Seele*, C. Maar, E. Pöppel, and T. Christaller (eds.). Rowohlt, 1996.

Dennett, D. (1998a). *Kinds of Minds*. New York: Basic Books.

Dennett, D. (1998b). The Myth of Double Transduction. In *Toward a Science of Consciousness II, The Second Tucson Discussions and Debates*, S. Hameroff, A.W. Kaszniak, and A. C. Scott (eds.), 97–107. Cambridge, Mass.: MIT Press. A Bradford Book.

Dennett, D. (1998c). Preston on exaltation: Herons, apples and eggs. *Journal of Philosophy* 95 (11): 576–580.

Dennett, D. (1998d). *Brainchildren*. Cambridge, Mass.: MIT Press. A Bradford Book.

Dennett, D. (forthcoming). Making tools for thinking. In *Metarepresentation*, D. Sperber (ed.). Vancouver Series in Cognitive Science. Oxford: Oxford University Press.

Dennett, D. (unpublished a). Memes: Myths, Misunderstandings, and Misgivings. Chapel Hill Colloquium, October, 1998.

Dennett, D. (unpublished b). The Evolution of Culture. The first Charles Simonyi Lecture, delivered at Oxford University, February, 1999. Available on the web at http://www.edge.org.

Dretske, F. (1981). *Knowledge and the Flow of Information*. Cambridge, Mass.: MIT Press. A Bradford Book.

Frank, R. (1988). *Passions within Reason: The Strategic Role of the Emotions*. New York: Norton.

Gould, S. J. (1982). Change in developmental timing as a mechanism of macroevolution. In *Evolution and Development*, J. Bonner (ed.). Dahlem Konferenzen (Berlin, Heidelberg, New York: Springer-Verlag).

Haugeland, J. (1998). *Having Thought*. Cambridge, Mass.: Harvard University Press.

Holland, J. (1995). *Hidden Order: How Adaptation Builds Complexity*. Reading, Mass.: Addison-Wesley.

Holland, J. (1998). *Emergence: From Chaos to Order*. Reading, Mass.: Addison-Wesley.

Lenat, D. and Guha, R. (1990). *Building Large Knowledge-based Systems: Representation and Inference in the CYC Project*. Reading, Mass.: Addison-Wesley.

Levine, J. (1995). Out of the closet: A qualophile confronts qualophobia. *Philosophical Topics* 22, 23: 107–126.

Orr, H. (1996). Dennett's strange idea (an enlarged republication of Orr's review in *Evolution*). *Boston Review* 21 (4).

Pinker, S. (1997). *How the Mind Works*. New York: Norton.

Preston, B. (1998). Why is a wing like a spoon? A pluralist theory of function. *Journal of Philosophy* 95 (5): 215–254.

Quine, W. v. O. (1960). *Word and Object*. Cambridge, Mass.: MIT Press.

Ramberg, B. (1999) Dennett's Pragmatism. *Revue Internationale de Philosophie* 53 (207): 61–86.

Sperber, D. (1985) Apparently irrational beliefs. In *On Anthropological Knowledge*. Cambridge: Cambridge University Press.

Westbury, C. and Dennett, D. (2000). Mining the past for the future. In *Memory, Brain, and Belief*, D. Schacter and E. Scarry (eds.). Cambridge, Mass.: Harvard University Press.

Name Index

Name Index

Subject Index

393

Subject Index

Eliminativism, 22, 90, 103, 120, 133,
136, 156, 159, 162, 201, 223–227,
245, 249, 359, 361–362, 366, 369
Emergence, 118–122
Empiricism, 18, 23, 63, 123–124, 156,
205
constructive, 123, 356
Engineering, 4, 28, 30–31, 55–73
biological, 28, 30–31, 55–73, 328–
329, 344
deliberative, 4–5
reverse, 4, 6
Entities, 134, 137–138, 141–142, 150–
151, 169, 182, 205
Entropy, 164
Epiphenomenalism, 141, 269–283, 357,
380–382
Epistemology, 8, 12, 26, 63–65, 88
Epoché, 8, 202, 206–209, 213, 216–
217, 363
Eros, 319–321
Error, 78–79, 83, 109, 173, 228, 230–
231, 349–351
Essentialism, 15–16, 23
Ethics, 1, 4–5, 12, 18, 46, 52, 309–324,
382–385
deontological, 309–312, 315–317,
321, 381–382
transcendental foundation for, 5
virtue, 12, 310–324, 382–385
Eudaimonia, 314
Evolution, 1, 5, 11–12, 14, 22, 27–37,
41–53, 107, 109, 111–112, 116, 119–
120, 140, 320, 328–333, 334, 336–
338, 340–344, 351, 354
cultural, 5, 7, 31–2, 329, 334–336,
354–355, 384–385
history of, 330
Lamarckian, 335–336
theory of, 27–37, 116, 203
Evolutionary
algorithm, 7, 41–53, 328–341
contingency, 14, 27–37, 41–53, 329–
332
design, 6, 25, 27–31, 41–53, 328–332,
336–344
gradualism, 14–15, 27–30, 329, 332–
334
history, 42, 67, 346
lineages, 28, 32–36, 328, 335–336
rationale, 41–53, 384
theory, 27–37, 120, 310, 312, 328–
344

Exaptations, 60–61, 347
Explanation, 100, 122, 124, 134–142,
149, 351–358, 360–361
causal, 68–69

First-person operationalism, 287–290,
297–303, 379
F-level, 224–228, 232, 245, 248–250,
366–367
Forced Moves, 7, 41–53, 336–337,
340–341
Free will, 4–5, 7, 13, 14, 20, 23–24,
147
Friendship, 320–324
Function, 1, 65, 67–68, 98–100, 17,
270
Functional analysis, 50–51, 56–58
Functionalism, 150, 263, 265, 275, 278,
368, 382

Genes, 30, 35–36, 52, 58, 114, 332,
359
Genetics, 30, 97, 114, 116, 153
Genome, 49–50
Good Tricks, 7, 41–53, 336–337, 340–
341, 352
Gradualism, 14, 27–30, 329, 332–
334
Guineafowl, 32–37, 328–332

Hardy-Weinberg law, 120
Hedonism, 313, 318
Heterophenomenological
interpretation, 225
stance, 221, 222, 227
world, 207–208, 210–212, 214, 216–
217, 225
Heterophenomenology, 158, 201, 207,
219–221, 225, 235–241, 245, 250–
252, 297, 301, 304, 351, 364
Higher-order thoughts (HOTs), 287–
289, 298–303, 375–380
Homunculi, 15, 250, 376

Idealism, 133–134, 214–215
Identities
behavioral, 266–282
functional, 263–265, 268–282, 380–
382
token, 132–133, 136, 159, 237, 357–
358
type, 83, 88–89, 133, 150
I-level, 224

394

Subject Index

DH

194
DEN